IMPLICIT MEASURES OF ATTITUDES

Implicit Measures of Attitudes

Edited by
BERND WITTENBRINK
NORBERT SCHWARZ

THE GUILFORD PRESS
New York   London

© 2007 The Guilford Press
A Division of Guilford Publications, Inc.
72 Spring Street, New York, NY 10012
www.guilford.com

Printed in the United States of America

This book is printed on acid-free paper.

Last digit is print number: 9 8 7 6 5 4 3 2 1

Library of Congress Cataloging-in-Publication Data

Implicit measures of attitudes / edited by Bernd Wittenbrink, Norbert Schwarz.
    p. cm.
  Includes bibliographical references and index.
  ISBN-10: 1-59385-402-1   ISBN-13: 978-1-59385-402-7 (hardcover)
  1. Attitude (Psychology)—Testing. 2. Social psychology—Research—Methodology.
I. Wittenbrink, Bernd. II. Schwarz, Norbert, Dr. phil.
  HM1181.I46 2006
  152.4028'7—dc22

                                                                    2006020538

About the Editors

Bernd Wittenbrink, PhD, is Professor of Behavioral Science in the Graduate School of Business and a member of the Center for Decision Research at the University of Chicago. His research concerns the roles that stereotypes and group attitudes play in social judgment and behavior. Dr. Wittenbrink's work has been published in, among others, the *Journal of Personality and Social Psychology*, the *Journal of Experimental Social Psychology*, and the *Personality and Social Psychology Bulletin*. He serves as Associate Editor for the premier journal in the field, the *Journal of Personality and Social Psychology*.

Norbert Schwarz, DrPhil, is Professor of Psychology, Research Professor in the Survey Research Center and the Research Center for Group Dynamics at the Institute for Social Research, and Professor of Marketing in the Ross School of Business at the University of Michigan. His research interests focus on human judgment and cognition. Dr. Schwarz is a Fellow of the American Academy of Arts and Sciences, the Association for Psychological Science, and the Society for Personality and Social Psychology. His publications include 20 books and more than 200 journal articles and book chapters.

Contributors

Mahzarin R. Banaji, PhD, Department of Psychology, Harvard University, Cambridge, Massachusetts

John A. Bargh, PhD, Department of Psychology, Yale University, New Haven, Connecticut

Galen V. Bodenhausen, PhD, Department of Psychology, Northwestern University, Evanston, Illinois

John T. Cacioppo, PhD, Department of Psychology, University of Chicago, Chicago, Illinois

Frederica R. Conrey, PhD, Department of Psychology, Indiana University, Bloomington, Indiana

Jan De Houwer, PhD, Department of Psychology, University of Ghent, Ghent, Belgium

Melissa J. Ferguson, PhD, Department of Psychology, Cornell University, Ithaca, New York

Bertram Gawronski, PhD, Department of Psychology, University of Western Ontario, London, Ontario, Canada

Anthony G. Greenwald, PhD, Department of Psychology, University of Washington, Seattle, Washington

Tiffany A. Ito, PhD, Department of Psychology, University of Colorado, Boulder, Colorado

Kristin A. Lane, MS, Department of Psychology, Harvard University, Cambridge, Massachusetts

Agnes Moors, PhD, Fund for Scientific Research, Flanders, Belgium

Brian A. Nosek, PhD, Department of Psychology, University of Virginia, Charlottesville, Virginia

Andreas Olsson, PhD, Department of Psychology, Columbia University, New York, New York

Elizabeth A. Phelps, PhD, Department of Psychology, New York University, New York, New York

Klaus Rothermund, PhD, Department of Psychology, University of Jena, Jena, Germany

Norbert Schwarz, DrPhil, Institute for Social Research, University of Michigan, Ann Arbor, Michigan

Denise Sekaquaptewa, PhD, Department of Psychology, University of Michigan, Ann Arbor, Michigan

Eliot R. Smith, PhD, Department of Psychology, Indiana University, Bloomington, Indiana

Patrick T. Vargas, PhD, Department of Advertising, University of Illinois at Urbana–Champaign, Urbana, Illinois

William von Hippel, PhD, School of Psychology, University of New South Wales, Sydney, Australia

Dirk Wentura, PhD, Department of Psychology, Saarland University, Saarbrucken, Germany

Bernd Wittenbrink, PhD, Center for Decision Research, University of Chicago, Chicago, Illinois

Contents

II. CRITICAL PERSPECTIVES

1 Introduction

Bernd Wittenbrink
Norbert Schwarz

Over the last two decades, few developments in social psychology have generated as much attention and excitement as the development of new implicit measures of attitudes, which promise to assess attitudes that respondents may not be willing to report directly or may not even be aware of themselves. The interest in these new measures has spurred significant research activity that has produced a growing number of available measures and a flurry of empirical studies concerning their effectiveness and potential limitations. This book offers a detailed introduction to this literature. Specifically, the contributions to Part I of this book describe implicit measurement procedures that have been most influential thus far. The chapters in this part outline the measures' underlying theoretical rationales, provide advice on the implementation of these measures, and review what has been learned through their use. The contributions to Part II offer diverging perspectives on implicit measures of attitudes, identify current theoretical controversies, and highlight avenues for future research. This introductory chapter provides an initial orientation for readers new to the area and offers a short preview of what is to come.

EXPLICIT AND IMPLICIT MEASURES OF ATTITUDES

Throughout the social and behavioral sciences, the dominant method of attitude measurement is the collection of explicit self-reports:

When we want to know people's attitudes toward a person, group, political issue, or product, we ask them to report them, usually by marking a rating scale or by selecting one of several response alternatives. But since the early days of attitude research, researchers have often been concerned that respondents may (sometimes) be unwilling or unable to report on their attitudes in an unbiased manner (for a review, see DeMaio, 1984). Moreover, the answers that research participants provide are highly context dependent and vary as a function of who asks, how they ask, and related variables (for reviews, see Schwarz, Groves, & Schuman, 1998; Sudman, Bradburn, & Schwarz, 1996; Tourangeau, Rips, & Rasinski, 2000). Some of the emerging context effects reflect strategic responding, whereas others reflect the cognitive and communicative processes involved in question comprehension and judgment formation. These different concerns gave rise to various methodological and theoretical answers.

Strategic Responding

Researchers' concern that participants may be unwilling to accurately report their attitudes prompted the development of three broad classes of methodological responses. One response maintains explicit self-reports as the key attitude measure and addresses respondents' presumed unwillingness to accurately report their attitudes by minimizing the incentives for socially desirable self-presentation. Relevant procedures range from simple assurances of anonymity and confidentiality to complex randomized response techniques (Bradburn, Sudman, & Warnsink, 2004). In the latter case, respondents are presented with two different questions, an innocuous one and a socially sensitive one, and draw a card that determines which one they are to answer. Given properly worded response alternatives, the interviewer remains unaware as to which question the answer pertains, thus ensuring the highest possible level of confidentiality. Other procedures create conditions that present a disincentive for socially desirable responding. For example, Sigall and Page's (1971) "bogus pipeline" technique involves convincing participants that the researcher can discern their true attitude independent of what they say, thus making lying an embarrassment. Empirically, these various techniques have been found to increase the frequency of socially undesirable answers. For example, people are more likely to admit that they enjoy pornography under randomized response conditions (Himmelfarb & Lickteig, 1982), and White participants are more likely to report that they dislike African Americans under bogus pipeline conditions (e.g., Allen, 1975). All of these procedures presume, however, that respondents know their attitude and merely hesitate to report it. Yet deception and self-presentation may not only be directed toward others, but may also be directed toward the self (e.g., Paulhus, 1984). Perhaps people sometimes hold attitudes of which they are not aware or which they do not even want to admit to themselves.

The second class of methodological responses addresses this concern by replacing explicit self-reports of attitudes with indirect measures. Because research participants are presumably unaware of the relationship between these measures and their attitudes, indirect measures also minimize the incentives and opportunities for strategic responding. Theoretically, the use of indirect measures is based on the assumption that attitudes exert a systematic influence on people's performance on a variety of tasks and that the size of this influence can serve as an index of the underlying attitude. Not surprisingly, the theoretical assumptions made have varied widely over the history of attitude research. From the early use of projective tests (e.g., Proshansky, 1943) to the current use of response latency measures (Lane, Banaji, Nosek, & Greenwald, Chapter 3, this volume; Wittenbrink, Chapter 2, this volume) and low-tech alternatives informed by the processing assumptions of social cognition research (Vargas, Sekaquaptewa, & von Hippel, Chapter 4, this volume), the selection of indirect measures mirrors historical shifts in the underlying conceptualization of attitudes, as Vargas and colleagues note. Throughout, the usefulness of indirect measures depends on the accuracy of the bridging assumptions that link the observed response to the presumed underlying attitude, as the theoretical controversies surrounding the currently dominant response latency measures illustrate (Chapters 7–11).

Finally, a third class of methodological approaches attempts to assess research participants' evaluative responses in ways that bypass any opportunity for strategic responding, relying on the assessment of physiological reactions and brain activity (Ito & Cacioppo, Chapter 5, this volume; Olsson & Phelps, Chapter 6, this volume).

Because the latter two approaches to attitude measurement do not involve explicit self-reports, the indicators they provide can be generically referred to as implicit measures of attitudes (although some authors would prefer a more restrictive definition; see De Houwer & Moors, Chapter 7, this volume).

CONTEXT DEPENDENCY

Whereas the possibility of strategic responding does not call the existence of stable and enduring attitudes into question, the observation that attitude reports vary as a function of numerous other contextual variables casts doubt on the assumption that attitudes are stable evaluations stored in memory. The theoretical responses to these doubts have taken a number of different forms. On one hand, attitude construal models hold that attitude reports are evaluative judgments that are made up on the spot, based on the declarative and experiential information that is accessible at the time (e.g., Schwarz & Bohner, 2001); from this perspective, the psychology of attitudes is the psychology of evaluative judgment. In contrast, others assume that context effects merely reflect noise that results from the deliberate consideration of contextual information and that attitudes are best assessed in ways that limit deliberate processing (see Ferguson & Bargh, Chapter 9, this volume, for a discussion). The most influential version of this argument conceptualizes attitudes as stored object–evaluation links that are automatically activated upon exposure to the attitude object (Fazio, 1995) and relies on evaluative priming procedures (described below and in Chapter 2) to assess the strength of the object–evaluation link. As Ferguson and Bargh (Chapter 9) emphasize, attitudes conceptualized and measured in this way are often "assumed to be contextually independent . . . , to the point that an implicit attitude measure was regarded as a potential 'bona fide pipeline' to people's inner attitudes" (p. 220). Hence, implicit measures of attitudes may not only provide an answer to the problem of strategic responding, but they have also been thought to limit the context dependency of attitude measurement. Next, we turn to these measures.

IMPLICIT MEASURES OF ATTITUDES: WHAT'S AVAILABLE?

Response Time Measures

The currently most widely used implicit measures of attitudes rely on response time measurement. These measures take advantage of one of two reliable observations, namely, (1) the observation that exposure to a stimulus facilitates subsequent responses to related stimuli or (2) the observation that a stimulus is responded to more slowly when it contains multiple features that each imply a different response.

Sequential Priming Procedures

As a large body of research in cognitive psychology indicates (for a review, see Neely, 1991), exposure to a concept (e.g., *doctor*) facilitates the subsequent recognition of related concepts (e.g., *nurse*). A common explanation for this phenomenon holds that exposure to the initial concept (the prime) activates semantically related concepts in memory, thus reducing the time needed for their identification.

Concept priming procedures take advantage of this facilitation effect to assess a person's associations with an attitude object. For example, Wittenbrink, Judd, and Park (1997) exposed participants to African American or White primes and assessed how quickly they could identify subsequently presented trait terms of positive versus negative valence, some of which were part of the cultural stereotype about the group and some were not. The observed facilitation patterns provide information bearing on three questions: (1) Does the exposure to the group activate associated stereotypical traits, independent of their valence? If so, stereotypical traits will be recognized faster than stereotype-unrelated traits. (2) Is the automatic activation evaluatively biased; for example, are negative stereotypical traits identified more quickly than positive ones? (3) Does exposure to the group prime activate general evaluative associations, independent of their stereotypicality?

Whereas concept priming procedures present target words with descriptive meaning and use decision tasks that require participants to identify the word, *evaluative priming* procedures (Fazio, Sanbonmatsu, Powell, & Kardes, 1986) present target words with general evaluative meanings (e.g., awful, pleasant) and ask participants to judge the words' evaluative connotation (good or bad). Of interest is whether exposure to an attitude object facilitates the evaluative response to negative or positive target words. Thus, evaluative priming assesses whether an attitude object triggers an automatic evaluation, whereas concept priming assesses descriptive associations that may have evaluative content.

Wittenbrink (Chapter 2, this volume) reviews these procedures, provides advice on their implementation, and summarizes representative findings.

Response Competition Procedures

Whereas the preceding procedures take advantage of priming effects, a second class of response time procedures is based on interference effects that may occur when different features of an attitude object imply different responses. The best known of these procedures is the Implicit Association Test (IAT) (Greenwald, McGhee, & Schwartz, 1998), reviewed by Lane, Banaji, Nosek, and Greenwald (Chapter 3, this volume).

The IAT presents two discrimination tasks that are combined in specific ways across a sequence of five steps. To assess attitudes toward African Americans and European Americans, for example, the first discrimination task may present names that are typical for the respective group and then ask participants to categorize each name as "White" versus "Black." They do so by pressing a response key assigned to "White" with the left hand or a response key assigned to "Black" with the right hand. Next, the second discrimination task presents words with pleasant (e.g., love) or unpleasant (e.g., poison) connotations, which participants classify as positive versus negative by pressing the left or right response key. At the third step, these two tasks are superimposed and participants press the left key when either a White name or a pleasant word is shown, but the right key when either a Black name or an unpleasant word is shown. As in the above facilitation paradigms, this task is easier when evaluatively associated categories share the same response key—for example, when White participants press the left key to categorize White names and pleasant words. Going beyond this assessment of response facilitation, the IAT involves two more steps. At the fourth step, the assignment of keys to White and Black names is reversed, so that participants who first used the left key for White names now use the left key for Black names. Finally, the two discrimination tasks are again superimposed, resulting in an assignment of "Black" and "pleasant" to the left response key and "White" and "unpleasant" to the right response key.

Of interest is the speed with which participants can perform the two superimposed discrimination tasks at step 3 and step 5. Do participants respond faster when a given response key pertains either to the pairing of White names + pleasant words or Black names + unpleasant words (step 3) than when this pairing is reversed and a given response key pertains either to White names + unpleasant words or Black names + pleasant words (step 5)? In the present example, a faster response at step 3 than at step 5 is thought to indicate that White names and positive evaluations, and Black names and negative evaluations, are more strongly associated than the reverse pairings.

Lane and colleagues (Chapter 3, this volume) review the underlying logic, report representative findings, and provide hands-on advice for the implementation and scoring of the IAT. Related response competition tasks include the Go/No-go Association Task (GNAT; Nosek & Banaji, 2001) and the Extrinsic Affective Simon Task (EAST; De Houwer, 2003).

Paper-and-Pencil Measures

Whereas the preceding measures require a high degree of instrumentation and technical sophistication, other implicit measures of attitudes are decidedly low-tech. Vargas, Sekaquaptewa, and von Hippel (Chapter 4, this volume) provide an informative review of a wide range of such low-tech measures and place them in the context of the history of attitude research.

Drawing on insights from social cognition research, some of these measures take advantage of the observation that attitudes and expectations have systematic effects on individuals' information processing. For example, people are more likely to spontaneously explain events that disconfirm rather than confirm their expectations (e.g., Hastie, 1984), suggesting that the amount of explanatory activity can serve as an indirect measure of a person's expectations. The Stereotypic Explanatory Bias (SEB) measure developed by Sekaquaptewa, Espinoza, Thompson, Vargas, and von Hippel (2003) builds on this observation and uses the number of explanations generated in response to stereotype-consistent versus stereotype-inconsistent behaviors as an implicit measure of stereotyping. Similarly, people describe expected or stereotype-consistent behaviors in more abstract terms than unexpected or stereotype-inconsistent behaviors, a phenomenon known as the Linguistic Intergroup Bias (LIB; see, e.g., Maass, Salvi, Arcuri, & Semin, 1989). The size of this bias can again be used as an indirect measure to gauge the underlying expectations. As Vargas and colleagues (Chapter 4, this volume) review, such measures have been found to predict prejudiced behaviors, although little is known about their psychometric qualities. Given their ease of use, the various measures reviewed by Vargas and colleagues deserve more systematic methodological exploration.

Physiological Responses and Brain Activity

Because of their involuntary and hard-to-control nature, physiological correlates of evaluative responses have long been of interest to attitude researchers who doubted respondents' explicit self-reports. Whereas early attempts to rely on the galvanic skin response (e.g., Rankin & Campbell, 1955) or on pupillary dilation or restriction (e.g., Hess, 1965) as indirect measures met with little success, recent progress in social psychophysiology and neuroscience suggests a more optimistic outlook, although a one-to-one mapping of neural and psychological processes is unlikely, as Ito and Cacioppo (Chapter 5, this volume) emphasize.

Ito and Cacioppo (Chapter 5, this volume) provide a tutorial overview of the available measures, ranging from autonomic responses, like cardiovascular and electrodermal activity, to facial electromyography and startle eyeblink modification or measures of brain activity, like functional magnetic resonance imaging and event-related brain potentials. Their review highlights the numerous intricacies of these measures, which require considerable specialized expertise for their implementation and interpretation. Olsson and Phelps's (Chapter 6, this volume) discussion of what we can and cannot learn from neuroimaging complements Ito and Cacioppo's overview and summarizes the neural underpinnings of social evaluations.

Summary

In combination, this first set of contributions (Chapters 2–6) provides an overview of the current state of the art in the implicit measurement of attitudes. These chapters review the currently available measures, offer advice on their implementation and interpretation, and summarize representative research findings. The remaining chapters provide different theoretical perspectives on the operation of these measures and address current controversies.

PERSPECTIVES AND CONTROVERSIES

What Makes a Measure "Implicit"?

Above, we distinguished between explicit and implicit measures of attitudes by virtue of their transparency and potential for strategic responding. In Chapter 7, this volume, De Houwer and Moors provide a thoughtful discussion of what qualifies a measure as "implicit." They adopt a more restrictive conceptualization that defines implicit measures as "measurement outcomes that reflect the to-be-measured construct by virtue of processes that are uncontrolled, unintentional, goal independent, purely stimulus driven, autonomous, unconscious, efficient, or fast" (pp. 188–189). Although all of the measures reviewed in Chapters 2–6 meet some of these criteria, few are likely to meet all of them. In fact, the extent to which even the most widely used measures meet some of these criteria is currently unknown, and De Houwer and Moors outline a research program that addresses these issues. Gawronski and Bodenhausen's (Chapter 11, this volume) discussion of conceptual and terminological ambiguities echoes these concerns.

Reiterating De Houwer and Moors's (Chapter 7, this volume) call for a more detailed analysis of the processes underlying implicit measures of attitudes, Wentura and Rothermund (Chapter 8, this volume) offer a plea for more basic research on the experimental paradigms on which implicit attitude measures are based. Their chapter raises several important questions about how response latency measures actually work and what exactly they measure. In general, it is assumed that latency-based measures capture associations between constructs and evaluations. In the case of the IAT, for example, a person is thought to respond faster to one set of key pairings because he or she holds relatively stronger associations for this pair than for the other. Wentura and Rothermund note that not all findings are perfectly consistent with such an associative account and, instead, offer an alternative explanation. In particular, they suggest that IAT effects reflect differences in the relative salience of the employed response categories. Although such salience differences themselves may be influenced by evaluative associations, there are other factors that likely impact salience as well and thus might limit the validity of the IAT as a measure of associative strength between an attitude object and an evaluation. Hence, the chapter by Wentura and Rothermund highlights the importance of future research on the mechanisms underlying implicit measurement procedures. Clarifying the exact mechanism by which these measures operate should improve our understanding of how to use and design effective implicit measurement tools.

Are Implicit Measures Context Dependent?

As Ferguson and Bargh (Chapter 9, this volume) highlight, the initial hope that responses to implicit measures of attitudes that limit deliberation may be less context dependent than responses to explicit attitude questions has not been supported. Instead, evaluative and conceptual priming procedures (Wittenbrink, Chapter 2, this volume) and response competition procedures like the IAT (Lane et al., Chapter 3, this volume) show pronounced context effects that usually parallel the context effects observed on explicit attitude measures. For example, Dasgupta and Greenwald (2001) observed that exposure to pictures of liked African Americans and disliked European Americans resulted in shifts on a subsequent IAT that parallel the effects of exposure to liked or disliked exemplars on explicit measures of attitudes (e.g., Bodenhausen, Schwarz, Bless, & Wänke, 1995). Similarly, Wittenbrink, Judd, and Park (2001) found that the same Black face primes elicited more negative automatic responses when the faces were presented on the background of an urban street scene rather than a church scene. Blair (2002) provides an extensive review of related findings.

Of particular interest is Lowery, Hardin, and Sinclair's (2001) observation that participants provided less negative automatic evaluations of African Americans when the experimenter was Black rather than White. This finding parallels the observed influence of interviewer race and ethnicity in the survey research literature (e.g., Hatchett & Schuman, 1976; Weeks & Moore, 1981). Yet the low transparency of Lowery and colleagues' implicit attitude measures makes it unlikely that participants' favorable attitude toward African Americans was based on deliberate strategic responding. Instead, it raises the possibility that experimenters and interviewers serve as highly accessible positive exemplars, thus increasing the favorability of the response as observed in studies that used names or pictures as exemplar primes (e.g., Bodenhausen et al.,1995; Dasgupta & Greenwald, 2001). This possibility would have far-reaching implications for the conceptualization of race of interviewer effects and the assumed role of socially desirable responding in their emergence.

To account for the context dependency of implicit measures, Ferguson and Bargh (Chapter 9, this volume) suggest that automatic attitudes are responses to object-centered contexts rather than to the attitude object in isolation. They conceptualize the underlying process in terms of a connectionist system, consistent with Smith and Conrey's (Chapter 10, this volume) assertion that "mental representations are states and not things."

From Smith and Conrey's (Chapter 10) perspective, the context sensitivity of implicit as well as explicit measures reflects the dynamic and context-sensitive nature of the mental representations on which evaluative responses are based. Only context-sensitive representations allow "the mind to respond efficiently and accurately to a constantly changing environment that calls for situated knowledge and behaviors" (p. 256). Hence, implicit measures of attitudes do not (solely) reflect previously learned object–evaluation links, but capture the current evaluative response to the attitude object in its present context, consistent with the observation that automatic evaluations can be obtained for novel objects, for which no previously acquired object–attitude links are stored in memory (Duckworth, Bargh, Garcia, & Chaiken, 2002).

Where To?

In the concluding Chapter 11, this volume, Gawronski and Bodenhausen identify important open issues, ranging from diverging theoretical conceptualizations of attitudes, to the (often lacking) correspondence between these conceptualizations and measurement procedures, and the conditions under which results obtained with different implicit measures may or may not converge. Their discussion provides welcome conceptual clarifications and suggests an ambitious but promising agenda for future research. In particular, Gawronski and Bodenhausen advocate the integration of existing small-scale explanations for how implicit assessment procedures work with broader, large-scale theories on the determinants of judgment and behavior and the interplay of affect and cognition. At present, accounts of the procedural underpinnings of implicit measures tend to involve concrete operational constructs that do not readily translate into the more abstract terminology of broader theories of social judgment and behavior. An integration of these divergent perspectives could prove immensely useful for furthering our understanding of the way attitudes determine behavior, as well as improve our ability to assess these influences.

Empirical and theoretical research in this area is progressing at a rapid pace, and an increasing number of researchers make use of implicit measures of attitudes. We hope that this book's introductory tutorials will provide useful guidance on the use and implementation of these measures and that the accompanying critical perspectives foster awareness of the numerous remaining ambiguities and open issues.

REFERENCES

Allen, B. P. (1975). Social distance and admiration reactions of "unprejudiced" whites. *Journal of Personality, 43,* 709–726.

Blair, I. V. (2002). The malleability of automatic stereotypes and prejudice. *Personality and Social Psychology Review, 6,* 242–261.

Bodenhausen, G. V., Schwarz, N., Bless, H., & Wänke, M. (1995). Effects of atypical exemplars on racial beliefs: Enlightened racism or generalized appraisals? *Journal of Experimental Social Psychology, 31,* 48–63.

Bradburn, N., Sudman, S., & Wansink, B. (2004). *Asking questions* (2nd ed.). San Francisco: Jossey-Bass.

Dasgupta, N., & Greenwald, A. G. (2001). On the malleability of automatic attitudes: Combating automatic prejudice with images of liked and disliked individuals. *Journal of Personality and Social Psychology, 81,* 800–814.

De Houwer, J. (2003). The Extrinsic Affective Simon Task. *Experimental Psychology, 50,* 77–85.

DeMaio, T. J. (1984). Social desirability and survey measurement: A review. In C. F. Turner & E. Martin (Eds.), *Surveying subjective phenomena* (Vol. 2, pp. 257–281). New York: Russell Sage.

Duckworth, K. L., Bargh, J. A., Garcia, M., & Chaiken, S. (2002). The automatic evaluation of novel stimuli. *Psychological Science, 13,* 513–519.

Fazio, R. H. (1995). Attitudes as object–evaluation associations: Determinants, consequences, and correlates of attitude accessibility. In R. E. Petty & J. A. Krosnick (Eds.), *Attitude strength* (pp. 247–282). Mahwah, NJ: Erlbaum.

Fazio, R. H., Sanbonmatsu, D. M., Powell, M. C., & Kardes, F. R. (1986). On the automatic activation of attitudes. *Journal of Personality and Social Psychology, 50,* 229–238.

Greenwald, A. G., McGhee, D. E., & Schwarz, J. L. K. (1998). Measuring individual differences in implicit cognition: The Implicit Association Test. *Journal of Personality and Social Psychology, 74,* 1464–1480.

Hastie, R. (1984). Causes and effects of causal attribution. *Journal of Personality and Social Psychology, 46,* 44–56.

Hatchett, S., & Schuman, H. (1976). White respondents and race-of-interviewer effects. *Public Opinion Quarterly, 39,* 523–528.

Hess, E. H. (1965). Attitude and pupil size. *Scientific American, 212,* 46–54.

Himmelfarb, S., & Lickteig, C. (1982). Social desirability and the randomized response technique. *Journal of Personality and Social Psychology, 43,* 710–717.

Lowery, B. S., Hardin, C. D., & Sinclair, S. (2001). Social influence on automatic racial prejudice. *Journal of Personality and Social Psychology, 81,* 842–855.

Maass, A., Salvi, D., Arcuri, L., & Semin, G. (1989). Language use in intergroup contexts: The linguistic intergroup bias. *Journal of Personality and Social Psychology, 57,* 981–993.

Neely, J. H. (1991). Semantic priming effects in visual word recognition: A selective review of current findings and theories. In D. Besner & G. W. Humphreys (Eds.), *Basic processes in reading: Visual word recognition* (pp. 264–336). Hillsdale, NJ: Erlbaum.

Nosek, B. A., & Banaji, M. R. (2001). The Go/No-go Association Task. *Social Cognition, 19*(6), 625–666.

Paulhus, D. L. (1984). Two-component models of socially desirable responding. *Journal of Personality and Social Psychology, 46*(3), 598–609.

Proshansky, H. M. (1943). A projective method for the study of attitudes. *Journal of Abnormal and Social Psychology, 38,* 393–395.

Rankin, R. E., & Campbell, D. T. (1955). Galvanic skin response to negro and white experimenters. *Journal of Abnormal and Social Psychology, 51,* 30–33.

Schwarz, N., & Bohner, G. (2001). The construction of attitudes. In A. Tesser & N. Schwarz (Eds.), *Blackwell handbook of social psychology: Intraindividual processes* (pp. 436–457). Malden, MA: Blackwell.

Schwarz, N., Groves, R., & Schuman, H. (1998). Survey methods. In D. Gilbert, S. Fiske, & G. Lindzey (Eds.), *Handbook of social psychology* (4th ed., Vol. 1, pp. 143–179). New York: McGraw-Hill.

Sekaquaptewa, D., Espinoza, P., Thompson, M., Vargas, P., & von Hippel, W. (2003). Stereotypic explanatory bias: Implicit stereotyping as a predictor of discrimination. *Journal of Experimental Social Psychology, 39,* 75–82.

Signall, H., & Page, R. (1971). Current stereotypes: A little fading, a little faking. *Journal of Personality and Social Psychology, 18,* 247–255.

Sudman, S., Bradburn, N. M., & Schwarz, N. (1996). *Thinking about answers: The application of cognitive processes to survey methodology.* San Francisco: Jossey-Bass.

Courageous, R., Rips, L. J., & Resins, K. (2000). *The psychology of survey response.* Cambridge, UK: Cambridge University Press.

Weeks, M. F., & Moore, R. P. (1981). Ethnicity-of-interviewer effects on ethnic respondents. *Public Opinion Quarterly, 45,* 245–249.

Writtenbrink, B., Judd, C. M., & Park, B. (1997). Evidence for racial prejudice at the implicit level and its relationships with questionnaire measures. *Journal of Personality and Social Psychology, 72,* 262–274.

Writtenbrink, B., Judd, C. M., & Park, B. (2001). Spontaneous prejudice in context: Variability in automatically activated attitudes. *Journal of Personality and Social Psychology, 81,* 815–827.

Part I Procedures and Their Implementation

2 Measuring Attitudes through Priming

Bernd Wittenbrink

In their efforts to achieve measurement accuracy, attitude researchers have developed a wide variety of measurement techniques (for a recent review, see Krosnick, Judd, & Wittenbrink, 2005). A set of new measures, which have become known collectively as *implicit attitude measures*, are an important recent addition to the many existing alternatives. They are designed to assess attitudinal responses, without the person being aware of or necessarily intending the attitude to affect his or her response.[1] The idea to capture attitudinal influences that are outside a respondent's awareness is not entirely new. Early unobtrusive assessment techniques were meant to do the same (e.g., Proshansy, 1943; Westie, 1953). What is new about the recent set of implicit measures is that they aim to assess *automatic evaluative responses* to an attitude object. Such responses occur fast, within a few hundred milliseconds after encountering the attitude object. They result from processes that are unintentional, resource efficient, and outside conscious awareness and control (Shiffrin & Schneider, 1977).

Considering the many existing alternatives, one might wonder about the need for yet another set of measures. Nevertheless, implicit attitude measures have received considerable attention during the relatively short time since their introduction in the 1980s. In fact, as illustrated by Figure 2.1, the interest in these new measures is growing at a rapid pace. There are two primary reasons for this attraction.

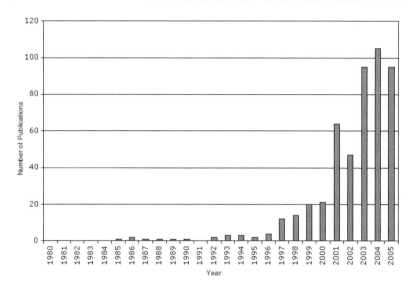

FIGURE 2.1. Number of yearly publications on implicit attitudes and related topics since 1980. The graph is based on an informal search of the PsychInfo database for articles that mention the terms *implicit attitude* or *automatic attitude*, or that make reference to one of the standard implicit attitude measurement techniques (e.g., IAT, evaluative priming) in their titles or abstracts. The count further includes articles containing the terms *implicit prejudice* or *implicit self-esteem*, two of the most frequently studied topics in this area.

The first is that implicit measures promise to address a long-standing and fundamental problem with standard self-report measures of attitudes: people do not necessarily tell the truth when asked about their attitudes toward socially sensitive issues. Instead, people may report attitudes that they believe are more socially desirable in order to present themselves in a favorable way to others and to themselves (Paulhus, 1984). Different strategies have been used to limit such self-presentational effects on attitude reports, ranging from the simple, such as ensuring respondents' anonymity (Gordon, 1987), to the highly elaborate, like the bogus pipeline procedure in which participants are led to believe that the researcher can otherwise determine the truthfulness of an answer (Sigall & Page, 1971). In general, these strategies do affect self-report measures, shifting the reported attitudes toward less socially desirable responses (Krosnick et al., 2005). However, even when such strategies are used, it remains unknown how much of a shift is really necessary to yield a correct attitude estimate, and in some cases it may even be doubtful whether the attitudes reported under low desirability conditions are any more accurate than those obtained under "normal" circumstances (Roese & Jamieson, 1993). In other words, although these strategies may have some influence on attitude reports, their overall effectiveness remains uncertain. Especially for research on socially sensitive attitudes like racial prejudice, the use of self-reports has continued to raise concerns in the field (e.g., Crosby, Bromley, & Saxe, 1980).

In contrast to self-report measures, implicit measures aim to assess attitudinal responses that do not stem from an active, intentional search for relevant information, but instead are the result of passive processes that run their course automatically following exposure to the attitude object. Because of its spontaneous nature this initial attitudinal response is not controllable and should therefore not be open to monitoring for purposes of self-presentation. As a result, implicit assessment techniques promise an innovative way to effectively assess attitudes free of intentional distortions or strategic manipulation. Descriptions of implicit measures generally emphasize this quality (Dovidio & Fazio, 1992; Fazio, Jackson, Dunton, & Williams, 1995; Greenwald, McGhee, & Schwartz, 1998), and, not surprisingly, among the areas where implicit measures have been most influential are those where distortions due to impression management are particularly likely (e.g., prejudice, self-esteem, risk-related health behavior). Thus, the potential to assess attitudes free of social desirability concerns explains to a significant degree the measures' recent popularity.

A second important factor driving the interest in implicit measures concerns the popularity of the specific process argument on which implicit measures are based; namely, that evaluations can occur automatically without any deliberation. Indeed, all contemporary accounts of how attitudes influence judgment and behavior argue that evaluations vary in the extent to which they are deliberate and effortful (e.g., Bargh, 1997; Chaiken, 1987; Fazio, 1990; Krosnick et al., 2005; Petty & Cacioppo, 1986; Strack & Martin, 1987; Wegener & Petty, 1997; Wilson, Lindsey, & Schooler, 2000). Likewise, the distinction between automatic associative processes and deliberative reasoning processes also plays an important role in more general models of behavior and judgment (Sloman, 1996; Smith & DeCoster, 2000; Strack & Deutsch, 2004). As a result, attitude research has been paying increasing attention to the circumstances under which evaluations occur without deliberation (for a review, see Wegner & Bargh, 1998). Implicit attitude measures provide the necessary tool for this work because they intend to capture automatic attitudinal responses, and separate such automatic responses from the more deliberate evaluations assessed by standard self-report measures.

Of the various implicit measures that have become popular in recent years, this chapter focuses on those that assess attitudes through
priming. This particular technique aims to determine automatic attitude activation from the impact that an attitude object has on the
speed with which a person can make certain judgments when such a
judgment is preceded (i.e., "primed") by the attitude object. Priming
measures were the first to start the trend toward the new implicit assessment techniques. They give researchers relatively stringent control over what psychological processes contribute to the attitudinal
response that is being assessed. They are also less invasive and easier
to administer than comparable techniques based on physiological
measures, although they require significantly more control over the
assessment situation than the Implicit Association Test (IAT), another common implicit technique based on response latency measures (see the corresponding chapters in this volume).

The goal of this chapter is to provide an overview of existing
priming measures for scholars interested in using such procedures for
their own research. The chapter offers an introduction to the basic
technique of priming as well as a review of relevant findings in order
to allow researchers a critical evaluation of what can and cannot be
accomplished with this kind of attitude measure. Specifically, I describe the procedures that have been employed, review explanations
for why and how priming works, and discuss a variety of variables
that influence the results obtained with priming measures. The chapter concludes with some comments on the usefulness of these measures for attitudes research.

PROCEDURE: HOW TO IMPLEMENT
PRIMING MEASURES?

A variety of priming procedures have been used to measure attitudes,
all derived from a classic paradigm in cognitive psychology.[2] In this
paradigm, which dates back to a seminal experiment by Meyer and
Schvaneveldt (1971), participants have to decide as quickly as possible whether a visually presented string of letters is an English word
(e.g., *BUTTER* vs. *BUTTIR*). In addition, the letter string is paired
with another word, the prime. The classic finding, replicated in numerous experiments, is that participants are faster in making such
lexical decisions when prime and target string are semantically related, when, for example, the string *butter* is paired with the prime
bread instead of an unrelated word like *doctor.* A common explanation for the effect is based on theories of spreading activation in

semantic networks and holds that the prime activates other semantically related concepts in long-term memory. As a result of this additional activation, related targets can be recognized and responded to faster (Neely, 1977; Posner & Snyder, 1975).

The original experiment presented both prime and target strings simultaneously in pairs. However, subsequent research modified the procedure by sequentially displaying first the prime and then the target string (e.g., Meyer, Schvaneveldt, & Ruddy, 1975; Neely, 1976). The modification has several advantages over the original paired display, most notably that it offers researchers more precise control over the stimulus input that participants use for their decisions, and that it allows researchers to vary the timing delay between prime and target. It has become the standard implementation of the paradigm in research on semantic priming (for a review, see Neely, 1991).

All priming procedures used for attitude measurement are based on this sequential variant of the semantic priming paradigm. The procedures generally present attitude objects as primes and pair them with targets that vary in their evaluative connotation (e.g., *spinach— pleasant* or *awful*) or on some other attitude-relevant dimension (e.g., *spinach—healthy* or *unhealthy*). The magnitude of facilitation observed for a given prime/target combination can then serve as an indicator of the degree with which a person relates the attitude object with a particular target. For example, in one of the first such adaptations Gaertner and McLaughlin (1983) assessed racial attitudes by pairing group primes (Blacks, Negroes, Whites) with positive and negative attributes (e.g., smart, lazy). Results indicated that White participants responded faster when positive attributes were paired with the prime "White" than with the primes "Blacks" or "Negroes." In other words, for the participants in these studies positive attributes were more closely linked to their representations of White people than of people of color.

Since the early demonstrations by Gaertner and McLaughlin as well as others (e.g., Fazio, Sanbonmatsu, Powell, & Kardes, 1986; Greenwald, Klinger, & Liu, 1989; Perdue & Gurtman, 1990), two particular strategies for how to use this general paradigm for the purpose of attitude measurement have emerged, *evaluative priming* and *concept priming*. The two share many features as they originate from the same paradigm. But because they address somewhat different research questions, and because different mechanisms seem to contribute to their operation, it is nevertheless important to distinguish these two variants of attitude priming.

The most common priming procedure used for attitude measurement was proposed by Fazio and his colleagues (1986). Fazio termed this procedure *evaluative priming*, although it has also been referred to as *affective priming* by others (e.g., Hermans, De Houwer, & Eelen, 1994; Klauer & Musch, 2003; Murphy & Zajonc, 1993; Wentura, 2002). For an evaluative priming procedure, primes are paired with target words of polarized valence (e.g., *pleasant, appealing*, or *delightful* vs. *awful, disgusting*, or *repulsive*), which participants classify for their evaluative connotation. That is, participants are asked to indicate as quickly as possible whether the meaning of the target implies either *good* or *bad*. Of interest is whether, across several trials with different targets, the attitude prime facilitates responses to positively valenced targets and/or responses to negatively valenced targets. The magnitude of such facilitation serves as a measure of automatic activation of a positive and/or negative evaluation.

The critical characteristic of this adaptation of sequential priming is that the target items vary in valence but are otherwise completely unrelated to the attitude object. In other words, the procedure investigates *evaluative* links between prime and target, rather than focusing on semantic associations as does semantic priming.

The initial experiments by Fazio and colleagues included a set of attitude primes for which participants held relatively strong positive or negative attitudes. For these primes, results showed that indeed the time needed to categorize the targets as either *good* or *bad* was significantly shorter when they were preceded by a prime of matching valence, as compared with primes of opposite valence. Such evaluative priming effects have since been replicated in many studies for a broad variety of attitudes, including mundane items such as *cake* as well as socially significant issues like war and race. They have been obtained with both words and photos as primes. Evaluative priming commonly uses the evaluative decision task described above, although the effect has also been found on occasion when participants performed a lexical decision task, or a pronunciation task in which they were asked to simply say the target aloud (for a review, see Fazio, 2001).

Because of its focus on evaluative links between an attitude prime and target words, evaluative priming aims to assess the extent to which the participant associates an attitude object with a positive or negative evaluation, and not whether the attitude object may activate other declarative memory contents with evaluative implications (e.g., spinach is healthy). The activation of such declarative memory contents is precisely the subject of a second basic variant of these priming measures, *concept priming*. Like the original semantic priming paradigm, concept priming investigates semantic links between prime and target. That is, it includes positive and negative target items that vary in how descriptive they are for the attitude object and presents them in the context of a lexical decision task (or sometimes a pronunciation task). For example, in our own lab we used concept priming for the assessment of group attitudes (Wittenbrink, Judd, & Park, 1997). In this procedure, African American and White group primes were paired with trait attributes known to be part of the cultural stereotype of each group. In addition, half of the target items for each stereotype were positive in valence, and half were of negative valence. In this kind of design, facilitation observed for the various combinations of primes and types of targets offers separate estimates for the degree to which a group prime yields activation of the group concept (i.e., stereotype), the extent to which this concept activation is evaluatively biased (i.e., whether primarily negative or positive attributes are activated), and the capacity for a group prime to trigger an overall evaluation (i.e., to facilitate any item of particular valence, independent of the stereotype).

I return to the different types of attitude estimates that can be calculated from priming data in the "Measures" section of this chapter. Before considering these various alternatives in detail, however, I will first describe the basic procedure for prime and target presentation. In large part, the procedures are identical for evaluative and concept priming.

In summary, then, the critical distinction between evaluative priming and concept priming concerns the kind of prime–target link that is being assessed. Whereas evaluative priming assesses evaluative links, concept priming assesses conceptual associations between prime and target. For this, the two variants differ in terms of the type of targets that they require and the decision task that they employ.

Basic Procedure

In principle, priming measures can be administered on any device capable of presenting stimuli and recording responses with sufficiently accurate timing. Commonly, this is a personal computer running standard experimentation software packages (e.g., *DirectRT* for Windows OS or *PsyScope* for the Macintosh).[3]

Because priming measures assess differences in response latencies that are relatively small in magnitude (typically between 20 and 50 msec) and because the stimuli are visible for only brief periods of time, it is critical that researchers take steps to keep participants from becoming distracted from the experimental task. For example, measures are best administered in individual sessions, or at least in a physical space that is private and free of distractors.

The presentation of priming materials is organized into trials. Figure 2.2 illustrates the basic sequence of events for each trial. It typically starts with a cue orienting the participant's attention to the stimulus display. The cue is then replaced with the prime, either a word referencing the attitude object or a picture of it. The prime is followed by the target, which in most implementations remains visible until the participant has indicated a response (for example, by pressing a button or by giving the response verbally).[4] The time period between onset of the prime and the target is denoted by the stimulus-onset asynchrony (SOA). Of critical interest is, of course, how long it takes the participant to respond to the target stimulus. This response latency is defined as the time that elapses between the onset of the target and the overt response (RT in Figure 2.2).

Response latency measures are not sufficiently reliable for them to be based on single trial assessments. Instead, an attitude object must be paired repeatedly with a target, or type of target, to yield useful data. For example, in the previously mentioned Wittenbrink and colleagues (1997) study on racial attitudes, a single group prime was paired 12 times with each type of target item (i.e., positive stereotypic White items, negative stereotypic White items, etc.). In addition, response latency measures are commonly calculated relative to a baseline response where a neutral prime or no prime at all precedes the target. As a result, priming measures require multiple trials for each attitude object. The trials follow in rapid succession, separated by short intertrial intervals (ITI; 2 to 4 sec). To limit participant fa-

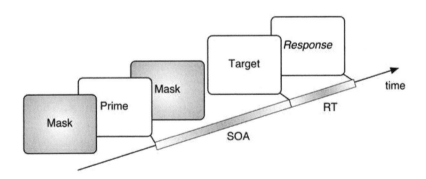

FIGURE 2.2. Sequential priming task with optional masking stimuli. SOA indicates the stimulus-onset asynchrony, the delay between the display onset of the prime and the target. RT indicates the central dependent measure in priming, the response time, measured as the time elapsed between onset of the target stimulus and the start of the overt response (e.g., a button press or the onset of a verbal response).

tigue, trials can be grouped into assessment blocks that are separated by short rest periods.

The response latency trials are typically described to the participant as being part of an experiment on word recognition. The participant is told that the task is to quickly identify the target words, or to determine the words' evaluative meaning if the measure uses an evaluative decision task. In addition, the primes are commonly described as distractors that are meant to make the task more difficult. The participant can be asked to respond only to the second stimulus (i.e., the target), or else he or she can be instructed to memorize the primes for later recall.[5] A different procedure for presenting the primes, which I describe in detail in the next section, involves displaying the primes below recognition threshold. In this case, no explanation is needed for the primes because they appear outside the participant's awareness.

Automatic Processing

A critical feature of priming measures is their ability to capture automatic responses to the attitude object. Several methods have been used to ensure that priming effects are limited to automatic activation (i.e., to preclude effects that could result from deliberate processing of the attitude prime). The most common approach is the use of a short SOA (the time period between onset of the prime and the target) of less than 300 msec between prime and target. Such a procedure effectively limits the time that the participant has available to process the prime before it is replaced by the target. Because automatic processes are thought to operate faster than controlled and effortful processes, automatic operations should dominate early stimulus processing, whereas controlled operations should become more prominent at later stages of processing. Thus, a procedure that allows only initial processing of the primes should favor automatic priming effects (Taylor, 1977).

Findings from semantic priming studies on the effects of task-induced expectations are also often cited in support of using a short SOA as a means to ensure automatic processing. In this work, participants are led to expect a particular kind of prime to be followed by a target that belongs to a category unrelated to the prime. For example, the prime *body* is said to be followed by targets that belong to the category *building parts* (e.g., *door*). A well-replicated finding then is that at short SOAs (e.g., 250 msec) these instructions have no effect on participants' response latencies (i.e., primes facilitate semantically related targets, independent of whether the target is expected to follow the prime or not); however, at longer SOAs (e.g., 1,000 msec), primes tend to have inhibitory effects on unexpected targets, actually slowing down responses to targets that are inconsistent with expectations (see, e.g., Neely, 1977). Following a proposition by Posner and Snyder (1975) that facilitatory effects result from automatic processing, whereas the expectation-driven inhibitory activity requires controlled processes, these findings have been interpreted as evidence that short SOA effects are due to automatic processing.

An alternative approach to this SOA manipulation has been the use of concealed primes that are presented below the participant's threshold for conscious recognition. In general, such subthreshold or "subliminal" primes yield overall smaller priming effects, making the procedure a potentially less sensitive measurement tool. A distinct advantage of this method, however, is its potential effectiveness in precluding controlled processes from influencing the response. After all, without conscious access to the prime no deliberate processing of it can occur (Balota, 1983). Three basic strategies have been used to implement subthreshold priming. The first involves the use of very short display times for the primes and pairing them with a masking stimulus. This combination of short exposure and additional stimulus input is meant to interfere with the conscious identification of the prime, while at the same time leaving intact the unconscious visual processing of the stimulus (Marcel, 1983). The masking stimuli used for this purpose are typically made up of scrambled elements of the priming stimuli. For example, if word primes are used, they may consist of scrambled letters or letter fragments. The primes then can be embedded in the mask by means of sandwich masking, a rapid sequential presentation in which the prime appears for only a few milliseconds, is preceded by a mask, and is again followed by another mask (Wittenbrink et al., 1997). In addition, such rapid displays can be combined with a response window that forces the participant to respond within a narrow time frame (about 100 msec) after presentation of the target stimulus (Greenwald, Draine, & Abrams, 1996).

This rapid presentation method obviously requires exact control over the display timing. It has become more feasible with the availability of fast personal computers and CRT displays, although more recent technical trends like multithreaded operating systems and LCD displays again complicate the use of standard computer equipment for reliable millisecond-accurate stimulus presentation.

In a second alternative for subthreshold presentation, prime and mask appear simultaneously. Using a dichoptic display, the prime is presented to the participant's nondominant eye while, simultaneously, the mask is displayed to the dominant eye (Greenwald et al., 1989). The method allows for substantially longer display times (about 100 msec); however, this benefit comes at the expense of having to rely on a stereoscopic viewing device and the need to determine the participant's dominant eye prior to administration of the measure (see Cheesman & Merikle, 1986, for a detailed description of this technique).

A somewhat different method for presenting primes below recognition threshold uses a parafoveal display of the prime. That is, the primes are displayed off center with their exact location varying across trials and with the orienting cue and target remaining in the display center. The procedure is based on evidence from Rayner (1978), who found that during text reading, words that appear in the parafoveal visual field (between 2° and 6° of visual angle) are processed to a certain extent without conscious awareness. In several studies, Bargh and his colleagues successfully employed such a parafoveal display, showing that words presented in this fashion can influence subsequent judgments without participants being able to identify the words (e.g., Bargh & Pietromonaco, 1982). The parafoveal display method can also be applied to sequential priming. For example, Bargh, Raymond, Pryor, and Strack (1995) presented primes and an accompanying mask randomly either 2 cm above or 2 cm below the orienting cue. Critically, the procedure does not rely on ultrashort display timing nor does it require a complicated viewing apparatus, making this parafoveal method potentially more useful for common measurement applications. However, the drawback of this approach is that, on a trial by trial basis, the method is less reliable in effectively concealing the prime. On any trial in which the participant does not follow instructions and correctly guesses the location of the prime display, the prime will be clearly visible. In situations where the assessment includes multiple attitude objects as primes, this does not pose much of a problem. But for the measurement of a single, or relatively few attitude objects, where the same primes are repeated multiple times across trials, parafoveal priming is less effective in concealing the prime.

More generally, the effectiveness of any of these methods of subthreshold presentation depends on a combination of multiple parameters including the mask and the content of the prime, as well as superficial characteristics of the prime like its size, font, brightness, and contrast with the background. In addition, other parameters such as the display timing, and factors related to the viewing conditions, like ambient lighting and seating distance to the display, also affect the integrity of the method. Obviously, such a large number of variables cannot be easily reduced to a simple formula that guarantees subthreshold priming will work as intended. A particular display timing, for example, does not in and of itself guarantee success. Instead, the exact same timing that produces subthreshold priming effects in one situation may leave primes easily visible in another when different words are used, or the words appear in a different font or on a different monitor. Pretesting for whether a given set of presentation parameters proves effective is therefore essential. Further adjusting these parameters for each individual participant may also be necessary (Balota, 1983).

The need for extensive pretesting of display parameters, as well as the level of procedural control that it requires, preclude the use of a subthreshold priming measure in many assessment contexts. Clearly, in those circumstances an SOA manipulation is the more appropriate alternative to ensure that the observed priming effects reflect automatic responses to the attitude object. Nevertheless, to the extent that it can be implemented effectively, subthreshold priming offers excellent control over how the primes are being processed. Subthreshold priming is also unique among all currently existing implicit measures in that it makes it possible to assess automatic attitudes without participants being able to link the assessment to the attitude object in question. Although other procedures may take steps to conceal their true purpose, this offers no guarantee that participants will actually remain ignorant. In the IAT, for example, it is evident to many participants what the procedure is meant to test (Monteith, Voils, & Ashburn-Nardo, 2001). Likewise, in a sequential priming measure with visible primes, participants may wonder why researchers chose Black and White faces as "distractors." This does not necessarily pose a problem for the automatic attitude measure itself, because even with full knowledge of what is being assessed participants still have limited control over their responses, nor does this knowledge necessarily allow participants to infer how exactly the attitude object impacts their responses. However, it does limit the use of these procedures in combination with other measures. In the case of socially sensitive attitudes, for example, awareness of what is being measured with an implicit measure likely compromises the diagnosticity of any other explicit attitude measure that might follow it. Thus, in such circumstances, subthreshold priming promises to be a particularly useful tool.

Measures

As discussed above, attitude estimates in priming are based on response latencies for the various prime/target combinations. Several steps are typically taken to prepare the latency data for computation of the attitude measure. First, latencies for trials with incorrect responses, when, for example, a target like *pleasant* is misclassified by the participant as *bad*, are excluded as these responses are influenced by extraneous factors. In addition, latency data typically include outliers in which responses are either started prior to the actual target stimulus or delayed because of temporary inattention. Such outliers are unavoidable in multitrial speeded response tasks and typically affect about 2–3% of the total number of responses. Therefore, researchers commonly set a priori criteria for excluding these outliers (e.g., responses faster than 150 msec and slower than two standard deviations above the individual participant's mean response time). Finally, because latency data are often characterized by skewness, they may require transformation prior to analyses (see Ratcliff, 1993).

Following these initial steps, the latency data can be used to calculate a variety of different attitude indices. The indices differ in terms of what research questions they address and what kind of design they require. Because the two basic variants of attitude priming— evaluative priming—and concept priming—differ in these regards, I review the attitude estimates that they offer separately for the two procedures.

Evaluative Priming Measures

Table 2.1 illustrates the typical design for an evaluative priming task. It pairs an attitude object with targets of positive and negative valence. The most basic attitude estimate that can be derived from such a design is a comparison of response latencies for the two types of targets (i.e., cells P_X vs. N_X in Table 2.1). Without any additional information, however, such a comparison is difficult to interpret because differences in responses to negative and positive targets could simply reflect re-

TABLE 2.1. Typical Design for an Evaluative Attitude Measure

Prime		Target	
		Positive	Negative
Attitude object X	Tulip	P_X	N_X
Attitude object Y	Snake	P_Y	N_Y
Neutral	XXXXX	P_N	N_N

Note. Cells P_X through N_N each represent multiple target items.

sponse differences that occur independent of the prime. For example, responses to negative target items could be generally faster irrespective of what prime precedes them. To control for such alternative influences, priming effects should therefore be assessed relative to another prime condition. For some attitudes, such a comparison condition may exist naturally (e.g., attitudes toward men vs. women), whereas other attitudes may imply an obvious comparison category (e.g., Republicans vs. Democrats). In these cases, it is possible to calculate attitude estimates relative to the contrasting category:

Relative Evaluation:
$$\text{Erel} = (P_Y - P_X) - (N_Y - N_X) \tag{1}$$

This index then captures the degree to which attitude object X, relative to object Y, yields faster responses for positive than negative targets. Thus, higher scores on this measure indicate that X yields more positive automatic evaluations than Y.

Such a measure can be quite informative for a variety of situations. For example, it may be of interest to know whether a person's automatic attitude toward Democrats is more positive than his or her automatic attitude toward Republicans. However, there are other situations where one needs to assess the attitude toward each attitude object separately. For example, a high Erel index for a given political party may result from very positive evaluations associated with that particular party or from very negative attitudes toward the opposing party. Obviously, the two interpretations describe very different attitudes. Likewise, in assessing attitudes toward social groups, for example, it is often of interest to differentiate positive evaluations of an ingroup (ingroup favoritism) from negative attitudes toward an outgroup (outgroup derogation; see Brewer, 2001).

Priming measures aim to accommodate this need for absolute attitude estimates by including a neutral prime condition. For example, a baseline condition that assesses responses to the targets when no prime is present has in some studies been used as such a neutral condition (see, e.g., Fazio et al., 1995). However, because primes in a sequential priming task also serve as warning signals that announce the target, such a no-prime baseline may actually overestimate the facilitatory effect that is due to the specific content of a prime (Jonides & Mack, 1984). Thus, control conditions that include an actual priming stimulus, rather than a no-prime baseline measure, should be more effective. For example, a nonword letter string (e.g., XXXXX) can serve this purpose if the procedure uses word primes.

The data from this neutral condition can then be used to calculate an estimate of absolute facilitation and inhibition that is observed for a given attitude prime, as well as the degree to which these effects differ for positive and negative targets:

Evaluation:

$$E_X = (P_N - P_X) - (N_N - N_X) \qquad (2)$$

Higher scores on this measure indicate that attitude object X triggers overall more positive than negative automatic evaluation. The measure can be further broken down into its positive and negative components in order to obtain separate estimates for positive and negative automatic evaluations (Cacioppo, Gardner, & Berntson, 1997).

Concept Priming Measures

Aside from capturing these general evaluative aspects of an attitude, priming measures can also be used for the assessment of other attitude-relevant dimensions. For example, researchers may not only be interested in determining whether people's attitudes toward a particular politician are generally positive, but may also be interested in what kinds of attributes and issues are associated with the politician. Is he or she perceived to be trustworthy, do they think of him or her as competent and experienced? To the extent that these associations are well learned and automatic, they can be assessed by priming measures as well.

The automatic activation of these cognitive aspects of the underlying attitude has received closer attention in recent work on group attitudes and prejudice. In this area, the attitude a person holds about a social group is generally distinguished from the stereotype, which consists of attributes the person believes characterize the group. Researchers have had a long-standing interest in the relationship between these two closely related constructs (cf. Stroebe & Insko, 1989), and several recent studies have used sequential priming procedures in order to assess the link between group attitudes and stereotypes (Kawakami, Dion, & Dovidio, 1998; Lepore & Brown, 1997; Wittenbrink et al., 1997). These studies modified the standard evaluative priming design depicted in Table 2.1 by including targets that vary in their stereotypicality instead of their evaluative connotation. Measures analogous to the evaluative measure that I just described can then be used to calculate estimates for the degree to which a participant links the stereotype to the primed social group. Moreover, by including target valence as an additional factor in the design and crossing it with target stereotypicality one can investigate the evaluative quality of automatically activated stereotypes. Thus, a design of this sort not only allows for the calculation of measures of the degree to which a person links a stereotype automatically to a social group, but also permits the calculation of measures that capture the extent to which such automatically activated stereotypes are positive or negative in evaluative quality. Table 2.2 shows an example of such a design from the previously mentioned study on racial attitudes by Wittenbrink and colleagues (1997). It makes it possible to calculate a variety of measures of interest to research on group attitudes, which, of course, can be easily translated to analogous issues in other domains.

First, collapsing across the two stereotypicality conditions, the design yields a measure of general automatic evaluation that is independent of the second target dimension (i.e., stereotypicality). Within the domain of intergroup attitudes, a negative attitude toward a group is commonly considered prejudice (Dovidio & Gaertner, 1986; Esses, Haddock, & Zanna, 1993). This measure therefore captures the general evaluative component of prejudice, a tendency to negatively evaluate a group (relative to another).

Generalized Prejudice:

$$GP = ((N_{AY} - N_{AX}) + (N_{BY} - N_{BX})) - ((P_{AY} - P_{AX}) + (P_{BY} - P_{BX})) \quad (3)$$

Generalized Prejudice is the analog to measure (1) *Erel* in evaluative priming. It captures the degree to which negative as opposed to positive targets, independent of their stereotypicality, are re-

TABLE 2.2. Typical Design for a Conceptual Attitude Measure

		Target		
Prime		Stereotypicality	Positive	Negative
Attitude object X	Black	(A) Black stereo	P_{AX}	N_{AX}
		(B) White stereo	P_{BX}	N_{BX}
Attitude object Y	White	(A) Black stereo	P_{AY}	N_{AY}
		(B) White stereo	P_{BY}	N_{BY}
Neutral	XXXXX	(A) Black stereo	P_{AN}	N_{AN}
		(B) White stereo	P_{BN}	N_{BN}

Note. Cells P_{AX} through N_{BN} each represent multiple target items.

sponded to faster when primed with group X as compared to group Y. Using a neutral prime condition, this measure can be decomposed into an outgroup and an ingroup portion. For White participants the two components would be captured in the present example by the following two indices:

Outgroup Derogation:

$$GP_X = ((N_{AN} - N_{AX}) + (N_{BN} - N_{BX})) - ((P_{AN} - P_{AX}) + (P_{BN} - P_{BX})) \quad (4)$$

Ingroup Favoritism:

$$GP_Y = ((P_{AN} - P_{AY}) + (P_{BN} - P_{BY})) - ((N_{AN} - N_{AY}) + (N_{BN} - N_{BY})) \quad (5)$$

These measures yield absolute estimates of each outgroup and ingroup evaluation that are equivalent to measure (2) E. As the labels suggest, higher scores on the outgroup measure indicate that the outgroup activates a more negative automatic evaluation, whereas the ingroup measure increases with a stronger positive automatic evaluation.

Aside from the fact that they are obtained with target items that are conceptually related to the primes, these three indices for concept priming are otherwise analogous to the measures obtained in evaluative priming. Including the second target attribute dimension in the analysis (i.e., stereotypicality), however, yields an additional set of estimates:

Stereotyping:

$$S = ((P_{BY} - P_{AX}) + (N_{BY} - N_{AX})) - ((P_{AY} - P_{BX}) + (N_{AY} - N_{BX})) \quad (6)$$

The stereotyping measure indicates the extent to which a person automatically activates the respective group stereotypes as represented by the target items. Higher scores reflect relatively faster responses on trials where the target stereotype matches the prime, independent of target valence. The stereotyping measure can also be separated into the two group components, which for White participants would be defined as:

Outgroup Stereotyping:

$$S_X = ((P_{AN} - P_{AX}) + (N_{AN} - N_{AX})) - ((P_{BN} - P_{BX}) + (N_{BN} - N_{BX})) \quad (7)$$

Ingroup Stereotyping:

$$S_Y = ((P_{BN} - P_{BY}) + (N_{BN} - N_{BY})) - ((P_{AN} - P_{AY}) + (N_{AN} - N_{AY})) \quad (8)$$

For both outgroup and ingroup stereotyping measures, higher scores indicate a stronger link between the group and its respective stereotype.

Taking into account both stereotypicality and valence of the targets makes it possible to assess stereotypic prejudice; that is, whether the strength of the stereotypic associations with the two group primes depends on the valence of the targets:

Stereotypic Prejudice:

$$SP = ((N_{AN} - N_{AX}) + (P_{BN} - P_{BY})) - ((P_{AN} - P_{AX}) + (N_{BN} - N_{BY})) \quad (9)$$

Higher scores indicate that the link between group X and its respective stereotype is stronger for negative targets than positive targets, when compared with the link between group Y and its stereotype. In other words, for White participants in the current example this measure would assess the degree to which there is an outgroup valence bias, whereby outgroup primes activate disproportionately negative stereotypic items, whereas ingroup primes are more likely to activate positive items. Again, this index can be broken up into its two separate group components:

Stereotypic Outgroup Derogation:
$$SP_X = (N_{AN} - N_{AX}) - (P_{AN} - P_{AX}) \quad\quad\quad (10)$$

Stereotypic Ingroup Derogation:
$$SP_Y = (P_{BN} - P_{BY}) - (N_{BN} - N_{BY}) \quad\quad\quad (11)$$

In more general terms, measures (9) through (11) assess whether the attributes that are automatically activated by an attitude object are disproportionately negative or positive in valence. As such, the measures address issues that are not only relevant to the domain of group attitudes, but that are likely relevant to any assessment context in which such attribute-specific associations are of interest (e.g., in marketing research, the features or qualities associated with a given brand).

MECHANISM: HOW DO PRIMING MEASURES WORK?

Research on how priming measures operate can draw from a large body of evidence and detailed theoretical analyses that have emerged from three decades of research on sequential priming. A detailed review of the existing empirical evidence on mechanisms is beyond the scope of this chapter but is available elsewhere (see, e.g., De Houwer, 2003; Klauer & Musch, 2003). In this chapter, I limit my discussion to a brief overview of several explanations that are most frequently offered.

Identification of the psychological mechanisms by which priming measures operate is important for at least two reasons. Pragmatically, better explanations for priming effects promise better measurement instruments. That is, a detailed account of how exactly a prime influences responses in a priming task should benefit our understanding of what a specific priming procedure actually measures, and how variations in the procedure will affect the assessment results. Aside from its practical relevance for attitude measurement, however, the identification of mechanisms should also improve our understanding of the processes by which attitudes shape judgment and behavior more generally.

Concept Priming

Explanations for concept priming can be readily adopted from the literature on semantic priming. The most common is derived from theories of spreading activation in semantic networks (Collins & Loftus, 1975). According to this account, the prime activates internal representations associated with that prime in memory. This activation spreads via existing links in the semantic network to other, associated representations. As a result of this spreading of activation in the network, the internal representation of a target related to the prime (but not an unrelated target) already receives some activation prior to the actual display of the target stimulus. Once the target appears, this additional input already present in the network reduces the time that is required for the target activation to reach recognition threshold. It thereby reduces the amount of time necessary for the target to be recognized and responded to (Neely, 1977; Posner & Snyder, 1975).

An alternative explanation attributes semantic priming effects to so-called postlexical mechanisms. That is, whereas spreading activation accounts argue that primes affect operations preceding the lexical identification of the target, this alternative explanation proposes that priming effects are due to processes that occur after lexical access or that are unrelated to lexical access. For example, Ratcliff and McKoon (1988) have suggested that prime and target are used in combination to access relevant representations in memory. Of these compound cues, those that yield a better match with contents in memory (e.g., related prime/target combinations) will seem more familiar. This sense of familiarity, then, is utilized for making a choice in a binary response decision (word/no word). Such familiarity-driven postlexical mechanisms cannot easily account for priming effects that occur with a pronunciation task (Neely, 1991) or with concealed, subthreshold primes (Klinger & Greenwald, 1995).

Evaluative Priming

As discussed earlier, evaluative priming is studied in much the same way as concept priming, the central difference being that instead of investigating conceptually driven relationships between primes and targets, evaluative priming studies focus on their evaluative associations. Thus, it is not surprising that evaluative priming effects, like concept priming effects, have been explained in terms of spreading activation accounts (e.g., Fazio, 2001). One possibility for applying this framework to evaluative associations is to argue that activation from the prime representation spreads in the network to other representations that are evaluatively consistent because they share an evaluative node in the network (e.g., they are both linked to a node representing positive valence; Bower, 1981). As with concept priming, this additional activation is thought to speed the recognition of related targets—in this case, evaluatively related targets.

However, an explanation of evaluative priming based on spreading activation has been criticized because it would require the activation from a prime of any given valence to spread to very large portions of the network, as the prime is thought to be linked to every other memory entry of similar valence. With so many links, activation would either quickly dissipate in a widely fanned system or, alternatively, it would flood the network with activation that is no longer diagnostic (see Bargh, Chaiken, Raymond, & Hymes, 1996). Aside from this theoretical concern, the account has also been challenged empirically, as a variety of studies have obtained evaluative priming effects that are inconsistent with a spreading activation explanation (for a review of findings, see Klauer & Musch, 2003).

An additional mechanism for evaluative priming focuses on the role of response competition in producing evaluative priming effects (De Houwer, Hermans, Rothermund, & Wentura, 2002; Klauer & Musch, 2003; Klinger, Burton, & Pitts, 2000; Wentura & Rothermund, 2003). The account is derived from explanations of classic paradigms like the Stroop task and its variants, in which responses must be made in the face of two conflicting stimulus inputs (MacLeod, 1991). Specifically, this account suggests that in the standard implementation of evaluative priming, when it is used with an evaluative decision task, priming effects can occur because the prime itself triggers an evaluative response that is either compatible or incompatible with the response required by the target. As a result, on trials where prime and target share the same valence, it will take less time to execute the response already triggered by the prime. However, when prime and target differ in valence, the response implied by the prime interferes with the target response and therefore slows down the response execution.

An important prediction of response competition accounts is that priming effects should occur only for attribute dimensions that are relevant to the decision task. In particular, evaluative priming should be observed when the experimental stimuli are being classified for their evaluative quality, but it should not occur when the procedure is based on a nonevaluative decision task, like a lexical decision task, or a pronunciation task. This prediction that priming effects should vary as a result of the decision task is generally supported empirically (De Houwer et al., 2002; Wittenbrink, Judd, & Park, 2001a). However, a response competition mechanism does not offer an easy explanation for those, albeit rare, instances in which evaluative priming has been observed with nonevaluative decision tasks (e.g., Bargh et al., 1996).

It seems quite plausible that the effects observed in evaluative priming procedures do not stem from a single, exclusive mechanism, but are instead multiply determined. For example, Fazio (2001) recently pointed out that some evaluative priming studies (Fazio et al., 1986) have relied on targets that are simply synonyms of the words *good* and *bad* (e.g., *appealing, delightful,* or *pleasant* vs. *repulsive, disgusting,* or *horrible*), whereas other studies (De Houwer et al., 2002) have used target words that are clearly valenced but otherwise more diverse in their meaning (e.g., *gold, sun,* or *candy* vs. *virus, dirt,* or *bomb*). One possibility suggested by Fazio is that evaluative priming obtained with the first type of targets could reflect spreading activation effects, where *good* or *bad* is part of the representation of the attitude object and activation to the object then spreads to synonyms of this particular attribute. In contrast, Fazio reasons that evaluative priming with more diverse target words could reflect response competition operations. Fazio's suggestion points to what is essentially the same distinction that I have used for this chapter in differentiating between evaluative priming and concept priming: whether a priming procedure investigates links between prime and target that are specific to the prime concept, or whether it taps more general similarities between prime and target in terms of their valence. In terms of this distinction, priming measures with *good/bad* synonyms are in effect a subset of conceptual priming procedures. They essentially pair primes with targets that are descriptive of the attitude object—in this case, descriptive with regard to one particular attribute dimension: *good/bad*. Fazio's argument regarding the use of target words does not solve all empirical puzzles in the literature on evaluative priming, but it does suggest an interesting starting point for a reconciliation of spreading activation accounts with response competition explanations and for reaching a more complete understanding of how evaluative priming works.[6]

VARIABLES: WHAT FACTORS INFLUENCE PRIMING EFFECTS?

The remaining uncertainties about how priming effects can be explained limit our ability to specify precisely the conditions under which priming should occur. However, there is a considerable amount of evidence on how particular variables influence priming effects, which is worth reviewing here. In this section, I focus on evidence on those characteristics of the procedure that have received the most attention thus far: attitude strength, the nature of the prime and the target, the kind of decision task used, and contextual aspects of the assessment situation.

Attitude Strength

A controversial issue in the literature on attitude priming has been the role of attitude strength in automatic evaluation. In their initial studies on evaluative priming, Fazio et al. (1986) found automatic evaluative priming effects only for primes for which participants had strong attitudes (e.g., *guns*) but not for primes associated with weak attitudes (e.g., *radiation*). A measure of attitude accessibility that preceded the priming task served as an indicator of attitude strength in these studies. The measure consisted of another response latency procedure in which participants had to quickly classify attitude objects as either good or bad. For each participant individually, the eight fastest and eight slowest objects were then determined and used as high accessibility attitude primes (considered strong attitudes) and low accessibility attitude primes (considered weak attitudes), respectively.

Subsequent studies have not always replicated this moderating effect of attitude strength, however. In particular, Bargh and his colleagues reported several experiments in which attitude strength, also measured as attitude accessibility, did not matter for the priming effect (Bargh, Chaiken, Govender, & Pratto, 1992; Bargh et al., 1996; Chaiken & Bargh, 1993; see also De Houwer, Hermans, & Eelen, 1998).

In an attempt to explain the discrepant findings, Bargh and colleagues suggested that the inclusion of the attitude accessibility measure as part of Fazio et al.'s procedure was partly responsible for the observed moderation effect because it required participants to deliberately evaluate the primes. Such deliberate rumination about one's evaluation of the attitude primes was thought to interfere with the automatic evaluation of attitude objects associated with weak attitudes. Specifically, Bargh and colleagues argued that the accessibility measure had the potential to temporarily increase the accessibility of conflicting evaluations for these objects. In fact, when the accessibility task was separated from the priming measure by a 2-day delay, the moderation effect went away and weak attitude primes also showed automatic priming effects (Bargh et al., 1992; Chaiken & Bargh, 1993). Bargh and colleagues further argued that, similarly, the evaluative decision task itself might also impact the temporary accessibility of an evaluation, because such a task may be more likely to lead participants to think about their evaluations of the primes. Thus, Bargh and his colleagues used a nonevaluative pronunciation task instead of an evaluative decision task and observed no moderation effects (Bargh et al., 1996).

Aside from their methodological implications for evaluative priming, Bargh and colleagues intended their studies on attitude strength to illustrate a more principled argument, namely, that automatic evaluation is universal and unconditional. Following Zajonc's (1980) *primacy of affect* hypothesis, evaluation is seen as a fundamental aspect of stimulus acquisition. Such evaluation does not require particular intentions and is not limited to particular kinds of objects. All it requires is the mere presence of the stimulus object (Bargh et al., 1996).

Be this as it may, even this universality argument does not negate the possibility that attitude strength still matters. Specifically, it is still possible that the outcomes of evaluative processes (automatic and controlled) will eventually become associated with the object. Because of frequent repetition this association will be strong for some objects. However, for others that are encountered infrequently, it may remain weak or may not be established at all. Variation in the strength of this association should then matter for attitude priming, just as many studies in the cognitive literature have demonstrated the effects of associative strength (Neely, 1991).

Prime

Aside from attitude strength, another relevant characteristic of the priming stimulus is whether it represents the attitude object pictorially or whether lexical references are used. From evidence in the cognitive literature, there is good reason to assume that pictures and words are processed in different ways and perhaps even represented differently (Farah, Wilson, Drain, & Tanaka, 1998; Glaser & Glaser, 1989; Paivio, 1991; Seymour, 1973). One aspect that differentiates words from pictures is that words often imply a particular categorization of the object they represent, whereas pictures remain ambiguous in this respect. For example, as compared with the word *firefighter,* which readily specifies a particular occupational category, a picture of a firefighter may be categorized in multiple ways. Instead of attending to the person's occupation, one might focus on the person's gender, race, age, attractiveness, and so on (see, e.g., Bodenhausen & Macrae, 1998; Gilbert & Hixon, 1991). Which categorization will dominate is likely to depend in part on the circumstances in which the picture is encountered. That is, aspects of the assessment situation, like task instructions or the salience of a particular attribute dimension, may influence the effects observed for such multiply classifiable picture primes. I return to this issue later in the section on assessment context.

A second implication of this difference in specificity between picture and word primes is that pictures always represent an attitude object as an exemplar of the category of objects. In contrast, words may explicitly reference the category of objects. This is potentially important because, depending on whether exemplar primes or category primes are used, priming measures may either tap into the evaluative responses to a specific attitude object or they may target responses to categories of objects instead. To the extent that exemplars vary in how representative they are of their respective categories, exemplars as compared with category references may activate somewhat different evaluations. For example, Livingston and Brewer (2002) varied the prototypicality of Black faces used as photo primes in a study on automatic racial attitudes. For faces that in pretesting had been rated as prototypical for the group of African Americans, the study found that the primes yielded more negative evaluations than did White faces, a common result in this area of research. However, primes that were low in prototypicality but nevertheless clearly recognizable as Black faces did not replicate this standard effect unless participants were first explicitly instructed to attend to the race of the face primes (see also Olson & Fazio, 2003).

Depending on the circumstances, exemplar-level evaluations may be exactly what an attitude measure is supposed to capture— for example, one might be concerned with a person's specific attitude toward John Kerry or George W. Bush. However, to the extent that attitudes toward a category of objects are of interest (e.g., attitudes toward the Democratic or Republican party), exemplar primes have to be representative of the larger category (e.g., a typical Democrat or typical Republican). Alternatively, as suggested by the Livingston and Brewer (2002) studies, the task instructions need to emphasize a particular kind of classification of primes (e.g., "Try to keep a mental tally of how many Democrats and how many Republicans you see during the experiment"; cf. Olson & Fazio, 2003).

Task Instructions

A variety of tasks have been used in priming measures. The most common are those mentioned earlier: the evaluative decision task, the lexical decision task, and, to a lesser degree, the pronunciation task. In addition, priming studies have on occasion used tasks that ask participants to identify certain target attributes, such as color (Hermans, Van den Broeck, & Eelen, 1998), letter case and grammatical category (Klauer & Musch, 2002), or animacy (Klinger et al., 2000). Still other studies require participants to make more complex classification decisions (e.g., could the target ever be true of the prime; Dovidio, Evans, & Tyler, 1986).

There is good evidence by now that the decision task critically influences automatic priming, with the effects typically being observed for prime attributes that are relevant for the decision task but not for attributes irrelevant for the decision task. For example, Wittenbrink and colleagues (2001a) varied the task instructions in a priming measure of racial attitudes. In the context of a lexical decision task, group primes showed facilitation for trait attributes associated with the respective group stereotype. Moreover, outgroup primes yielded disproportionately strong facilitation for negative stereotypic attributes as compared with ingroup primes. However, when the otherwise identical procedure was administered with an evaluative decision task, the stereotypicality of the target items did not matter for the observed priming effect. Outgroup primes produced overall stronger facilitation for any negatively valenced attribute. That is, in terms of the measures that I discussed earlier, the lexical decision task yielded conceptual priming effects, captured by indices (6) *stereotyping* and (9) *stereotypic prejudice*. In contrast, with the evaluative decision task the same procedure tapped into evaluative priming effects, identified by measure (3) *generalized prejudice.*

Parallel effects of task instructions were obtained by De Houwer and colleagues (2002), who had participants either perform an evaluative decision task or indicate whether the targets were people or objects. As in the Wittenbrink and colleagues research, priming effects emerged only for the task-relevant attribute dimension. Responses were relatively faster for evaluatively congruent targets when participants made evaluative decisions, but not when they made person/object decisions. In the latter case, the targets' conceptual congruency determined latencies instead. The conclusion that automatic priming effects depend on the relevance of the attribute dimension for the decision task is further supported in research by Klauer and Musch (2002) and by Klinger and colleagues (2000), who found such task dependency even with subthreshold primes.

Aside from the fact that task instructions affect what attribute dimension a priming measure may pick up, there is also evidence that the evaluative decision task and lexical decision task differ in their susceptibility to metacognitive influences like the experienced ease of retrieving relevant information from memory (Gawronski & Bodenhausen, 2005).

Another task sometimes used in priming procedures does not require participants to make binary classifications but instead asks them to simply say the target aloud. This pronunciation or naming task has been of interest to researchers because it is widely assumed to be a better measure of lexical access and thus a purer measure of activation (Balota & Chumbley, 1984). This is because in pronunciation a given response does not have to be mapped onto the available decision alternatives and therefore requires less postlexical processing. The lack of a response classification stage in pronunciation also makes the task a potentially useful tool in distinguishing between different explanations for priming effects. For example, as I mentioned earlier, priming effects obtained with the pronunciation task cannot be easily explained with response competition accounts precisely because these accounts attribute priming effects to such postlexical processes.

As is the case for the lexical decision task, the pronunciation task has reliably been found to yield automatic priming effects based on conceptual relations between prime and target (Neely, 1991). The results for evaluative links between prime and target, however, are much less conclusive when pronunciation is used. The already mentioned experiments by Bargh and colleagues (1996) consistently showed evaluative priming with a pronunciation task across three experiments. Evaluative priming effects were also observed by Hermans and colleagues (1994) and by Giner-Sorolla, Garcia, and Bargh

(1999). Yet, more recent attempts to replicate evaluative priming effects with a pronunciation task have been unsuccessful (Klauer & Musch, 2001; Spruyt, Hermans, Pandelaere, De Houwer, & Eelen, 2004) and in the case of studies by Glaser and Banaji (1999) have even resulted in *reverse* priming effects (i.e., priming facilitated responses for targets of opposite valence). At present it is not clear what particular factors explain these discrepancies, leaving the pronunciation task less useful for evaluative priming measures.

Target

It seems quite plausible that effects similar to those triggered by task instructions can also result from the composition of the target items themselves. That is, even without any explicit task instructions to categorize targets according to valence (as is the case in the pronunciation task), the exclusive use of clearly valenced target items may focus attention on the evaluative quality of the stimulus materials. To my knowledge, there is no direct evidence for this possibility, although it is clear that list composition can influence priming. That is, several studies have investigated so-called *relatedness proportion effects*, varying the relative number of targets that are evaluatively or conceptually related to the prime. In general, this work shows that a higher proportion of related prime/target pairs increases priming. For evaluative priming, this is especially the case at very short SOAs (Klauer, Roßnagel, & Musch, 1997). It would be interesting to know whether priming effects are similarly moderated by the proportion of targets evaluatively linked to the primes relative to those that are conceptually linked to the primes.

Another characteristic of the target that has received some attention in the semantic priming literature concerns the legibility of its display. This work indicates that target displays that are degraded in some form or another (e.g., displayed with visual noise, inverted, or combined with extraneous letters) yield overall stronger priming effects (Neely, 1991). De Houwer, Hermans, and Spruyt (2001) showed similar results for evaluative priming. Likewise, the earlier mentioned response window technique (Greenwald et al., 1996) may increase priming effects in part because it forces participants to respond before the target has been completely processed.

ASSESSMENT CONTEXT

Aside from the variables that I reviewed thus far, contextual aspects of the assessment situation can also influence priming effects. Several demonstrations of this sort now exist. For example, Wittenbrink, Judd, and Park (2001b) found that automatic responses to Black and White face primes depended on the background images against which those faces appeared. When displayed with the background of an urban street setting, Black face primes yielded more negative evaluations than when the same faces were displayed with a church interior as background. Likewise, Pratto and Shih (2000) observed increased outgroup prejudice on a priming measure for participants high in Social Dominance Orientation as a result of status threat. In an entirely different attitude domain, Sherman, Rose, Koch, Presson, and Chassin (2003) found that nicotine deprivation temporarily influenced cigarette smokers' automatic responses to cigarettes. Likewise, Ferguson and Bargh (2004) showed that evaluative priming is sensitive to participants' currently active goals.

To a certain extent, the fact that priming effects are sensitive to the assessment context seems to contradict the premise that priming measures capture automatic responses. Such responses are often described as invariant and unconditional reactions that occur reflexively in response to a certain stimulus (see, e.g., Bargh, 1999). Responses that vary across different assessment situations or that are conditional on other extraneous factors, like the experimenter's instructions, certainly do not fit such a description. However, few responses that are commonly considered to reflect *automatic* processing really fit the strict criteria of invariance and lack of conditionality. In fact, there is growing recognition that even basic perceptual processes are not unconditionally linked to a specific stimulus input and are indeed quite malleable—although they are nevertheless spontaneous, resource efficient, and often unconscious and uncontrollable. For example, it is generally agreed that the identification of auditory stimuli as a particular speech pattern is automatic (Shiffrin, Pisoni, & Castaneda-Mendez, 1974). Yet although these identification processes are effortless, resource efficient, and can occur involuntarily, without the perceiver's active control, they are not triggered in an unconditional fashion by a specified auditory stimulus. Instead, they can depend on people's expectations about the nature of the stimulus (e.g., whether or not they expect to hear "speech"; Remez, Rubin, Pisoni, & Carrell, 1981). With regard to semantic priming and visual word recognition more generally, similar evidence exists (e.g., Smith, Besner, & Miyoshi, 1994).

Elsewhere, I have argued that for theoretical reasons few responses can be truly conditional on only the perceiver's exposure to the stimulus cue (Wittenbrink et al., 2001b). That is, with the exception of those stimulus cues that can trigger responses without much evidence of higher-order cognitive mediation (LeDoux, 1996), any distal stimulus has to be somehow translated into a subjective percept. The mediating processes by which this translation occurs are determined not just by the particular stimulus in question but also by a variety of contextual factors like the perceiver's focus of attention, other stimulus features present in the environment, and so forth. The mediation may be spontaneous, fast, resource efficient, and uncontrollable, but it is hardly invariant, given the potential variation in input from factors other than the distal stimulus.

The argument is hardly new. It was put forth by Gestalt psychologists many years ago. Although the Gestalt approach emphasized the importance of consciousness and subjective experience, many of the phenomena to which it was applied clearly qualify as automatic by today's standards. For example, Wertheimer's (1923) work on perceptual organization shows that stimuli may be perceived as part of a grouped entity or as individual units, depending on the particular context in which they are placed. Again, the process by which the perceiver organizes the stimuli in such fashion is automatic: It is spontaneous, fast, resource efficient, and uncontrollable, but evidently not invariant.

Because such mediational processes are necessary to take place for any stimulus to acquire subjective reality, Gestalt psychologists argued that psychological functioning could not be explained based on an analysis of the "objective" stimulus features alone (Köhler, 1947). Likewise, one should not expect the responses assessed by priming measures to be determined solely by the primes themselves, even when the assessment effectively precludes controlled processes from influencing the responses.

USE: WHAT ARE PRIMING MEASURES GOOD FOR?

As I explained at the beginning of this chapter, one particular reason why researchers have been interested in priming measures is their potential to serve as effective means to unobtrusively measure attitudes. Although there have been several investigations on whether other types of implicit measures, namely the IAT, can be faked (Banse, Seise, & Zerbes, 2001; Egloff & Schmukle, 2002; Kim, 2003), I am not aware of any studies that have experimentally tested whether priming measures are susceptible to misrepresentation. Research has, however, considered the impact of individual differences in self-reported motivation to control a non-normative attitude (e.g., prejudice).

Intentional Misrepresentation

Theoretically, priming should not be affected by misrepresentation because automatic responses should be resistant to strategic control. Of course, the evidence on strategic control in priming procedures is not quite that simple. As the preceding review of task instructions and other procedural variables made clear, it is certainly the case that priming effects can be influenced by strategic considerations about what aspects of the situation the participant will consider as task relevant. However, the kinds of operations that in all likelihood contribute to these influences (attention selection, response mapping, etc.) are facile and can function under the time constraints of common priming procedures. For intentional misrepresentation to be effective in a similar manner, it would need to be based on an equally facile control process. There is some evidence that certain people may have automatized control processes for particular attitude objects and that these can be effective in priming procedures (e.g., racial attitudes; Devine, Plant, Amodio, Harmon-Jones, & Vance, 2002; Moskowitz, Salomon, & Taylor, 2000). However, such automatized control operations are usually attributed to individuals who are motivated to suppress a response because they genuinely disapprove of it. Otherwise, individual differences in people's motivation to control a certain attitude have not been found to affect priming measures (Devine et al., 2002; Dunton & Fazio, 1997).[7] Priming measures can also be implemented with subthreshold primes, in which case participants remain unaware of the attitude object altogether. Of course, responses cannot be misrepresented unless a participant at least knows what attitude is being assessed. In sum, priming measures should, under most circumstances, provide an effective means to assess attitudes free of intentional distortions.

Validity

Because of its effectiveness in this regard, priming has been described as an assessment technique that allows researchers to "get into the head" of the respondent, offering a bona fide measure of people's *true attitudes* (e.g., Fazio et al., 1995). Although this characterization is meant to capture the fact that participants cannot edit their responses, it can be misunderstood as implying that priming actually offers more accurate estimates of an attitude than conventional assessment techniques might provide. This is clearly not the case. Priming measures, and implicit techniques more generally, are not per se *better* attitude measures. After all, the automatic responses captured by priming are not the only input that influences a person's evaluation of an attitude object. To the extent that a person has the opportunity and is sufficiently motivated, automatic responses are followed by a more deliberate consideration of information relevant to his or her evaluation of the object. Such considerations may include thoughts about whether a response is appropriate and consistent with normative expectations (the person's own and those of others), as well as other information that is perhaps less accessible but nevertheless pertinent to the person's evaluation. Thus, deliberation is important to many attitudinal responses, yet by the very principle on which priming measures are based, they do not capture the inputs resulting from deliberation. In other words, priming will result in, at best, a true assessment of only some *aspect* or *component*, of the underlying attitude.

Consequently, priming measures should be diagnostic of evaluations when no further deliberation takes place, or when automatic and deliberate inputs favor the same response. That is, priming measures, like all other attitude measures, assess attitudes under specific processing conditions that determine what sources of input are available for the evaluation. They should be predictive of exactly those evaluations that occur under equivalent processing conditions. As such, priming measures are not inherently superior measures of attitudes. Certainly, there are many contexts in which evaluations are deliberate, and in which individuals will try to correct their automatic responses accordingly (e.g., Wegener & Petty, 1997).

At the same time, many everyday situations involve only quick and superficial evaluations in which people are unlikely to deliberate—for example, when choosing which person to sit next to on a subway train. And even evaluations that are potentially more consequential, and in which people would, in principle, be motivated to deliberate, may go by without such controlled consideration because they remain unnoticed (e.g., nonverbal expressions; Dovidio, Kawakami, & Gaertner, 2002). Moreover, many situations in everyday life impose significant cognitive demands, and as a result, one's capacity for deliberation may be limited or, in extreme circumstances, entirely lacking (Bargh, 1997; Correll, Park, Judd, & Wittenbrink, 2002; Gilbert, 1989). In all these cases, the automatic response should be a primary determinant of the evaluative response. To the extent that automatic and deliberate inputs to the evaluation differ, priming measures should be effective only in predicting an evaluative response that is dominated by the automatic inputs.

Several investigations have by now demonstrated the predictive validity of priming measures under these kinds of circumstances. The majority of these have considered the link between nonverbal or similar incidental behaviors and priming measures of related attitudes. For example, Fazio and colleagues (1995) found that an evaluative priming measure of racial attitudes predicted the general quality of brief interactions with a Black experimenter, as judged by the experimenter. A relationship with more specific measures of nonverbal behavior, such as the duration of eye contact or number of eyeblinks, was reported in two studies by Dovidio and his colleagues (Dovidio et al., 2002; Johnson, & Howard, 1997). Wilson, Damiani, and Shelton (as reported in Wilson et al., 2000) also found an evaluative priming measure of racial attitudes to predict how often White participants handed a pen to a Black confederate, as opposed to placing it on the table. Using a different group attitude, Bessenoff and Sherman (2000) observed a concept priming measure of attitudes toward obese people to be correlated with a seating-distance measure (Westie, 1953). Participants with more negative stereotypic attitudes chose to seat themselves farther away from an obese confederate. Finally, a study by Spalding and Hardin (1999) considered a different attitude domain, self-esteem. Here an evaluative priming measure of self-esteem predicted participants' expressions of anxiety in an interview on a self-relevant topic.

For all the studies mentioned, explicit attitude measures generally fared worse in predicting the critical behavior than did the priming measures. One reason why these kinds of responses may remain uninfluenced by deliberation is that they reflect superficial evaluations that people are not sufficiently motivated to monitor. A more likely explanation, however, is that people simply remain unaware of their nonverbal behavior and therefore fail to correct it if necessary (cf. Dovidio et al., 2002).

Recent studies from our own lab have used priming to predict responses where deliberation fails to impact the responses for different reasons. Specifically, these studies considered the link between priming measures of racial attitudes and decisions to shoot a potentially hostile target in the context of a video game. When a decision has to be made under time pressure, such responses have repeatedly been found to be influenced by the race of the target (e.g., Correll et al., 2002). In recent experiments, a conceptual priming measure collected several days prior to the video game task predicted the degree of race bias in the decision to shoot. In contrast, explicit self-reports of prejudice or stereotyping do not predict these types of responses (Wittenbrink, 2004).

Limitations

Taking these various lines of research together, there is encouraging evidence that priming measures have predictive validity, in particular for responses that are difficult to monitor or deliberate. However, the slightly more than 20 years of research on priming measures have not produced a staggering amount of evidence on the question of their validity. To some extent, this relative shortage of validation demonstrations reflects the limitations of priming measures.

First, priming measures are relatively complicated as compared with other implicit measures, most notably the IAT. Despite the many advances in computer technology, the implementation of priming procedures still requires significant technical resources and demands a certain level of technical expertise. Priming measures also take a substantial amount of time to administer, and they require close control over the experimental situation. Naturally, these challenges are even greater in the case of validation studies, in which the priming measure is supposed to be considered in relation to other dependent variables that, quite likely, cannot be collected in the confines of a computer cubicle.

The IAT, in comparison, fares significantly better when it comes to ease of administration and consequently has become the implicit measure of choice, despite several important features unique to priming measures (e.g., single attitude assessment, close control over the nature of prime processing, optional subthreshold presentation).

Another limitation that current priming procedures face is that they tend to produce relatively small effect sizes and are relatively low in reliability (Bosson, Swann, & Pennebaker, 2000; Cameron, Alvarez, & Bargh, 2000; Kawakami & Dovidio, 2001). This makes their findings potentially difficult to replicate and limits their sensitivity as measurement instruments.

Related to this issue, Payne, Cheng, Govorum, and Stewart (2005) recently proposed what appears to be an interesting alternative for attitude priming, referred to as affect misattribution procedure (AMP). A modified version of the Murphy and Zajonc (1993) procedure, the AMP is not based on response latencies but on liking judgments of unfamiliar target stimuli (Chinese ideographs) that are paired with attitude primes. As with response latency measures, primes in this paradigm tend to bias participants' target-related judgments. More positively valenced primes yield relatively higher liking judgments, even when participants are explicitly instructed to correct for any undue influences caused by the primes. In contrast to standard priming procedures, the AMP appears to yield relatively large effect sizes (average

$d = 1.25$ in the Payne et al. studies). Evidently, an assessment technique that produces a larger effect size is useful only as long as the effect relates to what is meant to be measured. However, to the extent that it proves effective in this respect, the AMP suggests a practical alternative for measuring attitudes through priming.

CONCLUSIONS

Compared to conventional assessment techniques, priming measures of attitudes are still quite young. As a result, there remain several important issues that must be addressed in future work to make priming more than a temporary fad in attitude research. With regard to theoretical matters, a more accurate identification of how different processing components contribute to the observed effect is one of the most critical challenges to priming research at this time. Methodologically, the investigation of the psychometric properties for various priming measures is still in its infancy. The use of attitude priming as a measurement tool would also benefit greatly from the development of a set of implementation standards for a variety of assessment purposes. Such standardized assessment procedures would allow for easier comparison of findings across different studies. And it would further address some of the practical limitations of priming, as those standardized procedures could be made available to researchers.

Nevertheless, it seems important to recognize that in the relatively short time since its introduction, a substantial body of evidence on attitude priming has already emerged. This work, in combination with the extensive literature on semantic priming, has resulted in significant advances in our understanding of priming as a technique, especially relative to what is known about other implicit measurement procedures. Indeed, the recent accumulation of knowledge on attitude priming puts the field on very strong footing to productively engage the outstanding theoretical and methodological questions. Thus, there is reason for optimism that, rather than being a passing fad, attitude priming will hold an important, permanent place in the field of social psychology.

NOTES

1. What specific quality the term *implicit* is supposed to convey and whether it adequately characterizes the procedures that are commonly referred to as implicit at-

titude measures has been widely debated (see De Houwer & Moore, Chapter 7, this volume). For the purposes of this chapter, I consider implicit measures to be those that aim to assess attitudinal influences that occur without awareness or intent. Similar interpretations have been used by Fazio and Olson (2003), Greenwald and Banaji (1995), and Krosnick and colleagues (2005).

2. A number of experimental techniques have been used to study priming. The present overview focuses on procedures that assess response latencies as estimates of accessibility effects.

3. Sample program scripts for running standard priming tasks under these software packages are available free of charge at the following websites:

DirectRT: *www.psych.uiuc.edu/~roese/mlhouse.htm*
DirectRT: *www.empirisoft.com/support*
PsyScope: *psyscope.psy.cmu.edu/scripts/index.html*

4. Some studies have used a short and fixed display time for the target, which is then erased even if a response has not yet been made. Moreover, in existing priming measures of attitudes, words typically serve as target stimuli. However, in principle, pictures could be used as well. In fact, there are several affective priming studies with pictorial target stimuli—although these do not explicitly address the measurement of attitudes (see, e.g., Murphy & Zajonc, 1993).

5. Bargh and colleagues (1992) found comparable priming effects independent of which type of instruction was used to justify the presence of the primes.

6. For example, it cannot account for all the results reported by Bargh and colleagues (1996). In their experiment 3, these authors found evaluative priming effects with valenced but otherwise unrelated targets (*bird, brother, lake* vs. *weapon, fire, trouble*). In fact, these targets were explicitly chosen to not be linked to a single attribute like *good*. Thus, spreading activation cannot easily account for the priming effects in this experiment. However, a response competition explanation does not apply either, because the procedure used a pronunciation task.

7. One effective strategy for interfering with response latency measures like priming is to simply delay one's responses. To the extent that the participant recognizes the purpose of the assessment task and is aware of this option, responses in a priming measure can be faked. However, an analysis of the overall response latencies allows for the identification of participants who might have used this strategy.

REFERENCES

Balota, D. A. (1983). Automatic semantic activation and episodic memory encoding. *Journal of Verbal Learning and Verbal Behavior, 22,* 88–104.

Balota, D. A., & Chumbley, J. I. (1984). Are lexical decisions a good measure of lexical access? The role of word frequency in the neglected decision stage. *Journal of Experimental Psychology: Human Perception and Performance, 10*(3), 340–357.

Banse, R., Seise, J., & Zerbes, N. (2001). Implicit attitudes towards homosexuality: Reliability, validity, and controllability of the IAT. *Zeitschrift für Experimentelle Psychologie, 48*(2), 145–160.

Bargh, J. A. (1997). The automaticity of everyday life. In R. S. Wyer (Ed.), *Advances in social cognition: Vol. 10. The automaticity of everyday life* (pp. 1–61). Mahwah, NJ: Erlbaum.

Bargh, J. A. (1999). The cognitive monster: The case against the controllability of automatic stereotype effects. In S. Chaiken & Y. Trope (Eds.), *Dual-process theories in social psychology* (pp. 361–382). New York: Guilford Press.only

Bargh, J. A., Chaiken, S., Govender, R., & Pratto, F. (1992). The generality of the automatic attitude activation effect. *Journal of Personality and Social Psychology, 62*(6), 893–912.

Bargh, J. A., Chaiken, S., Raymond, P., & Hymes, C. (1996). The automatic evaluation effect: Unconditional automatic attitude activation with a pronunciation task. *Journal of Experimental Social Psychology, 32*(1), 104–128.

Bargh, J. A., & Pietromonaco, P. (1982). Automatic information processing and social perception: The influence of trait information presented outside the conscious awareness on impression formation. *Journal of Personality and Social Psychology, 43,* 437–449.

Bargh, J. A., Raymond, P., Pryor, J. B., & Strack, F. (1995). Attractiveness of the underling: An automatic power - sex association and its consequences for sexual harassment and aggression. *Journal of Personality and Social Psychology, 68,* 768–781.

Bessenoff, G. R., & Sherman, J. W. (2000). Automatic and controlled components of prejudice toward fat people: Evaluation versus stereotype activation. *Social Cognition, 18*(4), 329–353.

Bodenhausen, G. V., & Macrae, C. (1998). Stereotype activation and inhibition. In R. S. Wyer (Ed.), *Advances in social cognition* (pp. 1–52). Mahwah, NJ: Erlbaum.

Bosson, J. K., Swann, W. B., & Pennebaker, J. W. (2000). Stalking the perfect measure of implicit self-esteem: The blind men and the elephant revisited? *Journal of Personality and Social Psychology, 79*(4), 631–643.

Bower, G. H. (1981). Emotional mood and memory. *American Psychologist, 36,* 129–148.

Brewer, M. B. (2001). Ingroup identification and intergroup conflict: When does ingroup love become outgroup hate? In R. D. Ashmore & L. Jussim (Eds.), *Social identity, intergroup conflict, and conflict reduction* (Rutgers Series on Self and Social Identity, Vol. 3, pp. 17–41). London: Oxford University Press.

Cacioppo, J. T., Gardner, W. L., & Berntson, G. G. (1997). Beyond bipolar conceptualizations and measures: The case of attitudes and evaluative space. *Personality and Social Psychology Review, 1*(1), 3–25.

Cameron, J. A., Alvarez, J. M., & Bargh, J. A. (2000). *Examining the validity of implicit measures of prejudice.* Paper presented at the first meeting of the Society for Personality and Social Psychology, Nashville, TN.

Chaiken, S. (1987). The heuristic model of persuasion. In M. P. Zanna & J. M. Olson (Eds.), *Social influence: The Ontario Symposium* (Vol. 5, pp. 3–39). Hillsdale, NJ: Erlbaum.

Chaiken, S., & Bargh, J. A. (1993). Occurrence versus moderation of the automatic attitude activation effect: Reply to Fazio. *Journal of Personality and Social Psychology, 64*(5), 759–765.

Cheesman, J., & Merikle, P. M. (1986). Distinguishing conscious from unconscious perceptual processes. *Canadian Journal of Psychology, 40*(4), 343–367.

Collins, A. M., & Loftus, E. F. (1975). A spreading-activation theory of semantic processing. *Psychological Review, 82*(6), 407–428.

Correll, J., Park, B., Judd, C. M., & Wittenbrink, B. (2002). The police officer's dilemma: Using ethnicity to disambiguate potentially threatening individuals. *Journal of Personality and Social Psychology, 83*(6), 1314–1329.

Crosby, F., Bromley, S., & Saxe, L. (1980). Recent unobtrusive studies of Black and White discrimination and prejudice: A literature review. *Psychological Bulletin, 87*, 546–563.

De Houwer, J. (2003). A structural analysis of indirect measures of attitudes. In J. Musch & K. C. Klauer (Eds.), *The psychology of evaluation: Affective processes in cognition and emotion* (pp. 219–244). Mahwah, NJ: Erlbaum.

De Houwer, J., Hermans, D., & Eelen, P. (1998). Affective and identity priming with episodically associated stimuli. *Cognition and Emotion, 12*(2), 145–169.

De Houwer, J., Hermans, D., Rothermund, K., & Wentura, D. (2002). Affective priming of semantic categorisation responses. *Cognition and Emotion, 16*(5), 643–666.

De Houwer, J., Hermans, D., & Spruyt, A. (2001). Affective priming of pronunciation responses: Effects of target degradation. *Journal of Experimental Social Psychology, 37*(1), 85–91.

Devine, P. G., Plant, E., Amodio, D. M., Harmon-Jones, E., & Vance, S. L. (2002). The regulation of explicit and implicit race bias: The role of motivations to respond without prejudice. *Journal of Personality and Social Psychology, 82*(5), 835–848.

Dovidio, J. F., Evans, N., & Tyler, R. (1986). Racial stereotypes: The contents of their cognitive representations. *Journal of Experimental Social Psychology, 22*, 22–37.

Dovidio, J. F., & Fazio, R. H. (1992). New technologies for the direct and indirect assessment of attitudes. In J. M. Tanur (Ed.), *Questions about questions* (pp. 204–236). New York: Russell Sage.

Dovidio, J. F., & Gaertner, S. L. (1986). Prejudice, discrimination, and racism: Historical trends and contemporary approaches. In J. F. Dovidio & S. L. Gaertner (Eds.), *Prejudice, discrimination, and racism* (pp. 1–34). Orlando, FL: Academic Press.

Dovidio, J. F., Kawakami, K., & Gaertner, S. L. (2002). Implicit and explicit prejudice and interracial interaction. *Journal of Personality and Social Psychology, 82*(1), 62–68.

Dovidio, J. F., Kawakami, K., Johnson, C., Johnson, B., & Howard, A. (1997). On the nature of prejudice: Automatic and controlled processes. *Journal of Experimental Social Psychology, 33*, 510–540.

Dunton, B. C., & Fazio, R. H. (1997). An individual difference measure of motivation to control prejudiced reactions. *Personality and Social Psychology Bulletin, 23*(3), 316–326.

Egloff, B., & Schmukle, S. C. (2002). Predictive validity of an implicit association test for assessing anxiety. *Journal of Personality and Social Psychology, 83*(6), 1441–1455.

Esses, V. M., Haddock, G., & Zanna, M. P. (1993). Values, stereotypes, and emotions as determinants of intergroup attitudes. In D. M. Mackie & D. L. Hamilton (Eds.), *Affect, cognition, and stereotyping: Integrative processes in group perception* (pp. 137–166). San Diego, CA: Academic Press.

Farah, M. J., Wilson, K. D., Drain, M., & Tanaka, J. N. (1998). What is "special" about face perception? *Psychological Review, 105*(3), 482–498.

Fazio, R. H. (1990). Multiple processes by which attitudes guide behavior: The MODE model as an integrative framework. In M. P. Zanna (Ed.), *Advances in experimental social psychology* (Vol. 23, pp. 75–109). San Diego, CA: Academic Press.

Fazio, R. H. (2001). On the automatic activation of associated evaluations: An overview. *Cognition and Emotion, 15*(2), 115–141.

Fazio, R. H., Jackson, J. R., Dunton, B. C., & Williams, C. J. (1995). Variability in automatic activation as an unobtrusive measure of racial attitudes: A bona fide pipeline? *Journal of Personality and Social Psychology, 69*, 1013–1027.

Fazio, R. H., & Olson, M. A. (2003). Implicit measures in social cognition research: Their meaning and uses. *Annual Review of Psychology, 54*, 297–327.

Fazio, R. H., Sanbonmatsu, D. M., Powell, M. C., & Kardes, F. R. (1986). On the automatic activation of attitudes. *Journal of Personality and Social Psychology, 50*, 229–238.

Ferguson, M. J., & Bargh, J. A. (2004). Liking is for doing: The effects of goal pursuit on automatic evaluation. *Journal of Personality and Social Psychology, 87*, 557–572.

Gaertner, S. L., & McLaughlin, J. P. (1983). Racial stereotypes: Associations and ascriptions of positive and negative characteristics. *Social Psychology Quarterly, 46*, 23–30.

Gawronski, B., & Bodenhausen, G. V. (2005). Accessibility effects on implicit social cognition: The role of knowledge activation and retrieval experiences. *Journal of Personality and Social Psychology, 89*, 672–685.

Gilbert, D. T. (1989). Thinking lightly about others: Automatic components of the social inference process. In J. S. Uleman & J. A. Bargh (Eds.), *Unintended thought* (pp. 189–211). New York: Guilford Press.

Gilbert, D. T., & Hixon, J. G. (1991). The trouble of thinking: Activation and application of stereotypic beliefs. *Journal of Personality and Social Psychology, 60*, 509–517.

Giner-Sorolla, R., Garcia, M. T., & Bargh, J. A. (1999). The automatic evaluation of pictures. *Social Cognition, 17*(1), 76–96.

Glaser, J., & Banaji, M. R. (1999). When fair is foul and foul is fair: Reverse priming in automatic evaluation. *Journal of Personality and Social Psychology, 77*(4), 669–687.

Glaser, W. R., & Glaser, M. O. (1989). Context effects in Stroop-like word and picture processing. *Journal of Experimental Psychology: General, 118*(1), 13–42.

Gordon, R. A. (1987). Social desirability bias: A demonstration and technique for its reduction. *Teaching of Psychology, 14*(1), 40–42.

Greenwald, A. G., & Banaji, M. R. (1995). Implicit social cognition: Attitudes, self-esteem, and stereotypes. *Psychological Review, 102*, 4–27.

Greenwald, A. G., Draine, S. C., & Abrams, R. L. (1996). Three cognitive markers of unconscious semantic activation. *Science, 273*, 1699–1702.

Greenwald, A. G., Klinger, M. R., & Liu, T. J. (1989). Unconscious processing of dichoptically masked words. *Memory and Cognition, 17*(1), 35–47.

Greenwald, A. G., McGhee, D. E., & Schwartz, J. L. K. (1998). Measuring individual differences in implicit cognition: The implicit association test. *Journal of Personality and Social Psychology, 74*, 1464–1480.

Hermans, D., De Houwer, J., & Eelen, P. (1994). The affective priming effect: Automatic activation of evaluative information in memory. *Cognition and Emotion, 8*(6), 515–533.

Hermans, D., Van den Broeck, A., & Eelen, P. (1998). Affective priming using a color-naming task: A test of an affective-motivational account of affective priming effects. *Zeitschrift Für Experimentelle Psychologie, 45*(2), 136–148.

Jonides, J., & Mack, R. (1984). On the cost and benefit of cost and benefit. *Psychological Bulletin, 96*, 29–44.

Kawakami, K., Dion, K. L., & Dovidio, J. F. (1998). Racial prejudice and stereotype activation. *Personality and Social Psychology Bulletin, 24*, 407–416.

Kawakami, K., & Dovidio, J. F. (2001). The reliability of implicit stereotyping. *Personality and Social Psychology Bulletin, 27*(2), 212–225.

Kim, D.-Y. (2003). Voluntary controllability of the Implicit Association Test (IAT). *Social Psychology Quarterly, 66*(1), 83–96.

Klauer, K. C., & Musch, J. (2001). Does sunshine prime loyal?: Affective priming in the naming task. *Quarterly Journal of Experimental Psychology A, 54A*(3), 727–751.

Klauer, K. C., & Musch, J. (2002). Goal-dependent and goal-independent effects of irrelevant evaluations. *Personality and Social Psychology Bulletin, 28*(6), 802–814.

Klauer, K. C., & Musch, J. (2003). Affective priming: Findings and theories. In J. Musch & K. C. Klauer (Eds.), *The psychology of evaluation: Affective processes in cognition and emotion* (pp. 7–50). Mahwah, NJ: Erlbaum.

Klauer, K. C., Roßnagel, C., & Musch, J. (1997). List-context effects in evaluative priming. *Journal of Experimental Psychology: Learning, Memory, and Cognition, 23*(1), 246–255.

Klinger, M. R., Burton, P. C., & Pitts, G. (2000). Mechanisms of unconscious priming: I. Response competition, not spreading activation. *Journal of Experimental Psychology: Learning, Memory, and Cognition, 26*(2), 441–455.

Klinger, M. R., & Greenwald, A. G. (1995). Unconscious priming of association judgments. *Journal of Experimental Psychology: Learning, Memory, and Cognition, 21*(3), 569–581.

Köhler, W. (1947). *Gestalt psychology* (rev. ed.). New York: Liveright.

Krosnick, J. A., Judd, C. M., & Wittenbrink, B. (2005). The measurement of attitudes. In D. Albarracín, B. T. Johnson & M. P. Zanna (Eds.), *Handbook of attitudes and attitude change: Basic principles* (pp. 21–76). Mahwah, NJ: Erlbaum.

LeDoux, J. E. (1996). *The emotional brain: The mysterious underpinnings of emotional life.* New York: Simon & Schuster.

Lepore, L., & Brown, R. (1997). Category and stereotype activation: Is prejudice inevitable? *Journal of Personality and Social Psychology, 72*, 275–287.

Livingston, R. W., & Brewer, M. B. (2002). What are we really priming?: Cue-based versus category-based processing of facial stimuli. *Journal of Personality and Social Psychology, 82*(1), 5–18.

MacLeod, C. M. (1991). Half a century of research on the Stroop effect: An integrative review. *Psychological Bulletin, 109*(2), 163–203.

Marcel, A. J. (1983). Conscious and unconscious perception: Experiments on visual masking and word recognition. *Cognitive Psychology, 15*(2), 197–237.

Meyer, D. E., & Schvaneveldt, R. W. (1971). Facilitation in recognizing pairs of words: Evidence of a dependence between retrieval operations. *Journal of Experimental Psychology, 90*, 227–234.

Meyer, D. E., Schvaneveldt, R. W., & Ruddy, M. G. (1975). Loci of contextual effects on visual word recognition. In P. M. A. Rabbitt & S. Dornic (Eds.), *Attention and performance: V* (pp. 98–118). New York: Academic Press.

Monteith, M. J., Voils, C. I., & Ashburn-Nardo, L. (2001). Taking a look underground: Detecting, interpreting, and reacting to implicit racial biases. *Social Cognition, 19*(4), 395–417.

Moskowitz, G. B., Salomon, A. R., & Taylor, C. M. (2000). Preconsciously controlling stereotyping: Implicitly activated egalitarian goals prevent the activation of stereotypes. *Social Cognition, 18*(2), 151–177.

Murphy, S. T., & Zajonc, R. B. (1993). Affect, cognition, and awareness: Affective priming with optimal and suboptimal stimulus exposures. *Journal of Personality and Social Psychology, 64*, 723–739.

Neely, J. H. (1976). Semantic priming and retrieval from lexical memory: Evidence for facilitatory and inhibitory processes. *Memory and Cognition, 4*(5), 648–654.

Neely, J. H. (1977). Semantic priming and retrieval from lexical memory: Roles of inhibitionless spreading activation and limited-capacity attention. *Journal of Experimental Psychology: General, 106*, 226–254.

Neely, J. H. (1991). Semantic priming effects in visual word recognition: A selective review of current findings and theories. In D. Besner & G. W. Humphreys (Eds.), *Basic processes in reading: Visual word recognition* (pp. 264–336). Hillsdale, NJ: Erlbaum

Olson, M. A., & Fazio, R. H. (2003). Relations between implicit measures of prejudice: What are we measuring? *Psychological Science, 14*(6), 636–639.

Paivio, A. (1991). Dual coding theory: Retrospect and current status. *Canadian Journal of Psychology, 45*(3), 255–287.

Paulhus, D. L. (1984). Two-component models of socially desirable responding. *Journal of Personality and Social Psychology, 46*(3), 598–609.

Payne, B., Cheng, C. M., Govorun, O., & Stewart, B. D. (2005). An inkblot for attitudes: Affect misattribution as implicit measurement. *Journal of Personality and Social Psychology, 89*(3), 277–293.

Perdue, C. W., & Gurtman, M. B. (1990). Evidence for the automaticity of ageism. *Journal of Experimental Social Psychology, 26*, 199–216.

Petty, R. E., & Cacioppo, J. T. (1986). The elaboration-likelihood model of persuasion. In L. Berkowitz (Ed.), *Advances in experimental social psychology* (Vol. 19, pp. 123–205). Orlando, FL: Academic Press.

Posner, M. I., & Snyder, C. R. (1975). Attention and cognitive control. In R. L. Solso (Ed.), *Information processing and cognition: The Loyola Symposium* (pp. 55–85). Hillsdale, NJ: Erlbaum.

Pratto, F., & Shih, M. (2000). Social dominance orientation and group context in implicit group prejudice. *Psychological Science, 11*(6), 515–518.

Proshansky, H. M. (1943). A projective method for the study of attitudes. *Journal of Abnormal and Social Psychology, 38*, 393–395.

Ratcliff, R. (1993). Methods for dealing with reaction time outliers. *Psychological Bulletin, 114*, 510–532.

Ratcliff, R., & McKoon, G. (1988). A retrieval theory of priming in memory. *Psychological Review, 95*(3), 385–408.

Rayner, K. (1978). Foveal and parafoveal cues in reading. In J. Requin (Ed.), *Attention and performance VIII* (pp. 149–161). Hillsdale, NJ: Erlbaum.

Remez, R. E., Rubin, P. E., Pisoni, D. B., & Carrell, T. D. (1981). Speech perception without traditional speech cues. *Science, 212*, 947–950.

Roese, N. J., & Jamieson, D. W. (1993). Twenty years of bogus pipeline research: A critical review and meta-analysis. *Psychological Bulletin, 114*(2), 363–375.

Seymour, P. H. (1973). A model for reading, naming and comparison. *British Journal of Psychology, 64*(1), 35–49.

Sherman, S. J., Rose, J. S., Koch, K., Presson, C. C., & Chassin, L. (2003). Implicit and explicit attitudes toward cigarette smoking: The effects of context and motivation. *Journal of Social and Clinical Psychology, 22*(1), 13–39.

Shiffrin, R. M., Pisoni, D. B., & Castaneda-Mendez, K. (1974). Is attention shared between the ears? *Cognitive Psychology, 6*, 190–215.

Shiffrin, R. M., & Schneider, W. (1977). Controlled and automatic human information processing: II. Perceptual learning, automatic attending, and a general theory. *Psychological Review, 84*, 127–190.

Sigall, H., & Page, R. (1971). Current stereotypes: A little fading, a little faking. *Journal of Personality and Social Psychology, 18*, 247–255.

Sloman, S. A. (1996). The empirical case for two systems of reasoning. *Psychological Bulletin, 119*(1), 3–22.

Smith, E. R., & DeCoster, J. (2000). Dual-process models in social and cognitive psychology: Conceptual integration and links to underlying memory systems. *Personality and Social Psychology Review, 4*(2), 108–131.

Smith, M. C., Besner, D., & Miyoshi, H. (1994). New limits to automaticity: Context modulates semantic priming. *Journal of Experimental Psychology: Learning, Memory, and Cognition, 20*, 104–115.

Spalding, L. R., & Hardin, C. D. (1999). Unconscious unease and self-handicapping: Behavioral consequences of individual differences in implicit and explicit self-esteem. *Psychological Science, 10*(6), 535–539.

Spruyt, A., Hermans, D., Pandelaere, M., De Houwer, J., & Eelen, P. (2004). On the replicability of the affective priming effect in the pronunciation task. *Experimental Psychology, 51*(2), 109–115.

Strack, F., & Deutsch, R. (2004). Reflective and impulsive determinants of social behavior. *Personality and Social Psychology Review, 8*, 220–247.

Strack, F., & Martin, L. (1987). Thinking, judging, and communicating: A process account of context effects in attitude surveys. In H. J. Hippler, N. Schwarz, & S. Sudman (Eds.), *Social information processing and survey methodology* (pp. 123–148). New York: Springer-Verlag.

Stroebe, W., & Insko, C. A. (1989). Stereotype, prejudice, and discrimination:

Changing conceptions in theory and research. In D. Bar-Tal, C. F. Graumann, A. W. Kruglanski, & W. Stroebe (Eds.), *Stereotyping and prejudice: Changing conceptions* (pp. 3–34). New York: Springer-Verlag.

Taylor, D. A. (1977). Time course of context effects. *Journal of Experimental Psychology: General, 106*(4), 404–426.

Wegener, D. T., & Petty, R. E. (1997). The flexible correction model: The role of naive theories of bias in bias correction. In M. P. Zanna (Ed.), *Advances in experimental social psychology* (Vol. 29, pp. 141–208). San Diego, CA: Academic Press.

Wegner, D. M., & Bargh, J. A. (1998). Control and automaticity in social life. In D. T. Gilbert, S. T. Fiske, & L. Gardner (Eds.), *Handbook of social psychology* (4th ed., Vol. 1, pp. 446–496). Boston: McGraw-Hill.

Wentura, D. (2002). Ignoring "brutal" will make "numid" more pleasant but "uyuvu" more unpleasant: The role of a priori pleasantness of unfamiliar stimuli in affective priming tasks. *Cognition and Emotion, 16*(2), 269–298.

Wentura, D., & Rothermund, K. (2003). The "meddling-in" of affective information: A general model of automatic evaluation effects. In J. Musch & K. C. Klauer (Eds.), *The psychology of evaluation: Affective processes in cognition and emotion* (pp. 51–86). Mahwah, NJ: Erlbaum.

Wertheimer, M. (1923). Untersuchungen zur Lehre der Gestalt, II. *Psychologische Forschung, 4*, 301–350.

Westie, F. R. (1953). A technique for the measurement of race attitudes. *American Sociological Review, 18*, 73–78.

Wilson, T. D., Lindsey, S., & Schooler, T. Y. (2000). A model of dual attitudes. *Psychological Review, 107*(1), 101–126.

Wittenbrink, B. (2004). *Stereotype activation and control as determinants of shooter bias.* Paper presented at the annual meeting of the Society of Experimental Social Psychology, Forth Worth, TX.

Wittenbrink, B., Judd, C. M., & Park, B. (1997). Evidence for racial prejudice at the implicit level and its relationship with questionnaire measures. *Journal of Personality and Social Psychology, 72*, 262–274.

Wittenbrink, B., Judd, C. M., & Park, B. (2001a). Evaluative versus conceptual judgments in automatic stereotyping and prejudice. *Journal of Experimental Social Psychology, 37*(3), 244–252.

Wittenbrink, B., Judd, C. M., & Park, B. (2001b). Spontaneous prejudice in context: Variability in automatically activated attitudes. *Journal of Personality and Social Psychology, 81*(5), 815–827.

Zajonc, R. B. (1980). Feeling and thinking: Preferences need no inferences. *American Psychologist, 35*, 151–175.

3 Understanding and Using the Implicit Association Test: IV

What We Know (So Far) about the Method

Kristin A. Lane
Mahzarin R. Banaji
Brian A. Nosek
Anthony G. Greenwald

Each time a latency in responding to a stimulus is measured, we owe a debt to F. C. Donders, who in the mid-19th century made the fundamental discovery that the time required to perform a mental computation reveals something fundamental about how the mind works. Donders expressed the idea in the following simple and optimistic statement about the feasibility of measuring the mind: "Will all quantitative treatment of mental processes be out of the question then? By no means! An important factor seemed to be susceptible to measurement: I refer to the time required for simple mental processes" (Donders, 1868/1969, pp. 413–414).

With particular variations of simple stimuli and subjects' choices, Donders demonstrated that it is possible to bring order to understanding invisible thought processes by computing the time that elapses between stimulus presentation and response production. A more specific observation he offered lies at the center of our own modern understanding of mental operations:

We made the subjects respond with the right hand to the stimulus on the right side, and with the left hand to the stimulus on the left side. . . . When movement of the right hand was required with stimulation on the left side or the other way round, then the time lapse was longer and errors common. (Donders, 1868/1969, p. 421)

With this modest test Donders opened up possibilities for studying mental processes, the effects of which are visible in behavioral and brain science even 150 years later. The idea underlying an entire family of response latency techniques remains the same as conjectured and tested by Donders: the easier a mental task, the quicker the decision point is reached and the fewer the errors that result. To make the right–right and left–left association is easier than the right–left and left–right association, and the difference in speed between the two tasks can serve as an indicator of their relative difficulty. With a psychology that relied on introspective access not yet born, Donders took for granted the logic underlying such a method—that mental states could be inferred on the basis of objective patterns of responses rather than relying on asking the subject the question, "Which of these two tasks is easier?"

Time as the variable to estimate the nature of mental computation underlies dozens of methods: the Stroop task, episodic or repetition priming, semantic priming, evaluation priming, and many others to assess attention, perception, memory and categorization. We focus on one such measure, the Implicit Association Test (IAT; Greenwald, McGhee, & Schwartz, 1998), which provides an estimate of the strength of association between concepts and attributes, much like the semantic priming measure does (see Wittenbrink, Chapter 2, this volume). In a grant proposal submitted by Banaji and Greenwald on January 13, 1994, the logic underlying the IAT was described as follows:

Experiment 3.8: Measurement of implicit attitude (B: Rapid classification method). The same materials as Expt. 3.7 are used, but without priming. Instead, two categories of words are assigned to each of two response keys. Subjects are asked to rapidly press (say) the right key whenever the stimulus word is *either* female-associated or pleasant in meaning, and the left key for words either male-associated or unpleasant in meaning. Through the course of a session, blocks of trials with the four combinations of category pairings and key assignments are intermixed. . . . The measure of implicit attitude . . . is the difference between latency with pleasant/male pairing versus pleasant/female pairing. To the extent that responding is faster with pleasant/female than with pleasant/male pairing, the latency-difference measure indicates greater positivity of the implicit attitude associated with female.

In 1995, Greenwald and Banaji argued that although many existing effects were already available as evidence of implicit social cognition, an individual difference measure with the sensitivity to detect variability among a population would be needed. They concluded their review of implicit social cognition with the following comment:

> In summary of existing efforts at indirect measurement of implicit social cognition: Research on latency decomposition, projective tests, and miscellaneous other procedures indicate that indirect measurement of individual differences in implicit social cognition is possible. At the same time, such measurement has not yet been achieved in the efficient form needed to make research investigation of individual differences in implicit social cognition a routine undertaking. When such measures do become available, there should follow the rapid development of a new industry of research on implicit cognitive aspects of personality and social behavior. (p. 20)

The IAT technique was developed to facilitate such progress, and in particular to generate new methods that would demonstrate large effect sizes and maintain reasonable reliability (Greenwald et al., 1998; for a discussion of the origins of the IAT, see Dasgupta, Greenwald, & Banaji, 2003). The technique was developed in the mid-1990s, following several years of parameter testing and refinement in labs at the University of Washington and Yale University. Distribution to any interested scientist preceded its first publication in 1998.

In the 9 years since its publication, the IAT method has received significant attention. At present, more than 200 papers report use of the method, hundreds of conference papers have been delivered, and more than 4.5 million tests have been taken at *www.implicit.harvard.edu*. In addition, a healthy skepticism about what the method is and does has produced commentaries on interpretation (see Nosek, Greenwald, & Banaji, in press, for a review). Specific reports of interest to readers include those that summarize results obtained using the IAT (Carney, Nosek, Greenwald, & Banaji, in press; Greenwald & Nosek, 2001; Nosek, Banaji, & Greenwald, 2002a; Nosek et al., in press), provide details on method and scoring development (Greenwald, Nosek, & Banaji, 2003; Nosek, Greenwald, & Banaji, 2005), and discuss the unique nature of reactions to the IAT (Banaji, 2001). In addition, stimulus materials and sample programs are available via web sites (see *www.people.fas.harvard.edu/~banaji*, *www.briannosek.com*, *www.faculty. washington.edu/agg*).

With these resources already available, this chapter focuses on an aspect of the work that is currently unavailable in a single location—a brief introduction to those who are new to the IAT and wish to become educated users of the technique and consumers of research that uses it. If successful, the chapter will provide a user-friendly guide to the IAT.

OVERVIEW OF THE IAT AND ITS INTERPRETATION

Like the semantic priming method used to understand semantic memory, the IAT measures the relative strength of association between pairs of concepts, labeled for pedagogical purposes as *category* and *attribute*. When completing an IAT, participants rapidly classify individual stimuli that represent category and attribute (in the form of words, symbols, or pictures) into one of four distinct categories with only two responses. The underlying assumption is that responses will be facilitated—and thus will be faster and more accurate—when categories that are closely associated share a response, as compared to when they do not. To intuitively understand how an IAT works, one might visit *www.implicit.harvard.edu* and try a test.

Structure of the Seven-Block IAT

Figure 3.1 presents a schematic overview of the structure of the first published IAT report, which assessed implicit attitudes toward flowers, relative to insects (Greenwald et al., 1998). It is described in detail here because it forms the basis of the rest of the chapter. At the heart of the measure is a pair of target concepts—in this example, flowers and insects—and a pair of attribute concepts—in this example, good and bad.

In Stage 1 of this sample task, participants rapidly classify words into the categories flower (by pressing the left computer key) and insect (by pressing the right computer key). They then repeat the same task for the categories good and bad (Stage 2). In Stage 3, the previous two tasks are combined and participants press the left computer key when any item in the category flower or good appears on the screen, and press the right computer key when any item in the category insect or bad appears on the screen (abbreviated as the *flower* + *good* or *insect* + *bad* pairing). Stage 4 repeats this procedure with an additional set of trials. In the next stage, the task in Stage 2 is reversed. Similarly, Stages 6 and 7 reverse the earlier combined pairings of Stages 3 and 4: flower + bad now share the left response key, and insect + good share the right response key. Because attitudes toward

Stage	Left key assignment	Right key assignment
1	FLOWER	INSECT
2	GOOD	BAD
3	FLOWER	INSECT
	GOOD	BAD
4	FLOWER	INSECT
	GOOD	BAD
5	BAD	GOOD
6	FLOWER	INSECT
	BAD	GOOD
7	FLOWER	INSECT
	BAD	GOOD

FIGURE 3.1. Schematic overview of the Implicit Association Test.

flowers are anticipated to be more positive than attitudes toward insects for most people, participants are expected to respond more rapidly, on average, when the category labels flower and good share one response, and insect and bad share the other response (Stages 3 and 4), as compared to the stage in which flower and bad share one response, and insect and good share the other response (Stages 6 and 7).

The difference in the latency to respond to particular pairings of concept and attribute (say, *insect + good* and *flower + bad*), compared to another set of pairings of concept and attribute (*insect + bad* and *flower + good*), provides an index of the relative strength of association between the first versus the second pairings. If the first set produces faster responses overall than the second (and does so even when the pairings' presentation order is reversed), we conclude that the relative strength of association between *flower + good* and *insect + bad* is greater than that between *flower + bad* and *insect + good* and therefore reflects a relative implicit preference for flowers over insects.

When young boys, compared with young girls, show a weaker preference for flowers over insects, we conclude that the group difference reflects a meaningful distinction in automatic preferences for these attitude objects (Banaji, in press; Baron & Banaji, 2006). When entomologists show a smaller effect on the same test, compared to a control group (Citrin & Greenwald, 1998)—that is, demonstrate a weaker relative preference for flowers over insects—we conclude that the IAT reveals individual differences in strength of association, using a known groups validation approach. That is, we begin with groups a priori expected to show differences in attitude and test this expected difference on the IAT measure. Furthermore, if individual differences in strength of association represent meaningful differences in attitude, the test should predict other behaviors such that those with stronger *insect + good* scores are more likely to spend time with insects and to act in favorable ways toward insects, such as feeding and caring for them and being invested in their survival. Taken together, these findings—that groups differ in strength of associations in predicted ways, that one's personal experience alters the magnitude of those associations, and that those associations relate reliably to other individual judgments and behaviors—would provide evidence of the usefulness of the measure to understand implicit social cognition.

Categories can represent any grouping, such as *insects* and *flowers*, *Ohio State* and *Michigan*, *psychology* and *chemistry*, *elderly* and *young*, *Mac* and *PC*, or *Coke* and *Pepsi* (see Nosek, 2005, for a list of over 50 pairings that have been tested and interpreted). The attribute concept can also vary in many ways. If attitude or preference is of interest, the attribute dimensions can be represented by the labels *good/bad*, *pleasant/unpleasant*, or *positive/negative*.

Alternatively, the association between a target category (*female* or *male*) and a specific trait or attribute provides a measure of what is commonly thought of as a *belief* or *stereotype*. For example, the group *male*, compared to the group *female*, is more strongly associated with *mathematics*, relative to *liberal arts* (Nosek, Banaji, & Greenwald, 2002b), *career* relative to *family* (Nosek et al., 2002a), and *strong* relative to *weak* (Rudman, Greenwald, & McGhee, 2001), indicating implicit gender stereotypes.

Moreover, the attribute dimension can be turned toward the *self*; a measure of association between the categories (say, PC/Mac) and self/other can be obtained as a measure of relative *identity* with the objects. For example, the pairing of self with gender provides a measure of gender identity (see, e.g., Greenwald & Farnham, 2000), of self with ethnic group offers a measure of ethnic identity (Devos & Banaji, 2005), and of self with math/arts provides a measure of an academic identity (Nosek et al., 2002b).

Likewise, association of self as the target category and attitude as the attribute dimension is assumed to provide a measure of implicit self-esteem. It is the relative strength of association between *self* (compared to another category such as *other*) and positive/negative concepts. The IAT to measure self-esteem is structured like the attitudinal measure described above, with *self* and *other* serving as the target concepts and *good* and *bad* terms as the attribute dimension (e.g., Bosson, Swann, & Pennebaker, 2000; Dijksterhuis, 2004; Greenwald & Farnham, 2000; Karpinski, 2004; Yamaguchi et al., 2006).

The IAT's main usage has been in the domain of implicit social cognition, and hence most of our examples reflect such practice. However, the IAT had been used in several other contexts, such as clinical (e.g., Egloff & Schmukle, 2002; Gemar, Segal, Sagrati, & Kennedy, 2001), developmental (Baron & Banaji, 2006), marketing (Maison, Greenwald, & Bruin, 2001), and health (Czopp & Monteith, 2003) applications, as well as in legal scholarship (Kang & Banaji, 2006) and business (Banaji, Bazerman, & Chugh, 2003). For example, clinical psychologists have adapted and used the IAT to understand the mechanisms that differentiate groups of individuals with and without particular disorders, in illuminating the cognitive changes that occur during psychological treatment, and in predicting the likelihood of engaging in behaviors that are known to be associated with clinical disorders (Egloff & Schmukle, 2002; Gemar et al., 2001; Gray, Brown, & MacCulloch, 2005; Gray, MacCulloch, Smith, Morris, & Snowden, 2003; Jordan, Spencer, Zanna, Hoshino-Browne, & Correll, 2003; Nock & Banaji, 2006; Teachman, Gregg, & Woody, 2001; Teachman & Woody, 2003). Domains as diverse as identity with nature (Schultz, Shriver, Tabanico, & Khazian, 2004), attitudes toward death (Bassett & Dabbs, 2003), and toward celebrities, foods, cities and geography, public opinion issues, and politics, have been studied (Nosek, 2005).

In this chapter, we review over 100 published and in-press studies that include at least one IAT. In order to decide if an IAT method is necessary or worth using, the reader must first be aware of the main results associated with the measure and the current status of research on the reliability and validity of the measure. With this in mind, we divide the chapter into three sections that present (1) an overview of the task and a summary of the most robust findings associated with it; (2) an overview of the evidence for the reliability and validity of the task; and (3) a how-to guide for researchers wanting to use the IAT themselves or to better evaluate experiments using the IAT.

THE IAT REVEALS ROBUST ASSOCIATIONS THAT OFTEN DIFFER FROM SELF-REPORTED ATTITUDES AND BELIEFS: EVIDENCE FROM WEB-BASED SAMPLES

By measuring associations between concepts and attributes, the IAT can reveal associations that often differ from those that are introspectively accessed and reported verbally. Table 3.1 summarizes the results of 17 different IATs, based on over 2.5 million tests completed at two public web sites. To facilitate comparison between implicit and explicit measures, means are reported as Cohen's d effect sizes of the difference from "no preference." At each site, visitors have an opportunity to complete one or more tests of their choice and receive feedback about the strength of their automatic associations.[1] Participants select a task, provide optional demographic data, and respond to explicit questions that parallel the IAT measure. Because of the large number of participants and the broad demographic range of respondents (compared to the typical undergraduate sample), these data provide insights into the variability among cognitions, offer estimates of correlations between implicit and explicit measures, and allow exploration of patterns of associations across different demographic groups. In addition, such large data sets can generate knowledge of the psychometric properties of the IAT and improve methodological and analytical techniques.

Two main findings are apparent from these data. First, subjects demonstrated strong and robust associations between social groups and basic evaluation (implicit attitude) or specific qualities (implicit stereotypes). Implicit attitudes toward culturally valued groups were shown to be positive; participants demonstrated, on average, greater positivity for White over Black, Other Peoples (non-Arab Muslims) over Arab Muslims, abled over disabled, young over old, and straight over gay. In addition, participants showed stereotype-consistent associations between White and American, male and science, and Black and weapons. These findings are consistent with laboratory data that used the IAT to measure the same constructs (e.g., Devos & Banaji, 2005; Greenwald et al., 1998, 2002; Hummert, Garstka, O'Brien, Greenwald, & Mellott, 2002; Jellison, McConnell, & Gabriel, 2004; Nosek et al., 2002b; Steffens & Buchner, 2003).

The second clear message from the web data is that patterns of cognitions can vary widely across implicit and explicit measures. For example, although participants showed strong implicit preference for White over Black (average Cohen's d of two race attitude tasks = 0.80), the effect of their self-reported bias was much weaker (average Cohen's d of two race attitude tasks = 0.31). It is not the case that the implicit measures always detect greater negativity than explicit measures, but in the case of attitudes toward social groups, that is a common result.

RELIABILITY AND VALIDITY OF THE IAT

Evaluating the IAT's validity is a somewhat different undertaking than that of evaluating the validity of a self-report scale. Because the

TABLE 3.1. Implicit and Explicit Attitudes for 17 Tasks Completed between July 2000 and May 2006 at Publicly Available Websites

Task	Higher numbers reflect association between:	Dates administered		IAT			Explicit		IAT-Explicit
		Begin	End	N	D	d	N	d	r
Age attitude	Young + Good/Old + Bad	7/2000	5/2006	351,204	0.49	1.23	356,308	0.51	.13
Race attitude	White + Good/Black + Bad	7/2000	5/2006	732,881	0.37	0.86	759,566	0.36	.31
Skin-tone attitude	Light skin + Good/Dark skin + Bad	3/2001	5/2006	122,988	0.30	0.73	72,735	0.25	.22
Child-race attitude	White + Good/Black + Bad	11/2001	5/2004	28,816	0.33	0.73	41,886	0.15	.29
Arab-Muslim attitude	Other Peoples + Good/Arab Muslims + Bad	11/2001	5/2006	77,254	0.14	0.33	37,499	0.58	.34
Religion attitude	Christian + Good/Jewish + Bad	8/2003	5/2006	66,092	-0.15	-0.34	43,711	-0.13	.38
Disability attitude	Abled + Good/Disabled + Bad	6/2003	5/2006	38,544	0.45	1.05	23,120	0.57	.14
Sexuality attitude	Straight People + Good/Gay People + Bad	2/2002	5/2006	269,683	0.35	0.74	168,498	0.54	.43
Weight attitude	Thin + Good/Obese + Bad	3/2001	5/2006	199,329	0.35	0.83	110,548	0.88	.20
Race-weapons stereotype	White + Harmless Objects/Black + Weapons	11/2001	5/2006	85,742	0.37	1.00	91,771	0.31	.15
American-native stereotype	White Am. + American/Native Am. + Foreign	5/2002	5/2006	44,878	0.23	0.46	41,966	-0.42	.18

(Continued)

67

TABLE 3.1. (*continued*)

Task	Higher numbers reflect association between:	Dates administered		IAT			Explicit		IAT-Explicit
		Begin	End	N	D	d	N	d	r
American-Asian stereotype	White + American/Asian + Foreign	3/2001	5/2006	57,569	0.26	0.62	27,734	0.45	.17
Gender-science stereotype	Male + Science/Female + Liberal Arts	7/2000	5/2006	299,298	0.37	0.93	139,182	0.79	.22
Gender-career stereotype	Male + Career/Female + Family	10/2002	5/2006	83,084	0.39	1.10	82,550	0.89	.16
Presidential attitude	Bush + Good/Other President + Bad[a]	5/2003	5/2006	68,123	-0.07	-0.15	73,595	-0.73	.54
Election 2004 attitude	Bush + Good/Gore + Bad	10/2003	5/2005	22,904	-0.14	-0.27	21,421	-0.42	.71
Election 2000 attitude	Bush + Good/Kerry + Bad	7/2000	2/2003	27,146	-0.09	-0.16	29,925	-0.20	.75
Total or median				2,575,535	0.33	0.73	2,122,015	0.36	.22

Note. From Nosek et al. (2006). *D* represents the IAT score calculated according to the recommendations of Greenwald et al. (2003).
[a]The comparison category to President Bush varied.

IAT represents a procedural format for measuring implicit cognition rather than a single measure of a specific construct, there is no single incantation of the IAT to be validated. Unlike traditional measures of attitude, such as the Modern Racism (McConahay, 1986) or Rosenberg Self-Esteem (Rosenberg, 1989) scales, and given that the IAT can be adapted to measure the constructs of stereotypes, self-esteem, identity, and attitudes toward concepts as diverse as gender, ethnicity, academic domains, and favorite foods, two IATs may have little in common other than the basic structure of the task. Thus, there are both general (format-specific) and specific (construct-specific) issues of reliability and validity to contend with in evaluating the IAT. By looking at issues of reliability and validity across content areas, we focus on the psychometric properties of the task in general. If IATs across multiple studies and multiple designs produce consistent effects, despite the variance associated with idiosyncratic design features, the generalizability of the findings should inspire greater confidence.

However, simply because the IAT format produces a reliable and valid task does not mean that any single IAT is necessarily a good measure of the target construct. Two IATs that measure attitudes toward the same construct may vary widely—one may use picture stimuli, and one may use verbal stimuli, or the exemplars of the category and attribute may differ quite a bit across task. As a result, features specific to construction of a particular IAT can produce unique variance.

Reliability

Error variance is easily introduced in response latency studies—a subject's sneeze, a car horn, or even an eyeblink, that coincides with the appearance of the stimulus can introduce task-irrelevant variability in response latency. Such factors are not typically given much importance in gauging the reliability of self-report scales, but they may dampen the reliability and stability of a measure based on quick responses. Indeed, the internal consistency of measures based on response latency is generally somewhat lower than that of those based on self-reports (Buchner & Wippich, 2000; Perruchet & Baveux, 1989).

In one study examining the internal consistency of a number of implicit measures, the IAT showed reasonable reliability (Cronbach's alpha = 0.78); notably, this was higher than that of an evaluative priming task and a modified version of the IAT included in the same session (Cunningham, Preacher, & Banaji, 2001). Additional studies that have reported the internal consistency of the IAT also indicate that it is generally acceptable (e.g., internal reliabilities averaged .79 across 50 studies in a meta-analysis conducted by Hofman, Gawronski, Gschwender, Le, & Schmitt, 2005).

The IAT has also shown reasonably good reliability over multiple assessments of the task. As shown in Table 3.2, in 20 studies that have included more than one administration of the IAT, test–retest reliability ranged from .25 to .69, with mean and median test–retest reliability of .50. Notably, in an analysis of seven implicit measures of self-esteem, the IAT's test–retest reliability (.69) was superior to the other implicit measures of self-esteem, which ranged from –.05 (Stroop task) to .63 (initials–birthday preference task) and averaged .30 (Bosson et al., 2000).

Validity

The traditional "multitrait–multimethod" (MTMM) (Campbell & Fiske, 1959) approach dictates not only that IATs measuring similar constructs should correlate with one another, but also that IATs assessing theoretically distinct concepts should not. It is important that, across methods, measures of similar traits should also converge with one another but measures of distinct traits should diverge from one another. In addition, multiple IATs assessing distinct constructs relate to each other in theoretically predicted patterns, providing evidence for the IAT's nomological validity. Evidence for its convergent validity with other implicit measures is more mixed. Discriminant validity is seen in studies indicating that cognitions that are predicted to be unrelated do, in fact, diverge from one another. That is, predicted relationships among different IATs are observed.

Nomological Validity: Theoretically Predicted Results Emerge across Studies

Greenwald and colleagues (2002) argued that the tendency toward cognitive consistency—as described almost a half century ago by balance (Heider, 1958) and dissonance (Festinger, 1957) theories—leads to cognitive balance among attitudes, stereotypes, identities, and self-esteem. For example, the higher a person's self-esteem, the more positive ingroup attitudes he or she should have in order to maintain cognitive consistency. This can be phrased as, "If I am good, and I am strongly tied to my group, then my group is good." Indeed, self-concept and attitudes related to gender and race (as measured by the IAT) adhered to this pattern, whereas explicit measures of these constructs did not. Similarly, the more women implicitly identified with

TABLE 3.2. Test–Retest Correlations of the IAT

Authors	Construct	Time period	r	N
Banse et al. (2001)	Attitudes toward homosexuality	Same session	.52	101
Bosson et al. (2000)	Self-esteem	4 weeks	.69	80
Cunningham et al. (2001)[a]	Racial attitudes	2 weeks between each of four sessions	.32	93
Dasgupta & Asgari (2004)	Gender stereotypes	1 year	.25	52
Dasgupta et al. (2001)	Racial attitudes	24 hours	.65	48
Dasgupta, McGhee, & Greenwald (2000)	Racial attitudes (name versus picture IAT)	Same session	.39	75
de Jong et al. (2003)	Fear association with spiders	4 months	.41	37
Egloff & Schmukle (2002)	Anxiety identity	1 week	.57	41
Egloff et al. (2005)	Anxiety identity	1 week	.58	65
		1 month	.62	39
		1 year	.47	36
Greenwald & Farnham (2000)	Self-esteem Two variants: an affective and an evaluative version	Same session	.43	145
	Gender self-concept Two variants: a generic and an idiographic version	Same session	.68	58
	Self-esteem	8 days	.52	44
Schmukle & Egloff[b] (2004)	Anxiety identity	Same session	.50	45
Shultz et al. (2004)	Implicit identity with nature	Same session	.45	32
		1 week	.46	33
		4 weeks	.40	33
Steffens & Buchner (2003)	Attitudes toward gay men	1 week	.50	84
		10 minutes	.52	107
Average			.50	
median			.50	

[a]Mean test–retest correlation of four IATs, each administered 2 weeks apart.

[b]Reflects control condition only. In the experimental condition, which was designed to elicit change in anxiety identity, participants completed a public speaking task in between administrations of the IAT. Correspondence between the two IAT scores was lower in this condition, $r = .21$.

their gender group and associated female with liberal arts (compared to math), the more they implicitly liked liberal arts (Nosek et al., 2002b). Students were also more likely to show implicit preference for their university over its main competitor to the extent that they showed both high implicit self-esteem and strong implicit university identity (Lane, Mitchell, & Banaji, 2005).

Cunningham, Nezlek, and Banaji (2004) examined whether implicit biases toward a range of stigmatized groups were related to one another. Such a pattern is predicted by traditional and modern theories of ethnocentrism and would therefore provide additional evidence of convergent validity. They found that attitudes toward five different stigmatized groups (involving race, sexuality, social class, religion, and nationality) loaded on a single factor of "implicit ethnocentrism." It is important to note that a conceptually unrelated IAT (measuring attitude toward trees and birds) did not load on this factor.

Convergent Validity: The Relationship of the IAT to Other Implicit Measures

Patterns of convergent validity among implicit measures that purport to measure that same construct are more mixed. Several studies have shown little overlap between implicit measures designed to assess the same construct. Bosson and colleagues (2000) examined the correlations among seven implicit and four explicit measures of self-esteem. Although the IAT was uncorrelated with the other implicit measures, it was not alone in failing to converge—among the 15 possible zero-order correlations between the six measures, only two pairs of implicit measures significantly correlated with each other. Most attention has focused on understanding when and how the two most widely used measures of implicit attitudes, evaluative priming tasks and the IAT, converge and diverge. In a typical use of the priming task measuring racial attitudes (Fazio, Jackson, Dunton, & Williams, 1995), participants classified words as positive or negative as quickly as possible. An image of a Black or a White face preceded each word, allowing the assessment of the relative facilitation of each social group to positive or negative concepts. The viewing of Black faces, as compared to White faces, facilitated judgments of negative words and interfered with judgments of positive words, indicating that Black faces automatically activated negative concepts.

IATs and priming tasks measuring implicit attitudes toward smoking (Sherman, Rose, Koch, Presson, & Chassin, 2003) and condom use (Marsh, Johnson, & Scott-Sheldon, 2001) were unrelated.

Fazio and Olson (2003) reported that across four studies in their lab, priming tasks and IATs measuring racial attitudes did not correlate. Other studies show greater promise. Stereotypes about gender authority (associations between female and low-status jobs), as measured by the IAT, were correlated with three indices of attitudes toward female authorities derived from the priming task (Rudman & Kilianski, 2000). Moreover, participants who tended to show strong implicit gender stereotypes (on the IAT) also showed more positive attitudes toward women on the priming measure, and political attitudes measured by a priming task and the IAT were reliably related (Nosek & Hansen, 2004).

What accounts for these sometimes less-than-robust correlations? As mentioned earlier, response-latency measures often have attenuated internal reliability, and on occasion this has been especially true of priming (Bosson et al., 2000). As a result, true relationships between measures may be masked by measurement error. Three implicit measures of racial preference (a standard IAT as well as response-window versions of both the priming task and IAT in which participants made responses in a very short window and that used error rates as the dependent measure) were completed during two sessions separated by a 2-week interval (Cunningham et al., 2001). Latent variable analysis revealed that this approach improved the stability of the measures. Moreover, the measures were correlated: Two versions of the IAT were strongly related, $r = .77$, as was the priming task with both the response-window IAT, $r = .53$, and the standard IAT, $r = .55$. In addition, all three implicit measures loaded onto a single "implicit bias" factor that was distinct from, but strongly correlated with, explicit bias. These findings suggest that when reliability is accounted for, implicit measures are more likely to be related.

Schwarz (1999) pointed out that many features of an explicit scale, such as the order of questions, response options, or slight wording changes, can affect the provided responses. Similarly, different implicit measures may tap into different features of an attitude object. One of the major distinctions between the priming task and the IAT is that the IAT requires explicit categorization by race, whereas the priming task does not. Noting this, Olson and Fazio (2003) suggested that participants completing the priming task evaluate exemplars of a group, whereas participants completing an IAT evaluate the overall social category. To support this contention, an IAT and a priming task measuring racial attitudes covaried only when participants completing the priming task were instructed to categorize the prime faces by their race; that is, when the subjects' task was made more similar to the IAT. However, this change also increased the split-half reliability of the priming task from .04 to .39 (Olson & Fazio, 2003), leaving open the possibility that the null relationship between the IAT and standard priming task was due to the relatively lower reliability of the standard priming task.

Given that correlations can be drastically attenuated when measures are unreliable, it is difficult to interpret null relations when one of the measures shows poor reliability. Based on the available evidence, we expect that additional investigations that use large samples, maximize reliability, and correct for measurement error through latent variable analysis will clarify the nature of the relationship between implicit measures.

Discriminant Validity

Overlap between IATs that are conceptually related would be poor evidence of the IAT's validity if measures that are conceptually distant also positively correlated with one another. For example, in the Cunningham and colleagues (2004) study, only attitudes toward social objects were related, consistent with theories of ethnocentric bias. The nonsocial attitude did not load onto the factor of "implicit prejudice" in their analysis. Their findings support the idea that implicit attitudes that are expected to be related do converge, whereas those that are conceptually distinct diverge.

Other studies, however, have found correlations between conceptually distinct IATs (McFarland & Crouch, 2002; Mierke & Klauer, 2003). Undoubtedly, as with any measure, there is variance in an IAT score that is attributable to an individual tendency to show IAT effects. Mierke and Klauer (2003) found that an IAT assessing novel associations covaried with both a flower–insect IAT and a shyness–self-concept IAT. Notably, after subjecting their data to the most recent suggested scoring procedures (Greenwald et al., 2003) for the IAT, method-specific variance was either removed (Study 2) or "markedly reduced" (p. 1188; see Back, Schmukle, Egloff, & Gutenberg, 2005, for a similar result). These findings suggest that when using statistical methods that better account for method variance—such as latent variable analysis or improved IAT scoring procedures, better discriminant validity is likely to be observed.

Using a method more directly analogous to the MTMM approach, Gawronski (2002) measured implicit and explicit attitudes toward Turks and Asians among German participants using the IAT. If the two IATs were tapping an individual difference in group-specific attitudes, he reasoned that the IAT measuring attitudes toward a particular group should relate only to explicit attitudes toward that group. This is the pattern that emerged—the IAT measuring attitudes toward Asians correlated only with explicit attitudes toward Asians, whereas the IAT measuring attitudes toward Turks correlated only with explicit attitudes toward Turks. Similarly, across seven attitude objects, Nosek and Smyth (in press) showed that, generally, each IAT-based measure of attitude correlated with an explicit measure of attitudes toward that object, but not with explicit attitudes toward the other target objects. Furthermore, while the IAT and explicit measures were related, they also retained unique components that were not reducible to shared method variance.

Criterion Validity

This section briefly summarizes research indicating the IAT's performance on tests of criterion validity. In short, the IAT can predict group membership based on theoretically predicted patterns of ingroup attitudes and identification, correlates with (but is distinct from) explicit measures of associated constructs, and successfully predicts judgments and behaviors.

Known-Groups Validity. If a new test is designed to be a valid test of math knowledge, then math majors should outperform non-math majors on it. This "known-groups" approach to validity argues that a good measure should reliably distinguish between members of different groups, based on a priori predictions or knowledge about those groups. The IAT has indeed demonstrated theoretically predicted patterns of strong ingroup liking. Japanese Americans exhibited strong preference for their group relative to Korean Americans, whereas Korean Americans showed the opposite pattern (Greenwald et al., 1998). Similarly, East and West Germans each exhibited preference for their ingroup (Kuhnen et al., 2001), and even members of groups artificially created in the laboratory showed preference for their ingroups (Ashburn-Nardo, Voils, & Monteith, 2001). Men and women associated their own gender strongly with self (Aidman & Carroll, 2003; Greenwald & Farnham, 2000), and women, consistent with the prevailing social stereotype, implicitly preferred the arts to math more than men did (Nosek et al., 2002b).

System justification theory (SJT) (Jost & Banaji, 1994) makes a more subtle theoretical prediction about ingroup preference. Specifically, SJT predicts that members of lower-status groups should show reduced implicit liking for their ingroup (compared to members of higher-status groups). Despite the ubiquity of ingroup preference, but consistent with SJT, the IAT is sensitive to differences in the societal evaluation of different groups (see Jost, Banaji, & Nosek, 2005, for a review). On the IAT, Black Americans showed reduced ingroup preference as compared to Whites (Ashburn-Nardo, Knowles, & Monteith, 2003; Livingston, 2002; Nosek et al., 2002a), and overweight and poor people (Rudman, Feinberg, & Fairchild, 2002) actually showed outgroup preference. Status also moderated the strength of ingroup preference among students at universities that varied in prestige (Jost, Pelham, & Carvallo, 2002), and lower ingroup preference has been shown in young children from disadvantaged groups, suggesting the early learning of justifying tendencies that are visible on implicit but not on explicit measures (Dunham, Baron, & Banaji, 2006b).

Successful discrimination between group members even extends to "groups" that are defined by behavior rather than demographic traits. In a study of subjects who were snake or spider phobic (Teachman & Woody, 2003), a composite measure of three IATs successfully classified 92% of participants according to which creature they feared. Smokers showed more positive attitudes toward and stronger identity with smoking than nonsmokers (Swanson, Rudman, & Greenwald, 2001). Although both light and heavy drinkers held negative implicit attitudes toward alcohol (as compared with soda), heavy drinkers strongly associated alcohol and arousal, whereas light drinkers did not (Wiers, van Woerden, Smulders, & de Jong, 2002). Gray and her colleagues (2003) recently investigated implicit attitudes about violence among psychopathic and nonpsychopathic murderers. Although all groups showed a preference for the concept peaceful, as compared to the concept violent, psychopathic murderers showed less dislike for violence than did nonpsychopathic murderers. In addition to providing evidence that the IAT can discriminate even between different types of deviance, this finding was taken to suggest that violent acts committed by psychopaths may be rooted in unusual beliefs about violence, unlike violent acts committed by nonpsychopaths, which may stem from other causes. In each of these cases, it is unclear whether the automatic cognitions influenced the subsequent behaviors, whether cognitions changed because of behavior, or both.

Relationship with Explicit Measures. The nature of the relationship between implicit and explicit attitudes has received a great deal of attention that has not answered the original proposed question: "Do implicit and explicit attitudes relate to one another?" As noted by Fazio and Olson (2003), the more appropriate question may be, "Under what conditions, and for what kind of people, are implicit and explicit measures related?" (p. 304). Useful answers may emerge from questions focused on the conditions under which implicit and explicit measures will covary.

There is a wide range in the extent to which implicit and explicit attitudes covary. As seen in Table 3.1, across 17 IATs that were available at public websites, correlations between implicit and explicit measures ranged from $r = .13$ to $r = .75$ (median $r = .22$). Laboratory studies have shown similar variability, with a number of studies revealing only slight or moderate (but generally positive) correlations between the IAT and explicit measures of the same construct (e.g., Bosson et al., 2000; de Jong, van den Hout, Rietbroek, & Huijding, 2003; Egloff & Schmukle, 2002; Greenwald et al., 1998; Karpinski & Hilton, 2001; Ottaway, Hayden, & Oakes, 2001; Rudman & Kilianski, 2000) and other studies showing strong and robust correlations between the IAT and explicit measures (e.g., Asendorpf, Banse, & Muecke, 2002; Cunningham et al., 2001; Greenwald & Farnham, 2000; Jellison et al., 2004; McConnell & Leibold, 2001; Wiers et al., 2002). A recent meta-analysis of such studies found that across 126 independent correlations, implicit–explicit correspondence ranged from $r = -.25$ to $r = .60$, with an average implicit–explicit correlation of .19 (Hofmann et al., 2005).

Consistent with the notion that implicit and explicit attitudes are distinct constructs (Greenwald & Banaji, 1995; Wilson, Lindsey, & Schooler, 2000), even when the IAT and explicit measures do correlate, implicit and explicit attitudes are separate constructs. Confirmatory factor analyses indicated that self-esteem and gender identity were better fit by a model in which implicit and explicit measures loaded onto two separate constructs, rather than a single, latent construct (Greenwald & Farnham, 2000). This finding parallels that of Cunningham and colleagues (2001), in which implicit (IAT and priming) racial attitudes were distinct from, but positively correlated with, explicit racial attitudes. This conclusion generalized to a wide variety of domains—across 57 different pairs of attitude objects, a two-factor solution fit much better than a single-factor solution even when implicit and explicit attitudes were highly correlated with one another (Nosek, 2005; Nosek & Smyth, in press). Further support for the distinction between implicit and explicit attitudes comes from findings that implicit and explicit attitudes predict unique variance in meaningful criterion variables (see, e.g., McConnell & Leibold, 2001; Nosek et al., 2002b).

Given that the extent to which implicit and explicit attitudes are correlated varies widely across studies, more recent work has turned to the issue of the conditions under which implicit and explicit attitudes will covary. Nosek (2005; see also Nosek & Banaji, 2002) identified factors that moderate the nature of the relationship between implicit and explicit attitudes: (1) self-presentational concerns, (2) attitude strength, (3) attitude dimensionality (the extent to which liking for one category appears to imply disliking of the contrasting category), and (4) attitude distinctiveness (the perception that an individual's attitude is distinct from others' attitudes). Also, consistent with the finding that implicit–explicit correlations will be higher for strongly held attitudes, participants who elaborated about an attitude or reported that an attitude was extremely important to them showed greater implicit–explicit correspondence than those who did not (Karpinski, Steinman, & Hilton, 2005).

This approach of examining aspects of the attitude object, as well as the attitude holder, when investigating the relationship between implicit and explicit measures will likely reveal additional personal and situational moderators of the relationship between implicit and explicit measures. The hunt for correlations may be most successful when large samples and rigorous statistical techniques, such as meta-analysis or latent variable modeling, are used, as these techniques are likely to provide the most reliable and stable correlations (be they negative, positive, or null).

The IAT Predicts Meaningful Behavior. Given psychologists' long-standing interest in understanding how attitudes predict behavior (Kraus, 1995; LaPierre, 1934), the pursuit of the IAT's ability to predict "real" behavior should not be surprising. In addition to successfully discriminating between groups of people who perform a behavior and those who do not (such as smoking, or avoidance of spiders), the IAT successfully predicts behavior. Poehlman, Uhlmann, Greenwald, and Banaji (2005) meta-analyzed 86 independent samples and found that the IAT predicted a range of criterion variables, including social judgments, physiological responses, and social action. In this section, we review some of the evidence that the IAT predicts behaviors and judgments in the domains that have received the most attention: stereotyping and prejudice, and health-related behaviors, such as food choices, alcohol use, and smoking.

Just as the first wave of research using the IAT centered on stereotyping and prejudice, the greatest focus in the attitude–behavior arena has been on behavior in intergroup settings. Implicit bias measured by the IAT predicts individual differences in behaviors and judgments. Stronger implicit stereotyping of Blacks covaried with more negative judgments of ambiguous actions by a Black target (Rudman & Lee, 2002; see Gawronski, Geschke, & Banse,

2003, for a similar result with a Turkish target). More negative attitudes toward Blacks (as compared to Whites) successfully predicted more negative nonverbal behaviors (e.g., less speaking time, less smiling, more speech errors) during an interaction with a Black experimenter (as compared to an interaction with a White experimenter; McConnell & Leibold, 2001). Similarly, spontaneous avoidance tendencies toward people with AIDS covaried with stronger negativity toward people with AIDS (as compared to healthy people; Neumann, Hulsenbeck, & Seibt, 2004). Most recently, Green, Carney, Pallin, Iezzoni, and Banaji (2006) found that doctors with stronger anti-Black attitudes and stereotypes were less likely to prescribe thrombolysis for myocardial infarction to African American patients diagnosed with the same condition as equivalent White Americans.

These studies focused on the prediction of behavior toward an outgroup; the IAT also effectively predicts behavior toward the ingroup. Greater anti-Black sentiment predicted Blacks' preference for a White partner over a Black partner on an anticipated intellectually challenging task (Ashburn-Nardo et al., 2003). Among gay men, more positive attitudes toward homosexuality on the IAT were related to more positive experiences in the gay community (Jellison et al., 2004). Stronger implicit romantic fantasies (the implicit association between romantic partners and chivalry and heroism) were linked to women's reported interest in pursuing powerful activities, such as attaining education or high-status jobs (Rudman & Heppen, 2003).

In addition to these macro-level behaviors, the IAT also predicts lower-level perceptual and cognitive events. The utility of the IAT to predict unobtrusive perceptual tasks and uncontrollable physiological measures suggests that more negative implicit attitudes toward a group leads to more top-down stereotypic processing. In a series of striking demonstrations, Hugenberg and Bodenhausen (2003) found that negativity toward Blacks on the IAT predicted a lowered threshold for detecting hostility on Black, but not White, faces. The reverse effect also held—subjects had a lowered threshold for judging racially ambiguous faces with hostile expressions as Black (Hugenberg & Bodenhausen, 2004). In addition, more negative attitudes may result in the depletion of cognitive resources when facing a member of the target group: After an interaction with a Black confederate, White participants with stronger anti-Black bias showed more cognitive decrements than participants with lower anti-Black bias, as measured by performance on a Stroop task (Richeson & Shelton, 2003). Moreover, the extent of activation in the right dorsolateral prefrontal cortex (DLPFC)—a brain region believed to be critical for executing cognitive control—when presented with unfamiliar Black faces was correlated with IAT scores and mediated the amount of interference on the Stroop task following interaction with a Black individual (Richeson et al., 2003). Other research using physiological measures points to the relationship between implicit intergroup attitudes and emotion. The IAT successfully predicted greater activation of the amygdala—an area of the brain associated with emotional, particularly fear, responses—to the presentation of unfamiliar Black (versus White) faces (Cunningham, Johnson, Gatenby, Gore, & Banaji, 2003; Phelps et al., 2000). Subsequent research (Cunningham et al., 2004) found that the IAT–amygdala relationship is stronger for subliminal than for supraliminal presentation of faces, indicating that the IAT reflects more automatic rather than controlled reactions to social groups.

Explicit reports of attitudes have been notoriously uninformative in accurately gauging health behaviors. Statistics regarding obesity, smoking, and sexually transmitted disease suggest that behaviors are not always congruent with people's best intentions to eat well, stop smoking, or practice safe sex. Although there are undoubtedly many reasons for this discrepancy, one possibility is that implicit processes play a role in determining behavior. These behaviors may be especially likely to be influenced by implicit mechanisms, because they may be susceptible to self-presentational concerns and often happen in the "heat of the moment" (such as the decision to use or not use a condom during sex) or in situations prone to low inhibition (such as at a bar with freely flowing alcohol).

Despite a widely reported initial failure to find a relationship between IAT scores and a choice between a healthy (apple) and less healthy (candy bar) snack (Karpinski & Hilton, 2001), when the studies ensure sufficient power to detect an effect, a relationship between implicit associations and food choices is obtained: attitudes toward the more global categories *snacks* and *fruits* successfully predicted the choice of fruit or a less healthy snack at the end of the experimental session (Perugini, 2005). IAT measures of attitudes toward soda, relative to fruit juices, and high-calorie foods, relative to low-calorie foods, were also associated with self-reports of food consumption (Maison et al., 2001).

Use of the IAT by researchers interested in less adaptive consumptions has led to a better understanding of the cognitive processes guiding such choices. For example, research examining implicit associations related to alcohol use suggests that it may be the perceived positive effects of alcohol that distinguish heavy from light drinkers. The IAT predicted the extent to which heavy drinkers showed arousal and the urge to drink in the presence of a glass of beer (Palfai & Ostafin, 2003). Positive, but not negative, associations with alcohol were significantly related to self-reports of alcohol use for the 30 days prior to the experimental session (Jajodia & Earley-wine, 2003). Similarly, among heavy drinkers, stronger associations between the concept *alcohol* and the attribute *approach* (relative to *electricity* and *avoid*) were correlated with frequency of binge drinking and quantity of alcohol consumed per drinking session during the month leading up to the experimental session (Palfai & Ostafin, 2003). In addition to retrospective reports, the IAT also predicted alcohol use in the month following administration of the task (Wiers et al., 2002).

Similarly, the IAT has helped to better elucidate the factors leading people to smoke. Although smokers and nonsmokers equally disliked smoking when it was contrasted with a positive health behavior or an even more strongly stigmatized behavior (stealing), smokers showed greater positivity when the contrasting category was *not smoking* and were more strongly identified with *smoking* at the implicit level. Moreover, smoking identity related to number of cigarettes smoked per day (Perugini, 2005; Swanson et al., 2001). Positive implicit attitudes toward smoking among mothers predicted the likelihood that their children would smoke (Chassin, Presson, Rose, Sherman, & Prost, 2002).

The IAT Measure Shifts in Response to Situational Cues. In light of the preceding evidence, one might conclude that implicit attitudes are stable characteristics that do not vary. Such an approach would be in line with views of the implicit system as slow to learn associations, and consequently slow to change (Smith & DeCoster, 2000). However, a growing number of studies indicate that implicit attitudes, including those measured by the IAT, often shift in relation to the current situation and new learning (Blair, Ma, & Lenton, 2001; Dasgupta & Greenwald, 2001; Gregg, Seibt, & Banaji, 2006; Lowery, Hardin, & Sinclair, 2001; Richeson & Ambady, 2003; see Blair, 2002, for a review). For example, race bias (as measured by the IAT) decreased after participants viewed pictures of admired African Americans and disliked White Americans, and such effects persisted after a 24-hour period (Dasgupta & Greenwald, 2001). Using a new procedure of individuals modulating their own implicit attitudes, Akalis, Nannapaneni, and Banaji (2006) showed that self-generated thoughts in ordinary people and yoga practitioners shifted attitudes in both negative and positive directions. Implicit self-concepts also appear susceptible to change: In a college-age sample, participants showed greater implicit identity with aggressive concepts after playing a violent video game than after playing a nonviolent video game (Uhlmann & Swanson, 2004).

Reconciling the findings that the IAT is able to predict meaningful criterion variables with findings that it is malleable may be an important avenue for future research. This area of inquiry will be especially important for applied researchers who desire a stable measure of implicit attitudes. The tendency for IAT-based attitudes or identities to shift in response to situational cues need not represent a challenge to its validity. Just as explicit attitudes may shift in response to the current situation, a particular situation may activate a specific set of associations, temporarily making certain category–target associations stronger. These associations, in turn, are reflected on the IAT. Understanding how the shifts in implicit cognitions relate to behavior may be an especially useful step in integrating these two lines of evidence.

FREQUENTLY ASKED QUESTIONS ABOUT THE IAT

This section briefly addresses some of the questions that are commonly asked of researchers using the IAT. Each of these questions has generated numerous studies and debates, and to fully address all of the issues raised by them is beyond the scope of this chapter. Here we outline the main issues involved in each matter.

• *Do IAT scores reflect attitudes of the individual or the culture?* In order for the IAT to function well in the purpose for which it was originally designed—measuring an individual difference in cognition— it needs to serve as more than a mirror of the culture. That is, it cannot be simply a tally of "the associations a person has been exposed to in his or her environment" (Karpinski & Hilton, 2001, p. 774), but should be useful in sorting among individuals within that culture. For instance, when a person shows a strong implicit preference for the Yankees over the Red Sox on the IAT, that person's score should not primarily reflect "extrapersonal associations" (Olson & Fazio, 2004) that come from living in New York; it should indicate a propensity to root for the Yankees and should be linked to the association between the person and the Yankees. We agree. In fact, IAT-based attitude measures do reliably relate to an individual's implicit cognitions about him- or herself (Greenwald et al., 2002) and also predict behavior (Poehlman et al., 2005).

If IAT scores were tapping environmental associations more than individual attitudes, they should correlate more reliably with self-reports of beliefs about widespread cultural preferences than with self-reports of a person's own preference. This is not the case; across 58 different attitude objects self-reported attitudes were consistently and reliably related to IAT performance, and estimates of the cultural attitudes such as beliefs about the "average person's" feelings were more related to self-reported attitudes than they were to the IAT (Nosek & Hansen, 2004). In fact, self-reported attitudes completely mediated the relationship between the IAT and perceptions of cultural attitudes.

• *Are implicit cognitions distinct from explicit ones? If so, are they the "true" attitudes, identities, or beliefs?* Just as implicit and explicit memory systems can diverge (Gabrieli, Fleischman, Keane, Reminger, & Morrell, 1995; Roediger, 1990, 2003), so too, it has been argued, can implicit and explicit attitudinal systems (Wilson et al., 2000). Although the IAT, like any other measure in this family, is not a process-pure measure—it seems to be affected by both automatic and controlled processes (Conrey, Sherman, Gawronski, Hugenberg, & Groom, 2005)—data indicate that the construct measured by the IAT differs from that assessed by self-reported measures. Correlations between implicit and explicit attitudes vary from close to zero to .90. We take these relationships seriously, especially when subject to appropriate statistical constraints, in inferring the degree of overlap between implicit and explicit measures. The question of whether these measures tap into different underlying representations is not one that is easy to answer. We focus, rather, on the empirical result showing varying levels of overlap in the hope that these patterns of results over time will give an indication about differences in underlying representation.

The fact that participants are often surprised by their IAT scores (Monteith, Ashburn-Nardo, Voils, & Czopp, 2002; Monteith, Voils, & Ashburn-Nardo, 2001) suggests that the IAT taps attitudes or beliefs that are not accessible by conscious introspection. In addition, the IAT and explicit measures explain unique variance in math performance (Nosek et al., 2002b) and differ in their ability to predict behavior across domains (Poehlman et al., 2005). Furthermore, the discrepancy between the two sets of cognitions is meaningful—individuals with high explicit but low implicit self-esteem showed greater narcissism, exhibited more ingroup bias in a minimal group paradigm, and reduced dissonant attitudes more than those with high explicit and implicit self-esteem (Jordan et al., 2003). Finally, the finding that the IAT relates to amygdala activation more strongly for faces presented subliminally than supraliminally suggests that it measures more automatic rather than controlled attitudes (Cunningham et al., 2004).

If these two cognitions—implicit and explicit—can exist simultaneously, is one of them the "real" one? To our knowledge, the only printed statements that the IAT measures a person's "true" sentiment are those that argue against such a position (Arkes & Tetlock, 2004; Karpinski & Hilton, 2001). A person's IAT score is no more a measure of his or her "true" attitude than that person's response to a Likert scale. The elusive "true" attitude seems not to exist—when an attitude depends on the measurement context, mood of the subject, and prior questions, how does one decide which is the true one? Indeed, routes to explicit attitude change are so numerous that the topic merits its own *Handbook* (Petty, Wheeler, & Tormala, 2003) and *Annual Review of Psychology* (Petty, Wegener, & Fabrigar, 1997) chapters, and the nascent research on implicit attitudes shows similar sensitivity to contextual cues (Blair, 2002).

If one were going to use predictive ability to determine the "true" attitude, a similar dead end would emerge. Implicit and explicit attitudes better predict discriminatory and consumer behaviors, respectively (Poehlman et al., 2005), suggesting that the ability of each type of attitude to predict behavior depends largely on the topic being studied. Based on this evidence, it seems sensible to say that implicit and explicit attitudes are equally authentic possessions of their holders.

• *What processes underlie IAT effects?* Several lines of inquiry have investigated the psychological processes involved in the IAT, with researchers proposing mechanisms such as a random walk (Brendl, Markman, & Messner, 2001), figure–ground asymmetries (Rothermund & Wentura, 2001, 2004; see also Greenwald, Nosek, Banaji, & Klauer, 2005), stimulus–response compatibility (De Houwer, 2001), and task set switching (Klauer & Mierke, 2005; Mierke & Klauer, 2001, 2003). These efforts have provided insight, for example, into the stronger influence of category-level (relative to stimulus-level) representations in producing IAT effects (De Houwer, 2001; Olson & Fazio, 2003). In addition, many of these theory-driven approaches have spurred methodological changes, such as improved scoring procedures (Greenwald et al., 2003), or better understandings of effects of block order (Klauer & Mierke, 2005). Future research into the mechanisms that cause people to exhibit IAT effects will likely improve an understanding of its relationship with its cousin implicit measures and spur further methodological improvements.

HOW TO BUILD AN IAT
Selecting Appropriate Categories and Exemplars

On one hand, the IAT is flexible—its structure allows the researcher to measure a broad range of constructs with one tool. This same flexibility, on the other hand, could potentially lead to a temptation to pick any four categories and throw them into an IAT. This approach would ignore the fact that the IAT's structure constrains what constructs it can best capture. In this section, we review the different stages of IAT construction.

Categories Matter

Two obvious choices in developing an IAT arise in determining how to represent the chosen categories. Both chosen category labels, and the specific stimuli presented, determine this construal of the concept. Data suggest that it is the construal of the category that determines how it is evaluated.

All judgments are made in some context. The IAT forces the researcher to be explicit about defining this context, as the structure of the task can change the perception of the target object being evaluated. De Houwer (2001) measured attitudes toward *British* (relative to *foreign*) among British subjects. Exemplars of each category included three positive (e.g., Princess Diana, Albert Einstein) and three negative (e.g., Margaret Thatcher, Adolf Hitler) stimuli. The superordinate category, rather than the stimuli's valence, determined response latencies to each item. De Houwer concluded that category membership, rather than valence of individual exemplars, is most important in determining IAT effects. Similarly, Mitchell, Nosek, and Banaji (2003) varied the categorization tasks as to whether they were based on race or occupation. They found that participants preferred a set of (well-liked) Black athletes to (disliked) White politicians when categorized on the basis of occupation, but preferred the politicians to the athletes when categorization was based on race. Taken together, these findings imply that the nature and construal of the categories play a large role in determining IAT effects.

These results suggest that the first step in designing an IAT is to precisely define the constructs of interest, and this will influence the choices of category labels to represent the constructs. Many categories (e.g., male) have an obvious comparison category (e.g., female), and such category pairs lend themselves particularly well to use of the IAT and interpretation of its effects. In the case where there is no obvious comparison category, it may be desirable to use an alternate implicit measure designed to measure single associations such as the Go/No-Go Association Task (Nosek & Banaji, 2001).

If the IAT is still the preferred method, a comparison category should be a sensible, mutually exclusive category that is ideally from the same domain (e.g., choosing *humanities* as the companion target category for the academic domain *science*), or presenting a category that represents the domain absent the target category (e.g., Arab Muslims, as compared to Other Peoples; see Table 3.1). Another alternative is to select an unrelated, neutral category. Some success has been realized in comparing social categories to (presumably) neutral categories such as "electricity" (Palfai & Ostafin, 2003) or "middle" (Lane & Banaji, 2004; Pinter & Greenwald, 2005), but such instantiations are not sufficiently understood to implement with confidence. One challenge is that no category is likely to be truly neutral, and interindividual variation in evaluation of the comparison category can introduce unwanted variance in effects. Second, the measurement effects of a relative comparison of a target category with an unrelated comparison are not understood.

Stimuli Matter

The popular press has suggested that citizens of some European nations (not to mention some Americans) love the nation America, but dislike its current administration (Bumiller, 2004). This idea would predict that America, when represented in an IAT by Dick Cheney and George Bush, would be evaluated negatively, but would be evaluated positively when denoted by pictures of the American flag and Golden Gate Bridge. In fact, stimulus exemplars do influence IAT effects. In addition to varying the category labels for Black athletes and White politicians, Mitchell and colleagues (2003) conducted a study in which they held the category labels constant and varied the stimuli used to represent the categories. When disliked Blacks and liked Whites represented the categories *Black* and *White*, participants exhibited strong and significant preference for Whites over Blacks. However, when liked Blacks and disliked Whites represented the categories, the typically seen preference for Whites was significantly diminished, with participants demonstrating nonsignificant preference for Whites (see also Govan & Williams, 2004; Steffens & Plewe, 2001). Similarly, inclusion of two images of lesbians as stimuli for the category *gay people* resulted in weaker implicit preference for straight over gay than when two images of gay men were included in the stimuli set (Nosek et al., 2005).

The prior examples represent changes in exemplars that were primarily designed to elicit different attitudes—by switching from liked Blacks/disliked Whites to disliked Blacks/liked Whites, the construal of the groups was changed and different patterns of preference were shown. Less drastic changes in category exemplars do not appear to shift implicit associations; when stimuli are chosen that do not alter the construal of the group, there are little to no effects of the chosen exemplars (Nosek et al., 2005). That is, if different stimuli represent the category in the same way, small differences among them are not likely to produce large differences in implicit attitudes, identities, or stereotypes. Stimuli that best represent the construal of the construct that a researcher is interested in will likely produce the most valid measure of implicit cognition.

For example, if a researcher assessing attitudes toward the category *Asian* were interested in attitudes toward Asian people, he or she would use faces easily identifiable as Asian, or names that can be quickly classified as Asian forenames or surnames. However, if the central research question focused on Asian culture or Asian nations, then a wider array of stimuli, including names of prominent cities or landmarks, would be appropriate. Note that the selection of stimuli does not guarantee that the construct is measured as intended.

Because the IAT relies on responses that are made without extensive deliberation, stimuli that are categorized easily and quickly will add the least error variance to the task. Pilot testing can ensure that participants can readily identify each item as denoting the appropriate category. Ambiguity about an item's appropriate categorization may slow reaction times, as may use of negations of words or phrases such as "unintelligent" that require additional time to be successfully negated and categorized correctly. Particularly when the IAT is used as an individual difference measure, these steps can help reduce task-related variability and maximize the variance the investigator cares about: that due to individual differences in the cognition.

Exemplars should be categorized solely on the basis of their membership in the appropriate category. That is, items should not be confounded with any of the other categories (Steffens & Plewe, 2001). An inadvertent confound—for example, all of the *good* words start with the letter C or are of more than seven letters, whereas all of the *bad* words start with the letter H or are of fewer than four letters—could provide subjects with a cue for sorting that is irrelevant to the task.

The addition of multiple cues for classification can reduce confusion or ambiguity about the task; for example, a researcher may choose to represent concept categories (such as *American* or *foreign*) with images, and attribute categories (such as *good* or *bad*) with words. Category and attribute items can be distinguished even when all stimuli are text by using a particular font and color for the concept items and a different font and color for the attribute items.

Once the criteria for stimuli are determined, how many should there be? Greenwald and colleagues (1998) indicated that stimulus sets of 25 items and of 5 items produced implicit preferences of equal magnitude. In a more extensive test of the effects of the number of exemplars, Nosek and colleagues (2005) varied the number of exemplars in both the target and attribute categories on three different measures of implicit cognition (Black/White attitude, old/young attitude, and gender/science academic stereotype). Even with fewer than four stimulus items for each category, the overall magnitude of implicit biases was consistent, and smaller numbers of stimuli did not impair the reliability of the task, nor did it increase the influences of potential confounding variables. Only when the categories were represented by one or two items were the psychometric properties (correlation with self-reported attitudes and split-half reliability) reduced. Thus, it seems that better construct validity will be obtained when researchers select the exemplars that best capture the construct of interest rather than trying to generate a longer list of exemplars that are not high-quality representations of the category.

Presentation of single-discrimination trials (Stages 1, 2, and 5 in Figure 3.1) such that the target concepts precede the attribute traits allows the initial category construal to be uninfluenced by the subsequent attributes. Within each of the combined-task blocks (Stages 3, 4, 6, and 7), alternating stimuli from the attribute and trait categories provides participants a means of using the relevant features (category or attribute) for the task.

Study Design

Number of Trials

There are three main categorization tasks in the IAT: single-category classifications (Stages 1, 2, and 5 in Figure 3.1), one configuration of double categorizations (Stages 3 and 4), and an alternative configuration of double categorizations (Stages 6 and 7). The order of the two double configuration tasks is usually counterbalanced between subjects. Evidence indicates that including 20 trials in Stages 3 and 6 (the first sets of each combined pairing) and 40 trials in Stages 4 and 7 (the second sets of each combined pairing) yields good psychometric properties (Greenwald et al., 1998; Nosek et al., 2005) for the IAT, and it is not clear that there is any benefit to using more trials.

One of the most common artifacts observed on the IAT is the tendency for the first combined configuration to interfere with performance in the second combined configuration. For example, participants completing a gender-science stereotype IAT typically show larger IAT effects when the stereotype-consistent Male + Math block precedes the stereotype-inconsistent Female + Math block than vice versa. Nosek and colleagues (2005) varied the number of trials in Stage 4 of the IAT, during which the subject practices the single-category classification before beginning the second set of combined pairings. Use of 40 single-categorization trials at this stage reduced this undesirable order effect.

Order of Measures

Researchers face at least two decisions about counterbalancing measures when developing study designs. First, when the IAT is used as a predictor or criterion variable, in what order should measures be completed? Effects of the order of measures have been most widely considered as a potential moderator of the relationship between implicit and explicit measures. If completing explicit measures makes concepts more accessible (Fazio, 1995), then providing self-reports before the IAT may increase the extent to which the two measures tap a similar construct, thus inflating the correlation between them (see Bosson et al., 2000, for such a result). Contrary to this logic, however, Hofmann and colleagues' (2005) meta-analysis found that implicit–explicit correspondence did not differ when explicit measures preceded the IAT (52 independent observations, $\rho = .23$), as compared to when the IAT was completed first (48 independent observations, $\rho = .21$). Similarly, in an experimental investigation of this issue, Nosek and colleagues (2005) systematically varied the order of implicit and explicit measures of three IATs on a publicly available website and found that the relationship between implicit and explicit measures did not vary as a function of the order in which measures were completed (average $r = .23$ in both orders of presentation). Additional data from a large Internet sample ($N > 11,000$) indicated that across a larger number of attitude objects ($N = 57$), presentation order did not affect the relationship between implicit and explicit measures (Nosek, 2005).

These data appear to suggest that the order of implicit measures does not systematically affect the relationship between implicit and explicit measures. However, at least occasionally, the relationship between implicit and explicit measures does vary as a function of the order in which the IAT and explicit measures are completed (Bosson et al., 2000). Design decisions are best made after giving careful thought to the appropriate order of measures.

The second question is related to the IAT's structure: Should the order of the combined conditions be counterbalanced? Because the well-documented order effects on the IAT may not always be eliminated even by additional practice trials in Stage 4 (Nosek et al., 2005), it is essential that researchers interested in the overall magnitude of the IAT effect counterbalance the presentation order of the combined pairings. Fixing the order may lead to an overestimate (if, for example, the flower + good stage in Figure 3.1 is always presented first) or underestimate (if, for example, the flower + bad stage in Figure 3.1 is always presented first) of the magnitude of the effect, as compared to other studies that counterbalance blocks.

Similarly, if the IAT is used as a predictor or criterion variable, the variability potentially added by counterbalancing block orders may make it more difficult for existing relationships to emerge. This intuition may suggest fixing the order of the blocks when interested in the predictive value of implicit cognitions. In practice, use of counterbalancing tends to have little effect on observed correlations with IAT measures. In Hofmann and colleagues' (2005) meta-analysis, correlations between the IAT and explicit measures were slightly higher when the presentation order of the combined pairings was counterbalanced (89 independent observations, $\rho = .25$) than when they were fixed (26 independent observations, $\rho = .18$). This difference is presumably due to decisions about counterbalancing having covaried with features of the task that at least mildly moderated implicit–explicit relationships, such as the attitude domain's social sensitivity. There has been no experimental analogue of this finding, although correspondence between implicit and explicit measures did not vary across the two possible task orders (Nosek et al., 2005). A researcher who wishes to account for the potential variability attributed to IAT order can include dummy variables that code for presentation order; this approach allows both estimation of mean IAT effects and accounts for variability due to counterbalancing.

Other Design Issues

The effects of a number of other features that can vary across IATs have been examined. By including error feedback (a red X that appears when an incorrect response is made) and requiring subjects to make the correct response before proceeding to the next trial, the researcher can ensure that items are categorized as intended. The amount of time between the response to a given stimulus and presentation of the next stimulus is typically greater than 150 msec. Varying these intertrial intervals up to 750 msec did not affect the IAT results (Greenwald et al., 1998). In addition, a number of studies have ruled out differential familiarity as a plausible explanation for implicit biases as measured by the IAT (Dasgupta et al., 2003; Dasgupta, McGhee, Greenwald, & Banaji, 2000; Ottaway et al., 2001).

These findings represent knowledge based on large numbers of tests, but researchers are likely to encounter situations in which alterations may improve task performance. When time is a constraint, an investigator may choose to use fewer trials. When the task is likely to be especially challenging to a subject population, additional practice tasks may improve performance. Systematic variations of task features will likely lead to improvements of the task in general, or to development of specific variants of the task that are appropriate for particular contexts or populations; for example, systematic examination of task features led to the development of a child-friendly version of the IAT (Baron & Banaji, 2006; Dunham, Baron, & Banaji, 2006b).

DATA ANALYSIS AND INTERPRETATION

An Improved Scoring Algorithm

Until recently the majority of studies that included one or more IATs reported the IAT effect as the difference in mean (usually log-transformed) response latencies between the second of the two combined pairings (depicted as Stages 4 and 7 in Figure 3.1), with some adjustments for excessively slow or fast responses (see Greenwald et al., 1998). More recently, Greenwald and colleagues (2003), based on analyses of large data sets available from the public websites, developed an improved scoring method for IAT data. They identified the psychometrically best-functioning scoring procedure from a large number of candidate scoring methods. The recommended algorithm was the one that worked best to minimize (1) the correlation between IAT effects and individual subjects' average response latencies, (2) the effect of the order of the IAT blocks, and (3) the effect of previously completing one or more IATs on IAT scores, while (4) retaining strong internal consistency and (5) maximizing the correlation between implicit and explicit measures.

Based on these criteria, Greenwald and colleagues (2003) recommended the measure that they identified as D to replace the previously conventional scoring method. D is computed as the difference in average response latency between the IAT's two combined tasks (e.g., flower + good, flower + bad), divided by an "inclusive" standard deviation of subject response latencies in the two combined tasks. Table 3.3 provides an overview of the specific stages of this approach.

Other Interpretation Issues

One of the structural features of the IAT is its relative nature—IAT effects are always a function of two target categories. Some researchers have used subsets of response latencies to each target category as an index for absolute attitudes. Nosek and colleagues (2005) examined the feasibility of this analysis strategy and concluded that such an approach is not appropriate. If absolute attitudes could be distilled from IAT data, they reasoned, such attitudes should correspond more highly with absolute explicit attitudes than relative explicit attitudes (Campbell & Fiske, 1959). In addition to calculating the standard (relative) IAT effect, they decomposed scores into two "absolute IAT" scores. Across four IATs, the separate components of the IAT, as well as the standard (relative) IAT score, had higher correspondence with relative, rather than absolute, self-reported attitudes. Responses to stimuli in the IAT are made in the framework of a comparison to a contrasting category, and this comparison is reflected in each trial response. Absolute implicit attitudes may be best assessed

---

TABLE 3.3. Summary of IAT Scoring Procedures Recommended by Greenwald et al. (2003)

1 Delete trials greater than 10,000 msec

2 Delete subjects for whom more than 10% of trials have latency less than 300 msec

3 Compute the "inclusive" standard deviation for all trials in Stages 3 and 6 and likewise for all trials in Stages 4 and 7

4 Compute the mean latency for responses for each of Stages 3, 4, 6, and 7

5 Compute the two mean differences (Mean$_{Stage\ 6}$ – Mean$_{Stage\ 3}$) and (Mean$_{Stage\ 7}$ – Mean$_{Stage\ 4}$)

6 Divide each difference score by its associated "inclusive" standard deviation

7 D = the equal-weight average of the two resulting ratios

Note. From Greenwald, Nosek, and Banaji (2003, Table 4). Copyright 2003 by the American Psychological Association. Adapted by permission. This computation is appropriate for designs in which subjects must correctly classify each item before the next stimulus appears. If subjects can proceed to the next stimulus following an incorrect response, the following steps may be taken between Steps 2 and 3 in the table: (1) compute mean latency of correct responses for each combined Stage (3, 4, 6, 7); (2) replace each error latency with an error penalty computed optionally as "Stage mean + 600 msec" or "Stage mean + twice the *SD* of correct responses for that Stage." Proceed as above from Step 3 using these error-penalty latencies. Stage numbers refer to the stages depicted in Figure 3.1. SPSS and SAS syntax for implementing the new scoring algorithm are available at faculty.washington.edu/agg/iat_materials.htm and www.briannosek.com, respectively.

using an alternative implicit measure (De Houwer, 2003; Nosek & Banaji, 2001).

CONCLUSIONS

Because of the rapid dissemination of the IAT, researchers have correctly called for intensive investigation into its underlying psychometric properties and mechanisms. In the past few years investigations into these features have led to identification of confounding influences (Greenwald & Nosek, 2001; Greenwald et al., 2003; McFarland & Crouch, 2002; Mierke & Klauer, 2001), improvements to scoring strategies (Greenwald et al., 2003), and improvements in study designs (Nosek et al., 2005).

Nevertheless, a number of issues remain open and in critical need of analysis. A better understanding of the mechanism of the IAT is needed (Greenwald, Nosek, Banaji, & Klauer, 2005; Mierke & Klauer, 2003; Rothermund & Wentura, 2001, 2004). In addition, exploration of the relationship between changes in implicit cognitions and changes in behavior may help to identify mechanisms of behavioral change as well as consequences of the well-documented malleability effects. Rather than simply asking if the IAT converges with other implicit and explicit measures and covaries with meaningful criterion variables—because there is evidence that it does—the next generation of questions will likely continue the current shift to identifying when and why these patterns emerge. Answers to these questions will help in building theories of implicit social cognition, because methods are a central route to theory development.

ACKNOWLEDGMENTS

The research and writing of this chapter were supported by a grant from the National Institute of Mental Health and the Third Millennium Foundation as well as a fellowship from the Radcliffe Institute for Advanced Study to Mahzarin R. Banaji. We thank Dolly Chugh for her comments on a prior version of this chapter.

NOTE

1. Of course, we are not suggesting that the sample at the demonstration websites is random (see Nosek et al., 2002a, for a discussion of the benefits and challenges of conducting this kind of research over the Internet). The demonstration website (now at *www.implicit.harvard.edu*) has been operating continuously since Sep-

tember 1998. In addition, the Southern Poverty Law Center (SPLC) maintains a website devoted to educating visitors about bias in various forms. This website had included a component that, as at the demonstration site, allowed participants to select and complete one or more IATs and receive feedback on each test completed.

REFERENCES

Aidman, E. V., & Carroll, S. M. (2003). Implicit individual differences: Relationships between implicit self-esteem, gender identity, and gender attitudes. *European Journal of Personality, 17*, 19–37.

Akalis, S. A., Nannapaneni, J., & Banaji, M. R. (2006). *Do-it-yourself mental makeovers: Self-generated implicit attitude shifts in college students and yoga practitioners.* Unpublished manuscript.

Arkes, H. R., & Tetlock, P. E. (2004). Attributions of implicit prejudice, or would Jesse Jackson "fail" the Implicit Association Test? *Psychological Inquiry, 15*, 257–278.

Asendorpf, J. B., Banse, R., & Muecke, D. (2002). Double dissociation between implicit and explicit personality self-concept: The case of shy behavior. *Journal of Personality and Social Psychology, 83*, 380–393.

Ashburn-Nardo, L., Knowles, M. L., & Monteith, M. J. (2003). Black Americans' implicit racial associations and their implications for intergroup judgment. *Social Cognition, 21*, 61–87.

Ashburn-Nardo, L., Voils, C. I., & Monteith, M. J. (2001). Implicit associations as the seeds of intergroup bias: How easily do they take root? *Journal of Personality and Social Psychology, 81*, 789–799.

Back, M., Schmukle, S. C., Egloff, B., & Gutenberg, J. (2005). Measuring task-switching ability in the Implicit Association Test. *Experimental Psychology, 52*, 167–179.

Banaji, M. R. (2001). Implicit attitudes can be measured. In H. L. Roediger III, J. S. Nairne, I. Neath, & A. Surprenant (Eds.), *The nature of remembering: Essays in honor of Robert G. Crowder* (pp. 117–150). Washington, DC: American Psychological Association.

Banaji, M. R. (in press). Toward an understanding of the origins of attitudes. In R. E. Petty, R. H. Fazio, & P. Briñol (Eds.), *Attitudes: Insights from the new wave of implicit measures.* Mahwah, NJ: Erlbaum.

Banaji, M. R., Bazerman, M. H., & Chugh, D. (2003). How (un)ethical are you? *Harvard Business Review, 30*, 1–20.

Banse, R., Seise, J., & Zerbes, N. (2001). Implicit attitudes toward homosexuality: Reliability, validity, and controllability of the IAT. *Zeitschrift für Experimentelle Psychologie, 48*, 145–160.

Baron, A. S., & Banaji, M. R. (2006). The development of implicit attitudes: Evidence of race evaluations from ages 6, 10, and adulthood. *Psychological Science, 17*, 53–58.

Bassett, J. F., & Dabbs, J. M. (2003). Evaluating explicit and implicit death attitudes in funeral and university students. *Mortality, 8*, 352–371.

Blair, I. V. (2002). The malleability of automatic stereotypes and prejudice. *Personality and Social Psychology Review, 6*, 242–261.

Blair, I. V., Ma, J. E., & Lenton, A. P. (2001). Imagining stereotypes away: The moderation of implicit stereotypes through mental imagery. *Journal of Personality and Social Psychology, 81,* 828–841.

Bosson, J. K., Swann, W. B. J., & Pennebaker, J. W. (2000). Stalking the perfect measure of implicit self-esteem: The blind men and the elephant revisited? *Journal of Personality and Social Psychology, 79,* 631–643.

Brendl, C. M., Markman, A. B., & Messner, C. (2001). How do indirect measures of evaluation work?: Evaluating the inference of prejudice in the Implicit Association Test. *Journal of Personality and Social Psychology, 81,* 760–773.

Buchner, A., & Wippich, W. (2000). On the reliability of implicit and explicit memory measures. *Cognitive Psychology, 40,* 227–259.

Bumiller, E. A. (2004, June 26). Bush gets chilly reception on eve of meeting in Ireland. *New York Times,* p. 7.

Campbell, D. T., & Fiske, D. W. (1959). Convergent and discriminant validation by the multitraitmultimethod matrix. *Psychological Bulletin, 56,* 81—105.

Carney, D. R., Nosek, B. A., Greenwald, A. G., & Banaji, M. R. (in press). Implicit Association Test (IAT). In R. F. Baumeister & K. D. Vohs (Eds.), *Encyclopedia of social psychology.* Thousand Oaks, CA: Sage.

Chassin, L., Presson, C., Rose, J., Sherman, S. J., & Prost, J. (2002). Parental smoking cessation and adolescent smoking. *Journal of Pediatric Psychology, 27,* 485–496.

Citrin, L. B., & Greenwald, A. G. (1998). *Measuring implicit cognition: Psychologists' and entomologists' attitudes toward insects.* Paper presented at the Midwestern Psychological Association, Chicago.

Conrey, F. R., Sherman, J. W., Gawronski, B., Hugenberg, K., & Groom, C. J. (2005). Separating multiple processes in implicit social cognition: The quad model of implicit task performance. *Journal of Personality and Social Psychology, 89,* 469–487.

Cunningham, W. A., Johnson, M. K., Gatenby, J. C., Gore, J. C., & Banaji, M. R. (2003). Neural components of social evaluation. *Journal of Personality and Social Psychology, 85,* 639–649.

Cunningham, W. A., Johnson, M. K., Raye, C. L., Gatenby, J. C., Gore, J. C., & Banaji, M. R. (2004). Separable neural components in the processing of Black and White faces. *Psychological Science, 15,* 806–813.

Cunningham, W. A., Nezlek, J., & Banaji, M. R. (2004). Implicit and explicit ethnocentrism: Revisiting the ideologies of prejudice. *Personality and Social Psychology Bulletin, 30,* 1332–1346.

Cunningham, W. A., Preacher, K. J., & Banaji, M. R. (2001). Implicit attitude measures: Consistency, stability, and convergent validity. *Psychological Science, 12,* 163–170.

Czopp, A. M., & Monteith, M. J. (2003). Confronting prejudice (literally): Reactions to confrontations of racial and gender bias. *Personality and Social Psychology Bulletin, 29,* 532–544.

Dasgupta, N., & Asgari, S. (2004). Seeing is believing: Exposure to counterstereotypic women leaders and its effect on the malleability of automatic gender stereotyping. *Journal of Experimental Social Psychology, 40,* 642–658.

Dasgupta, N., & Greenwald, A. G. (2001). On the malleability of automatic attitudes: Combating automatic prejudice with images of admired and disliked individuals. *Journal of Personality and Social Psychology, 81*, 800–814.

Dasgupta, N., Greenwald, A. G., & Banaji, M. R. (2003). The first ontological challenge to the IAT: Attitude or mere familiarity? *Psychological Inquiry, 14*, 238–243.

Dasgupta, N., McGhee, D. E., Greenwald, A. G., & Banaji, M. R. (2000). Automatic preference for White Americans: Eliminating the familiarity explanation. *Journal of Experimental Social Psychology, 36*, 316–328.

De Houwer, J. (2001). A structural and process analysis of the Implicit Association Test. *Journal of Experimental Social Psychology, 37*, 443–451.

De Houwer, J. (2003). The extrinsic affective Simon task. *Experimental Psychology, 50*, 77–85.

de Jong, P. J., van den Hout, M. A., Rietbroek, H., & Huijding, J. (2003). Dissociations between implicit and explicit attitudes toward phobic stimuli. *Cognition and Emotion, 17*, 521–545.

Devos, T., & Banaji, M. R. (2005). American = White? *Journal of Personality and Social Psychology, 88*, 447–466.

Dijksterhuis, A. (2004). I like myself but I don't know why: Enhancing implicit self-esteem by subliminal evaluative conditioning. *Journal of Personality and Social Psychology, 86*, 345–355.

Donders, F. C. (1969). On the speed of mental processes. *Acta Psychologica, 30*, 413–421. (Original work published 1868)

Dunham, Y., Baron, A. S., & Banaji, M. R. (2006a). From American city to Japanese village: The omnipresence of implicit race attitudes. *Child Development, 77*, 1268–1281.

Dunham, Y., Baron, A. S., & Banaji, M. R. (2006b). *The person and the group: A developmental analysis of consistency in implicit social cognition.* Unpublished manuscript.

Egloff, B., & Schmukle, S. C. (2002). Predictive validity of an Implicit Association Test for assessing anxiety. *Journal of Personality and Social Psychology, 83*, 1441–1455.

Egloff, B., Schwerdtfeger, A., & Schmukle, S. C. (2005). Temporal stability of the Implicit Association Test. *Anxiety, 84*, 82–88.

Fazio, R. H. (1995). Attitudes as object–evaluation associations: Determinants, consequences, and correlates of attitude accessibility. In R. E. Petty & J. A. Krosnick (Eds.), *Attitude strength: Antecedents and consequences* (pp. 247–282). Mahwah, NJ: Erlbaum.

Fazio, R. H., Jackson, J. R., Dunton, B. C., & Williams, C. J. (1995). Variability in automatic activation as an unobstrusive measure of racial attitudes: A bona fide pipeline? *Journal of Personality and Social Psychology, 69*, 1013–1027.

Fazio, R. H., & Olson, M. A. (2003). Implicit measures in social cognition research: Their meaning and use. *Annual Review of Psychology, 54*, 297–327.

Festinger, L. (1957). *A theory of cognitive dissonance.* Oxford, UK: Row, Peterson.

Gabrieli, J. D. E., Fleischman, D. A., Keane, M. M., Reminger, S. L., & Morrell, F. (1995). Double dissociations between memory systems underlying explicit and implicit memory in the human brain. *Psychological Science, 6*, 76–82.

Gawronski, B. (2002). What does the Implicit Association Test measure? A test of the convergent and discriminant validity of prejudice-related IATs. *Experimental Psychology, 49*, 171–180.

Gawronski, B., Geschke, D., & Banse, R. (2003). Implicit bias in impression formation: Associations influence the construal of individuating information. *European Journal of Social Psychology, 33*, 573–589.

Gemar, M. C., Segal, Z. V., Sagrati, S., & Kennedy, S. J. (2001). Mood-induced changes on the Implicit Association Test in recovered depressed patients. *Journal of Abnormal Psychology, 110*, 282–289.

Govan, C. L., & Williams, K. D. (2004). Changing the affective valence of the stimulus items influences the IAT by re-defining the category labels. *Journal of Experimental Social Psychology, 40*, 357—365.

Gray, N. S., Brown, A. S., & MacCulloch, M. J. (2005). An implicit test of the associations between children and sex in pedophiles. *Journal of Abnormal Psychology, 114*, 304–308.

Gray, N. S., MacCulloch, M. J., Smith, J., Morris, M., & Snowden, R. J. (2003). Violence viewed by psychopathic murderers. *Nature, 423*, 497–498.

Green, A., Carney, D. R., Pallin, D., Iezzoni, L., & Banaji, M. R. (2006). *Physicians' implicit biases predict differential treatment of Black versus White patients.* Unpublished manuscript.

Greenwald, A. G., & Banaji, M. R. (1995). Implicit social cognition: Attitudes, self-esteem, and stereotypes. *Psychological Review, 102*, 4–27.

Greenwald, A. G., Banaji, M. R., Rudman, L. A., Farnham, S. D., Nosek, B. A., & Mellott, D. S. (2002). A unified theory of implicit attitudes, stereotypes, self-esteem, and self-concept. *Psychological Review, 109*, 3–25.

Greenwald, A. G., & Farnham, S. D. (2000). Using the Implicit Association Test to measure self-esteem and self-concept. *Journal of Personality and Social Psychology, 79*, 1022–1038.

Greenwald, A. G., McGhee, D. E., & Schwartz, J. L. K. (1998). Measuring individual differences in implicit cognition: The Implicit Association Test. *Journal of Personality and Social Psychology, 74*, 1464–1480.

Greenwald, A. G., & Nosek, B. A. (2001). Health of the Implicit Association Test at age 3. *Zeitschrift für Experimentelle Psychologie, 48*, 85–93.

Greenwald, A. G., Nosek, B. A., & Banaji, M. R. (2003). Understanding and using the Implicit Association Test: I. An improved scoring algorithm. *Journal of Personality and Social Psychology, 85*, 197–216.

Greenwald, A. G., Nosek, B. A., Banaji, M. R., & Klauer, K. C. (2005). Validity of the salience asymmetry interpretation of the IAT: Comment on Rothermund and Wentura, 2004. *Journal of Experimental Psychology: General, 134*, 420–425.

Gregg, A. P., Seibt, B., & Banaji, M. R. (2006). Easier done than undone: Asymmetry in the malleability of implicit preferences. *Journal of Personality and Social Psychology, 90*, 1–20.

Heider, F. (1958). *The psychology of interpersonal relations.* New York: Wiley.

Hofmann, W., Gawronski, B., Gschwender, T., Le, H., & Schmitt, M. (2005). A meta-analysis on the correlation between the Implicit Association Test and explicit self-report measures. *Personality and Social Psychology Bulletin, 31*, 1369–1385.

Hugenberg, K., & Bodenhausen, G. V. (2003). Facing prejudice: Implicit prejudice and the perception of facial threat. *Psychological Science, 14*, 640–643.

Hugenberg, K., & Bodenhausen, G. V. (2004). Ambiguity in social categorization: The role of prejudice and facial affect in race. *Psychological Science, 15*, 342–345.

Hummert, M. L., Garstka, T. A., O'Brien, L. T., Greenwald, A. G., & Mellott, D. S. (2002). Using the Implicit Association Test to measure age differences in implicit social cognitions. *Psychology and Aging, 17*, 482–495.

Jajodia, A., & Earleywine, M. (2003). Measuring alcohol expectancies with the Implicit Association Test. *Psychology of Addictive Behaviors, 17*, 126–133.

Jellison, W. A., McConnell, A. R., & Gabriel, S. (2004). Implicit and explicit measures of sexual orientation attitudes: Ingroup preferences and related behaviors and beliefs among gay and straight men. *Personality and Social Psychology Bulletin, 30*, 629–642.

Jordan, C. H., Spencer, S. J., Zanna, M. P., Hoshino-Browne, E., & Correll, J. (2003). Secure and defensive high self-esteem. *Journal of Personality and Social Psychology, 85*, 969–978.

Jost, J. T., & Banaji, M. R. (1994). The role of stereotyping in system-justification and the production of false consciousness. *British Journal of Social Psychology, 33*, 1–27.

Jost, J. T., Banaji, M. R., & Nosek, B. A. (2005). A decade of system justification theory: Accumulated evidence of conscious and unconscious bolstering of the status quo. *Political Psychology, 25*, 881–919.

Jost, J. T., Pelham, B. W., & Carvallo, M. R. (2002). Non-conscious forms of system justification: Implicit and behavioral preferences for higher status groups. *Journal of Experimental Social Psychology, 38*, 586–602.

Kang, J., & Banaji, M. R. (2006). Fair measures: A behavioral realist revision of "affirmative action." *California Law Review*, pp. 1063–1118.

Karpinski, A. (2004). Measuring self-esteem using the Implicit Association Test: The role of the other. *Personality and Social Psychology Bulletin, 30*, 22–34.

Karpinski, A., & Hilton, J. L. (2001). Attitudes and the Implicit Association Test. *Journal of Personality and Social Psychology, 81*, 774–788.

Karpinski, A., Steinman, R. B., & Hilton, J. L. (2005). Attitude importance as a moderator of the relationship between implicit and explicit attitude measures. *Personality and Social Psychology Bulletin, 31*, 949–962.

Klauer, K. C., & Mierke, J. (2005). Task-set inertia, attitude accessibility, and compatibility-order effects: New evidence for a task-set switching account of the Implicit Association Test effect. *Personality and Social Psychology Bulletin, 31*, 208–217.

Kraus, S. J. (1995). Attitudes and the prediction of behavior: A meta-analysis of the empirical literature. *Personality and Social Psychology Bulletin, 21*, 58–75.

Kuhnen, U., Schiessl, M., Bauer, N., Paulig, N., Pohlmann, C., & Schmidthals, K. (2001). How robust is the IAT? Measuring and manipulating implicit attitudes of East- and West-Germans. *Zeitschrift für Experimentelle Psychologie, 48*, 135–144.

Lane, K. A., & Banaji, M. R. (2004). *Implicit intergroup bias: The contributions of ingroup liking and outgroup disliking.* Paper presented at the 5th annual meeting of the Society for Personality and Social Psychology, Austin, TX.

Lane, K. A., Mitchell, J. P., & Banaji, M. R. (2005). Me and my group: Cultural status can disrupt cognitive consistency. *Social Cognition, 23,* 353–386.

LaPierre, R. (1934). Attitudes and actions. *Social Forces, 13,* 230–237.

Livingston, R. W. (2002). The role of perceived negativity in the moderation of African Americans' implicit and explicit racial attitudes. *Journal of Experimental Social Psychology, 38,* 405–413.

Lowery, B. S., Hardin, C. D., & Sinclair, S. (2001). Social influence effects on automatic racial prejudice. *Journal of Personality and Social Psychology, 81,* 842–855.

Maison, D., Greenwald, A. G., & Bruin, R. (2001). The Implicit Association Test as a measure of implicit consumer attitudes. *Polish Psychological Bulletin, 32,* 61–69.

Marsh, K. L., Johnson, B. T., & Scott-Sheldon, L. A. J. (2001). Heart versus reason in condom use: Implicit versus explicit attitudinal predictors of sexual behavior. *Zeitschrift für Experimentelle Psychologie, 48,* 161–175.

McConahay, J. B. (1986). Modern racism, ambivalence, and the modern racism scale. In J. F. Dovidio & S. L. Gaertner (Eds.), *Prejudice, discrimination and racism* (pp. 91—126). San Diego, CA: Academic Press.

McConnell, A. R., & Leibold, J. M. (2001). Relations among the Implicit Association Test, discriminatory behavior, and explicit measures of racial attitudes. *Journal of Experimental Social Psychology, 37,* 435–442.

McFarland, S. G., & Crouch, Z. (2002). A cognitive skill confound on the Implicit Association Test. *Social Cognition, 20,* 483–510.

Mierke, J., & Klauer, K. C. (2001). Implicit association measurement with the IAT: Evidence for effects of executive control processes. *Zeitschrift für Experimentelle Psychologie, 48,* 107–122.

Mierke, J., & Klauer, K. C. (2003). Method-specific variance in the Implicit Association Test. *Journal of Personality and Social Psychology, 85,* 1180–1192.

Mitchell, J. P., Nosek, B. A., & Banaji, M. R. (2003). Contextual variations in implicit evaluation. *Journal of Experimental Psychology: General, 132,* 455–469.

Monteith, M. J., Ashburn-Nardo, L., Voils, C. I., & Czopp, A. M. (2002). Putting the brakes on prejudice: On the development and operation of cues for control. *Journal of Personality and Social Psychology, 83,* 1029–1050.

Monteith, M. J., Voils, C. I., & Ashburn-Nardo, L. (2001). Taking a look underground: Detecting, interpreting, and reacting to implicit racial biases. *Social Cognition, 19,* 395–417.

Neumann, R., Hulsenbeck, K., & Seibt, B. (2004). Attitudes towards people with AIDS and avoidance behavior: Automatic and reflective bases of behavior. *Journal of Experimental Social Psychology, 40,* 543–550.

Nock, M., & Banaji, M. R. (2006). *Assessing suicide risk implicitly.* Unpublished manuscript.

Nosek, B. A. (2005). Moderators of the relationship between implicit and explicit evaluation. *Journal of Experimental Psychology: General, 134,* 565–584.

Nosek, B. A., & Banaji, M. R. (2001). The Go/No-go Association Task. *Social Cognition, 19*, 625–666.

Nosek, B. A., & Banaji, M. R. (2002). (At least) two factors moderate the relationship between implicit and explicit attitudes. In R. K. Ohme & M. Jarymowicz (Eds.), *Natura Automatyzmów* (pp. 49–56). Warsaw: WIP PAN & SWPS.

Nosek, B. A., Banaji, M. R., & Greenwald, A. G. (2002a). Harvesting implicit group attitudes and beliefs from a demonstration web site. *Group Dynamics, 6*, 101–115.

Nosek, B. A., Banaji, M. R., & Greenwald, A. G. (2002b). Math = male, me = female, therefore math is not equal to me. *Journal of Personality and Social Psychology, 83*, 44–59.

Nosek, B. A., Greenwald, A. G., & Banaji, M. R. (2005). Understanding and using the Implicit Association Test II: Method variables and construct validity. *Personality and Social Psychology Bulletin, 31*, 166–180.

Nosek, B. A., Greenwald, A. G., & Banaji, M. R. (in press). The Implicit Association Test at age 7: A methodological and conceptual review. In J. A. Bargh (Ed.), *Automatic processes in social thinking and behavior.* Hove, UK: Psychology Press.

Nosek, B. A., & Hansen, J. J. (2004). *The associations in our head belong to us: Searching for attitudes and knowledge in implicit cognition.* Unpublished manuscript.

Nosek, B. A., & Smyth, F. L. (in press). A multitrait–multimethod validation of the Implicit Association Test: Implicit and explicit attitudes are related but distinct constructs. *Experimental Psychology.*

Nosek, B. A., Smyth, F. L., Hansen, J. J., Devos, T., Linder, N., Smith, C. T., et al. (2006). *Pervasiveness and variability in implicit bias.* Unpublished manuscript.

Olson, M. A., & Fazio, R. H. (2003). Relations between implicit measures of prejudice: What are we measuring? *Psychological Science, 14*, 636–639.

Olson, M. A., & Fazio, R. (2004). Reducing the influence of extrapersonal associations on the Implicit Association Test: Personalizing the IAT. *Journal of Personality and Social Psychology, 86*, 653–667.

Ottaway, S. A., Hayden, D. C., & Oakes, M. A. (2001). Implicit attitudes and racism: Effects of word familiarity and frequency on the Implicit Association Test. *Social Cognition, 19*, 97—144.

Palfai, T. P., & Ostafin, B. D. (2003). Alcohol-related motivational tendencies in hazardous drinkers: Assessing implicit response tendencies using the modified-IAT. *Behaviour Research and Therapy, 41*, 1149–1162.

Perruchet, P., & Baveux, P. (1989). Correlational analyses of explicit and implicit memory performance. *Memory and Cognition, 17*, 77–86.

Perugini, M. (2005). Predictive models of implicit and explicit attitudes. *British Journal of Social Psychology, 44*, 29–45.

Petty, R. E., Wegener, D. T., & Fabrigar, L. R. (1997). Attitudes and attitude change. *Annual Review of Psychology, 48*, 609–647.

Petty, R. E., Wheeler, S. C., & Tormala, Z. L. (2003). Persuasion and attitude change. In T. Millon & M. J. Lerner (Eds.), *Handbook of psychology: Personality and social psychology* (Vol. 5, pp. 353–382). Hoboken, NJ: Wiley.

Phelps, E. A., O'Connor, K. J., Cunningham, W. A., Funayama, E. S., Gatenby, J.

C., Gore, J. C., et al. (2000). Performance on indirect measures of race evalua-tion predicts amygdala activation. *Journal of Cognitive Neuroscience, 12,* 729–738.

Pinter, B., & Greenwald, A. G. (2005). Clarifying the role of the "other" category in the self-esteem IAT. *Experimental Psychology, 52,* 74–79.

Poehlman, A., Uhlmann, E., Greenwald, A. G., & Banaji, M. R. (2005). *Under-standing and using the Implicit Association Test III: A meta-analysis of pre-dictive validity.* Unpublished manuscript.

Richeson, J. A., & Ambady, N. (2003). Effects of situational power on automatic racial prejudice. *Journal of Experimental Social Psychology, 39,* 177–183.

Richeson, J. A., Baird, A. A., Gordon, H. L., Heatherton, T. F., Wyland, C. L., Trawalter, S., et al. (2003). An fMRI investigation of the impact of interracial contact on executive function. *Nature Neuroscience, 6,* 1323–1328.

Richeson, J. A., & Shelton, J. N. (2003). When prejudice does not pay: Effects of interracial contact on executive function. *Psychological Science, 14,* 287–290.

Roediger, H. L. III. (1990). Implicit memory: Retention without remembering. *American Psychologist, 45,* 1043–1056.

Roediger, H. L. III. (2003). Reconsidering implicit memory. In J. S. Bowers & C. J. Marsolek (Eds.), *Rethinking implicit memory* (pp. 3–18). New York: Oxford University Press.

Rosenberg, M. (1989). *Society and the adolescent self-image* (Rev. ed.). Middle-town, CT: Wesleyan University Press.

Rothermund, K., & Wentura, D. (2001). Figure–ground asymmetries in the Im-plicit Association Test (IAT). *Zeitschrift für Experimentelle Psychologie, 48,* 94–106.

Rothermund, K., & Wentura, D. (2004). Underlying processes in the Implicit As-sociation Test: Dissociating salience from associations. *Journal of Experi-mental Psychology: General, 133,* 139–165.

Rudman, L. A., Feinberg, J., & Fairchild, K. (2002). Minority members' implicit attitudes: Automatic ingroup bias as a function of group status. *Social Cogni-tion, 20,* 294–320.

Rudman, L. A., Greenwald, A. G., & McGhee, D. E. (2001). Implicit self-concept and evaluative implicit gender stereotypes: Self and ingroup share desirable traits. *Personality and Social Psychology Bulletin, 27,* 1164–1178.

Rudman, L. A., & Heppen, J. B. (2003). Implicit romantic fantasies and women's interest in personal power: A glass slipper effect? *Personality and Social Psy-chology Bulletin, 29,* 1357–1370.

Rudman, L. A., & Kilianski, S. E. (2000). Implicit and explicit attitudes toward fe-male authority. *Personality and Social Psychology Bulletin, 26,* 1315–1328.

Rudman, L. A., & Lee, M. R. (2002). Implicit and explicit consequences of expo-sure to violent and misogynous rap music. *Group Processes and Intergroup Relations, 5,* 133–150.

Schmukle, S. C., & Egloff, B. (2004). Does the Implicit Association Test for assess-ing anxiety measure trait *and* state variance? *European Journal of Personal-ity, 18,* 483–494.

Schultz, P. W., Shriver, C., Tabanico, J. J., & Khazian, A. M. (2004). Implicit connections with nature. *Journal of Environmental Psychology, 24,* 31–42.

Schwarz, N. (1999). Self-reports: How the questions shape the answers. *American Psychologist, 54,* 93—105.

Sherman, S. J., Rose, J. S., Koch, K., Presson, C. C., & Chassin, L. (2003). Implicit and explicit attitudes toward cigarette smoking: The effects of context and motivation. *Journal of Social and Clinical Psychology, 22,* 13–39.

Smith, E. R., & DeCoster, J. (2000). Dual-process models in social and cognitive psychology: Conceptual integration and links to underlying memory systems. *Personality and Social Psychology Review, 4,* 108–131.

Steffens, M. C., & Buchner, A. (2003). Implicit Association Test: Separating transsituationally stable and variable components of attitudes toward gay men. *Experimental Psychology, 50,* 33–48.

Steffens, M. C., & Plewe, I. (2001). Items' cross-category associations as a confounding factor in the Implicit Association Test. *Zeitschrift für Experimentelle Psychologie, 48,* 123–134.

Swanson, J. E., Rudman, L. A., & Greenwald, A. G. (2001). Using the Implicit Association Test to investigate attitude–behaviour consistency for stigmatised behaviour. *Cognition and Emotion, 15,* 207–230.

Teachman, B. A., Gregg, A. P., & Woody, S. R. (2001). Implicit associations for fear-relevant stimuli among individuals with snake and spider fears. *Journal of Abnormal Psychology, 110,* 226–235.

Teachman, B. A., & Woody, S. R. (2003). Automatic processing in spider phobia: Implicit fear associations over the course of treatment. *Journal of Abnormal Psychology, 112,* 100–109.

Uhlmann, E., & Swanson, J. (2004). Exposure to violent video games increases automatic aggressiveness. *Journal of Adolescence, 27,* 41–52.

Wiers, R. W., van Woerden, N., Smulders, F. T. Y., & de Jong, P. J. (2002). Implicit and explicit alcohol-related cognitions in heavy and light drinkers. *Journal of Abnormal Psychology, 111,* 648–658.

Wilson, T. D., Lindsey, S., & Schooler, T. Y. (2000). A model of dual attitudes. *Psychological Review, 107,* 101–126.

Yamaguchi, S., Greenwald, A. G., Banaji, M. R., Murakami, F., Chen, D., Shiomura, K., et al. (2006). *Comparisons of implicit and explicit self-esteem among Chinese, Japanese, and North American university students.* Unpublished manuscript.

4 Armed Only with Paper and Pencil

"Low-Tech" Measures of Implicit Attitudes

Patrick T. Vargas
Denise Sekaquaptewa
William von Hippel

Indirect measures of attitudes were developed to help researchers assess attitudes that respondents were unwilling or unable
to report. For example, in the past 50 years it has become increasingly unacceptable to publicly express antipathy toward members of
ethnic minority groups. Yet prejudice persists and has simply moved
"underground" (e.g., Crosby, Bromley, & Saxe, 1980), becoming
harder to assess directly. To circumvent these "willing and able"
problems, researchers developed attitude measures that did not require respondents to intentionally retrieve stored attitudes. These indirect measures took a variety of different forms, but were similar in
that none require the intentional recollection and reporting of stored
evaluative tendencies.

Other chapters in this book address contemporary implicit measures that require a certain level of technological sophistication to be
administered (see particularly Ito & Cacioppo, Chapter 5, this volume).
In this chapter we discuss implicit measures that may be administered
in a decidedly more "low-tech" manner; these measures require nothing more than respondents, paper, and pencil. First we review the logic
underlying the operation of these types of measures and note similarities and differences with response-time-based implicit measures. Then

we review specific measures that have been used in each of three broad areas: attitudes, stereotyping and prejudice, and the self-concept.

ON THE INTERDEPENDENCE
OF ATTITUDE THEORY AND MEASUREMENT

In the past 10 years there has been an explosion of interest in attitudes that is due, in no small part, to the development of implicit measures that are remarkably robust. Fazio, Jackson, Dunton, and Williams's (1995) Evaluative Priming Task (EPT) and Greenwald, McGhee, and Schwartz's (1998) Implicit Association Test (IAT) have led the way, but numerous other implicit measures have been developed and employed in a wide variety of contexts. Here we see clearly the influence of measurement on theory. The ease with which these measures can be used and the large effect sizes that they often obtain have led to their widespread use, which in turn is driving theorizing about the nature of the attitude construct (Fazio & Olson, 2003; Greenwald et al., 2002; Wilson, Lindsey, & Schooler, 2000).

Consider the following definitions of attitude: Allport (1935) referred to attitude as "a mental and neural state of readiness, organized through experience, exerting a directive or dynamic influence upon the individual's response to all objects and situations with which it is related" (p. 810). Krech and Crutchfield (1948) conceptualized attitude as "an enduring organization of motivational, emotional, perceptual, and cognitive processes with respect to some aspect of the individual's world" (p. 152). These older definitions of attitude differ markedly from the more contemporary definitions of attitude that predate the current surge in implicit measurement, such as Eagly and Chaiken's (1993) widely cited definition, "a psychological tendency that is expressed by evaluating a particular entity with some degree of favor or disfavor" (p. 1).

As is evident in these definitions, early scientific conceptualizations of the attitude construct were far broader than current ones. Indeed, Allport might have invoked attitude to refer to the position of a sprinter awaiting the starting gun, or a student slumped in his chair after an exceedingly difficult exam. In this sense, early use of the attitude construct is consistent with contemporary everyday use of the term *attitude*. When someone remarks that George "has an attitude problem," or "a bad attitude," one may safely infer that George has an unpleasant disposition that causes him to respond nastily and behave badly. The problem with such conceptualizations, however, is the inherent difficulty in measuring such a complex construct (see Smith, Bruner, & White, 1956). As Ostrom (1989) noted, attempting to measure Allport's version of attitude would be akin to asking a carpenter to measure a chair. Just as there are dozens of ways to measure a chair, with classic definitions of attitude there were too many dimensions to allow for a simple quantitative measure. Thurstone's (1928) paired comparisons measure focused on the evaluative dimension of attitude; Osgood, Suci, and Tannenbaum (1957) focused on three dimensions: evaluation, potency, and activity (but found the evaluative dimension to account for the most variance and therefore referred to it as the attitude). Since that time, attitude has become synonymous with evaluation, and most explicit measures clearly reflect this conceptualization. The process(es) by which implicit measures operate, however, may bring us back to earlier writers' conceptualizations of attitude.

CLASSES OF ATTITUDE MEASURES

In 1964, Cook and Selltiz identified five classes of attitude measures that, remarkably, still encompass attitude measures available today. Three of their classes, self-report, behavioral, and physiological measures, are rather straightforward in meaning. Self-report measures are now often referred to as explicit measures; behavioral measures are rarely used, as behavior has emerged as more of an outcome than a predictor (but see Albarracin & Wyer, 2000; Ouelette & Wood, 1998; Patterson, 2001); and physiological measures are covered elsewhere in this volume (Ito & Cacioppo, Chapter 5, this volume). Cook and Selltiz's other two classes, partially structured measures and measures based on performance on objective tasks, are more pertinent to the present discussion.

Partially structured measures require the presentation of stimuli that can be interpreted in multiple ways—for example, a picture of a person looking out to sea, or the beginning of a sentence referring to a member of a minority group. Although these measures do not attempt to disguise the attitude object under consideration, partially structured measures are implicit, in that they do not require respondents to intentionally recollect and report their attitudes to the object. Instead, respondents are asked to describe a scene, a character, or the behavior of some third person. These measures rely on the notion that "perception of stimuli that are not clearly structured is influenced by the perceiver's own needs and dispositions . . . the expressed response corresponds directly to the individual's attitude" (Cook & Selltiz, 1964, pp. 47–48). Presumably, respondents are largely unaware of the biasing effects of their attitudes, believing that they are simply reporting what they perceive (Vargas, 2004). Note here the similarity to Allport's (1935) and Krech and Crutchfield's (1948) definitions of attitude. Partially structured measures rely on the tendency for the individual's attitude to exert some influence on the way he or she perceives the world.

Measures based on performance on objective tasks require the presentation of "specific tasks to be performed; they are presented as tests of information or ability, or simply as jobs that need to be done" (Cook & Selltiz, 1964, p. 50). Contemporary reaction-time-based implicit measures (e.g., IAT, EPT) clearly fall into this category of measures, as they require respondents to categorize words or images as quickly as possible (see Lane, Banaji, Nosek, & Greenwald, Chapter 3, and Wittenbrink, Chapter 2, this volume). In Cook and Selltiz's day there were no response-time measures of attitudes. More typical of measures belonging to this category was a prejudice measure requiring respondents to judge the validity of emotionally charged but logically flawed arguments (Thistlethwaite, 1950; see also Saucier & Miller, 2003). Again, there is no attempt to disguise the attitude object under consideration, but these measures are implicit because they do not require respondents to intentionally provide an evaluation of the attitude object. Measures relying on performance on objective tasks operate on the assumption that "performance may be influenced by attitude, and that a systematic bias in performance reflects the influence of the attitude" (Cook & Selltiz, 1964, p. 50). This class of measures relies on the tendency for attitudes to "exert a directive or dynamic influence upon the individual's response" (Allport, 1935, p. 810).

In the current analysis, these two classes of attitude measures have more important similarities than differences. Partially structured measures and those based on performance on objective tasks are both implicit, and both rely on the tendency for attitudes to influence perceptions of and responses to attitude objects. They differ only in the types of tasks they require of respondents—partially structured measures require some type of interpretive response to an ambiguous stimulus, whereas performance on objective tasks requires more discrete, determinant–choice responses. Although these two classes still neatly encompass contemporary implicit measures, we suggest modifying Cook and Selltiz's distinction in favor of a new distinction that is inspired by advances in attitude measurement.

Based on a variety of dual-process or continuum-based models of social cognition (e.g., Fazio's [1990] MODE model), we propose that implicit attitude measures may be differentiated by the amount of cognitive deliberation required by the measure. Many contemporary implicit measures are based on response time, or the speed with which respondents can perform some task (see Lane et al., Chapter 3, and Wittenbrink, Chapter 2, this volume); others severely constrain the amount of time in which respondents are permitted to respond and are based on the number of errors respondents make (see, e.g., Draine & Greenwald, 1998). These measures are designed to tap respondents' automatic responses by minimizing the extent to which respondents carefully and deliberately process information. At the other extreme are partially structured implicit measures like the Thematic Apperception Test (TAT; Murray, 1965), wherein respondents are asked to write stories or describe scenes. Respondents may spend 20 seconds examining a stimulus, and then take 5 minutes or so to write approximately 200 words about the stimulus. These measures may tap automatic responses to some degree, but they do not constrain participants' information processing as contemporary implicit measures do, thereby allowing for much greater influence by controlled processes.

One way to distinguish between such measures is to label response-time measures as *spontaneous*, and measures that require more thoughtful responses as *deliberative*. The problem with such labels, however, is that they suggest a dichotomy between the two types of processing. Because no measure is "process pure," relying exclusively on either spontaneous or deliberative information processing, it makes little sense to dichotomize measures into two categories. It is more likely that all attitude measures involve different degrees of spontaneous and deliberative information processing. Response-time measures minimize deliberative processing and thereby rely primarily on spontaneous information processing; interpretive measures require substantial deliberative processing and thereby minimize the role of spontaneous processing. Thus, different implicit measures may be best conceptualized as lying along a continuum of information processing levels. Although measures at both ends of the continuum are largely implicit, they may nevertheless measure different aspects of the attitude construct, and this is the primary reason why level of information processing may be a useful way of parsing implicit measures. For this reason, and for the sake of simplicity, we refer to implicit measures as spontaneous or deliberative as a shorthand way of indicating where on the information processing continuum they appear to lie.

WHY SHOULD LEVEL OF INFORMATION
PROCESSING MATTER?

Implicit measures have traditionally been used primarily when social desirability concerns are expected to limit the efficacy of explicit measures. We believe, however, that implicit measures might be used fruitfully in addition to explicit measures, even when social desirability is not a concern (Vargas, von Hippel, & Petty, 2004). If the evaluative dimension of attitudes is but one component of the attitude construct, as suggested by early researchers, then explicit measures tapping evaluative tendencies may be just scratching the surface of attitudes. Spontaneous and deliberative implicit measures may each tap unique aspects of attitudes beyond the evaluative component assessed by most explicit measures. Moreover, the use and classification of such implicit measures may allow researchers to avoid Ostrom's (1989) problem of "measuring the chair" by providing guidelines concerning which aspects of an expanded and rather rich construct of attitude are being measured.

Responses to any attitude measure are jointly determined by the individual's attitude toward the object, "other characteristics of the individual" such as motivation and expressive style, and "other characteristics of the situation" such as proscriptions on behavior, the presence of others, and so forth (Cook & Selltiz, 1964, p. 37; see also Fishbein & Ajzen, 1974; Wicker, 1969). Thus, there are innumerable attitude-irrelevant factors that can influence responses to (both implicit and explicit) attitude measures. However, the irrelevancies affecting implicit measures differ from those affecting explicit measures, and indeed the irrelevancies affecting spontaneous implicit measures are likely to differ from those affecting deliberative implicit measures. For example, the IAT may be influenced by factors that guide the interpretation of category labels (Govan & Williams, 2004), whereas this issue will often be irrelevant for deliberative measures that do not require categorization. By creating heterogeneity of irrelevancies, the use of multiple implicit measures to assess attitudes can thereby be advantageous (Cunningham, Preacher, & Banaji, 2001). But perhaps more important is the fact that spontaneous and deliberative measures are likely to tap different aspects of attitudes (see Wittenbrink, Chapter 2, this volume).

Implicit measures that require primarily spontaneous information processing, such as the IAT and EPT, rely on the automatic activation of attitudes. These measures likely tap the evaluative component of attitudes, as well as the accessibility of the evaluative component. Measures that require more deliberative information processing likely tap aspects of attitudes other than just evaluation and evaluative accessibility. Deliberative measures may tap the extent to which attitudes influence perceptions of, or cognitions about, attitude-relevant objects or events. For example, Sekaquaptewa and colleagues (Sekaquaptewa & Espinoza, 2004; Sekaquaptewa, Espinoza, Thompson, Vargas, & von Hippel, 2003; von Hippel, Sekaquaptewa, & Vargas, 1997) developed deliberative implicit measures of stereotyping that draw on individuals' tendencies to explain away stereotype-incongruent information. Vargas, von Hippel, and Petty (2004) developed deliberative implicit measures of attitudes that draw on individuals' tendencies to contrast others' social judgments away from their own. And von Hippel, Lakin, and Shakarchi (2005) developed deliberative implicit measures of the self-concept that draw on individuals' tendencies to emphasize successful over unsuccessful performance. To the extent that these different measures of attitudes, stereotyping, and the self-concept are not isomorphic with the associated evaluations and their accessibility, then deliberative implicit measures may predict unique variance beyond spontaneous implicit measures (and beyond explicit measures as well).

Behavior is driven by factors other than attitudes, and thus it seems reasonable to suggest that it is driven by attitudinal factors other than the evaluative component. For example, different individuals may perceive a dog wandering the streets without either leash or owner as threatening, in need of assistance, cuddly, or a yard-defiling menace. These different perceptions of the dog are evaluative, but they are distinctly more complex than merely good or bad. And these different perceptions are likely to lead to different behaviors: flight, cautious approach, warm approach, or shoo-and-chase, respectively. Attitude measures that go beyond evaluative tendencies might help predict such different behaviors.

For these various reasons, pencil-and-paper-based deliberative implicit measures have a lot to offer. They have the potential to add predictive power beyond what can be achieved with explicit measures or spontaneous implicit measures, and they may often be useful even when social desirability concerns are minimal. Just as important, these measures are easy to use, they require no special equipment, and they can be administered to large groups of respondents at the same time, even in the field. For these reasons, the primary goal of this chapter is to review deliberative implicit measures, but it should be noted that a number of spontaneous measures have also been adapted for use with paper and pencil, so we turn first to a brief description of these measures.

SPONTANEOUS, BUT LOW-TECH, IMPLICIT MEASURES

There are two types of low-tech measures that rely on spontaneous information processing: first, there are "manual" versions of computer-mediated implicit measures; second, there are measures that tap category or construct accessibility. With regard to the former, there are at least two low-tech versions of the IAT. One version features on each page a column of stimuli from the target and attribute categories (e.g., *daffodil, rainbow, cockroach, vomit*). Respondents categorize the stimuli by marking circles on either side of the column. The critical dependent measure is the difference in the number of stimuli correctly categorized in a fixed amount of time (30 seconds in Mast, 2004; 20 seconds in Lemm, Sattler, Khan, Mitchell, & Dahl, 2002) between evaluatively congruent and incongruent blocks. A second low-tech version of the IAT features lists of stimuli from the target and attribute categories, but instead of marking circles, respondents are asked to categorize by tapping one knee or the other (Kitayama & Uchida, 2003). The critical dependent measure in this version is the difference in speed with which respondents can get through the different lists.

The Lemm and colleagues (2002) research has the advantage that it compared different versions of the IAT. The investigators administered two different versions of the IAT, one on computer and one via paper and pencil. One version featured Black and White names as stimuli, and another featured cropped pictures of Black and White faces. Lemm and colleagues found that the low-tech name version of the IAT produced a larger effect size, better test–retest reliability, and higher correlations with a computerized IAT than did the low-tech picture version of the IAT.

At least one other computer-based, spontaneous implicit measure may easily be administered in a low-tech version. In Payne, Cheng, Govorun, and Stewart's Affect Misattribution Procedure (AMP; 2005) respondents are presented with a series of trials in which an attitude object is shown and then followed immediately by an ambiguous stimulus that respondents evaluate. Findings from this research suggest that automatically activated evaluative responses to the attitude object influence explicit evaluations of the ambiguous stimuli, even when the attitude objects are presented for up to 1,500 msec, and when respondents are forewarned of the effect. A computerized version of this measure assessing political attitudes was reliably correlated with explicit measures of political attitudes. Because the AMP does not rely on response time and tends to produce robust effects, it should be a relatively simple matter to administer a low-tech version.

A final, spontaneous low-tech implicit measure that is widely used relies on word production. Typically, participants may be primed or presented with the attitude object and then asked to work on word fragments or anagrams that may be completed in different ways. They may also be asked to generate first associates to a randomly selected letter from the alphabet, or to neutral words. Respondent-generated words can then be coded for affective valence (Isen, Labroo, & Durlach, 2004), stereotype-congruency (Gilbert & Hixon, 1991), or content (Sia, Lord, Blessum, Thomas, & Lepper, 1999). To the best of our knowledge, these word production measures have not been extensively compared with either computer-mediated implicit measures or traditional explicit attitude measures, but they have been used very effectively to assess activation of attitudes, stereotypes, and the like.

The studies cited above testify to the fact that spontaneous implicit attitudes can be effectively measured, at least in some circumstances, with only paper and pencil. Low-tech versions of such measures are clearly helpful in a variety of circumstances when different limitations preclude the use of computer-mediated response time measures. As we noted above, however, deliberative implicit measures are intended to allow ample time for responding, and thus deliberative implicit measures are just as well suited for measurement with paper and pencil as they are for computer-mediated measurement. For this reason, deliberative implicit measures are well suited for low-tech environments, and thus the rest of this chapter is devoted to the review of deliberative implicit measures that assess attitudes, stereotyping and prejudice, and the self-concept.

ATTITUDES

The classic low-tech deliberative implicit attitude measure is Hammond's (1948) information error test, which was presented to respondents as a simple multiple-choice test of their knowledge. Hammond devised two different types of questions: those in which the response options provided were equidistant and in opposite directions from the truth (e.g., "The percentage of US citizens living in poverty by the end of George W. Bush's first term was (a) 8.5%, (b) 15.3%"), and others in which the response options were indeterminate (e.g., "President George W. Bush is known around the world for his (a) affable (b) bumbling demeanor"). Hammond found that both of these types of questions enabled him to differentiate between known groups of responders.

A conceptually related measure examined respondents' proclivity to accept or reject logically flawed, but emotionally charged arguments toward a socially sensitive topic. In one such study (Thistlethwaite, 1950) respondents from Northern and Southern colleges were shown a series of premises and conclusions about integration and were asked to evaluate the validity of the arguments. Prejudiced students tended to accept flawed arguments that were emotionally charged and attitude congruent, but to reject more neutral, attitude-congruent arguments (see also Lord, Ross, & Lepper, 1979; Saucier & Miller, 2003).

More recently Vargas and colleagues (2004) developed a low-tech implicit measure in which respondents were presented with a series of vignettes featuring individuals behaving in somewhat conflicting ways. For example, one of the vignettes designed to assess attitudes toward religion featured a person who claimed to be very religious, watched religious television programs on TV, but had not attended church services in several years. When asked to judge how religious this individual was, respondents tended to contrast her away from their own attitudes. Religious respondents tended to view her as nonreligious, whereas nonreligious respondents tended to view her as religious. Similar results obtained for measures designed to assess attitudes toward dishonesty and politics. Further, these deliberative implicit measures tended to be uncorrelated with explicit measures. Most important, these deliberative implicit measures reliably predicted unique variance in self-reported and actual behavior, beyond what was predicted by the IAT or explicit measures, regardless of social desirability concerns.

Perhaps the most deliberative of low-tech implicit measures is the projective test. In a classic study of projective measures of attitude, Proshansky (1943) presented students known to have pro- and anti-labor-union attitudes with a series of images previously judged to be neither pro- nor anti-labor and asked the students to write about each picture. Three judges coded the responses as either favorable or unfavorable toward labor. Proshansky's projective technique was found to be highly correlated with a traditional measure of attitudes toward labor unions.

Since this study, little work has been done using projective attitude tests because of concerns about reliability (see Lemon, 1974), and the difficulty in scoring such tests. Nevertheless, personality researchers have convincingly demonstrated the predictive power of such projective tests. In one such study, Winter, John, Stewart, Klohnen, and Duncan (1998) obtained explicit measures of extraversion and projective measures of the need for affiliation. These measures were weakly correlated with each other and interacted to predict (among other things) relationship dissatisfaction and low levels of intimacy, 30 years after the projective measures had been administered! Women who were extraverted, but low in implicit affiliation motive, and women who were introverted, but high in implicit affiliation motive (i.e., those who showed an implicit–explicit conflict) suffered more dissatisfaction and experienced more low points in intimacy.

These deliberative measures appear to be operating implicitly, but they also have the potential to be at least somewhat sensitive to social desirability concerns. That is, to the degree that respondents infer that their responses provide a clue about their relevant attitude, they can easily adjust their scores on the measures. Consistent with this possibility, implicit deliberative attitudes toward dishonesty in a study by Vargas and colleagues (2004) were sensitive to social desirability concerns, although they still predicted actual dishonest behavior. Despite this potential for contamination, implicit deliberative measures can be designed that are more opaque and thus less sensitive to socially desirable responding. In one such study, Vargas and von Hippel (2005) relied on a category accessibility measure to examine effects of social desirability on implicit versus explicit deliberative measures. In this study, smoking and nonsmoking male respondents were introduced (individually) to an attractive female confederate under the guise of an impression formation task. The participant and confederate exchanged information about themselves, including the critical, between-subjects social desirability manipulation: whether the confederate liked or disliked smoking. Thus, both smokers and nonsmokers were randomly assigned to believe that the confederate either approved or disapproved of their behavior. Next, participants were asked to complete a questionnaire packet, which included both explicit and implicit measures of smoking attitudes. Respondents were led to believe that their completed questionnaires would be given to the confederate to help her decide whether she wanted further interaction with a respondent.

We expected that the explicit (semantic differential) measure would be affected by the social desirability manipulation, but that the implicit measure would not. Indeed, we found that smokers and nonsmokers alike explicitly reported that they liked smoking when the confederate liked it, and disliked smoking when the confederate disliked it. The implicit measure presented respondents with ambiguous behaviors and asked them to generate reasons for the behaviors. Some of the behaviors could be explained by smoking-related attributions (e.g., went outside for his break even though it was freezing cold; was nervous and fidgety on the cross-country flight), whereas others were unrelated to smoking (e.g., was overjoyed when strangers came knocking at her door; didn't lace up her sneakers). Smokers were more likely than nonsmokers to generate smoking-related attributions for the smoking-ambiguous behaviors, regardless of the confederate's attitude toward smoking. Thus, these data suggest that at least with some types of social desirability pressure, and at least with some types of low-tech deliberative implicit measures, contamination via social desirability is unlikely.

STEREOTYPING AND PREJUDICE

Perhaps the first low-tech measure to be used in research on stereotyping and prejudice was word fragment completion (WFC). In a WFC task, respondents are presented with letter strings with missing letters indicated by blanks. Their task is to fill in the blanks with letters to form a complete word. To assess activation of a particular stereotype (e.g., that of Asians), word fragments are developed so that they can be completed with a target word associated with that stereotype (e.g., SMART) or with a neutral word (e.g., START). Greater completion with target words indicates activation of the stereotype (Gilbert & Hixon, 1991). Although WFC tasks have been widely used as implicit evidence that a stereotype has been activated, that is, as a dependent measure (Gilbert & Hixon, 1991; Sinclair & Kunda, 1999; Spencer, Fein, Wolfe, Fong, & Dunn, 1998; Steele & Aronson, 1995), WFC can be used as a predictor variable as well.

In one such study (Son Hing, Li, & Zanna, 2002), WFC was used in conjunction with measures of explicit racism to identify aversive racists (individuals who endorse egalitarianism but are nevertheless thought to retain unconscious negative feelings toward racial outgroups; Gaertner & Dovidio, 1986). Implicit prejudice toward Asians was indicated by the number of word fragments completed with negative Asian stereotypic target words (e.g., SLY, SHORT), minus the number completed with positive Asian stereotypic target words (e.g., SMART, POLITE). Participants who scored low on an explicit measure of prejudice (the Asian Modern Racism Scale) but high on the implicit WFC measure were identified as aversive racists, and their responses were compared to those of individuals who scored low on both measures. Participants identified as aversive racists felt more guilty and showed less discrimination toward Asians after being reminded of previous racist transgressions against Asians (consistent with aversive racism and prejudice reduction theories;

Monteith, 1996), whereas these outcomes did not emerge among individuals who scored low on both measures.

The WFC task appears to tap accessibility of stereotypes and thus may lie closer to the spontaneous end of the continuum, but another class of low-tech implicit measures is more clearly deliberative in nature. These measures assess the degree to which information processing is biased by stereotyping and thus reflects individual differences in the tendency to engage in stereotype-biased processing (von Hippel, Sekaquaptewa, & Vargas, 1995). Biases in information processing emerge in many forms, any of which might be adapted for use as an implicit bias measure. For example, the Linguistic Intergroup Bias (LIB; Maass, Salvi, Arcuri, & Semin, 1989) represents a bias in the way that information about ingroups and outgroups is conveyed, and measurement of this bias is readily adapted for use as an implicit prejudice measure. The LIB is evinced by the tendency to describe stereotype-consistent events in abstract trait terms ("LaKeisha is athletic"), and stereotype-inconsistent events in concrete behavioral terms ("Sue Ellen dribbled the basketball"). As such, abstract inferences are made and communicated from instances of stereotype-confirming but not stereotype-disconfirming behavior, contributing to maintenance of the original stereotype (Karpinski & von Hippel, 1996; Wigboldus, Semin, & Spears, 2000). Perhaps just as important, individuals who engaged in the LIB regarding African Americans also perceived a Black panhandler as more threatening than a White panhandler who displayed identical behavior (von Hippel et al., 1997). Moreover, the tendency to engage in the LIB was correlated with a measure of biased attributional processing, to which we now turn.

Information that is inconsistent with stereotypic expectations is often processed in a manner that resolves or dismisses the inconsistency, thereby maintaining the original expectancy. One such bias is evident in the attributions provided for stereotype-inconsistent versus stereotype-consistent behaviors. As Hastie (1984) has shown, people are more likely to spontaneously explain behaviors that disconfirm their expectancies than behaviors that confirm their expectancies. If one expects Jane to be poor at mathematics, learning that Jane received an A on the math test may instigate attributional processing in an attempt to make sense of the incongruity (e.g., perhaps it was an easy test). Learning that Jane received the lowest grade in the math class, however, is unlikely to instigate attributional processing. In this way explanatory biases enable people to reconcile stereotype-incongruent information with their overall impression of the individual or group by making the event appear situationally rather than dispositionally determined. We have termed this tendency the Stereotypic Explanatory Bias, or SEB, which we defined as the greater likelihood of engaging in attributional processing when confronted with stereotype inconsistency than with stereotype consistency (Sekaquaptewa et al., 2003).

To assess SEB, we adapted a sentence completion task from Hastie (1984). In this task participants are given a series of sentence beginnings and are asked to add words to form a grammatically correct sentence. The sentence beginnings describe group members performing behaviors that are either consistent or inconsistent with their group stereotypes. To create an SEB score, the sentence completions are coded as to whether they explain the behavior in the sentence stem. SEB is evidenced when more explanations are provided for stereotype inconsistency over stereotype consistency. One advantage of the SEB measure is that it is readily modified to assess implicit stereotyping of different social groups by developing sentence stems that reflect behaviors consistent or inconsistent with stereotypes relevant to the target group of interest (gender, race, religion, etc.).

Increasing evidence supports the utility of SEB as a measure of implicit stereotyping. Research on SEB has demonstrated that it is correlated with an EPT measure of stereotyping, but not with an IAT measure of prejudice, supporting a conceptual distinction between implicit stereotyping and prejudice (Sekaquaptewa et al., 2003). SEB is exacerbated by factors known to increase stereotyping, such as mortality salience (Schimel et al., 1999), threats to collective self-esteem (Carlisle & von Hippel, 2000), positive mood (Chartrand, van Baaren, & Bargh, 2006), and suggestions that stereotyping is normative (Gonsalkorale, Carlisle, & von Hippel, 2005). SEB is also greater for targets of low social status than for high-status targets (Sekaquaptewa & Espinoza, 2004), and SEB predicts stereotype-congruent recall (Espinoza & Sekaquaptewa, 2001; Sekaquaptewa, Vargas, & von Hippel, 1996).

Perhaps the most important findings regarding SEB involve its utility in predicting intergroup behavior. As is the case with other implicit measures (e.g., see Dovidio, Kawakami, Johnson, Johnson, & Howard, 1997), SEB seems to be a better predictor than explicit measures of subtle or nonverbal behaviors displayed toward outgroup members. In one study of gender SEB, male participants engaged in a mock job interview with a female or male job applicant (Vargas et al., 2004). Male interviewers chose from pairs of questions pretested such that one question was worded in a somewhat sexist fashion, whereas the other was neutrally worded. Gender SEB predicted men's choice of the sexist question over the neutral question, such that males with high SEB chose to ask the sexist questions of the female but not of the male job applicant. This result was conceptually replicated in a second study using a measure of African American SEB and White or Black job applicants (Sekaquaptewa et al., 2003, Experiment 1). In both studies, explicit measures of prejudice (the Attitudes toward Women scale and the Modern Racism Scale) did not emerge as significant predictors of question choice.

The measure of African American SEB was also used to predict the quality of an interracial interaction (Sekaquaptewa et al., 2003, Experiment 2). In this study, White participants played a game with a Black or White male partner (a confederate). After playing two rounds of the game, the experimenter left the two alone for a period of 2 minutes to give the participant unstructured interaction time with the confederate. SEB predicted the Black but not the White confederate's rating of the social interaction. Furthermore, this study was the first to examine the type of attribution provided on the SEB. Analyses revealed that engaging in external SEB (attributing stereotype inconsistency to external or situational forces) predicted Whites having more negative social interactions with the African American confederate. Conversely, engaging in internal SEB (attributing stereotype inconsistency to internal dispositions) predicted Whites having more positive social interactions with the African American confederate. This pattern may emerge because external SEB is associated with stereotype maintenance, as stereotype inconsistency is attributed to less controllable and perhaps fleeting situational forces. Internal SEB, however, is associated with stereotype change, as stereotype inconsistency is attributed to stable and enduring characteristics of the actor. These data suggest that an important feature of the SEB is that it can predict positive as well as negative social interactions, although replication of this result will be necessary before it can be interpreted with confidence.

SELF-CONCEPT

Most attitudes regarding the self should be accessible via implicit measurement, but the bulk of the literature has focused on assessment of implicit self-esteem. The most widely used measure of implicit self-esteem is assessment of the name letter effect, or the tendency to prefer letters that are in one's own initials (Nuttin, 1985). Interest in this measure stems not only from its ease of use, but also from its reliability, predictive validity, and robustness even in cultures in which people do not report high levels of explicit self-esteem (Kitayama & Karasawa, 1997; Koole, Dijksterhuis, & van Knippenberg, 2001). For example, Pelham and colleagues have shown that name letter preferences are associated with having nurturing parents (DeHart, Pelham, & Tennen, 2006), manifest themselves in occupational and geographic preferences (Pelham, Mirenberg, & Jones, 2002), and are sensitive to threats to the self-concept (Jones, Pelham, Mirenberg, & Hetts, 2002). In addition, people who have high explicit self-esteem but weak name letter preferences display greater self-enhancement than people who have high explicit self-esteem and strong name letter preferences (Bosson, Brown, Zeigle-Hill, & Swann, 2003). Beyond assessment of the name letter effect (and the associated birthday number effect), a variety of other procedures have taken advantage of the association between various symbols and the self to measure implicit self-esteem. For example, implicit measures of self-esteem have been based on signature size (see, e.g., Stapel & Blanton, 2004) and the tendency to complete word stems with positive or negative words after answering questions about the self (Hetts, Sakuma, & Pelham, 1999).

These measures all rely on the tendency for symbols associated with the self to take on the affective quality that is experienced with regard to the self. Although these measures are not designed to ensure automatic responding that is relatively free from deliberative processes, they involve only minimal interpretive processing and appear to be closer to the spontaneous than the deliberative end of the continuum (see Koole et al., 2001). Other measures do exist, however, that tap more deliberative responses to the self. For example, Tafarodi (1998) presented participants with ambiguous statements that they were to imagine were used by an acquaintance to describe them. Participants' interpretations of these ambiguous statements as reflecting positive or negative meaning were then used as an assessment of implicit self-esteem. Our recommendation for use of this procedure would be to avoid the imagination component by convincing people that these statements really had been used by an interaction partner to describe them (e.g., a friend vs. a relative stranger) and then indirectly assessing the manner in which the statements are interpreted.

Of the various implicit self-concept measures available, this procedure developed by Tafarodi probably maps most closely onto Cook and Selltiz's (1964) original description of partially structured measures, but there are other procedures that measure deliberative implicit attitudes regarding the self. One example of such a procedure that taps aspects of the self other than self-esteem can be found in a recent measure of self-serving bias, in which participants were given success and failure feedback on two novel tasks and asked which task appeared to be more important (von Hippel et al., 2005). Participants who rated the task at which they succeeded as more important than the task at which they failed also tended to engage in other self-serving behaviors when they could rationalize their actions. Specifically, these self-serving participants were more likely to cheat on a math task when they could justify their cheating as unintentional, but not when their cheating could only be construed as intended. This relationship between a relatively indirect measure of self-serving bias and rationalized cheating suggests that implicit measures of the self-concept have the potential to predict behavior that is both theoretically and practically meaningful.

CONCLUSION

The theoretical richness of the attitude construct as it was first introduced by Allport (1935), Krech and Crutchfield (1948), and others was largely abandoned in favor of simpler and more direct conceptualizations of attitudes, owing to the inherent difficulties in measuring such a complex construct. Seventy years later, the boom in measurement of implicit attitudes is again providing theoretical and empirical justification for the possibility that attitudes might be much more than just stored evaluations (Fazio & Olson, 2003; Greenwald et al., 2002; Wilson et al., 2000). The original arsenal of implicit paper-and-pencil measures failed to adequately support such a complex notion of attitudes. In combination with modern theories of information processing and techniques for measuring automatic attitudes, however, the possibility is now reemerging that paper-and-pencil measures of implicit attitudes might play a key role in expanding our conception of what it means to hold an attitude. Despite their rather low profile, paper-and-pencil measures of implicit attitudes are not only the original forebears of the modern approach to implicit attitude measurement, but they still retain their vitality and utility for modern researchers. Such low-tech measures are particularly useful when situations or budgets preclude complex measurement machinery, but because deliberative implicit attitude measures appear to capture a component of the attitude unmeasured by other procedures, these measures can also be useful even for researchers armed with fMRI, IATs, and subliminal EPTs.

REFERENCES

Albarracin, D., & Wyer, R. S., Jr. (2000). The cognitive impact of past behavior: Influences of beliefs, attitudes, and future behavioral decisions. *Journal of Personality and Social Psychology, 79*, 5–22.

Allport, G. W. (1935). Attitudes. In C. Murchison (Ed.), *Handbook of social psychology* (pp. 133–175). Worcester, MA: Clark University Press.

Bosson, J. K., Brown, R. P., Zeigler-Hill, V., & Swann, W. B., Jr. (2003). Self-enhancement tendencies among people with high explicit self-esteem: The moderating role of implicit self-esteem. *Self and Identity, 2*, 169–187.

Carlisle, K., & von Hippel, W. (2000). *Threat to collective self-esteem and implicit stereotyping.* Paper presented at the 72nd annual meeting of the Midwestern Psychological Association, Chicago.

Chartrand, T. L., van Baaren, R. B., & Bargh, J. A. (2006). Linking automatic evaluation to mood and information processing style: Consequences for experienced affect, impression formation, and stereotyping. *Journal of Experimental Psychology: General, 135*, 70–77.

Cook, S. W., & Selltiz, C. (1964). A multiple-indicator approach to attitude measurement. *Psychological Bulletin, 62*, 36–55.

Crosby, F., Bromley, S., & Saxe, L. (1980). Recent unobtrusive studies of Black and White discrimination and prejudice: A literature review. *Psychological Bulletin, 87*, 546–563.

Cunningham, W. A., Preacher, K. J., & Banaji, M. R. (2001). Implicit attitude measures: Consistency, stability, and convergent validity. *Psychological Science, 12*, 163–170.

DeHart, T., Pelham, B. W., & Tennen, H. (2006). What lies beneath: Parenting style and implicit self-esteem. *Journal of Experimental Social Psychology, 42*, 1–17.

Dovidio, J., Kawakami, K., Johnson, C., Johnson, B., & Howard, A. (1997). On the nature of prejudice: Automatic and controlled processes. *Journal of Experimental Social Psychology, 33*, 510–540.

Draine, S. C., & Greenwald, A. G. (1998). Replicable unconscious semantic priming. *Journal of Experimental Psychology: General, 127*, 286–303.

Eagly A. E., & Chaiken S. (1993). *The psychology of attitudes.* Fort Worth, TX: Harcourt Brace Jovanovich.

Espinoza, P., & Sekaquaptewa, D. (2001). *Perceiving racial outgroup members as "all the same": Outgroup homogeneity as an individual-difference racial bias.* Paper presented at the 73nd annual meeting of the Midwestern Psychological Association, Chicago.

Fazio, R. H. (1990). Multiple processes by which attitudes guide behavior: The MODE model as an integrative framework. In M. P. Zanna (Ed.), *Advances in experimental social psychology* (Vol. 23, pp. 75–109). San Francisco: Academic Press.

Fazio, R. H., Jackson, J. R., Dunton, B. C., & Williams, C. J. (1995). Variability in automatic activation as an unobtrusive measure of racial attitudes: A bona fide pipeline? *Journal of Personality and Social Psychology, 69*, 1013–1027.

Fazio, R. H., & Olson, M. A. (2003). Implicit measures in social cognition research: Their meaning and use. *Annual Review of Psychology, 54,* 297–327.

Fishbein, M., & Ajzen, I. (1974). Attitudes toward objects as predictors of single and multiple behavioral criteria. *Psychological Review, 81,* 59–74.

Gaertner, S. L., & Dovidio, J. F. (1986). The aversive form of racism. In J. F. Dovidio & S. L. Gaertner (Eds.), *Prejudice, discrimination, and racism* (pp. 61–89). San Diego: Academic Press.

Gilbert, D. T., & Hixon, J. G. (1991). The trouble of thinking: Activation and application of stereotypic beliefs. *Journal of Personality and Social Psychology, 60,* 509–517.

Gonsalkorale, K., Carlisle, K., & von Hippel, W. (2005). *Effects of threat and consensus on implicit stereotyping.* Unpublished manuscript, University of New South Wales, Sydney.

Govan, C. L., & Williams, K. D. (2004). Changing the affective valence of the stimulus items influences the IAT by re-defining the category labels. *Journal of Experimental Social Psychology, 40,* 357–365.

Greenwald, A. G., Banaji, M. R., Rudman, L. A., Farnham, S. D., Nosek, B. A., & Mellott, D. S. (2002). A unified theory of implicit attitudes, stereotypes, self-esteem, and self-concept. *Psychological Review, 109,* 3–25.

Greenwald, A. G., McGhee, D., & Schwartz, J. L. K. (1998). Measuring individual differences in implicit cognition: The Implicit Association Test. *Journal of Personality and Social Psychology, 74,* 1364–1480.

Hammond, K. R. (1948). Measuring attitudes by error choice: An indirect method. *Journal of Abnormal and Social Psychology, 43,* 38–48.

Hastie, R. (1984). Causes and effects of causal attribution. *Journal of Personality and Social Psychology, 46,* 44–56.

Hetts, J. J., Sakuma, M., & Pelham, B. W. (1999). Two roads to positive regard: Implicit and explicit self-evaluation and culture. *Journal of Experimental Social Psychology, 35,* 512–559.

Isen, A. M., Labroo, A. A., & Durlach, P. (2004). An influence of product and brand name on positive affect: Implicit and explicit measures. *Motivation and Emotion, 28,* 43–63.

Jones, J. T., Pelham, B. W., Mirenberg, M. C., & Hetts, J. J. (2002). Name letter preferences are not merely mere exposure: Implicit egotism as self-regulation. *Journal of Experimental Social Psychology, 38,* 170–177.

Karpinski, A., & von Hippel, W. (1996). The role of the linguistic intergroup bias in expectancy maintenance. *Social Cognition, 14,* 141–163.

Kitayama, S., & Karasawa, M. (1997). Implicit self-esteem in Japan: Name letters and birthday numbers. *Personality and Social Psychology Bulletin, 23,* 736–742.

Kitayama, S., & Uchida, Y. (2003). Explicit self-criticism and implicit self-regard: Evaluating self and friend in two cultures. *Journal of Experimental Social Psychology, 39,* 476–482.

Koole, S. L., Dijksterhuis, A., & van Knippenberg, A. (2001). What's in a name: Implicit self-esteem and the automatic self. *Journal of Personality and Social Psychology, 80,* 669–685.

Krech, D., & Crutchfield, R. (1948). *Theory and problems of social psychology.* New York: McGraw-Hill.

Lemm, K., Sattler, D. N., Khan, S., Mitchell, R. A., & Dahl, J. (2002, February). *Reliability and validity of a paper-based implicit association test*. Paper presented at the fourth annual convention of the Society for Personality and Social Psychology, Savannah, GA.

Lemon, N, (1973). *Attitudes and their measurement*. New York: Wiley.

Lord, C. G., Ross, L., & Lepper, M. (1979). Biased assimilation and attitude polarization: The effects of prior theories on subsequently considered evidence. *Journal of Personality and Social Psychology, 37*, 2098–2109.

Maass, A., Salvi, D., Arcuri, L., & Semin, G. (1989). Language use in intergroup contexts: The Linguistic Intergroup Bias. *Journal of Personality and Social Psychology, 57*, 981–993.

Mast, M. S. (2004). Men are hierarchical, women are egalitarian: An implicit gender stereotype. *Swiss Journal of Psychology, 63*, 107–111.

Monteith, M. J. (1996). Affective reactions to prejudice-related discrepant responses: The impact of standard salience. *Personality and Social Psychology Bulletin, 22*, 48–59.

Murray, H. A. (1965). Uses of the Thematic Apperception Test. In B. I. Murstein (Ed.), *Handbook of projective techniques* (pp. 425–432). New York: Basic Books.

Nuttin, J. M. (1985). Narcissism beyond Gestalt and awareness: The name letter effect. *European Journal of Social Psychology, 15*, 353–361.

Osgood, C. E., Suci, G. J., & Tannenbaum, P. H. (1957). *The measurement of meaning*. Urbana: University of Illinois Press.

Ostrom, T. M. (1989). The interdependence of attitude theory and measurement. In A. R. Pratkanis, S. J. Breckler, & A. G. Greenwald (Eds.), *Attitude structure and function* (pp. 11–36). Hillsdale, NJ: Erlbaum.

Ouellette, J. A., & Wood, W. (1998). Habit and intention in everyday life: The processes by which past behavior predicts future behavior. *Psychological Bulletin, 124*, 54–74.

Patterson, M. L. (2001). Toward a comprehensive model of non-verbal communication. In W. P. Robinson & H. Giles (Eds.), *The new handbook of language and social psychology* (pp. 159–176). Hoboken, NJ: Wiley.

Payne, B. K., Cheng, C. M., Govorun, O., & Stewart, B. D. (2005). An inkblot for attitudes: Affect misattribution as implicit measurement. *Journal of Personality and Social Psychology, 89*, 277–293.

Pelham, B. W., Mirenberg, M. C., & Jones, J. T. (2002). Why Susie sells seashells by the seashore: Implicit egotism and major life decisions. *Journal of Personality and Social Psychology, 82*, 469–487.

Proshansky, H. M. (1943). A projective method for the study of attitudes. *Journal of Abnormal and Social Psychology, 38*, 393–395.

Saucier, D. A., & Miller, C. T. (2003). The persuasiveness of racial arguments as a subtle measure of racism. *Personality and Social Psychology Bulletin, 29*, 1303–1315.

Schimel, J., Simon, L., Greenberg, J., Pyszczynski, T., Solomon, S., Waxmonsky, J., et al. (1999). Stereotypes and terror management: Evidence that mortality salience enhances stereotypic thinking and preferences. *Journal of Personality and Social Psychology, 77*, 905–926.

Sekaquaptewa, D., & Espinoza, P. (2004). Biased processing of stereotype-incongruency is greater for low than high status groups. *Journal of Experimental Social Psychology, 40,* 128–135.

Sekaquaptewa, D., Espinoza, P., Thompson, M., Vargas, P., & von Hippel, W. (2003). Stereotypic explanatory bias: Implicit stereotyping as a predictor of discrimination. *Journal of Experimental Social Psychology, 39,* 75–82.

Sekaquaptewa, D., Vargas, P., & von Hippel, W. (1996). *Process prejudice predicts biased processing of information about women.* Paper presented at the 68th annual meeting of the Midwestern Psychological Association, Chicago.

Sia, T. L., Lord, C. G., Blessum, K. A., Thomas, J. C., & Lepper, M. R. (1999). Activation of exemplars in the process of assessing social category attitudes. *Journal of Personality and Social Psychology, 76,* 517–532.

Sinclair, L., & Kunda, Z. (1999). Reactions to a Black professional: Motivated inhibition and activation of conflicting stereotypes. *Journal of Personality and Social Psychology, 77,* 885–904.

Smith, M. B., Bruner, J. S., & White, R. W. (1956). *Opinions and personality.* New York: Wiley.

Son Hing, L. S., Li, W., & Zanna, M. P. (2002). Inducing hypocrisy to reduce prejudicial responses among aversive racists. *Journal of Experimental Social Psychology, 38,* 71–78.

Spencer, S. J., Fein, S., Wolfe, C., Fong, C., & Dunn, M. (1998). Stereotype activation under cognitive load: The moderating role of self-image threat. *Personality and Social Psychology Bulletin, 24,* 1139–1152.

Stapel, D. A., & Blanton, H. (2004). From seeing to being: Subliminal social comparisons affect implicit and explicit self-evaluations. *Journal of Personality and Social Psychology, 87,* 468–481.

Steele, C. M., & Aronson, J. (1995). Stereotype threat and the intellectual test performance of African-Americans. *Journal of Personality and Social Psychology, 69,* 797–811.

Tafarodi, R. W. (1998). Paradoxical self-esteem and selectivity in the processing of social information. *Journal of Personality and Social Psychology, 74,* 1181–1196.

Thistlethwaite, D. L. (1950). Attitude and structure as factors in the distortion in reasoning. *Journal of Abnormal and Social Psychology, 45,* 442–458.

Thurstone, L. L. (1928). Attitudes can be measured. *American Journal of Sociology, 33,* 529–554.

Vargas, P. (2004). On the relations among implicit and explicit attitude measures, and behavior: A 2 × 2 typology of attitude measures. In G. Haddock & G. R. O. Maio (Eds.), *Contemporary perspectives on the psychology of attitudes.* London: Psychology Press.

Vargas, P. T., Sekaquaptewa, D., & von Hippel, W. (2004). It's not just what you think, it's also how you think: Prejudice as biased information processing. In W. N. Lee & J. Williams (Eds.), *Diversity in advertising* (pp. 93–119). Mahwah, NJ: Earlbaum.

Vargas, P. T., & von Hippel, W. (2005). *Now we're smoking: Faking explicit but not implicit attitudes toward cigarettes.* Unpublished manuscript, University of Illinois.

Vargas, P. T., von Hippel, W., & Petty, R. E. (2004). Using "partially structured" attitude measures to enhance the attitude–behavior relationship. *Personality and Social Psychology Bulletin, 30,* 197–211.

von Hippel, W., Lakin, J. L., & Shakarchi, R. J. (2005). Individual differences in motivated social cognition: The case of self-serving information processing. *Personality and Social Psychology Bulletin, 31,* 1347–1357.

von Hippel, W., Sekaquaptewa, D., & Vargas, P. (1995). On the role of encoding processes in stereotype maintenance. *Advances in Experimental Social Psychology, 27,* 177–254.

von Hippel, W., Sekaquaptewa, D., & Vargas, P. (1997). The Linguistic Intergroup Bias as an implicit indicator of prejudice. *Journal of Experimental Social Psychology, 33,* 490–509.

Wicker, A. W. (1969). Attitudes versus actions: The relationship of verbal and overt behavioral responses to attitude objects. *Journal of Social Issues, 25,* 41–78.

Wigboldus, D., Semin, G. R., & Spears, R. (2000). How do we communicate stereotypes? Linguistic bases and inferential consequences. *Journal of Personality and Social Psychology, 78,* 5–18.

Wilson, T. D., Lindsey, S., & Schooler, T. Y. (2000). A model of dual attitudes. *Psychological Review, 107,* 101–126.

Winter, D. G., John, O. P., Stewart, A. J., Klohnen, E. C., & Duncan, L. E. (1998). Traits and motives: Toward an integration of two traditions in personality research. *Psychological Review, 105,* 230–250.

5 Attitudes as Mental and Neural States of Readiness

Using Physiological Measures to Study Implicit Attitudes

Tiffany A. Ito
John T. Cacioppo

In the mid-1950s a patient known as H. M. underwent surgery for the treatment of intractable epilepsy. The resulting bilateral resection of the medial portions of his temporal lobes was successful in reducing seizures, but also had unexpected and profound effects on his memory. Initially, it appeared that H. M. completely lacked the ability to learn new information, but further testing revealed that he could perform new tasks even when he could not remember learning them (Scofield & Milner, 1957). This provocative memory dissociation had important implications for the understanding of memory, leading to the current acceptance of the distinction between explicit, semantic memory and implicit, procedural memory. The impact of these initial observations has since been extended beyond the domain of memory, as this book illustrates.

The study of implicit attitudes by social psychologists has relied heavily on the behavioral methods of social cognition, including response competition (Greenwald, McGhee, & Schwartz, 1998), se-

125

mantic (Wittenbrink, Judd, & Park, 1997) and evaluative (Fazio, Jackson, Dunton, & Williams, 1995) priming, and topographical learning (Crawford & Cacioppo, 2002). Given the role of human neuroscience research in initially highlighting the presence of implicit processes, however, it seems fitting to consider how the theories and methods from the neurosciences might be applied to the study of implicit attitudes. Accordingly, in this chapter we review seven physiological measures that have been used to assess implicit attitudinal processes. For each measure, we discuss methodological issues relevant for validating its use in assessing implicit processes, and note its strengths and weakness. Before doing so, we consider more explicitly the rationale for using physiological measures to assess implicit attitudes. This requires a consideration of the different ways in which the term *implicit* has been applied to the study of attitudes, which we discuss next.

THE REFERENT IN IMPLICIT ATTITUDE PROCESSES

The term *attitudes* refers to global and enduring favorable or unfavorable predispositions to respond toward a stimulus or class of stimuli. The notion that people are not always willing or able to report their attitudes is an old one in social psychology (see review by Cacioppo & Sandman, 1981). For the past decade, however, the term *implicit* has been applied to attitudes in at least three different ways: (1) when considering the lack of awareness of the information-processing operations that underlie attitudes, (2) when the attitude itself is implicit (i. e., nonverbalizable), and (3) when the attitude is implicitly measured. Physiological measures can address each of these issues.

Few would doubt that the brain is the organ of the mind, and in attitude research this point extends back at least as far as Allport (1935), who defined an attitude as "a mental and neural state of readiness" (p. 810). But it has also been long recognized that the psychological processes leading to evaluation and judgment are typically introspectively unavailable (Nisbett & Wilson, 1977). As a consequence, self-reported responses may reflect the products of higher-order thought processes (e. g., the attitude judgment) or lay theories of cause and effect, but bear little resemblance to the actual computations that produce them. By directly tracking the physiological processes that form the basis of attitude judgments, physiological measures provide access to the implicit information-processing operations that underlie them.

A second way in which attitudes have been considered implicit corresponds to situations in which the attitude itself fails to reach conscious awareness. This is the meaning that is probably typically intended by the term *implicit attitudes*, which Greenwald and Banaji (1995) define as "introspectively unidentified (or inaccurately identified) traces of past experience that mediate favorable or unfavorable feeling, thought, or action toward social objects" (p. 8). It is assumed that even though the attitude may not be subjectively available, it can nevertheless impact behavior and judgments. Physiological measures are obviously useful for measuring implicit attitudes because they do not rely on a participant's subjective awareness of the attitude. Nor do physiological measures typically require participants to be accurately informed of the psychological construct of interest. For instance, participants are unlikely to correctly infer that attitudes are being measured by electrodes placed on the surface of the skin, making most physiological measures nonreactive. In this regard, physiological measures can be used in a manner similar to other indirect measures of implicit attitudes, such as response latency measures based on spreading of activation (e. g., Fazio, Sanbonmatsu, Powell, & Kardes, 1986).

A final consideration comes into play in domains where social desirability may be a concern, such as when measuring attitudes toward stigmatized groups. This is often considered a class of implicit attitude processes, not because of the implicit process underlying the attitude or because the attitude itself might be implicit, but because use of an implicit (i. e., indirect) measure can decrease the influence of response biases. The ability of physiological measures to indirectly measure attitudes is therefore also relevant to this last consideration. In addition, the excellent temporal resolution of many physiological measures allows them to index responses occurring very quickly in processing, before explicit motivations to alter overt responses are likely to have operated.

In each of these referents for the term *implicit*, neural processes that reflect the unfolding of the implicit attitude process should be identifiable without assuming there is a one-to-one mapping of the neural-to-implicit psychological process (Cacioppo et al., 2003). That is, physiological measures can be used to inform our understanding of implicit attitudes without assuming we have identified an invariant marker of implicit attitudes or reducing the attitude phenomenon to the physiological response. In the sections that follow, we review several physiological methods that have been used to study attitudes. The measures vary in many important dimensions, such as the physiological response being measured and the cost and ease of measurement. They also differ in the aspect of implicit attitude process that can be assessed. Across these measures, it is useful to keep in mind that (1) there are foci of neural activity in which changes mark particular psychological processes; (2) inhibitory as well as excitatory changes in neural activity may mark psychological processes; (3) changes in neural activity are patterned temporally as well as spatially (i. e., spatiotemporal response patterning); and (4) changes in neural activity become less evident as the distance of measurement from the point of activation increases. These principles are fundamental to interpreting the first approach to be discussed, functional brain imaging.

Functional Brain Imaging

As the name implies, functional brain imaging involves quantification of brain activity. This can be done with a number of techniques (for a review, see Savoy, 2001), but most applications in the study of attitudes have used either functional magnetic resonance imaging (fMRI) or event-related brain potentials (ERPs). Our discussion therefore focuses on these methods. Because they quantify brain activity with an emphasis on either the spatial location (fMRI) or the timing (ERP) of events, brain imaging measures are the best suited among the measures we review here for examining the actual neural mechanisms that underlie attitudes. As will be shown, they can also be used to assess the two other ways in which attitudes have been considered implicit.

Functional Magnetic Resonance Imaging

fMRI represents the newest application of brain imaging to the study of attitudes (as well as other social processes). It is based on the observation that increases in neuronal activity are associated with increased local blood flow. An important aspect is that there is a mismatch following increased metabolism, with blood flow typically increasing in excess of oxygen use. As a result, venus circulation near the area of increased neural activity actually exhibits a *decrease* in the concentration in deoxygenated hemoglobin. This is, in turn, important because deoxyhemoglobin is paramagnetic and distorts local magnetic fields, which allows inferences to be made about local hemodynamic activity from measurements of local magnetic fields (Jezzard, Matthews, & Smith, 2001).

fMRI has been applied to the study of attitudes only recently, but is perhaps the most powerful measure currently available for identifying the neural mechanisms underlying attitudes because of it high spatial resolution. Much research has focused on the role of the amygdala (located bilaterally in the medial temporal lobe) in both explicit and implicit evaluative processes. Initial associations between the amygdala and evaluative responses came from work on the acquisition of conditioned fear responses (see, e.g., LaBar, Gatenby, Gore Le Doux, & Phelps, 1998; for a review, see LeDoux, 2000). In addition to its association with conditioned evaluative reactions, amygdala activation has been associated with emotional processes more generally, especially those involving threat and fear (Whalen, 1998). This is seen, for instance, in increased amygdala activation during viewing of fearful as compared to happy faces (Morris et al., 1996), both of which tend to increase activation relative to neutral faces or baseline levels.

Studies using very brief presentations of stimuli show that the amygdala is also involved during implicit evaluative responses. Whalen and colleagues (1998) exposed participants to 33 msec presentations of happy and fearful facial expressions that were immediately backward masked by faces showing neutral expressions. Although participants reported seeing only the neutral expressions, amygdala activation was significantly greater in response to fearful than to happy faces. The involvement of the amygdala with socially relevant information is not limited to emotional expressions. Faces idiosyncratically judged as untrustworthy are associated with greater amygdala activation. This occurs both when perceivers are explicitly attending to trustworthiness, and when attending to another dimension (age) (Winston, Strange, O'Doherty, & Dolan, 2002).

The studies reviewed to this point examine general evaluative and affective processes. More recent research has also examined amygdala activation associated with attitudinal judgments (Cunningham, Johnson, Gatenby, Gore, & Banaji, 2003). Greater amygdala activation has been observed during the processing of names associated with negative (e. g., Adolph Hitler) as opposed to positive (e. g., Mahatma Gandhi) attitudes. Moreover, this effect occurred both when names were explicitly being evaluated as good and bad and when they were being judged along a nonevaluative dimension (whether the names referred to current or historical persons). Thus, amygdala activation does not require the conscious evaluative processing of a stimulus, but the activation of the amygdala is nevertheless typically in accord with what one might expect from explicit ratings of stimuli.

The association of amygdala activation with implicit evaluative processes has led to studies of amygdala activation in the context of racial attitudes. Several studies have now examined whether amygdala

activation differs during the perception of racial outgroup as compared to ingroup members. In one of the first demonstrations, Hart
and colleagues (2000) had White and Black participants view pictures of White and Black faces showing neutral expressions. Greater
amygdala activation was found for racial outgroup faces. This effect,
however, was confined to the second block of stimulus presentation.
In the first block, ingroup and outgroup faces were associated with
similarly high levels of amygdala activation. This may reflect the involvement of the amygdala in vigilance (Whalen, 1998) and the
faster loss of threat relevance from ingroup than outgroup members.
In another study, Phelps and colleagues (2000) found no differences
in amygdala activation in response to racial ingroup and outgroup
faces. However, greater ingroup bias on both an Implicit Association
Test (IAT) and in the pattern of evaluative differentiation of startle
eyeblink responses (this measure is discussed in more detail in a later
section) were correlated with relatively greater amygdala activation
in response to outgroup members.

Cunningham and colleagues have suggested that discrepancies
between more negative implicit but more positive explicit reactions
to outgroup members account for the failure to consistently obtain
greater amygdala activation to racial outgroup faces (Cunningham,
Johnson, Raye, et al., 2004). Given that fMRI reflects changes in metabolism across a relatively wide temporal window (see discussion
below), the presence of conflicting evaluative reactions could obscure
differences in initial implicit reactions when activation is measured in
response to relatively long presentations of ingroup and outgroup exemplars. To separately assess implicit reactions, Cunningham, Johnson, Raye, and colleagues (2004) had White participants view brief,
30-msec, and longer, 525-msec, presentations of White and Black
faces. In both cases, faces were immediately followed by a pattern
mask. Consistent with the presence of differences in implicit attitudes
toward ingroup and outgroup members, greater amygdala activation
occurred when participants were viewing the briefly presented outgroup faces than when similarly viewing ingroup faces. Outgroup
faces viewed at longer durations were also associated with greater
amygdala activation, but only when using a lowered statistical threshold, whereas the effect reached conventional levels of statistical significance in the subliminal presentation condition.

It may be tempting to conclude from the preceding discussion that
the amygdala represents the neural mechanism underlying attitudes,
and that amygdala activation can serve as an index of attitudes. Assuming a one-to-one relation between amygdala activation and negativity, however, is inappropriate for several reasons (Cacioppo &

Tassinary, 1990). At the most general level, care should be taken in attributing any complex psychological process to localized changes in brain activation. From an anatomical perspective, distributed neural mechanisms are much more likely, especially when considering a complex process (for a more detailed discussion of this issue, see Cacioppo et al., 2003). This is, in fact, supported by fMRI studies of attitudinal processes. In addition to the amygdala, areas of the right inferior prefrontal cortex (PFC) have been associated with implicit and explicit evaluations. Explicit evaluations, especially those involving conflicting valences at the explicit level (ambivalence) or conflict in valence between implicit and explicit evaluations, have been associated with medial and right ventrolateral PFC activation (Cunningham et al., 2003; Cunningham, Johnson, Raye, et al., 2004). The involvement of these latter areas may reflect the need to coordinate multiple representations and/or implement cognitive control when evaluations of conflicting valences are activated (cf. Johnson & Reeder, 1997).

The assumption of distributed neural mechanisms underlying attitudes is also consistent with an investigation of implicit racial bias in a patient with bilateral amygdala damage (Phelps, Cannistraci, & Cunningham, 2003). If the amygdala represents a necessary neural substrate for implicit evaluations, the ability to make evaluative differentiations at the implicit level should be compromised following bilateral lesions to the amygdala. However, this patient did not differ from control participants in either implicit attitudes toward Blacks (as measured with the IAT) or explicit attitudes (as measured with the Modern Racism Scale [MRS]). In the case of the IAT, both the patient with the amygdala lesion and control participants showed implicit bias favoring Whites as compared to Blacks. The involvement of other brain areas in implicit evaluations, still intact in this particular patient, may explain the dissociation between amygdala damage and implicit bias.

It is also not yet clear how valence and amygdala activation are related. Increases in amygdala activation are most consistently associated with negative stimuli (e. g., in perception of fearful faces or unpleasant odors (Morris et al., 1996; Zald & Pardo, 1997)), but greater amygdala activation is sometimes observed in response to positive as compared to neutral stimuli (Canli, Sivers, Whitfield, Gotlib, & Gabrieli, 2002; Hamann & Mao, 2002). Whalen (1998) has suggested that amygdala activation in response to negative stimuli occurs because the amygdala is important for modulating vigilance. From this perspective, amygdala activation may be seen most consistently in response to negative, especially threatening, stimuli but should also be seen in response to any stimulus signaling biological relevance.

Another perspective on the relation between valence and the amygdala is suggested by Cunningham, Raye, and Johnson (2004), who note that the valence and intensity dimensions of stimuli used in fMRI studies have not always been separately considered. The tendency for negative stimuli to often be more intense than positive stimuli (cf. Ito & Cacioppo, 2000) raises the possibility that negative stimuli more consistently increase amygdala activation simply because they are typically more intense. Cunningham and colleagues assessed the relative roles of valence and intensity in amygdala activation by regressing amygdala activation in response to positive and negative attitude object labels (e. g., the words *murder, freedom, technology, immigration*) on participants' valence and intensity ratings of the stimuli, obtained after scanning. Only intensity judgments significantly predicted amygdala activation, with more intense stimuli of both valences associated with greater amygdala activation. (Nevertheless, a J-shaped association was found, with amygdala activation highest in response to negative stimuli, lowest to neutral stimuli, and intermediate to positive stimuli.) This relation was obtained when participants judged whether the stimuli represented something abstract versus concrete, as well as when they made explicit evaluative judgments, demonstrating that the effect occurs when evaluation is both implicit and explicit.

Finally, Norris, Chen, Zhu, Small, and Cacioppo (2004) examined the independent and interactive effects of affective and social stimuli on brain activation. Whole-brain images were acquired while participants viewed and categorized affective pictures that varied on two dimensions: emotional content (i. e., neutral, emotional) and social content (i. e., faces/people, objects/scenes). Patterns of activation were consistent with past findings demonstrating that the amygdala and part of the visual cortex were more active in response to emotionally evocative pictures than to neutral pictures. Of special relevance here is that the activation of the amygdala showed evidence of additive effects. This result suggests that the amygdala is primarily implicated in processing biologically or personally relevant stimuli, regardless of the nature of the relevance (i. e., social, emotional, or both).

To summarize, what precisely amygdala activation reflects is not yet clear. Among the functions that have been ascribed to it are evaluations of the threatening nature of a stimulus, assessments of the attentional demands of the stimulus, assessments of the biological or personal significance of a stimulus, and the binding together of information (e. g., a conditioned and unconditioned stimulus) to form a coherent unit of information, to name but a few. What is clear from the extant literature is that amygdala activation does not *require* conscious recognition of a stimulus, and that the activation of the amygdala is nevertheless typically in accord with what one might expect from explicit ratings of stimuli. Thus, amygdala activation is greater in response to negative and positive than to neutral stimuli. In addition, amygdala activation appears to reflect a J-shaped function such that negative stimuli are also associated with somewhat more activation than positive stimuli, although issues of low statistical power appear to render this comparison nonsignificant in some studies. Although amygdala activation is often increased in response to negative stimuli, it is clear is that amygdala activation cannot be taken as prima facie evidence that a stimulus is evaluated more negatively (cf. Cacioppo & Tassinary, 1990).

Even though the exact function of the amygdala (or many other brain areas, for that matter) has not yet been fully specified, the studies reviewed here nevertheless demonstrate how fMRI can been used to investigate all three forms of implicit attitude processes noted in the introduction. In understanding the neural mechanisms that underlie attitudes, the amygdala and areas of the right inferior PFC are implicated in both implicit and explicit evaluative processes. Additional areas such as the medial PFC and right ventrolateral PFC may be involved in explicit evaluative processes, especially when more controlled, reflective processes are required. This may be especially likely with ambivalent attitudes because of the coactivation of opposing evaluations, or when implicit and explicit attitudes conflict in evaluation. Studies on attitude items shown below conscious awareness examine evaluative processes about which participants are unaware, and dissociations between amygdala activation and explicit racial attitudes may be instances where indirect attitude measurement reveals a response participants choose not to report.

An important strength of fMRI is its spatial resolution, but an important limitation is its poor temporal resolution. Rather than directly quantifying brain electrical activity or actual changes in brain metabolism, fMRI indirectly quantifies brain activity through changes in regional cerebral blood flow. As a result, the temporal resolution of fMRI is dependent on the time course of blood flow changes, which lag behind actual neuronal changes. Although the hemodynamic response can vary, depending on factors such as the particular brain location being studied and the duration of stimulation, change in the fMRI signal typically does not start until about 2 sec after stimulus onset. The response typically reaches its peak within 4–6 sec after stimulus onset and returns to baseline 10–14 sec after stimulus onset (Menon & Kim, 1999). Event-related fMRI designs and various analytic methods (e. g., deconvolution) have improved the temporal resolution one can achieve with fMRI, but decomposing theoretically separable processes of interest can still be difficult. For instance, the measured activation of a particular area might include activation due to both implicit and explicit processes (cf. Cunningham, Johnson, Raye, et al., in 2004). Procedural dissociations where stimuli are presented below conscious awareness can be used to separately assess activation due to implicit processes, but activation due to implicit and explicit processes cannot be easily separated in situations where both are thought to occur (e. g., when stimuli are presented above threshold). We therefore turn next to a brain imaging methodology that has complementing strengths and weaknesses that allow for better quantification of implicit processes—that of ERPs.

Event-Related Brain Potentials

The second main type of brain imaging used to study implicit attitude processes is derived from the direct measurement of the electrical echoes of brain activity that can be measured at the surface of the scalp with the use of electroencephalography. ERPs have a higher temporal resolution (on the order of milliseconds) than fMRI, allowing for investigation of information-processing operations that occur in close temporal proximity, such as implicit and explicit attitudinal processes. Time-locked positive and negative deflections in the ERP waveform are referred to as *components*.[1] The importance of ERPs to the study of psychological processes derives from the association of individual ERP components with distinct information-processing operations (Gehring, Gratton, Coles, & Donchin, 1992). This allows inferences about the timing (revealed in component latency) and degree (revealed in component amplitude) of various psychological operations to be drawn from ERPs. Another positive aspect of ERP measurement is its lower cost relative to fMRI. High-quality amplifiers capable of simultaneously recording from many scalp sites can be reasonably purchased and maintained by a single lab.

What ERPs offer in temporal resolution, they lack in spatial resolution. ERPs are typically recorded noninvasively from the surface of the scalp. At this distance from the brain, electrodes are sensitive to activity from a relatively wide area. In addition, to be registered on the scalp surface, electrical activity from the brain must be of sufficient strength. It is generally thought that scalp-recorded ERPs reflect time-varying sums of the activity of large populations of neurons in the brain (Fabiani, Gratton, & Coles, 2000), with little sensitivity to deeper brain structures. Source modeling techniques can be used to infer possible sources of ERP activity, but field distortion caused by the skull and the inverse problem (i. e., innumerable unique combinations of neural generators that could account for the same scalp-recorded activity) limit the utility of such source estimates.

The use of ERPs to investigate implicit and explicit attitudes and attitude processes preceded the use of fMRI, with the first studies of attitudinal processes measuring the late positive potential (LPP), a complex component related to the P300, whose amplitude increases as a function of task-relevant discrepancies between stimuli.[2] Early research on cognitive processes indicated that when participants are instructed to count the occurrences of infrequent high-pitched tones presented in a stream of tones of a different pitch, P300s are larger to the infrequent tones (e. g., Donchin, 1981). Effects such as these led to the conclusion that P300 amplitude reflects updates to working memory that serve to maintain an accurate mental model of the external environment.

In the original P300 research, physical characteristics such as tone pitch served to differentiate classes of stimuli. Cacioppo and colleagues reasoned that an individual's attitude could also serve as the criterion for classification, and using a variation of the oddball paradigm that has been used to study pitch classifications, they discovered that the amplitude of the LPP (peaking at around 550 rather than 300 msec) varied as a function of the discrepancy between the attitude toward a target stimulus and the attitudes toward the preceding attitudinally homogeneous set of stimuli (Cacioppo, Crites, Berntson, & Coles, 1993). In a typical study, stimuli from one evaluative category (e. g., positive attitude items) are presented most frequently and LPP responses to evaluatively consistent (e. g., another positive item) and inconsistent (e. g., a negative item) stimuli are compared, revealing larger LPPs to evaluatively inconsistent stimuli. It has since been repeatedly demonstrated that LPP amplitude is sensitive to the evaluative discrepancy between stimuli using written labels of attitude objects (e. g., liked and disliked fruits and vegetables) (Cacioppo et al., 1993; Crites & Cacioppo, 1996) and trait labels (Cacioppo, Crites, Gardner, & Berntson, 1994; Crites, Cacioppo, Gardner, & Berntson, 1995), as well as with more general affective stimuli such as affect-laden pictures (Ito, Larsen, Smith, & Cacioppo, 1998; Ito & Cacioppo, 2000). In addition, the LPP varies as a function of the *degree* of evaluative inconsistency. A stimulus that is extremely evaluatively incongruent with the preceding stimuli (e. g., a very positive attitude item shown among a majority of very negative attitude items) will elicit a larger LPP than a moderately

evaluatively incongruent stimulus (e. g., a moderately positive attitude item shown among a majority of very negative attitude items)
(Cacioppo et al., 1994).

A much smaller, earlier, and faster component, the P1, has also
been investigated in the context of attitudes. The P1 is a positive-
going component associated with visual attention that peaks at 100–
150 msec after stimulus onset.[3] Typically largest over the occipital
lobe, the P1 has been linked with activity in the extrastriate area of
the visual cortex (Clark & Hillyard, 1996). Capitalizing on this sensitivity, Smith, Cacioppo, Larsen, and Chartrand (2003) examined
P1 responses to positive, negative, and neutral pictures to determine
if the general bias toward negative information seen in behavioral responses also manifests as differences in early attentional processes.
Their results reveal an attentional bias in which negative pictures at-
tracted more attention than positive or neutral pictures as quickly as
110 msec after stimulus onset. Presumably, the attentional component indexed by the P1 is implicit. Similarly greater attention to negative stimuli has been revealed in temporally later ERP components
associated with selective attention, such as the P200 (Carretié,
Martín-Loeches, Hinojosa, & Mercado, 2001; Carretié, Mercado,
Tapia, & Hinojosa, 2001).

Together, these studies have several implications for understanding the implicit mechanisms involved in attitudes. The greater attention to negative than positive stimuli shown in the P1 and P200 demonstrates the speed at which bias toward negative information can
occur (Carretié, Martín-Loeches, et al., 2001; Carretié, Mercado, et
al., 2001; Smith et al., 2003). Evaluatively-inconsistent negative stimuli also elicit larger LPPs than equally rare and evaluatively extreme
positive stimuli, providing evidence of an evaluative bias toward negative information slightly later in processing (Ito et al., 1998). Both
effects are consistent with the existence of different response functions
governing negative and positive evaluations, with the response function for negative evaluative processes responding more intensely than
the one for positivity (Cacioppo, Gardner, & Berntson, 1997). Moreover, examination of the spatial distribution of LPP evaluative effects
reveals that they are maximal at right parietal areas (Cacioppo,
Crites, & Gardner, 1996). The P300, which is thought to be a component of the LPP (see note 2), has been linked with activity in the
association cortex (Yamaguchi & Knight, 1991). Right lateralization
of responses associated with evaluative categorization is therefore
consistent with right hemisphere dominance for affective judgments
(Etcoff, 1989; Tucker & Frederick, 1989) and with involvement of
the right association cortex in evaluative categorizations.

Other studies demonstrate that LPP amplitude can be sensitive to attitudes that participants are unwilling or unable to report. When LPPs were compared when participants truthfully reported versus misreported their attitudes, LPP amplitude was sensitive to the underlying evaluative percept and not to the untruthful explicit attitude report (Crites, Cacioppo, Gardner, & Berston, 1995). For instance, LPPs to positive attitude objects toward which participants reported a negative attitude did not differ from responses to positive attitude objects that were truthfully reported as positive. The LPP also appears to be sensitive to implicit evaluative processes. When participants were shown positive and negative pictures but were explicitly instructed to categorize the stimuli in terms of whether people were present or absent, LPP amplitude nevertheless increased to evaluatively inconsistent stimuli (Ito & Cacioppo, 2000). Similarly, participants show larger LPPs to self-relevant information even when they are explicitly attending to the color of ink in which the information is presented (Gray, Ambady, Lowenthal, & Deldin, 2004).

In light of findings that the LPP can reflect both evaluative responses that participants do not want to report as well as responses about which they are unaware, the LPP has also been used to assess racial bias. Ito, Thompson, and Cacioppo (2004) presented White participants with pictures of Black and White males shown in the context of either primarily positive or negative pictures. Participants reported their liking for each picture seen. Although equally high liking was reported for Blacks and Whites, LPPs showed evidence of racial bias. Those participants with more negative attitudes toward Blacks (as indicated by MRS scores obtained in a prior session) viewed individual Black exemplars as more negative than White exemplars. When viewed in the context of primarily positive pictures, this manifested as relatively larger LPPs to Blacks than Whites (i. e., Blacks were more evaluatively inconsistent with positive pictures than were Whites). When viewed in the context of primarily negative pictures, this manifested as relatively larger LPPs to Whites than Blacks (i. e., Whites were more evaluatively inconsistent with negative pictures than were Blacks). Thus, in light of equally positive evaluative responses to individual exemplars, LPP amplitude was sensitive to underlying individual differences in racial attitudes.

The study just reviewed examined dissociations between ERPs and later self-reported responses. Dissociations between more implicit and explicit responses have also been examined by comparing ERP components that occur earlier versus later in processing. An example of this type of application is shown by studies examining whether alcohol impairs more explicit forms of processing while leaving more implicit processing unimpaired. In one study, this was assessed by first showing paragraphs that described the typical behavior of unfamiliar individuals to participants who received either a placebo or a moderate or high dose of alcohol (Bartholow, Pearson, Gratton, & Fabiani, 2003). The paragraphs were intended to create a strong trait expectation for each individual. Participants then read sentences describing subsequent behavior performed by these individuals as ERPs were recorded. Regardless of alcohol dose, sentences describing negative behaviors were associated with larger N100s than sentences describing positive behaviors. The N100, which peaked in this study with a mean latency of 110 msec, has been associated with selective attention (Fabiani et al., 2000). In the face of alcohol's known impairment of more reflective processing, the absence of alcohol effects on the N100 suggests that greater attention to undesirable behaviors is a more implicit response. In contrast, ERP responses that occurred later in processing, and were therefore more likely to also assess more reflective processes, were influenced by alcohol. Consistent with prior demonstrations that the LPP is sensitive to incongruency, sentences that violated a prior positive behavioral expectation were associated with larger LPPs among sober participants. That is, negative expectancy-incongruent sentences were associated with larger LPPs than positive, expectancy-congruent sentences. This effect, however, was not seen among intoxicated individuals (for a conceptually similar demonstration, see also Bartholow, Dickter, & Sestir, 2006).

As with fMRI, this review demonstrates that ERPs have been used to assess all three forms of implicit attitude processes reviewed in the introduction. Larger P1, N100, P200, and LPP responses to negative than positive or neutral stimuli, for instance, provide information on the implicit mechanisms that underlie attitudes. Early attitude effects, as shown in the P1 and the sensitivity of the LPP to spontaneous evaluations, both show the sensitivity of ERPs to attitude processes about which participants are likely to be unaware. Finally, studies on racial prejudice demonstrate how ERPs have been used to index attitude responses participants may not wish to report.

ELECTROMYOGRAPHY

Measures of brain activity as reflected in fMRI and ERPs represent the newest application of physiological measures to the study implicit attitudes. Given their basis of measurement (i. e., brain activity), they also provide the best means for examining the implicit neutral mech-

anisms of attitude processes. Measures of other physiological processes, including activity of the somatic muscles and of the autonomic nervous system, have a longer history of use in the study of
attitudes and have been used primarily in instances in which the attitude is implicit (i. e., nonverbalizable) and when it is desirable to
measure the attitude implicitly.

This can be seen in the study of facial electromyography (EMG),
which is recorded by small electrodes placed on the surface of the
skin over facial muscles of interest. Although facial expressions are
often associated with changes in affective state, it is also recognized
that many factors can make visible expressions an imperfect marker
of affective state (Cacioppo, Bush, & Tassinary, 1992). For instance,
affect may be experienced only briefly or at a level too low to produce overt changes in expression, or norms about emotional display
may mask overt expressions. By measuring the electrical activity of
muscles typically involved in facial expressions, incipient activity can
be detected even in the absence of changes in overt expression.

Cacioppo and colleagues were the first to demonstrate the value
of facial EMG in assessing both cognitive and affective processing
components underlying attitudes (see Cacioppo & Petty, 1981).
Building on the work of McGuigan (e. g., 1970) and Schwartz and
colleagues (e. g., Schwartz, Fair, Salt, Mandel, & Klerman, 1976a,
1976b), Cacioppo and Petty (1979) demonstrated that attitude valence was reflected in the EMG activity over the brow (corrugator
supercillii) and cheek (zygomaticus major) muscle regions, and extent of silent language processing was indexed over the perioral
(orbiularis oris) muscle region. Similar patterns of EMG activity over
brow and cheek regions have since been observed in responses to
affect-laden pictures, film clips, words, and sounds (Bush, Barr,
McHugo, & Lanzetta, 1989; Cacioppo, Bush, & Tassinary, 1992;
Cacioppo, Petty, Losch, & Kim, 1986; Dimberg, 1986; Greenwald,
Cook, & Lang, 1989). Although pleasant stimuli typically elicit
greater EMG activity over the cheek region and less activity over the
brow region than do unpleasant stimuli, the relative form and
strength of affective influences on activity over the zygomaticus major and corrugator supercilii muscle regions were investigated recently by Larsen, Norris, and Cacioppo (2003). Self-reported positive and negative affective reactions and facial EMG were collected
as participants were exposed to series of affective pictures, sounds,
and words. Consistent with the known properties of the neurophysiology of the facial musculature, results revealed a stronger lin-
ear effect of valence on activity over the corrugator supercilii (brow)
muscle region than the zygomaticus major (cheek) muscle region. In

addition, positive and negative affect ratings indicated that positive and negative affective stimuli have opposite effects on activity over the corrugator supercilii region but not over the zygomaticus major region.

Facial muscles, like response latencies, can be controlled consciously but in carefully constructed paradigms can be used to investigate implicit affective/evaluative processes by measuring responses to stimuli about which participants are unaware. Using backward masking with a neutral face, Dimberg, Thunberg, and Elmehed (2000) showed participants 30 msec presentations of happy and angry faces. Presentations of masked happy faces were associated with greater cheek area activity, whereas angry faces were associated with increased brow area activity, even though participants reported no awareness of the non-neutral faces. Using an even shorter presentation duration, Winkielman and Cacioppo (2001) presented contour outlines of common objects (e. g., a desk) for 16 msec, immediately masked by simple line drawings. Participants were not consciously aware of the priming contours, but perceptual fluency effects suggest that perception of the target object should be facilitated when the contour prime and target match. Consistent with arguments that perceptual fluency is associated with increased positive affect, greater cheek area activity was obtained when the contour prime matched rather than mismatched the target picture.

In the area of ingroup bias, studies using facial EMG have addressed dissociations between more positive self-reported reactions and more negative affective reactions to outgroup members. In one series of studies, facial EMG and various self-report measures were collected as White participants imagined cooperative interactions with either Black or White partners (Vanman, Paul, Ito, & Miller, 1997). Situational factors theoretically relevant to cooperative outcomes, such as presence of a joint or independent reward structure, had similar effects on self-report and EMG. In the case of reward structure, for instance, participants reported more liking for their partners and showed greater cheek but less brow area activity when imagining a situation in which their rewards did not depend on the performance of their partners. In contrast, partner race had differing effects on self-report and facial EMG. Participants reported equally high liking and positive affect to Black and White partners, but EMG revealed greater brow and less cheek area activity in response to Black partners. This pattern of results suggests that participants were unconcerned about expressing their reactions to structural variables such as reward structure, but consciously or unconsciously modified their initial affective reactions when considering partner race. This explanation is further supported by a study that manipulated the social sensitivity of the outgroup (Ensari et al., 2004). Self-reported reactions were more favorable toward members of socially sensitive groups (Blacks and homosexuals) as opposed to nonsensitive groups (undergraduate major and graduate/undergraduate status), but facial EMG revealed more negative affect toward members of the socially sensitive groups. Interestingly, the relation between facial EMG and self-reported responses differed when members of the outgroup were believed to have insulted the participants. In the presence of an insult, which should provide a justification for expressing negative reactions even to members of socially sensitive groups, facial EMG and self-report revealed equally negative reactions toward the socially sensitive and nonsensitive outgroups.

The major advantages of facial EMG in the study of implicit attitudes derive from its ease of measurement and strong relation to affective processes. In terms of measurement, facial EMGs can be more easily acquired than ERPs in most applications (e. g., fewer channels of data are typically recorded, requiring less preparation and fewer amplifiers), but two important limitations of facial EMGs as measures of implicit attitudes should be noted. First, although response biases may have less of an impact on facial EMG than on self-reported responses because the measurement interest of the former can be more easily disguised, facial muscles can nevertheless be consciously controlled. Using their activity to reflect implicit processes therefore requires consideration of whether participants can discern that facial muscle activity is being measured as a reflection of affective processes. One way to address this is through the use of carefully constructed paradigms (e. g., presentation of stimuli below conscious awareness) or cover stories that direct attention away from the measurement interest. Second, although EMG responses reflect the output of a loquacious servant of the central nervous system (CNS), they are not equally sensitive to all aspects of CNS functioning. Specifically, EMG responses are motor outputs expressed through the final common pathway—the lower motor neurons. As such, they are more sensitive to response organizations and predispositions than to attentional or integrative actions per se. In this respect, EMG measures and startle eyeblink modulation, reviewed in the next section, are similar. In both cases, affective responses appear to be organized in a reciprocal fashion. That is, increases in positivity are associated with decreases in negativity (for a more detailed discussion, see Ito & Cacioppo, 1999).

The reciprocal relation between positive and negative affective and evaluative states seen in facial EMG diverges from the more bivariate organization seen at levels higher in the neuraxis and reflected in measures of brain activity. As noted in our discussion of ERP studies, for instance, ERP research supports the existence of separate response functions that govern positive and negative evaluations, consistent with the assumption that positivity and negativity are governed by stochastically and functionally independent evaluative systems (Cacioppo & Berntson, 1994; Cacioppo, Gardner, & Berntson, 1997). Functional demands are likely to explain this difference in patterning across the neuraxis. Although separable positive and negative evaluative substrates may underlie evaluative reactions, behavior is most efficiently governed by bivalent action tendencies. Measures at the level of the somatic nervous system, such as facial EMG, would be expected to reflect this more bivalent, reciprocal organization between positivity and negativity. This analysis highlights the fact that implicit attitudinal events are not solitary or unitary processes. Different physiological measures within a specific measurement paradigm will bear on different implicit and explicit attitude processes.

STARTLE EYEBLINK MODIFICATION

The eyeblink is a reliable and durable component of the whole-body startle response and has the further benefit of being relatively easy to elicit and measure. In experimental contexts, it occurs reliably in response to short, intense blasts of noise (referred to as the startle probe) and is typically measured by a pair of electrodes placed below the eye, over the obicularis oculi (periocular) muscle region. Startle eyeblink is of interest to psychologists because, like other reflexes, its magnitude can be modified by contextual factors. In particular, both attention and affective state can influence startle blink magnitude.

Attentional effects are consistently obtained when a foreground stimulus (e. g., a visual stimulus) precedes the startle probe by 500 msec or less. With this short lead interval to the startle probe, eyeblink magnitude is inhibited relative to a blink elicited by the probe alone. The attenuation of the blink response is thought to reflect automatic sensorimotor gating that briefly protects processing of the foreground stimulus from other distracting stimuli (Graham, 1975). The foreground stimuli that precede the startle probe are often very simple, such as auditory tones (Anthony, 1985; Filion, Dawson, & Schell, 1998), but attentional effects are also seen with affect-laden stimuli. Both positive and negative stimuli are known to attract more attention than neutral stimuli (Bradley, Cuthbert, &

Lang, 1990), which results in startle inhibition to both positive and negative stimuli as compared to neutral stimuli at short lead intervals (Bradley, Cuthbert, & Lang, 1993; Vanman, Boehmelt, Dawson, & Schell, 1996). In addition, the degree of startle inhibition varies as a function of the degree of attention directed at the stimulus preceding the startle (e. g., Filion, Dawson, & Schell, 1993). To the extent that attentional capture varies as a function of affective intensity, the degree of startle inhibition following positive or negative foreground stimuli should reflect the intensity of the foreground stimulus.

At longer lead intervals (500 msec or greater), startle eyeblink magnitude is sensitive to affective valence, with startle facilitation when the individual is in a negative affective state and inhibition when in a positive state, relative to neutral affective states or blinks that are elicited in the absence of an affective stimulus (Lang, Bradley, & Cuthbert, 1990). This has been obtained with a wide variety of affect-eliciting stimuli, including affective visual stimuli (Lang et al., 1990), imagery (Cook, Hawk, Davis, & Stevenson, 1991), and classically conditioned stimuli (Lipp, Sheridan, & Siddle, 1994). Lang and colleagues have proposed a motivational priming account for the affective modulation effects. In this view, an individual's current affective state augments motivationally congruent reflexive responses but inhibits incongruent ones (Lang, 1995; Lang et al., 1990; Lang, Bradley, & Cuthbert, 1992). The startle response is considered a defensive reflex, resulting in facilitation of the reflex when presented in the context of a negative affective foreground stimulus.

Relative to some of the other measures reviewed here, startle eyeblink modification has been less frequently applied to the study of attitudes. Two recent notable exceptions have examined attitudes toward gays and racial attitudes. To assess attitudes toward homosexuals, Mahaffey, Bryan, and Hutchison (2005a, 2005b) showed participants pictures of nude or seminude men and women, and nude or seminude gay, lesbian, and heterosexual couples. Startle probes were presented 4000 msec after picture onset in some trials. Startle blink magnitude in response to photos showing nude males (alone or as a couple) was related to self-reported homophobia, with higher homophobia associated with greater startle facilitation. Given the use of a long lead interval, the startle facilitation suggests a more negative attitude or affective reaction in response to the nude male stimuli as homophobia increased.

Startle probes presented at both short lead and long lead intervals were used by Amodio, Harmon-Jones, and Devine (2003) to examine racial attitudes. Participants with differing levels of internal and external motivation to control prejudice toward Blacks were shown pictures of Black and White male faces, with startle probes delivered either 400 msec or 4,000 msec after picture onset. At short lead intervals, participants who were high in internal motivation but low in external motivation showed larger blinks to Black faces than did participants who were low in internal motivation to control prejudice (regardless of their level of external motivation) or who had high levels of both internal and external motivation. In other research, participants who were high in internal but low in external motivation to control prejudice have been shown to demonstrate the lowest levels of prejudice (Devine, Plant, Amodio, Harmon-Jones, & Vance, 2002). Based on this result, Amodio and colleagues interpret the larger blinks to Black faces by these participants as evidence of decreased affective activation relative to other participants. Motivations to control prejudice did not affect startle blink modification to White faces.

At long lead intervals, participants high in internal but low in external motivation once again differed from those who were low in internal motivation or high in both internal and external motivation in their responses to Black faces, but this time they showed smaller blinks than the other participants. Given that negative affect facilitates responses at long lead intervals, these responses converge with the short lead responses to suggest less negative responses to Blacks among participants high in internal but low in external motivation to control prejudice. As with the short lead responses, level of internal and external motivation did not affect blink responses to White faces.

As this review indicates, startle eyeblink has hitherto been primarily used as an indirect attitude measure in cases where response bias is of concern. Given the onset of the startle probe relative to the psychological process of interest, startle probes presented at short lead intervals are probably best suited to assess attitudes that are unaffected by response presentation issues, but even at long lead intervals it may be difficult for participants to determine how attitudes are being measured in a study containing occasional noise bursts and electrodes below the eye. As a result, startle eyeblink modification at long lead intervals may also be sensitive to responses participants are unaware of or may not express if explicitly asked. At the same time, at long lead intervals such as those used by Mahaffey and colleagues (2005a, 2005b) and Amodio and colleagues (2003), sufficient time elapses after the onset of the attitude object to allow controlled processes to affect the initial psychological state elicited by the attitude object. It is therefore possible that responses measured at long lead intervals reflect the activation of explicit responses. In the Amodio and colleagues study, there is no strong evidence that participants did in fact implement control strategies, as shown in the similar effects of motivation to control prejudice at the short and long lead intervals. If participants were altering their initial attitudinal responses, participants high in external motivation to control prejudice may have been expected to try to initiate more positive responses.

Because startle eyeblink is most commonly quantified by measuring activity of a periocular muscle, its measurement carries many of the same considerations noted in the section on facial EMG. Two important points of similarity are the ease of acquisition and the reciprocal relation between positivity and negativity seen at long lead intervals, but an important point of departure is seen in sensitivity to less arousing affective states. Whereas cheek and brow area activity as measured with facial EMG is sensitive to stimuli that are of only moderate affective intensity, startle eyeblink modification is typically observed only with highly arousing stimuli (Lang et al., 1992). This may be a particularly relevant consideration in the measurement of implicit attitudes, where evaluative processes that fail to reach consciousness may also be more subtle responses.

It is also important to note that the measure we discuss here—startle eyeblink modification—should not be confused with the simple measure of startle amplitude. Startle eyeblink modification reflects the moderation of this reflexive response by attentional or affective processes. It is quantified by comparing amplitude of the startle response presented in the context of a foreground stimulus relative to a control foreground stimulus, or a startle elicited in the absence of a foreground stimulus.

AUTONOMIC RESPONSES

Measurement of autonomic responses was originally thought to assess arousal associated with the emotional component of attitudes, but we now know that autonomic responses are complexly determined (cf. Berntson, Cacioppo, & Quigley, 1991). The measurement contexts for clear interpretations of autonomic responses have proven more important, and the aspects of attitudinal processes that autonomic responses can be used to gauge have proven to be richer than originally thought. In this section, we discuss three measures—heart rate, the pattern of cardiac output and vasomotor responses, and electrodermal activity (EDA). Heart rate and electrodermal activity are the most frequently used and easy-to-acquire measures of autonomic nervous system activity, but their use in studying implicit attitudes is limited by their insensitivity to attitude valence (Cacioppo et al., 1986). Because both strong positive and negative affective or evaluative reactions can activate the autonomic nervous system, increases in heart rate or EDA provide ambiguous valence information unless there is some prior knowledge regarding attitude valence.

For heart rate, attitude assessment in a context where prior information about the individuals' attitudes is known is illustrated by a study in which men who had previously completed a measure of attitudes toward gays were shown sexually explicit pictures involving two men. Heart rate increases were highest among men with more negative attitudes toward gays (Sheilds & Harriman, 1984). Similarly, Marinelli and Kelz (1973) found higher heart rates during an interaction with a physically disabled confederate among individuals with the most negative attitudes toward cosmetic disabilities. Physiological considerations, however, suggest then even when attitude valence is known, heart rate can be an imperfect measure of attitude intensity. Several researchers have proposed that heart rate is a relatively insensitive autonomic measure because it can be influenced by many factors other than attitude intensity, such as the metabolic demands associated with an affective state (Cacioppo, Berntson, Klein, & Poehlmann, 1997; Lang et al., 1990; Zajonc & McIntosch, 1992). From this perspective, attitude measurement contexts that lack strong metabolic consequences may have little effect on heart rate. This may explain instances in which heart rate fails to differ as a function of attitude, such as in Vanman and colleagues (1997), who obtained facial EMG differences to imagined interactions with Blacks versus Whites, but no heart rate differences.

Rather than recording a single measure of cardiovascular activity, Blascovich and colleagues suggest that patterns of cardiovascular responses in conjunction with vasomotor activity can differentiate between challenged versus threatened motivational states (Blascovich, Mendes, Hunter, & Lickel, 2000; Bascovich & Tomaka, 1996). Challenge appraisals arise from the perception that personal resources exceed environmental demands. They are associated with an adaptive pattern of cardiovascular changes including an increase in ventricular contractility and cardiac output coupled with vasodilation. Threat appraisals arise from the perception that environmental demands exceed personal resources. They are also associated with increased ventricular contractility, but without the decreased cardiac resistance associated with challenge appraisals. Instead, decreases in vascular resistance are actually inhibited during threat appraisals. Across multiple studies, interacting with individuals from stigmatized groups, such as socioeconomically disadvantaged individuals, Blacks, and individuals with a physical stigma, has been associated with cardiovascular responses indicative of threat (Blascovich, Mendes, Hunter, Lickel, & Kowai-Bell, 2001; Mendes, Blascovich, Lickel, & Hunter, 2002). These effects occur even in situations where participants report more positive reactions to the members of stigmatized groups (see, e. g., Mendes et al., 2002).

These results suggest that multiple measures of cardiovascular activity can be used to differentiate reactions to attitude objects, but Wright and Kirby (2003) have questioned this interpretation. They have raised numerous methodological issues about this line of research, including (1) the conception of demand, (2) the definitions of goal-relevant and evaluative situations, (3) the assertion regarding primary and secondary appraisal determinants of challenge and threat, and (4) the cardiovascular predictions. They further argue that the studies are difficult to interpret because the cardiovascular results obtained across studies are only partially consistent with predictions, the comparison of cardiovascular responses has included groups that bear an uncertain relationship to the primary and secondary appraisal criteria specified for the production of challenge and threat effects, and self-reported challenge and threat appraisals have not always been shown to differ as a function of challenge and threat manipulations. Wright and Kirby have suggested that cardiovascular responses may reflect effort instead. This is an important controversy that awaits additional research to resolve.

EDA is another important class of autonomic nervous system (ANS) measures used to assess attitudes. EDA measurement dates back to Fere (1888) and is among the earliest physiological measures used by psychologists (see Dawson, Schell, & Filion, 2000). Measures of EDA reflect the activity of the eccrine sweat glands, which is quantified by measuring changes in skin resistance as a small external current is passed across the skin. This current is typically introduced via two small electrodes placed on the surface of the hand and is so small as to be unnoticeable and present no threat of shock. Unlike heart rate, activity in the eccrince sweat glands is controlled primarily by the sympathetic nervous system (Wallin, 1981). The postganglionic neurotransmitter is acetylcholine, rather than the norepinephrine more typical of the sympathetic nervous system, which makes the eccrine system unique among sympathetic effector systems (Fowles, 1986). Psychological research over the past century has shown EDA to be a highly sensitive but nonspecific measure (cf. Cacioppo & Tassinary, 1990; Landis, 1930).

Given the ease of acquisition, EDA has been used in many attitude studies where prior information about the individuals' attitudes is known. These include studies of implicit attitudes, though inferences about attitudes based on EDA have been limited primarily to affective intensity. An early study of attitudes and EDA is provided by Rankin and Campbell (1955). Participants were told that their word associations were being studied, but the real interest was how they responded to close contact by White and Black experimenters, which occurred in the context of supposed needs to adjust the physiological recording equipment. EDA was greater following adjustments by the Black experimenter, which Rankin and Campbell recognized could reflect differences in attitudes toward Blacks and Whites over which participants had little control.

Dissociations between implicit and explicit evaluative processes have been assessed with EDA in various contexts as well. In the domain of classical conditioning, this has been done by presenting the conditioned stimulus below conscious awareness. For example, Esteves, Parra, Dimberg, and Öhman (1994) used 30 msec presentations of angry and happy faces immediately masked with neutral faces as the CS+ and CS–. Hand shock served as the conditioned stimulus. Participants expressed no awareness of the happy and angry faces during the conditioning phase, but later showed larger skin conductance responses to the CS+ during extinction, when both the CS+ and CS– were presented for 500 msec. Evidence that EDA reflects implicit evaluative associations is also found in studies of risky decision making (Bechara, Damasio, Tranel, & Damasio, 1997). Participants were given monetary rewards or punishments based on their choice of cards from decks with differing reward contingencies. The contingencies were not conveyed in advance, so participants could come to understand them only through experience with the decks. Participants began to advantageously choose from the decks with the best expected value before they could explicitly identify the decks that were the best, displaying implicit evaluative responses to the decks. Of importance was that anticipatory skin conductance responses were generated in response to the disadvantageous decks before participants became explicitly aware of the differences in the decks. Finally, individuals with prosopagnosia, who lack the ability to consciously recognize familiar faces, such as those of family members, nevertheless show some degree of recognition as reflected by increased skin conductance responses (Tranel & Damasio, 1985).

As with all the measures we have reviewed, the use of ANS measures to assess implicit attitudes requires consideration of both their strengths and weakness. Ease of acquisition and the strong link between motivational states and changes in ANS activity are two factors that recommend their use. This helps explain the enduring popularity of ANS measures in the assessment of both implicit (nonverbalizable) attitudes and attitudes that participants may not wish to express. For heart rate and EDA, however, their lack of sensitivity to valence information may often limit their use. In addition, heart rate is sensitive to metabolic demands and so should be expected to change only in situations with strong enough metabolic consequences. As we noted when discussing startle eyeblink modification's relative insensitivity to low-arousing states, this may not always occur in the context of attitude assessment. EDA is typically a more sensitive measure than heart rate, showing changes even when metabolic consequences are low, but this too can be problematic. EDA is so sensitive that it responds to factors other than just affective/evaluative intensity, which increases the difficulty in using EDA responses as a marker of attitude intensity. Inferential power may be increased by examining patterns of cardiovascular and vasomotor responses because the likelihood that a configuration of physiological responses has been brought about by something other than the psychological construct of interest is decreased relative to measurement of a single response (Blascovich, 2000; Cacioppo & Tassinary, 1990). Although the general approach of quantifying configurations of physiological responses is recommended, additional research may be required to clarify the ability of cardiovascular and vasomotor responses to differentiate attitude responses (Wright & Kirby, 2003).

CONCLUSION

From the simple pair of EDA electrodes used by Fere in the late 1800s to study EDA to the million dollar fMRI scanners used with increasing frequency in the last decade, attitudes and attitude processes have been probed with a variety of physiological responses. Each measure has its own unique considerations, which we have highlighted in each section. Across measures, there are emergent themes worth considering when using or interpreting physiological measures in the study of implicit attitude processes.

First, it is useful to remember that although attitudes are conceptualized as enduring positive or negative evaluative predispositions toward a stimulus or class of stimuli, they are themselves multifaceted. Because an attitude may at once encompass the neural mechanisms associated with the evaluative percept, attentional effects of the attitude, response competition aroused by the attitude object, metabolic changes to support the action tendency implied by the attitude, and overt behavioral expression, to name but a few, the most appropriate measure will vary depending on the specific focus of interest. Even when confining one's interest to implicit attitudes, our discussion of the multiple ways in which attitude processes can be considered implicit suggests that many different types of measures may be appropriate. From these considerations it should be obvious that no single physiological measure is inherently better than another, and physiological measures as a class are not inherently better than other types of measures of attitude processes. Their appropriateness depends on the research question and experimental design. Nevertheless, the great benefit of physiological measures comes from their relevance in many different situations, their ability to track attitude processes across time, and their suggestion of the nature of the attitude processes based on the nature of the physiological response, as illustrated by the research reviewed in this chapter.

A second important point that emerges from this review is the recognition that measures of different physiological responses, or of the same response in different contexts, provide information about different aspects of implicit and explicit attitude processes. The brain imaging methods of fMRI and ERPs, with their emphasis on either the spatial distribution or timing of brain activity, are well suited for examining the implicit underlying mechanisms for attitudes. When this is the primary research interest, these measures are most appropriate. When considering other implicit aspects of attitudes, all the methods we reviewed have been used to varying degrees as indirect measures of attitudes to examine those of which participants are not consciously aware or do not wish to express. When this is the primary research interest, a wider range of measures is relevant. Dimensions such as expense and ease of measurement may become considerations in determining which to use.

Another factor that can be considered when choosing among different physiological measures is the organization of evaluative predispositions at the level of the neuraxis being measured. Brain imaging and lesion studies support the presence of separable substrates governing positive and negative affective/evaluative processes (Berntson & Cacioppo, in press), but a bivariate organization is more often seen lower in the neuraxis (Ito & Cacioppo, 1999). As we noted in our discussion of facial EMG, overt behavior is most efficiently governed by bivalent action tendencies. Since the somatic nervous system provides the means for behavioral expression, somatic and reflex responses tend to reflect this more bivalent organization.

Regardless of which physiological measure is used, care should be taken in how the measure is implemented. Social psychologists have long recognized that the experimental context can influence participants' reactions, and the novelty of physiological measures may make the experimental context even more potentially impactful. Luckily, this can be counteracted relatively easily through common-sense procedures such as allowing participants time to habituate after affixing measurement devices and providing full explanations about the measurement procedures to lower anxiety.

Finally, when differences in brain images or physiological events (Φ) are found in tasks that are thought to differ only in one or more cognitive functions (Ψ), the data are often interpreted prematurely as showing that brain structure (or event) Φ is associated with cognitive function (Ψ). These data are also treated as revealing much the same information that would have been obtained had brain structure (or event) Φ been stimulated or ablated and a consequent change in cognitive function Ψ been observed. This form of interpretation reflects the explicit assumption that there is a fundamental localizability of specific cognitive operations, and the implicit assumption that there is an isomorphism between Φ and Ψ (Sarter, Berntson, & Cacioppo, 1996). Interpreting studies of the form $P(\Phi/\Psi)$, which characterizes most of the studies reviewed here, as equivalent to studies of the form $P(\Phi/\Psi)$ is misleading unless one is dealing with 1:1 relationships.[4] This is a premise that needs to be tested rather than treated as an assumption. With attention to details of this kind, we anticipate that the methodological and theoretical importance of a social neuroscience approach to attitudes and attitude processes will be increasingly important in the years ahead.

NOTES

1. The term *components* has various meanings in this literature, and morphological features of the waveform provide only one means of identifying components. The interested reader may consult Fabiani, Gratton, and Coles (2000) for more details.
2. Principal component analyses of the LPP suggests it consists of two factors or "components," one of which is the P300. For this reason, the term *late positive potential* rather than P300 has been used to describe this ERP.
3. In most naming conventions in ERP research, P and N are used to designate the polarity of a component. The number that follows either designates the order of the component relative to stimulus onset (e. g., the P1 is the first positive-going component) or the typical peak latency of the component (e. g., the P300 is a positive-going component with a peak latency around 300 msec in many paradigms).
4. Research in which psychological or behavioral factors serve as the independent (or blocking) variables and physiological structures or events serve as the dependent variables can be conceptualized as investigating the $P(\Phi/\Psi)$. Research in which physiological structures or events serve as the independent (or blocking) variables

and psychological or behavioral factors serve as the dependent variables, in contrast, can be conceptualized as investigating the $P(\Psi/\Phi)$. These conditional probabilities are equal only when the relationship between Ψ and Φ and is 1:1 (Cacioppo & Tassinary, 1990). Accordingly, approaches such as stimulation and ablation studies provide complementary rather than redundant information to studies in which physiological (e. g., fMRI) measures serve as dependent measures. This is because stimulation and ablation studies bear on the relationship $P(\Psi/\Phi)$, whereas studies in which physiological variables serve as dependent measures provide information about $P(\Phi/\Psi)$.

REFERENCES

Allport, G. (1935). Attitudes. In C. Murchison (Ed.), *Handbook of social psychology* (pp. 798–844). Worcester, MA: Clark University Press.

Amodio, D. M., Harmon-Jones, E., & Devine, P. G. (2003). Individual differences in the activation and control of affective race bias as assessed by startle eyeblink response and self-report. *Journal of Personality and Social Psychology, 8,* 738–753.

Anthony, B. J. (1985). In the blink of an eye: Implications of reflex modification for information processing. In P. K. Ackles, J. R. Richards, & M. G. H. Coles (Eds.), *Advances in psychophysiology* (Vol. 1, pp. 167–218). Greenwich, CT: JAI Press.

Bartholow, B. D., Dicker, C. D., & Sestir, M. (2006). *Stereotype activation and control of prejudiced responses: Cognitive control of inhibition and its impairment by alcohol.* Manuscript under review.

Bartholow, B. D., Peason, M. A., Gratton, G., & Fabiani, M. (2003). Effects of alcohol on person perception: A social cognitive neuroscience approach. *Journal of Personality and Social Psychology, 85,* 627–638.

Bechara, A., Damasio, J., Tranel, D., Damasio, A. R. (1997). Deciding advantageously before knowing the advantageous strategy. *Science, 275,* 1293–1295.

Berntson, G. G., & Cacioppo, J. T. (in press). The neuroevolution of motivation. In J. Shah & W. Gardner (Eds.), *Handbook of motivation science.* New York: Guilford Press.

Berntson, G. G., Cacioppo, J. T., & Quigley, K. S. (1991). Autonomic determinism: The modes of autonomic control, the doctrine of autonomic space, and the laws of autonomic constraint. *Psychological Review, 98,* 459–487.

Blascovich, J. (2000). Using physiological indexes of psychological processes in social psychological research. In H. T. Reis & C. M. Judd (Eds.), *Handbook of research methods in social and personality psychology* (pp. 117–137). Cambridge, UK: Cambridge University Press.

Blascovich, J., Mendes, W. B., Hunter, S. B., & Lickel, B. (2000). Stigma, threat, and social interactions. In T. F. Heatherton, R. E. Kleck, M. R. Hebl, & J. G. Hull (Eds.), *Social psychology of stigma* (pp. 307–333). New York: Guilford Press.

Blascovich, J., Mendes, W. B., Hunter, S. B., Lickel, B., & Kowai-Bell, N. (2001).

Perceiver threat in social interactions with stigmatized others. *Journal of Personality and Social Psychology, 80*(2), 253–267.

Blascovich, J., & Tomaka, J. (1996). The biopsychosocial model of arousal regulation. *Advances in Experimental Social Psychology, 28*, 1–51.

Bradley, M. M., Cuthbert, B. N., & Lang, P. J. (1990). Startle reflex modification: Emotion or attention? *Psychophysiology, 27, 513–522.*

Bradley, M. M., Cuthbert, B. N., & Lang, P. J. (1993). Pictures as prepulse: Attention and emotion in startle modification. *Psychophysiology, 30, 541–545.*

Bush, L. K., Barr, C. L., McHugo, G. J., & Lanzetta, J. T. (1989). The effects of facial control and facial mimicry on subjective reactions to comedy routines. *Motivation and Emotion, 13, 31–52.*

Cacioppo, J. T., & Berntson, G. G. (1994). Relationship between attitudes and evaluative space: A critical review, with emphasis on the separability of positive and negative substrates. *Psychological Bulletin, 115,* 401–423.

Cacioppo, J. T., Berntson, G. G., Klein, D. J., & Poehlmann, K. M. (1997). The psychophysiology of emotion across the lifespan. *Annual Review of Gerontology and Geriatrics, 17,* 27–74.

Cacioppo, J. T., Berntson, G. G., Lorig, T. S., Norris, C. J., Rickett, E., & Nusbaum, H. (2003). Just because you're imaging the brain doesn't mean you can stop using your head: A primer and set of first principles. *Journal of Personality and Social Psychology, 85,* 650–661.

Cacioppo, J. T., Bush, L. K., & Tassinary, L. G. (1992). Microexpressive facial actions as a function of affective stimuli: Replication and extension. *Personality and Social Psychology Bulletin, 18, 515–526.*

Cacioppo, J. T., Crites, S. L., Jr., Berntson, G. G., & Coles, M. G. H. (1993). If attitudes affect how stimuli are processed, should they not affect the event-related brain potential? *Psychological Science, 4,* 108–112.

Cacioppo, J. T., Crites, S. L., & Gardner, W. L. (1996). Attitudes to the right: Evaluative processing is associated with lateralized late positive event-related brain potentials. *Personality and Social Psychology Bulletin, 22,* 1205–1219.

Cacioppo, J. T., Crites, S. L., Jr., Gardner, W. L., & Berntson, G. G. (1994). Bioelectrical echoes from evaluative categorizations: I. A late positive brain potential that varies as a function of trait negativity and extremity. *Journal of Personality and Social Psychology, 67,* 115–125.

Cacioppo, J. T., Gardner, W. L., & Berntson, G. B. (1997). Beyond bipolar conceptualizations and measures: The case of attitudes and evaluative space. *Personality and Social Psychology Review, 1,* 3–25.

Cacioppo, J. T., & Petty, R. E. (1979). Attitudes and cognitive response: An electrophysiological approach. *Journal of Personality and Social Psychology, 37,* 2181–2199.

Cacioppo, J. T., & Petty, R. E. (1981). Electromyograms as measures of extent and affectivity of information processing. *American Psychologist, 36,* 441–456.

Cacioppo, J. T., Petty, R. E., Losch, M. E., & Kim, H. S. (1986). Electromyographic activity over facial muscle regions can differentiate the valence and intensity of affective reactions. *Journal of Personality and Social Psychology, 50,* 260–268.

Cacioppo, J. T., & Sandman, C. A. (1981). Psychophysiological functioning, cognitive responding, and attitudes. In R. E. Petty, T. M. Ostrom, & T. C. Brock (Eds.), *Cognitive responses in persuasion* (pp. 81–104). Hillsdale, NJ: Erlbaum.

Cacioppo, J. T., & Tassinary, L. G. (1990). Inferring psychological significance from physiological signals. *American Psychologist, 45*, 16–28.

Canli, T., Sivers, H., Whitfield, S. L., Gotlib, I. H., & Gabrieli, J. D. E. (2002). Amygdala response to happy faces as a function of extraversion. *Science, 296*, 2191.

Carretié, L., Martín-Loeches, M., Hinojosa, J. A., & Mercado, F. (2001). Emotion and attention interactions studied through event-related potentials. *Journal of Cognitive Neuroscience, 13*(8), 1109–1128.

Carretié, L., Mercado, F., Tapia, M., & Hinojosa, J. A. (2001). Emotion, attention, and the "negativitiy bias," studied through event-related potentials. *International Journal of Psychophysiology, 41*, 75–85.

Clark, V. P., & Hillyard, S. A. (1996). Spatial selective attention affects early extrastriate but not striate components of the visual evoked potential. *Journal of Cognitive Neuroscience, 8*, 387–402.

Cook, E. W., Hawk, L. W., Jr., Davis, T. L., & Stevenson, V. E. (1991). Affective individual differences and startle reflex modulation. *Journal of Abnormal Psychology, 100*, 5–13.

Crawford, L. E., & Cacioppo, J. T. (2002). Learning where to look for danger: Integrating affective and spatial information. *Psychological Science, 13*, 449–453.

Crites, S. L., Jr., & Cacioppo, J. T. (1996). Electrocortical differentiation of evaluative and nonevaluative categorizations. *Psychological Science, 7*, 318–321.

Crites, S. L., Jr., Cacioppo, J. T., Gardner, W. L., & Berntson, G. G. (1995). Bioelectrical echoes from evaluative categorizations: II. A late positive brain potential that varies as a function of attitude registration rather than attitude report. *Journal of Personality and Social Psychology, 68*, 997–1013.

Cunningham, W. A., Johnson, M. K., Gatenby, J. C., Gore, J. C., & Banaji, M. R. (2003). Neural components of social evaluation. *Journal of Personality and Social Psychology, 85*, 639–649.

Cunningham, W. A., Johnson, M. K., Raye, C. L., Gatenby, J. C., Gore, J. C., & Banaji, M. R. (2004). Separable neural components in the processing of Black and White faces. *Psychological Science, 5*, 806–813.

Cunningham, W. A., Raye, C. L., & Johnson, M. K. (2004). Implicit and explicit evaluation: fMRI correlates of valence, emotional intensity, and control in the processing of attitudes. *Journal of Cognitive Neuroscience, 16*, 1717–1729.

Dawson, M. E., Schell, A. M., & Filion, D. L. (2000). The electrodermal system. In J. T. Cacioppo, L. G. Tassinary, & G. G Berntson (Eds.), *Handbook of psychophyiology* (2nd ed., pp. 200–223). Cambridge, UK: Cambridge University Press.

Devine, P. G., Plant, E. A., Amodio, D. M., Harmon-Jones, E., & Vance, S. L. (2002). The regulation of explicit and implicit race bias: The role of motivations to respond without prejudice. *Journal of Personality and Social Psychology, 82*(5), 835–848.

Dimberg, U. (1986). Facial reactions to fear-relevant and fear-irrelevant stimuli. *Biological Psychology, 23*, 153–161.

Dimberg, U., Thunberg, M., & Elmehed, K. (2000). Unconscious facial reactions to emotional facial expressions. *Psychological Science, 11,* 86–89.

Donchin, E. (1981). Surprise! . . . Surprise? *Psychophysiology, 18,* 493–513.

Ensari, N., Kenworthy, J. B., Urban, L., Canales, C. J., Vasquez, E., Kim, D., et al. (2004). Negative affect and political sensitivity in crossed categorization: Self-reports versus EMG. *Group Processes and Intergroup Relations, 7,* 55–75.

Esteves, F., Parra, C., Dimberg, U., & Öhman, A. (1994). Nonconscious associative learning: Pavlovian conditioning of skin conductance responses to masked fear-relevant facial stimuli. *Psychophysiology, 31,* 375–385.

Etcoff, N. L. (1989). Asymmetries on recognition of emotion. In F. Boller & J. Grafman (Eds.), *Handbook of neuropsychology* (Vol 3, pp. 363–382). Amsterdam: Elsevier.

Fabiani, M., Gratton, G., & Coles, M. G. H. (2000). Event-related brain potentials. In J. T. Cacioppo, L. G. Tassinary, & G. G Berntson (Eds.), *Handbook of psychophysiology* (2nd ed., pp 53–84). Cambridge, UK: Cambridge University Press.

Fazio, R. H., Jackson, J. R., Dunton, B. C., & Williams, C. J. 1995). Variability in automatic activation as an unobtrusive measure of racial attitudes: A bona fide pipeline? *Journal of Personality and Social Psychology, 69,* 1013–1027.

Fazio, R. H., Sanbonmatsu, D. M., Powell, M. C., & Kardes, F. C. (1986). On the automatic activation of attitudes. *Journal of Personality and Social Psychology, 50,* 229–238.

Fere, C. (1888). Note on changes in electrical resistance under the effect of sensory stimulation and emotion. *Comptes Rendus des Seances de la Societe de Biologie, Series 9, 5,* 217–219.

Filion, D. L., Dawson, M. E., & Schell, A. M. (1993). Modification of the acoustic startle-reflex eyeblink: A tool for investigating early and late attentional processes. *Biological Psychology, 35,* 185–200.

Filion, D. L., Dawson, M. E., & Schell, A. M. (1998). The psychological significance of human startle eyeblink modification: A review. *Biological Psychology, 47,* 1–43.

Fowles, D. C. (1986). The eccrine system. In M. G. H. Coles, E. Donchin, & S. W. Porges (Eds.), *Psychophysiology: Systems, processes, and applications.* New York: Guilford Press.

Gehring, W. J., Gratton, G., Coles, M. G. H., & Donchin, E. (1992). Probability effects on stimulus evaluation and response processes. *Journal of Experimental Psychology: Human Perception and Performance, 18,* 198–216.

Graham, F. K. (1975). The more or less startling effects of weak pre-stimulation. *Psychophysiology, 12,* 238–248.

Gray, H. M., Ambady, N., Lowenthal, W. T., & Deldin, P. (2004). P300 as an index of attention to self-relevant stimuli. *Journal of Experimental Social Psychology, 40,* 216–224.

Greenwald, A. G., & Banaji, M. R. 1995). Implicit social cognition: Attitudes, self-esteem, and stereotypes. *Psychological Review, 102,* 4–27.

Greenwald, A. G., McGhee, D. E., & Schwartz, J. L. K. (1998). Measuring individual differences in implicit cognition: The Implicit Association Test. *Journal of Personality and Social Psychology, 74,* 1464–1480.

Greenwald, M. K., Cook, E. W., & Lang, P. J. (1989). Affective judgment and psychophysiological response: Dimensional covariation in the evaluation of pictorial stimuli. *Journal of Psychophysiology, 3,* 51–64.

Hamann, S., & Mao, H. (2002). Positive and negative emotional verbal stimuli elicit activity in the left amygdala. *NeuroReport, 13,* 15–19.

Hart, A. J., Whalen, P. J., Sin, L. M., McInerney, S. C., Fischer, H., & Rauch, S. L. (2000). Differential response in the human amygdala to racial outgroup vs. ingroup face stimuli. *NeuroReport, 11,* 2351–2355.

Ito, T. A., & Cacioppo, J. T. (1999). The psychophysiology of utility appraisals. In D. Kahneman, E. Diener, & N. Schwarz (Eds.), *Well-being: The foundations of hedonic psychology* (pp. 470–488). New York: Russell Sage Foundation.

Ito, T. A., & Cacioppo, J. T. (2000). Electrophysiological evidence of implicit and explicit categorization processes. *Journal of Experimental Social Psychology, 36,* 660–676.

Ito, T. A., Larsen, J. T., Smith, N. K., & Cacioppo, J. T. (1998). Negative information weighs more heavily on the brain: The negativity bias in evaluative categorizations. *Journal of Personality and Social Psychology, 75,* 887–900.

Ito, T. A., Thompson, E., & Cacioppo, J. T. (2004). Tracking the timecourse of social perception: The effects of racial cues on event-related brain potentials. *Personality and Social Psychology Bulletin, 30,* 1267–1280.

Jezzard, P., Matthews, P. M., & Smith, S. M. (2001). *Functional MRI: An introduction to methods.* New York: Oxford University Press.

Johnson, M. K., & Reeder, J. A. 1997). Consciousness as meta-processing. In J. D. Cohen & J. W. Schooler (Eds.), *Scientific approaches to consciousness* (pp. 261–293). Mahwah, NJ: Erlbaum.

LaBar, K. S., Gatenby, J. C., Gore, J. C., LeDoux, J. E., & Phelps, E. A. (1998). Human amygdala activation during conditioned fear acquisition and extinction: A mixed-trial fMRI study. *Neuron, 20,* 937–945.

Landis, C. (1930). Psychology and the psychogalvanic reflex. *Psychological Review, 37,* 381–398.

Lang, P. J. (1995). The emotion probe: Studies of motivation and attention. *American Psychologist, 50,* 372–385.

Lang, P. J., Bradley, M. M., & Cuthbert, B. N. (1990). Emotion, attention, and the startle reflex. *Psychological Review, 97,* 377–395.

Lang, P. J., Bradley, M. M., & Cuthbert, B. N. (1992). A motivational analysis of emotion: Reflex-cortex connections. *Psychological Science, 3,* 44–49.

Larsen, J. T., Norris, C. J., & Cacioppo, J. T. (2003). Effects of positive and negative affect on eletromyographic activity over zygomaticus major and corrugator supercilii. *Psychophysiology, 40,* 776–785.

LeDoux, J. E. (2000). Emotion circuits in the brain. *Annual Review of Neuroscience, 23,* 155–184.

Lipp, O. V., Sheridan, J., & Siddle, D. A. T. (1994). Human blink startle during aversive and nonaversive Pavlovian conditioning. *Journal of Experimental Psychology: Animal Behavior Processes, 20,* 380–389.

Mahaffey, A. L., Bryan, A., & Hutchison, K. E. (2005a). Sex differences in affective responses to homoerotic stimuli: Evidence for an unconscious bias among heterosexual men, but not heterosexual women. *Archives of Sexual Behavior, 35, 537–545.*

Mahaffey, A. L., Bryan, A., & Hutchison, K. E. (2005b). Using startle eye blink to measure the affective component of antigay bias. *Basic and Applied Social Psychology, 35, 537–545.*

Marinelli, R. P., & Kelz, J. W. (1973). Anxiety and attitudes toward visibly disabled persons. *Rehabilitation Counseling Bulletin, 16, 198–205.*

McGuigan, F. J. (1970). Covert oral behavior during silent language performance of language tasks. *Psychological Bulletin, 74, 309–326.*

Mendes, W. B., Blascovich, J., Lickel, B., & Hunter, S. (2002). Challenge and threat during social interactions with white and black men. *Personality and Social Psychology Bulletin, 28, 939–952.*

Menon, R. S., & Kim, S. (1999). Spatial and temporal limits in cognitive neuroimaging with fMRI. *Trends in Cognitive Sciences, 3, 207–216.*

Morris, J. S., Frith, C. D., Perrett, D. I., Rowland, D., Young, A. W., Calder, A. J., et al. (1996). A differential neural response in the human amygdala to fearful and happy facial expressions. *Nature, 383, 812–815.*

Nisbett, R. E., & Wilson, T. D. (1977). Telling more than we can know: Verbal reports on mental processes. *Psychological Review, 84, 231–259.*

Norris, C. J., Chen, E. E., Zhu, D. C., Small, S. L., & Cacioppo, J. T. (2004). The interaction of social and emotional processes in the brain. *Journal of Cognitive Neuroscience, 16, 1818–1829.*

Phelps, E. A., Cannistraci, C. J., & Cunningham, W. A. (2003). Intact performance on an indirect measure of race bias following amygdala damage. *Neuropsychologia, 41, 203–208.*

Phelps. E. A., O'Connor, K. J., Cunningham, W. A., Funayama, E. S., Gatenby, J. C., Gore, J. C., et al. (2000). Performance on indirect measures of race evaluation predicts amygdala activation. *Journal of Cognitive Neuroscience, 12, 729–738.*

Rankin, R. E., & Campbell, D. T. (1955). Galvanic skin response to negro and white experimenters. *Journal of Abnormal and Social Psychology, 51, 30–33.*

Sarter, M., Berntson, G. G., & Cacioppo, J. T. (1996). Brain imaging and cognitive neuroscience: Toward strong inferences in attributing function to structure. *American Psychologist, 51, 13–21.*

Savoy, R. A. (2001). History and future directions of human brain mapping and functional neuroimaging. *Acta Psychologica, 107, 9–42.*

Scofield, W. B., & Milner, B. (1957). Loss of recent memory after bilateral hippocampal lesions. *Journal of Neurology, Neurosurgery, and Psychiatry, 20, 11–21.*

Schwartz, G. E., Fair, P. L., Salt, P., Mandel, M. R., & Klerman, G. L. (1976a). Facial expression and imagery in depression: An eletromyographic study. *Psychosomatic Medicine, 38(5), 337–347.*

Schwartz, G. E., Fair, P. L., Salt, P., Mandel, M. R., & Klerman, G. L. (1975b). Facial muscle patterning to affective imagery in depressed and nondepressed subjects. *Science, 192, 489–491.*

Shields, S. A., & Harriman, R. E. (1984). Fear of male homosexuality: Cardiac responses of low and high homonegative males. *Journal of Homosexuality, 10,* 53–67.

Smith, N. K., Cacioppo, J. T., Larsen, J. T., & Chartrand, T. L. 2003). May I have your attention, please: Electrocortical responses to positive and negative stimuli. *Neuropsychologia, 41,* 171–183.

Tranel, D., & Damasio, A. R. (1985). Knowledge without awareness: An autonomic index of facial recognition by prosopagnosics. *Science, 228,* 1453–1454.

Tucker, D. M., & Frederick, S. L. (1989). Emotion and brain lateralization. In H. Wagner & A. Manstead (Eds.), *Handbook of social psychophysiology* (pp. 27–70). Chichester, UK: Wiley.

Vanman, E. J., Boehmelt, A. H., Dawson, M. E., & Schell, A. M. (1996). The varying time courses of attentional and affective modulation of the startle eyeblink reflex. *Psychophysiology, 33,* 691–697.

Vanman, E. J., Paul, B. Y., Ito, T. A., & Miller, N. (1997). The modern face of prejudice and structural features that moderate the effect of cooperation on affect. *Journal of Personality and Social Psychology, 73,* 941–959.

Wallin, B. G. (1981). Sympathetic nerve activity underlying electrodermal and cardiovascular reactions in man. *Psychophysiology, 18,* 470–476.

Whalen, P. J. (1998). Fear, vigilance, and ambiguity: Initial neuroimaging studies of the human amygdala. *Current Directions in Psychological Science, 7*(6), 177–188.

Whalen, P. J., Rauch, S. L., Etcoff, N. L., McInerney, S. C., Lee, M. B., & Jenike, M. A. (1998). Masked presentations of emotional facial expressions modulate amygdala activity without explicit knowledge. *Journal of Neuroscience, 18*(1), 411–418.

Winkielman, P., & Cacioppo, J. T. (2001). Mind at ease puts a smile on the face: Psychophysiological evidence that processing facilitation elicits positive affect. *Journal of Personality and Social Psychology, 81*(6), 989–1000.

Winston, J. S., Strange, B. A., O'Doherty, J., & Dolan, R. J. (2002). Automatic and intentional brain responses during evaluation of trustworthiness of faces. *Nature Neuroscience, 5*(3), 277–283.

Wittenbrink, B., Judd, C. M., & Park, B. (1997). Evidence of racial prejudice at the implicit level and its relationship with questionnaire measures. *Journal of Personality and Social Psychology, 72,* 262–274.

Wright, R. A., & Kirby, L. D. (2003). Cardiovascular correlates of challenge and threat appraisals: A critical examination of the biopsychosocial analysis. *Personality and Social Psychology Review, 7,* 216–233.

Yamaguchi, S., & Knight, R. T. (1991). Anterior and posterior association cortex contributions to the somatosensory P300. *Journal of Neuroscience, 11,* 2039–2054.

Zajonc, R. B., & McIntosh, D. N. (1992). Emotions research: Some promising questions and some questionable promises. *Psychological Science, 3,* 70–74.

Zald, D. H., & Pardo, J. V. (1997). Emotion, olfaction, and the human amygdala: Amygdala activation during aversive olfactory stimulation. *Proceedings of the National Academy of Sciences of the United States of America, 94,* 4119–4124.

6 Understanding Social Evaluations

What We Can (and Cannot) Learn from Neuroimaging

Andreas Olsson
Elizabeth A. Phelps

The behavioral and psychophysiological methods that have been utilized over the past 50 years to investigate social evaluations have been developed and refined over centuries. In contrast, although there has been no lack of interest, it is only during the past two decades that modern neuroscience has allowed us to begin relating these measures to processes occurring in the central nervous system. In spite of their relatively recent emergence, neuroimaging techniques, in particular functional magnetic resonance imaging (fMRI), have made a significant contribution to our understanding of the neural systems involved in the perception and evaluation of social stimuli. Together with advances in behavioral research on humans and an increased awareness of cross-species similarities contributed by evolutionary paradigms, this knowledge plays a key role in the construction of a mechanistic model that describes and explains the way humans are relating to their social environment.

Here, we provide a commentary on how recent findings in neuroscience, gained through the application of neuroimaging techniques, especially fMRI, have affected our understanding of the neural mechanisms supporting social evaluations. We focus on findings that are tightly related to phenomena on other levels of explanation, such as the psychological and behavioral. Although the prospect of linking descriptions on a neural level directly to complex social phenomena currently seems remote, the aim should be to establish firm ties between these explanatory levels. Making sure that descriptions of human behavior at different levels are compatible with each other through rigorous experimentation will promote a more reliable and complete science of human social behavior. However, in spite of such optimism, it is important to be aware of the limitations of neural data in describing and predicting behavior. For example, even though we can use neural responses to make limited predictions about the probability of simple behaviors, such as the likelihood of recognizing a particular individual face in a recognition task (Mitchell, Macrae, & Banaji, 2004) or responding more slowly when categorizing a racial outgroup face than an ingroup face (Phelps et al., 2000), these data have a restricted bearing on more complex social evaluations and behaviors. It would therefore, for example, be wrong to claim that information about neural functions can be used to predict social behaviors more accurately than information derived from examining behavior itself (Phelps & Thomas, 2003).

All measures provided by neuroimaging tools can be described as "implicit" in the sense that, like measures of metabolic-dependent activity in other bodily organs, they contain a richness of signals that are neither consciously accessible nor under the intentional control of the responder. In addition, within the boundaries of their sensitivity to activity linked to neural processes, imaging measures do not distinguish between the limited range of processes that are explicitly represented in a person's awareness, and the larger share of neural events coding for information and information processing that is not accessible to explicit awareness. They simply estimate all events taking place within a given temporal and spatial range. It is then the difficult task of the researcher to design experimental conditions that aim at distinguishing neural events corresponding to explicit and implicit processes, respectively.

Studies investigating the neural mechanisms underlying social evaluations in humans can be broadly divided into two classes: (1) research examining the influence of physical features of the social stimulus, such as the emotional expression or race of a face, and (2) research examining the influence of added information about the target individual's traits or past behaviors, which may be transmitted indirectly through biographical information or direct interaction.

We begin by addressing findings in the first category, which represents the major part of the research aiming to understand the neural correlates of implicit social evaluations, as well as the efforts to control them. The main strength of this first category of work is the high level of control that can be exerted over the manipulated variables, which is helping to constrain the interpretations of the observed brain activations in terms of meaningful psychological and behavioral mechanisms. However, whereas this promotes tighter links between explanatory levels, it lacks in ecological validity. Social evaluations practiced outside the laboratory are almost invariably more complex. The second line of research comprises experimental advances that aim at creating more naturalistic social settings in which the neural bases of social evaluations can be studied. These two approaches are complementary and each is important in its own right, but they are especially fruitful when used together to integrate descriptions of neural events with descriptions of psychological and behavioral phenomena. By means of integration, neural descriptions will help to constrain higher-level theorizing, whereas psychological theories, in turn, will help to formulate meaningful hypotheses to be tested.

EVALUATING THE GOOD AND BAD IN THE FACE

Most behavioral work on social evaluations has been examining responses to social stimuli associated with values on a continuum ranging from good to bad. A common way of describing this polarized dimension is in terms of values that motivate either approach or withdrawal behavior (Davidson, Ekman, Saron, Senulis, & Friesen, 1990), a distinction that aligns well with data on the neural foundation of motivated behaviors across animals (LeDoux, 2000; Schultz, 2006). In addition to a large body of research on nonhuman animals, studies on patients and imaging work in healthy humans have contributed to the rich literature that exists on the mapping of the neural functions supporting approach and withdrawal behaviors. Many of the neural components critical for approach and withdrawal responses in processing appetitive and aversive stimuli, respectively, generally apply to behaviors elicited by both social and nonsocial stimuli (Breiter, Aharon, Kahneman, Dale, & Shizgal, 2001; Öhman & Mineka, 2001). However, as discussed below, social evaluations have been argued to recruit a unique set of additional neural functions. Because negatively valenced states are easier to experimentally induce and measure, research of this kind dominates the field. Following this, the majority of findings reviewed here will be drawn from this pool of studies.

The amygdala, an almond-shaped structure in the temporal lobes, is known to play a key role in a range of evaluative responses. Since the seminal findings by Klüver and Bucy (1939), reporting severe impairments in a variety of social and emotional behaviors in monkeys following bilateral temporal lobectomy, this structure has become the most studied region in a neural network known to support learning and evaluation of aversive stimuli (Phelps & LeDoux, 2005). The amygdala has been shown to be critical to the acquisition, storage, and implicit (physiological) expression of conditioned fear (LaBar, Gatenby, Gore, LeDoux, & Phelps, 1998; LaBar, LeDoux, Spencer, & Phelps, 1995; LeDoux, 2000) and, more recently, to be involved in indirectly attained fears transmitted through social observation and verbal communication (Olsson, Nearing, & Phelps, 2006; Phelps et al., 2001).

The speedy approach of a predator or the swift alternation of facial expressions, signaling a change from benevolent to adversarial intentions in a conspecific, illustrates rapidly occurring changes that may have fatal implications for the individual if not responded to adaptively. Thus, it has been argued that in response to such environmental challenges, a neural system for rapid detection of potentially harmful cues in the environment, centered on the amygdala, has evolved (Adolphs, 2006; Anderson, 2005; de Gelder, Snyder, Greve, Gerard, & Hadjikhani, 2004; LeDoux, 2000; Öhman & Mineka, 2001; Whalen et al., 1998). This system is thought to quickly assemble perceptual and attentional resources to allow for a more detailed analysis of the situation and to initiate an appropriate behavior. Consistent with this assumption, the processing of emotionally significant properties of social stimuli, known to involve the amygdala, has been reported to influence early visual and attentional processing (Anderson & Phelps, 2001; Morris, Öhman, & Dolan, 1998a; Phelps, Ling, & Carrasco, 2006; Vuilleumier, Richardson, Armony, Driver, & Dolan, 2004) and action representations (de Gelder et al., 2004). However, the precise mechanisms underlying the amygdala's influence on a distributed network of cortical areas remains unclear and is currently attracting a considerable amount of research and debate (McGaugh, 2004; Phelps, 2006). Nevertheless, it is clear that this system for detection of potentially threatening stimuli contributes important information to the rest of the cognitive system at an early stage of the evaluative process. Indeed, research shows that social stimuli can automatically access this brain system, even in the absence of the perceiving individual's conscious awareness of their presence.

For example, a series of studies by Öhman and colleagues has demonstrated conditioned responses as measured by physiological arousal to subliminally presented images of angry faces that had been previously paired with a shock (e.g., Soares & Öhman, 1993). More recent imaging studies, employing a similar technique to present facial stimuli without the subjects' conscious awareness, have highlighted the role of the amygdala (Cunningham et al., 2004; Morris et al., 1998b; Whalen et al., 1998). Morris et al. (1998b) showed that the amygdala discriminated between both supra- and subliminally presented aversively conditioned angry faces, when another angry face served as the control stimuli. Using a comparable presentation technique, Whalen and colleagues found that fearful faces elicited greater amygdala activation than happy faces when presented both supra- and subliminally (Whalen et al., 1998).

The link between the amygdala and implicit responses is substantiated by research on patients with amygdala damage, showing impairment in implicit emotional (physiological) responding to fully visible stimuli that acquired their aversive properties through fear conditioning (Bechara et al., 1995; LaBar et al., 1995). However, the ability to express an explicit understanding of the learning contingencies remains intact in spite of amygdala lesion. In contrast, patients with damage to the hippocampal complex, another temporal brain structure known to be involved in the formation of episodic memories, but whose amygdalae are intact, lack the explicit awareness of the contingency learning but retain their implicit emotional responses to the conditioned stimuli (Bechara et al., 1995; LaBar & Phelps, 2005). Other research targeting the neural bases of the conscious "feeling" component of emotional evaluations has implicated somatosensory cortices, such as the anterior insular (Adolphs, 2006; Critchley, Wiens, Rotshtein, Öhman, & Dolan, 2004).

Together, these findings suggest that different, but closely interacting brain structures critically involved in the processing of explicit versus implicit information can be functionally dissociated. These neural dissociations are reminiscent of dissociations reported between explicit versus implicit behavioral measures (Phelps & Banaji, 2006). Although there are still relatively few, an increasing number of studies are now directly linking specific brain regions with implicit physiological and behavioral assessments of social evaluations (Cunningham et al., 2004; Phelps et al., 2000).

Many of the studies on the role of the amygdala have suggested that this neural structure is particularly sensitive to facial stimuli expressing fear (Adolphs et al., 2005; Whalen et al., 1998), although it may also respond to other facial expressions under specific circumstances (Anderson, Christoff, Panitz, DeRosa, & Gabrieli, 2003;

Canli, Sivers, Whitfield, Gotlib, & Gabrieli, 2002; Kim, Somerville, Johnstone, Alexander, & Whalen, 2003). A recent study by Adolphs and colleagues (2005) suggests that the amygdala not only is sensitive to fear and other emotional expressions, but may also contribute to the generation of actions favoring the detection of fear. This study reports that the inability to recognize fear expressions in a patient with bilateral amygdala lesions is due to the lack of making spontaneous use of information in the eye region—a region that is particularly diagnostic for fear expressions. Interestingly, when the patient was explicitly instructed to look at the eye region, she performed entirely normally on a fear recognition task.

Apart from expanding our understanding of the function of the amygdala, this study also underscores the complexity and potential pitfalls in closely aligning behaviors with certain neural functions. Certain brain circuits may simply serve multiple functions, some of them more general than what we initially would expect based on earlier data. For example, as suggested by the study by Adolphs and colleagues (2005), the amygdala may serve a more general function of exploring emotionally relevant cues in the social environment, a domain that is inherently interactive and that demands rapid and concerted responding of different cognitive, emotional, and motor functions. In order to better specify the functions subserved by particular brain regions, it is imperative that, when possible, imaging studies (which are inherently correlational) are followed up by lesions studies that can determine whether a particular brain region is necessarily involved in a given task.

EVALUATING SAME-RACE AND OTHER-RACE FACES

The emotional expressiveness in faces has been the most widely manipulated variable in studies exploring the neural bases of social evaluations. However, recently there have been investigations of evaluation linked to other facial attributes, among them the racial belonging of a face (Cunningham et al., 2004; Hart et al., 2000; Lieberman, Hariri, Jarcho, Eisenberger, & Bookheimer, 2005; Phelps et al., 2000). Partly because of progress made in social psychology in developing behavioral and psychophysiological measures of biases dependent on racial stereotypes (see Phelps & Banaji, 2006), these questions have recently received increased attention from cognitive neuroscientists.

It has been demonstrated that the amygdala shows greater activation to racial outgroup versus ingroup faces (Cunningham et al.,

2004; Hart et al., 2000). Consistent with research suggesting that the amygdala may mediate some forms of nonconscious evaluation (Phelps & LeDoux, 2005), the strength of this amygdala response has been linked to indirect, but not direct, measures of race bias (Cunningham et al., 2004; Phelps et al., 2000). Interestingly, although the amygdala seems to be automatically engaged in these tasks (Cunningham et al., 2004), research has shown that its response can be moderated or altered through either consciously applying control strategies (Amodio et al., 2004; Cunningham et al., 2004) or by altering the task demands to focus on different aspects of the stimuli, such as individual traits (Wheeler & Fiske, 2005) and the verbal label of the race (Lieberman et al., 2005). Following a growing interest in the neural correlates of racially based evaluations, recent studies have attempted to outline the neural mechanisms involved in controlling and modulating negatively biased evaluations, which may involve the interaction of the amygdala and regions of the prefrontal cortex (Amodio et al., 2004; Cunningham et al., 2004). It remains unknown how or if controlled strategies can be made to operate unconsciously (Richeson et al., 2003).

Facial characteristics indicating racial group not only influence aspects of evaluation, but also later memory for a face. Research in psychology has shown that people more readily recognize faces of their own race (e.g., Chance & Goldstein, 1996). This effect, called the *same-race advantage*, is in line with other studies arguing that individuals are immediately and automatically categorized based on their belonging to a certain racial group (Stangor, Lynch, Duan, & Glass, 1992). Research has also reported that racial group information can affect the way we learn to associate others with an emotional event. For example, a recent study has shown that a fear response to a racial outgroup member can be more persistent than to a racial group ingroup member (Olsson, Ebert, Banaji, & Phelps, 2005).

Research on the neural bases of face perception has suggested that a specific portion of the inferior temporal lobe, the fusiform face area (FFA), is specialized in the processing of human faces (Kanwisher, 2000; but see Gauthier, Skudlarski, Gore, & Anderson, 2000). An fMRI study examining the perception of racial outgroup versus ingroup faces found that ingroup faces elicited significantly greater activation in the FFA than outgroup faces (Golby, Gabrieli, Chiao, & Eberhardt, 2001). These data indicate a specialization of visual processing for facial information that is dependent on racial group belonging. It is possible that this is the result of the different amounts of exposure that people have to certain groups, although it is also possible that social learning of the cultural definition of ingroup versus outgroup may mediate this effect (Eberhardt, personal communication).

Although there are now a number of neuroimaging studies investigating the neural systems underlying the processing of racial ingroup versus outgroup members, several questions remain. It has yet to be determined if the observed effects are due to the physical dissimilarities of faces that vary by race, cultural biases and stereotypes of racial groups, or simply the designation of ingroup versus outgroup. Only through the sophisticated experimental manipulations of these variables will we be able to understand the significance of these initial results.

EVALUATING TRAITS AND MENTAL STATES

Many of the basic aversive evaluations discussed above seem to align fairly well with the research on evaluative processes in nonhuman animals. However, because both the complexity of social interactive patterns and the cognitive capacity in humans far exceed those of other animals (and these two components may have coevolved), humans' evaluations of each other often involve more complex judgments that are detached from the physical features of the target individual. Research has shown that even thin temporal slices of visual information can result in social evaluations that are quite sophisticated and surprisingly reliable. For example, a recent study shows that a viewing time as short as 100 msec allows a person to form an impression about a target person's likeability, trustworthiness, competence, and aggressiveness that is highly correlated with impressions made in the absence of time constraints (Willis & Todorov, 2006), which resonates well with previous imaging studies reporting that the amygdala is involved in the automatic evaluation of trustworthiness (Winston, Strange, O'Doherty, & Dolan, 2002). That some of these immediate evaluations can have real and important implications outside the laboratory is evidenced by the fact that an impression of competence formed about a face within 1 sec has been shown to predict U.S. congressional elections better than chance (Todorov, Mandisodza, Goren, & Hall, 2005). Still, other research has demonstrated that peoples' evaluations of social stimuli can be subjected to manipulation without their noticing, suggesting that the internal representation of the evaluated stimuli may not be as stable as previously thought (Johansson, Hall, Sikström, & Olsson, 2005).

Since the time of Phineas Gage, one of the most well-cited cases of damage to the prefrontal cortex (PFC) in the history of neurology, which was recorded in the mid-19th century, we know that subparts of the frontal region are important for social evaluations and behaviors (Damasio, 1994). These evaluations may include inferred conclusions about another person's mental cognitive and emotional states or intentions (Blakemore & Decety, 2001; Frith & Frith, 2006). A growing literature suggest that the medial portion of the PFC is especially important in reasoning about other peoples' minds (Gallagher & Frith, 2003; Mitchell, Heatherton, & Macrae, 2002; Ochsner et al., 2001). The attribution of emotional states to others seems to recruit additional regions in the dorsal portions of the PFC as well as the anterior insula (Morrison, Lloyd, di Pellegrino, & Roberts, 2004; Olsson et al., 2006; Singer et al., 2004). Because these activations overlap with regions that are involved in the personal experience of the corresponding emotional state, much theoretical and empirical work is currently focused on the role of mental simulation as a basis for social evaluations and the extent to which this ability is dependent on mirror neurons or mirror circuits—neural assemblies representing both one's own and others' mental states (Adolphs, 2006; Gallese, Keysers, & Rizzolatti, 2004; Preston & deWaal, 2001). The way these mentalizing functions interact with more basic evaluative processes, such as those dependent on the amygdala, remains to be explored.

Finally, although different regions in the PFC have been attributed specific social functions, it still remains a possibility that these functions are subserved by more general mental abilities recruited in tasks involving complex thinking and which are known to depend on overlapping areas of the PFC (Adolphs, 2006; Ridderinkhof, Ullsperger, Crone, & Nieuwenhuis, 2004). However, regardless of the degree of specialization found in the PFC, social variables may influence the operation of mental functions, traditionally investigated as independent processes, such as attention, visual perception, learning, and memory, in a way similar to what has been claimed for emotional factors (and it can be argued that social variables are emotional per se), may influence the operation of other mental functions that have traditionally been investigated as independent processes, such as attention, visual perception, and learning and memory.

EVALUATING SOCIAL INFORMATION BEYOND THE FACE

The research reviewed above covers mainly evaluations of still images depicting faces. The second class of neuroimaging work on social evaluations discussed here involves adding socially relevant information about the individual (real or fictive) who is the target of evaluation. Although simple stimuli, such as faces displaying discrete emotional expressions and racial features, are important for well-controlled experimentation, the ecological validity is admittedly low. Few of these simple stimuli match the interactive and meaningful features that characterize a natural social context. Fortunately, new imaging methods and refined experimental designs now allow us to extend the investigation into the interactive realm (Montague et al., 2002). As alluded to above, social cognition does not consist of mere reactions to the social environment, "it is instrumental" (Adolphs, 2006, p. 32). Depending on our social goals, we often need more information than what is available through a sole visual assessment, and different nonverbal and verbal strategies may be used to probe other individuals to gain additional information. Behavioral research has demonstrated that quite complex social interactions can be experimentally induced without the involved agents being aware of their causes (Chartrand & Bargh, 1999; Kosfeld, Heinrichs, Zak, Fischbacher, & Fehr, 2005).

Like those of other social animals, most of our human daily activities are either directly or indirectly dependent on others. Social cooperation and competition are universal phenomena that have been extensively studied by both biologists and economists. One analytic tool that is often used to study strategic interaction between social agents when resources are limited is to model the interaction as a game (for an overview on game theory, and its relevance to experimental research in behavioral science, see Camerer, 2003). Although the designs of most games are based on oversimplifications of everyday social interactions, they do capture some fundamental elements of human interaction that are based on social evaluations, such as trust, altruism, and defection. An additional advantage of using interactive games in cognitive neuroscience experiments is that the behavioral results can be interpreted in the light of a vast literature on nonhuman and human behavior in game-like situations.

In line with the different possible outcomes in a game situation, imaging research using games to model social interaction examines the neural bases of both positive (e.g., trust) and negative (e.g., distrust) social evaluations and their impact on the agent's own behavior. The information that serves as a basis for the evaluations and behavior is acquired through the biographical information presented, interaction with the target, or a combination of both. Because of its simplicity and reliance on evaluations of trust, the trust game has been most widely used in imaging studies (Delgado, Frank, & Phelps,

2005; King-Casas et al., 2005; McCabe, Houser, Ryan, Smith, & Trouard, 2001). In brief, in a trust game two or more social players are sending money back and forth in an economic interaction that is more likely to be mutually beneficial if each player acts trustworthy and evaluates the partner(s) as such (Berg, Dickhaut, & McCabe, 1995; Camerer, 2003).

A common observation is that brain systems known to be involved in reward processing more generally, including dopaminergic projection regions of the striatum and the PFC, are recruited when partners cooperate with each other (King-Casas et al., 2005; Rilling et al., 2002) or when defectors are punished (de Quervain et al., 2004). These studies suggest that cooperation feels good partly because it involves a system that promotes prosocial behaviors. A recent experiment that simultaneously scanned two interacting partners shows that the dynamic development of trust between the partners is mirrored by the activation in the reward system (Montague et al., 2002). In this study, in which anonymous partners acquired reputations through repeated trials of the trust game, responses in the striatum were modified over time, much in the same way they are modified through nonsocial trial and error learning of stimuli that predict rewards (Delgado, Miller, Inati, & Phelps, 2005).

However, the dynamics of the reward circuitry are altered not only in learning to trust another through trial and error, but also by prior knowledge of the moral characteristics of the playing partner (Delgado, Frank, & Phelps, 2005). A recent study provided subjects with information about the moral characteristics of trust game partners by describing events from the partners' lives suggesting good, bad, or neutral moral character. These simple vignettes significantly diminished the striatum's typical reward response during trial and error learning, especially for the "good" partner, suggesting that the moral information may alter the reliance on neural signals of reward important for learning through trial and error (Delgado, Frank, & Phelps, 2005). These findings provide some initial insight into why moral information may significantly alter the choices we make.

Although the responses in the reward circuitry have been the focus of most studies investigating the neural circuitry of interactive games, a number of other brain regions have been shown to be influenced by dynamic social interactions. For example, being excluded from a situation in which others are playing a game increases the recruitment of brain areas associated with experience of physical pain and disgust, such as the insular cortex and anterior cingulate (Eisenberger, Lieberman, & Williams, 2003). The medial regions of the PFC are involved when people are (or believe they are) playing games against a human rather than a computer (McCabe et al., 2001), corroborating the assumption that mental attributions may play a role in the social evaluations taking place in interactive tasks. The amygdala is observed when players are bluffing, which is likely to reflect an evaluation of the social risk of being caught defecting (Kahn et al., 2002).

These studies and others highlight the importance of investigating neural systems, characterized by interactions of specific brain regions, when exploring the neural basis of social behavior. Historically, neuroscience research has focused on investigating individual brain regions, in part because lesion studies in humans and most techniques with nonhumans do not allow for the investigation of multiple brain regions simultaneously. However, neuroimaging is one of the few techniques in which activity throughout the brain can be measured. Although, for the sake of simplicity and ease of interpretation, human neuroimaging studies often emphasize responses in specific brain areas, these regions are rarely the only ones in which changes observed. As both neuroimaging analysis techniques and our understanding of the functions of the human brain become more sophisticated, we are likely to see greater discussion of the neural *systems* of social behavior, and less emphasis on assigning complex behaviors to individual brain structures.

CONCLUSIONS

In this chapter we have attempted to provide an overview of what has been learned from neuroimaging studies of social evaluation. However, we have also highlighted a number of caveats that are important to keep in mind as the influence of neuroimaging data in our understanding of social behavior continues to grow. Neuroimaging is a correlational technique. Only by combining neuroimaging with lesion studies or animal models can we begin to understand the critical functions of brain circuits. In addition, it is not possible to interpret the behavioral significance of signals derived from neuroimaging without a sophisticated understanding of the behavior assessed and a careful experimental design. Because neuroimaging results are primarily derived from comparing responses in two or more conditions, creative and detailed experimental manipulations are critical.

The power of neuroimaging, and studies of the brain more broadly, is that these techniques both confirm assumptions about the organization of social behavior derived from psychological research and provide new insights into these behaviors. Although the constraints of these techniques make it difficult to assess complex social behaviors, such research is starting to emerge. As we progress in our efforts to take advantage of neuroimaging to understand social evaluations, advances in the psychological techniques for investigating the questions raised will become increasingly important.

REFERENCES

Adolphs, R. (2006). How do we know the minds of others?: Domain-specificity, simulation, and enactive social cognition. *Brain Research, 1079,* 25–35.

Adolphs, R., Gosselin, F., Buchanan, T. W., Tranel, D., Schyns, P., & Damasio, A. R. (2005). A mechanism for impaired fear recognition after amygdala damage. *Nature, 433,* 68–72.

Amodio, D. M., Harmon-Jones, E., Devine, P. G., Curtin, J. J., Hartley, S. L., & Covert, A. E. (2004). Neural signals for the detection of unintentional race bias. *Psychological Science, 15,* 88–93.

Anderson, A. K. (2005). Affective influences on the attentional dynamics supporting awareness. *Journal of Experimental Psychology: General, 34,* 258–281.

Anderson, A. K., Christoff, K., Panitz, D., DeRosa, E., & Gabrieli, J. D. (2003). Neural correlates of the automatic processing of threat facial signs. *Journal of Neuroscience, 23,* 5627–5633.

Anderson, A. K., & Phelps, E. A. (2001). The human amygdala supports affective modulatory influences on visual awareness. *Nature, 411,* 305–309.

Bechara, A., Tranel, D., Damasio, H., Adolphs, R., Rockland, C., & Damasio, A. R. (1995). Double dissociation of conditioning and declarative knowledge relative to the amygdala and hippocampus in humans. *Science, 269,* 1115–1118.

Berg, J., Dickhaut, J., & McCabe, K. (1995). Trust, reciprocity, and social history. *Games and Economic Behavior, 10,* 122–142.

Blakemore, S. J., & Decety, J. (2001). From the perception of action to the understanding of intention. *Nature Review Neuroscience, 2,* 561–567.

Breiter, H. C., Aharon, I., Kahneman, D., Dale, A., & Shizgal, P. (2001). Functional imaging of neural responses to expectancy and experience of monetary gains and losses. *Neuron, 30,* 619–639.

Camerer, C. (2003). *Behavioral game theory: Experiments in strategic interaction.* Princeton, NJ: Princeton University Press.

Canli, T., Sivers, H., Whitfield, S. L., Gotlib, I. H., & Gabrieli, J. D. 2002. Amygdala response to happy faces as a function of extraversion. *Science, 296,* 2191.

Chance, J. E., & Goldstein, A. G. (1996). The other-race effect and eyewitness identification. In S. L. Sporer, R. S. Malpass & G. Koeknken (Eds.), *Psychological issues in eyewitness identification.* (pp. 153–176). Mahwah, NJ: Erlbaum.

Chartrand, T. L., Bargh, J. A. (1999). The chameleon effect: the perception-behavior link and social interaction. *Journal of Personality and Social Psychology, 76,* 893–910.

Critchley, H. D., Wiens, S., Rotshtein, P., Öhman, A., & Dolan, R. J. (2004). Neural systems supporting interoceptive awareness. *Nature Neuroscience, 7,* 189–195.

Cunningham, W. A., Johnson, M. K., Raye, C. L., Chris Gatenby, J., Gore, J. C., & Banaji, M. R. (2004). Separable neural components in the processing of black and white faces. *Psychological Science, 15,* 806–313.

Damasio, A., (1994). *Descartes' error: Emotion, reason, and the human brain.* New York: Avon Books.

Davidson, R. J., Ekman, P., Saron, C. D., Senulis, J. A., & Friesen, W. V. (1990). Approach–withdrawal and cerebral asymmetry: Emotional expression and brain physiology. *Journal of Personality and Social Psychology, 58,* 330–341.

de Gelder, B., Snyder, J., Greve, D., Gerard, G., & Hadjikhani, N. 2004. Fear fosters flight: A mechanism for fear contagion when perceiving emotion expressed by a whole body. *Proceedings of the National Academy of Sciences USA, 101,* 16701–16706.

Delgado, M. R., Frank, R., & Phelps, E. A. (2005). Perception of moral character modulates the neural circuitry of reward during the trust game. *Nature Neuroscience, 8,* 1611–1618.

Delgado, M. R., Miller, M. M., Inati, S., & Phelps, E. A. (2005). An fMRI study of reward-related probability learning. *NeuroImage, 24,* 862–873.

de Quervain, D. J., Fischbacher, U., Treyer, V., Schellhammer, M., Schnyder, U., Buck, A,. et al. (2004). The neural basis of altruistic punishment. *Science, 305,* 1254–1258.

Eisenberger, N. I., Lieberman, M. D., & Williams, K. D. (2003). Does rejection hurt?: An fMRI study of social exclusion. *Science, 302,* 290–292.

Frith, C. D., & Frith, U. (2006). How we predict what other people are going to do. *Brain Research, 1079,* 36–46.

Gallagher, H. L., & Frith, C. D. (2003). Functional imaging of "theory of mind." *Trends in Cognitive Science, 7,* 77–83.

Gallese, V., Keysers, C., & Rizzolatti, G. (2004). A unifying view of the basis of social cognition. *Trends in Cognitive Science, 8,* 396–403.

Gauthier, I., Skudlarski, P., Gore, J. C., & Anderson, A. W. (2000). Expertise for cars and birds recruits brain areas involved in face recognition. *Nature Neuroscience, 3,* 191–197.

Golby, A. J., Gabrieli, J. D., Chiao, J. Y., & Eberhardt, J. L. (2001). Differential responses in the fusiform region to same-race and other-race faces. *Nature Neuroscience, 4,* 845–850.

Hart, A. J., Whalen, P. J., Shin, L. M., McInerney, S. C., Fischer, H., & Rauch, S. L. (2000). Differential response in the human amygdale to racial outgroup vs. ingroup face stimuli. *NeuroReport, 11,* 2351–2355.

Johansson, P., Hall, L., Sikström, S., & Olsson, A. (2005). Failure to detect mismatches between intention and outcome in a simple decision task. *Science, 310,* 116–119.

Kahn, I., Yeshurun, Y., Rotshtein, P., Fried, I., Ben-Bashat, D., & Hendler, T. (2002). The role of the amygdala in signaling prospective outcome of choice. *Neuron, 33,* 983–994.

Kanwisher, N. (2000). Domain specifity in face perception. *Nature Neuroscience, 3,* 759–763.

Kim, H., Somerville, L. H., Johnstone, T., Alexander, A. L., & Whalen, P. J. (2003). Inverse amygdala and medial prefrontal cortex responses to surprised faces. *NeuroReport, 14,* 2317–2322.

King-Casas, B., Tomlin, D., Anen, C., Camerer, C. F., Quartz, S. R., & Montague, P. R. (2005). Getting to know you: Reputation and trust in a two-person economic exchange. *Science, 308,* 78–83.

Klüver, H., & Bucy, P. (1939). Preliminary analysis of functioning of the temporal lobes in monkeys. *Archives of Neurological Psychiatry, 42,* 979–1000.

Kosfeld, M., Heinrichs, M., Zak, P. J., Fischbacher, U., & Fehr, E. (2005). Oxytocin increases trust in humans. *Nature, 435,* 673–676.

LaBar, K. S., Gatenby, C., Gore, J. C., LeDoux, J. E., & Phelps, E. A. (1998). Human amygdala activation during conditioned fear acquisition and extinction: A mixed trial fMRI study. *Neuron, 20,* 937–945

LaBar, K. S., LeDoux, J. E., Spencer, D. D., & Phelps, E. A. (1995). Impaired fear conditioning following unilateral temporal lobectomy in humans. *Journal of Neuroscience, 15,* 6846–6855.

LaBar, K. S., & Phelps, E. A. (2005). Reinstatement of conditioned fear in humans is context dependent and impaired in amnesia. *Behavioral Neuroscience, 119,* 677–686.

LeDoux, J. E. (2000). Emotion circuits in the brain. *Annual Review of Neuroscience, 23,* 155–184.

Lieberman, M. D., Hariri, A., Jarcho, J. M., Eisenberger, N. I, & Bookheimer, S. Y. (2005). An fMRI investigation of race-related amygdala activity in African-American and Caucasian-American individuals. *Nature Neuroscience, 8,* 720–722.

McCabe, K., Houser, D., Ryan, L., Smith, V., & Trouard, T. (2001). A functional imaging study of cooperation in two-person reciprocal exchange. *Proceedings of the National Academy of Sciences USA, 98,* 11832–11835.

McGaugh, J. L. (2004). The amygdala modulates the consolidation of memories of emotionally arousing experiences. *Annual Review of Neuroscience, 27,* 1–28.

Mitchell, J. P., Heatherton, T. F., & Macrae, C. N. (2002). Distinct neural systems subserve person and object knowledge. *Proceedings of the National Academy of Science, 99,* 15238–15243.

Mitchell, J. P., Macrae, C. N., & Banaji, M. R. (2004). Encoding-specific effects of social cognition on the neural correlates of subsequent memory. *Journal of Neuroscience, 24,* 4912–4917.

Montague, P. R., Berns, G. S., Cohen, J. D., McClure. S. M., Pagnoni, G., Dhamala, M., et al. (2002). Hyperscanning: Simultaneous fMRI during linked social interactions. *NeuroImage, 16,* 1159–1164.

Morris, J. S., Friston, K. J., Buchel, C., Frith, C. D., Young, A. W., Calder, A. J., et al. (1998b). A neuromodulatory role for the human amygdala in processing emotional facial expressions. *Brain, 121,* 47–57.

Morris, J. S., Öhman, A., & Dolan, R. J. (1998a). Conscious and unconscious emotional learning in the amygdala. *Nature, 393,* 467–470.

Morrison, I., Lloyd, D., di Pellegrino, G., & Roberts, N. (2004). Responses to pain in anterior cingulate cortex: Is empathy a multisensory issue? *Cognitive Affective Behavioral Neuroscience, 4,* 270–278.

Öhman, A., & Mineka, S. (2001). Fears, phobias, and preparedness: Toward an evolved module of fear and fear learning. *Psychological Review, 108,* 483–522.

Olsson, A., Ebert, J. P., Banaji, M. R., & Phelps, E. A. (2005). The role of social groups in the persistence of learned fear. *Science, 309,* 785–787.

Olsson, A., Nearing, K., & Phelps, E. A. (2006). *Learning by observing: neural correlates of fear learning through social observation.* Manuscript submitted for publication.

Phelps, E. A. (2002). The cognitive neuroscience of emotion. In M. S. Gazzaniga, R. B. Ivry, & G. R. Mangun (Eds.), *Cognitive neuroscience: The biology of mind* (2nd ed., pp. 536–537). New York: Norton.

Phelps, E. A. (2006). Emotion and cognition: Insights from studies of the human amygdala. *Annual Review of Psychology, 57,* 27–53.

Phelps, E. A., & Banaji, M. R. (2006). Animal models of human attitudes: Intergations across behavioral, cognitive, and social neuroscience. In J. T. Cacioppo, P. S. Visser, & C. L. Pickett (Eds.), *Social neuroscience: People thinking about thinking people* (pp. 229–243). Cambridge, MA: MIT Press.

Phelps, E. A., & LeDoux, J. E. (2005). Contributions of the amygdala to emotion processing: From animal models to human behavior. *Neuron, 48,* 175–187.

Phelps, E. A., Ling, S., & Carrasco, M. (2006). Emotion facilitates perception and potentiates the perceptual benefit of attention. *Psychological Science, 17,* 292–299.

Phelps, E. A., O'Connor, K. J., Cunningham, W. A., Funayma, E. S., Gatenby, J. C., Gore, J. C., et al. (2000). Performance on indirect measures of race evaluation predicts amygdala activity. *Journal of Cognitive Neuroscience, 12,* 1–10.

Phelps, E. A., O'Connor, K. J., Gatenby, J. C., Gore, J. C., Grillon, C., & Davis, M. (2001). Activation of the left amygdala to a cognitive representation of fear. *Nature Neuroscience, 4,* 437–441.

Phelps, E. A., & Thomas, L. A. (2003). Race, behavior and the brain: The role of neuroimaging in understanding complex human behaviors. *Political Psychology, 24,* 747–758.

Preston, S. D., & de Waal, F. B. (2001). Empathy: Its ultimate and proximate bases. *Behavioral and Brain Sciences, 25,* 1–20.

Richeson, J. A., Baird, A. A., Gordon, H. L., Heatherton, T. F., Wyland, C. L., Trawalter, S., et al. (2003). An fMRI investigation of the impact of interracial contact on executive function. *Nature Neuroscience, 6,* 1323–1328.

Ridderinkhof, K. R., Ullsperger, M., Crone, E. A., & Nieuwenhuis, S. (2004). The role of the medial frontal cortex in cognitive control. *Science, 306,* 443–447.

Rilling, J., Gutman, D., Zeh, T., Pagnoni, G., Berns, G., & Kilts, C. (2002). A neural basis for social cooperation. *Neuron, 35,* 395–405.

Schultz, W. (2006). Behavioral theories and the neurophysiology of reward. *Annual Review of Psychology, 57,* 87–115.

Singer, T., Seymour, B., O'Doherty, J., Kaube, H., Dolan, R. J., & Frith, C. D.

(2004). Empathy for pain involves the affective but not sensory components of pain. *Science, 303,* 1157–1162.

Soares, J. J., & Öhman, A. (1993). Backward masking and skin conductance responses after conditioning to nonfeared but fear-relevant stimuli in fearful subjects. *Psychophysiology, 30,* 460–466.

Stangor, C., Lynch, L., Duan, C., & Glass, B. (1992). Categorization of individuals on the basis of multiple social features. *Journal of Personality and Social Psychology, 62,* 207–218.

Todorov, A., Mandisodza, A. N., Goren, A., & Hall, C. C. (2005). Inferences of competence from faces predict election outcomes. *Science, 308,* 1623–1626.

Vuilleumier, P., Richardson, M. P., Armony, J. L., Driver, J., & Dolan, R. J. (2004). Distant influences of amygdala lesion on visual cortical activation during emotional face processing. *Nature Neuroscience, 7,* 1271–1278.

Whalen, P. J., Rauch, S. L., Etcoff, N. L., McInerney, S. C., Lee, M. B., & Jenike, M. A. (1998). Masked presentations of emotional facial expressions modulate amygdala activity without explicit knowledge. *Journal of Neuroscience, 18,* 411–418.

Wheeler, M. E., & Fiske, S. T. (2005). Controlling racial prejudice: Social-cognitive goals affect amygdale and stereotype activation. *Psychological Science, 16,* 56–63.

Willis, J., & Todorov, A. (2006). First impressions: Making up your mind after a 100-ms exposure to a face. *Psychological Science, 17,* 592–598.

Winston, J. S, Strange, B. A., O'Doherty, J., & Dolan . R. J. (2002). Automatic and intentional brain responses during evaluation of trustworthiness of faces. *Nature Neuroscience, 5,* 277–283.

Part II Critical Perspectives

7 How to Define and Examine the Implicitness of Implicit Measures

Jan De Houwer
Agnes Moors

In less then a decade, implicit measures of attitudes, stereotypes, and other cognitive constructs have become popular in research disciplines as diverse as social, clinical, health, personality, and consumer psychology. Several types of implicit measures have been developed, including reaction-time-based tasks such as the affective priming task (Fazio, Jackson, Dunton, & Williams, 1995; Fazio, Sanbonmatsu, Powell, & Kardes, 1986), the Implicit Association Test (IAT; Greenwald, McGhee, & Schwartz, 1998), and the (extrinsic) affective Simon task (De Houwer, 2003; De Houwer & Eelen, 1998). Despite the popularity of these tasks, it is often not clear what it means to say that a measure is implicit. In this chapter, we start from the definition of implicit measures that was recently provided by De Houwer (2006) and will try to make this definition more precise by linking it with the analysis of the concept *automaticity* that we recently proposed elsewhere (Moors & De Houwer, 2006). In doing so, we will try to make clear how the term *implicit measure* is linked to a variety of features of automatic processes and explain how these features can be examined in order to test the implicit nature of measures.

179

IMPLICIT MEASURES AS AUTOMATICALLY
PRODUCED MEASUREMENT OUTCOMES

The definition of implicit measures that De Houwer (2006) provided originated from the insight that the term *measure* can refer either to a measurement procedure or to a measurement outcome. Take the example of measuring how much someone weighs. There are several possible procedures for achieving this, one of which is to ask the person to step onto a weighing scale and to read the value that appears on the scale. One can say that this particular course of action constitutes a measure of weight. In this sense, the concept *measure* thus refers to a procedure, that is, to a specific set of guidelines about which actions to take. Following a measurement procedure generates a measurement outcome, for example, a numerical value of weight in terms of pounds or kilograms. One can also say that such a numerical value is a measure of weight. In that sense, the term *measure* refers to a measurement outcome.

The same analysis holds for measures of cognitive constructs such as attitudes. The term *attitude measure* can refer to a procedure, such as a particular questionnaire or reaction time task, or it can refer to the outcome of a procedure. Take the example of a racial IAT (see, e.g., Greenwald et al., 1998). As a procedure, this involves giving instructions to participants, presenting certain stimuli in a certain manner, and registering and transforming reaction times in a certain way. When one says that the racial IAT is a measure of racial attitudes, it thus refers to the fact that the racial IAT is a set of guidelines that can be followed in order to obtain an estimate of racial attitudes. Yet one can also say that the outcome of the IAT procedure (e.g., a difference between reaction times in the compatible or incompatible block or a *d* value as calculated according to the guidelines of Greenwald, Nosek, & Banaji, 2003) is a measure of racial attitudes. Hence, the score on a racial IAT is a measurement outcome that is assumed to reflect racial attitudes.

De Houwer (2006) argued that it does not make sense to use the adjective *implicit* when the concept *measure* is understood as a measurement procedure. There is nothing implicit about a measurement procedure, because it is simply an objective set of guidelines about what to do.[1] It is, however, meaningful to use the adjective *implicit* in the context of measurement outcomes. A measurement outcome is meant to reflect a certain construct, such as weight or attitudes. It can do so only by virtue of the processes by which the to-be-measured construct is translated into the outcome. For instance, the value on a weighing scale reflects the weight of the person because of certain physical and mechanical processes such as gravity and resistance.

Likewise, if someone's score on a racial IAT reflects the racial attitudes of that person, it can only be because there are certain processes by which the actual attitude is activated and somehow influences reaction time performance and thus the IAT score. De Houwer
argued that the concept *implicit measure* actually refers to the idea
that the processes by which the to-be-measured construct is translated into the measurement outcome have certain features, that is,
that they operate under certain conditions. For instance, one can say
that a measure of racial attitudes is implicit because the measurement
outcome reflects racial attitudes even though the participants are not
aware of the fact that they possess those attitudes, do not realize that
the measurement outcome reflects those attitudes, or have no control
over the fact that or degree to which the measurement outcome reflects their racial attitudes. Put more precisely, this means that the
processes that translate the racial attitudes into the measurement outcome operate even when participants are not aware of the attitudes,
even when they do not realize that the outcome reflects racial attitudes, or regardless of efforts to control the outcome of those processes. Based on these considerations, we can thus provide a first approximate definition of the concept *implicit measure*: *An implicit
measure is a measurement outcome that reflects the to-be-measured
construct by virtue of processes that have certain features.*

As De Houwer (2006) pointed out, this definition has clear implications for how the concept *implicit measure* should be used and
understood. First, the concept has little or no meaning if one does
not specify the features to which one is referring. For instance, rather
than saying that an IAT score *is* an implicit measure, one needs to
specify *in which sense* the IAT score is an implicit measure. For example, one can say that racial IAT scores provide an implicit measure
of racial attitudes in the sense that participants have little control
over these scores (and thus over the processes by which the racial attitudes are translated in the IAT scores). Second, one cannot merely
claim that a measurement outcome is implicit in a certain sense, one
also needs to provide evidence that the measurement outcome is implicit in that sense, or more precisely, that the processes underlying
the measurement outcome do possess those features. For instance,
before one can claim that scores in a racial IAT provide an implicit,
in the sense of uncontrolled, measure of racial attitudes, one first
needs to demonstrate that participants indeed do not intentionally
produce a certain score (see Steffens, 2004, for some recent evidence).

Although the definition of *implicit measure* that we provided
above already has important implications, it is obviously limited in
that it does not specify which features can be considered typical of

implicit measures. De Houwer (2006) noted that the term *implicit* is often regarded as synonymous with *unconscious*. When *implicit* is understood in this manner, one could argue that only features related to consciousness (e.g., of the to-be-measured construct, of the fact that the outcome reflects the to-be-measured construct, and of the processes by which the construct is translated into the outcome) should be taken into account when defining implicit measures. However, in the existing literature, features that are not related to consciousness have also been mentioned as typical of implicit measure. For instance, measurement outcomes have been described as implicit in the sense that participants have little control over (the processes underlying) them. In order to solve this issue, De Houwer suggested that the concept *implicit* should be regarded as a synonym for the concept *automatic*. The concept *automatic* is typically defined in terms of a set of features that includes features related to consciousness, but also other features such as uncontrolled, unintentional, efficient, and fast. Moreover, the term *automatic* and its features are commonly used to describe the nature of processes. Hence, the term and its features can also be used to characterize the processes that underlie measurement outcomes. Finally, there is a long tradition of theorizing and research on (the features linked to) automaticity. Linking research on implicit measures with this tradition can therefore provide many new insights into the nature of implicit measures.

If one accepts the proposal that *implicit* should be understood as synonym for *automatic*, then the definition of implicit measures can be further specified as follows: *An implicit measure is a measurement outcome that reflects the to-be-measured construct by virtue of processes that have the features of automatic processes.* However, this definition leaves unanswered the question of which features are typical for automatic processes, what those features exactly mean, how they are related to each other, and how they can be examined. De Houwer (2006) sidestepped this issue and thus left a large degree of ambiguity in his definition of implicit measures. In this chapter, we try to remove this ambiguity by drawing on the conceptual analysis of automaticity that we recently put forward (Moors & De Houwer, 2006). In the next part of this chapter, we briefly summarize this analysis. In the third and final part, we then discuss the implications of this analysis for the definition of and research on implicit measures.

A CONCEPTUAL ANALYSIS OF AUTOMATICITY

To say that a process is automatic implies that the process can operate under certain conditions. To say that a process possesses a particular feature of automaticity means that it operates under one particular subset of those conditions. One historically important view on automaticity is that there are two sets of mutually exclusive processes, one being nonautomatic or controlled processes and the other being automatic processes. According to this view, which is known as the all-or-none view of automaticity, all nonautomatic processes have the same features (i.e., occur only when certain conditions are fulfilled), whereas all automatic processes have the opposite features (i.e., can occur when those conditions are not fulfilled). Features that have been attributed to nonautomatic processes include the features conscious, intentional, controlled, effortful, and slow. Typically, these features are meant to refer to the fact that these processes operate only when people are conscious of them and have the intention to engage in them, that the operation of the processes can be controlled, and that their operation depends on the availability of cognitive resources and time. Automatic processes, however, have been characterized as unconscious, unintentional, uncontrollable, effortless, and fast, meaning that they operate even when people are not conscious of the processes and do not have the intention to engage in them, that the operation of the processes cannot be controlled, and that the processes operate even when cognitive resources are scarce and time is limited.

It has become clear, however, that this all-or-none view is incorrect. Studies have demonstrated that most processes possess features typical of nonautomatic processes but also features typical of automatic processes. Evidence from Stroop studies, for instance, suggests that the processing of word meaning is automatic in that it does not depend on intention, resources, or time, but at the same time occurs only when attention is directed toward the word (see Logan, 1985, 1989, for a review). This and other evidence led Bargh (1989) to the conclusion that "all automaticity is conditional; it is dependent on the occurrence of some specific set of circumstances. A cognitive process is automatic *given* certain enabling circumstances, whether it be merely the presence of the triggering proximal stimulus, or that plus a specific goal-directed state of mind and sufficient attentional resources" (p. 7, original emphasis).

An important implication of this conclusion is that one cannot simply characterize a process as automatic or nonautomatic. Rather, it is necessary to always specify the sense in which a process is automatic, that is, to specify which automaticity features it possesses and which automaticity features it does not possess. Hence, one needs to adopt a decompositional, feature-based approach of the concept *automaticity*. Although there are some alternative approaches (e.g., Logan, 1988), it is now widely accepted that a decompositional approach is necessary in order to diagnose whether a process or a certain behavior is automatic (see Moors & De Houwer, 2006, for a detailed justification of this claim). However, a decompositional approach makes sense only if it is clear what the different automaticity features are and only if these features can be clearly defined and conceptually separated from each other. In our recent paper on automaticity (Moors & De Houwer, 2006), we considered a variety of features and argued that most of them can indeed be characterized in such a manner that the overlap between them is minimal. We now summarize our definitions of the automaticity features.

Many features, such as (un)intentional, goal directed, goal (in)dependent, (un)controlled/(un)controllable, and autonomous, are somehow related to goals. An overview of the goal-related features and their definitions can be found in Table 7.1. Perhaps the most central of these is the feature *controlled*. To say that a process is controlled implies that one has a goal regarding the process (i.e., the goal to engage in, alter, stop, or avoid the process) and that having this goal actually causes the achievement of the end state put forward in the goal (i.e., the actual occurrence, change, interruption, or prevention of the process). To say that a process is *uncontrolled* can have different meanings. It can refer to the fact that the state of a process alters (i.e., that the process occurs, changes, is interrupted) in the absence of a goal to achieve this alteration. But it can also refer to the fact that one has a certain goal but the desired effect does not occur. For instance, a process can be called uncontrolled in the sense that the process occurs even when the goal to prevent the occurrence of the process is present. A more subtle meaning of the term *uncontrolled* refers to a situation in which both the goal and the desired effect are present, but in which the effect was not caused by the goal. Imagine that you have the goal to kneel down in front of your loved one in order to propose marriage. Suppose that you do kneel down, not because of your goal but because you are pushed by someone who happens to pass by. In this case, both the goal and the desired effect are present, but it would be wrong to regard this act as controlled, because the goal did not cause the desired effect. Hence, the act is uncontrolled. Note that labeling a process or act as controlled thus requires a demonstration of causality, something that may not always be easy to achieve.

Several other goal-related features are closely related to the feature (un)controlled. To say that a process is *intentional* means that one has the goal to engage in a process and that this goal results in the occurrence of the process. Hence, intentional is identical to con-

TABLE 7.1. Overview of Goal-Related (Non)automaticity Features and the Conditions and Effects to Which They Refer

Features	Conditions	Effect
Controlled	• Goal pertaining to process (i.e., to engage, alter, stop, or avoid process) is present.	• Intended effect is present and caused by the goal.
Uncontrolled	• Goal pertaining to process is absent. • Goal pertaining to process is absent. • Goal pertaining to process is present. • Goal pertaining to process is present.	• Effect is absent. • Effect is present. • Intended effect is absent. • Intended effect is present but not caused by goal.
Intentional	• Goal to engage in process is present.	• Process is present and caused by goal.
Unintentional	• Goal to engage in process is absent. • Goal to engage in process is present.	• Process is present. • Process is present but not caused by goal.
Goal dependent	• Goal is present.	• Process is present and caused by goal.
Goal independent	• Goal is absent. • Goal is present.	• Process is present. • Process is present but not caused by goal.
Purely stimulus driven	• Stimulus (+ usual background conditions).	• Process is present and caused by stimuli and background conditions.
Autonomous	• Goal to engage in process is absent or present. • And goal to alter, stop, or avoid process is absent or present.	• Process is present or process is present but not caused by goal. • Effect is absent. • Intended effect is absent.

trolled in the sense of the goal to engage in (rather than the goal to alter, stop, or avoid) the process. Intentional processes are thus a subset of controlled processes. Likewise, *unintentional* processes are a subset of uncontrolled processes. Like the concept *uncontrolled*, *unintentional* can refer to a variety of situations. It can refer to the fact that the process occurs without the intention to engage in the process, that the goal to engage does not lead to the engagement in the process, or that there is a goal to engage in the process and the process occurs but not because of the goal.

The feature *autonomous* also refers to process-related goals. Moors and De Houwer (2006) defined *autonomous* as *uncontrolled* in terms of every possible processing goal. A process is autonomous when its occurrence does not causally depend on the goal to engage in the process (i.e., is unintentional or uncontrolled in the sense of the goal to engage in) and when the goal to alter, stop, or avoid the process does not result in a change, interruption, or prevention of the process (i.e., uncontrolled in the sense of the goal to alter, stop, or avoid the process). In other words, one can say that an autonomous process is a process that is uncontrolled in every possible sense.

Another feature that is closely related to (un)controlled is the feature goal (in)dependent. The main difference is related to the type of goals. Whereas (un)controlled processes are defined in terms of goals related to various aspects of the process itself (i.e., the proximal goals of engaging in, changing, stopping, or avoiding the process), goal (in)dependent processes are defined in terms of any possible goal, including goals that are not related to the process at hand (i.e., remote goals). Moreover, goal (in)dependence refers only to conditions under which the process occurs, not to conditions necessary for changing, stopping, or avoiding the process. A process is *goal dependent* when the occurrence of the process depends on the presence of (any type of) goal. For instance, the act of moving one's arm toward an apple may depend on the goal to eat an apple. It is possible that the act of moving the arm is as such not caused by the (conscious or unconscious) proximal goal to move the arm (and can therefore be regarded as unintentional or uncontrolled in the sense of engaging in that act) but the act is goal dependent in that its occurrence does depend on the remote goal to eat an apple. Goal-dependent processes are thus not necessarily intentional or controlled (because their occurrence may depend on goals other than those related to engaging in a process), but intentional processes are by definition goal dependent. Unintentional processes are, however, not necessarily goal independent. That is, the occurrence of a process may not causally depend on the goal to engage in the process (i.e., be unintentional) but may still depend on other goals. A process is *goal independent* only when its occurrence does not causally depend on the presence of any type of goal.

A subclass of goal-independent processes are *purely stimulus-driven* processes. These are processes that in addition to being goal independent (i.e., do not causally depend on any type of goal), also do not depend on other factors such as awareness or attention. The occurrence of these processes depends only on the presence of a stimulus and certain basic conditions that ensure that the stimulus can be physically registered (e.g., in case of visual stimuli, that the eyes are not closed). It should be clear from the above that it is difficult, if not impossible, to demonstrate that a process is entirely goal independent or purely stimulus driven. The best one can do is to demonstrate that the process does not depend on certain remote goals or enabling conditions and to make these goals and conditions explicit when describing the process as goal independent or purely stimulus driven.

Now that we have discussed all goal-related features, we turn our attention to the features *conscious* and *unconscious*. It is notoriously difficult to define the concepts *conscious* and *unconscious*, which is one of the reasons we do not like to put these features at the heart of our definition of *automatic* or *implicit*. But if one does want to use these features when characterizing processes, it is crucial to specify what is considered to be conscious or unconscious because these features can be used as a predicate of several things. They can be applied to (1) the stimulus input that evokes the process, (2) the output of the process, (3) the process itself, or (4) the consequences of the process, such as its influence on subsequent processing (e.g., Bargh, 1994). Therefore, when using the term *unconscious*, one needs to specify what it is a predicate of.

It is important to note that there is no complete overlap between the feature (un)conscious and goal-related features. For instance, it may seem reasonable to assume that all intentional processes are conscious in the sense that one needs to be conscious of the goal to engage in a process. However, recent research has convincingly demonstrated that unconsciously activated goals to engage in a process can also be causally effective. The same is true for other process-related goals. Hence, one can have an intention or control without being aware of it. It is therefore important to clearly distinguish between the feature (un)conscious and goal-related features. One way to do this is to use the term *(un)conscious* as a predicate of goal-related terms such as *intentional* and *controlled*. For instance, when a process occurs only in the presence of the conscious goal to engage in the process, the process needs to be described as consciously intentional rather than as simply intentional.

Another correlate of automaticity is the feature *(non)efficient*. A process is defined as efficient when it consumes little or no processing resources or attentional capacity. Efficiency leads to the subjective experience that processing is effortless. Because of this, the terms *efficient* and *effortless* have often been used interchangeably. Again, there is no complete overlap between efficiency and goal-related features or consciousness. Whereas goals are related to the *direction* of attention (goals may determine the focus of attention), efficiency is related to the *amount* of attention. Likewise, although attention and consciousness are closely linked, some authors have suggested that there is a phenomenal aspect or type of consciousness that can occur outside the focus of attention (Block, 1995). Moreover, some evidence suggests that unconscious processing also depends on attention (e.g., Naccache, Blandin, & Dehaene, 2002).

The final features we consider are the features fast and slow. These can be used to refer either to the duration of the process or to the duration of the stimulus input on which the process operates. These features are clearly gradual. There is no objective threshold for calling something fast or slow, so investigators need to rely on commonsense arguments for calling some interval short or long or for deciding whether a process is fast or slow. There is a clear link between the feature fast and other features. Processes that are efficient are typically faster than nonefficient processes. Some researchers even consider processing speed as evidence for efficiency (e.g., Smith & Lerner, 1986). Likewise, awareness of the process and of the stimulus input is related to the duration of the process and the input, respectively. Some processes occur so fast that one cannot become aware of them. Some stimuli are presented so briefly that one cannot perceive them consciously. Finally, the duration of the process or stimulus input may also have an effect on the (conscious) implementation of goals and thus on the features intentional and controlled. Certain stimulus durations are so brief that they prevent the implementation of the goal to engage in some process, and certain processes occur so rapidly that they cannot be altered or stopped. Despite the overlap between the feature fast and these other features, it is very difficult to set a priori time intervals that prevent the processing of goals or consciousness from taking effect. This may be especially difficult considering that the factors time, attention, and intensity (of stimulus input or process) may be interrelated. For example, higher levels of attention and/or stimulus strength (salience) may compensate for short stimulus durations.

APPLYING THE CONCEPTUAL ANALYSIS
TO THE DEFINITION AND CHARACTERIZATION
OF IMPLICIT MEASURES

Based on our conceptual analysis, we can now define implicit measures as *measurement outcomes that reflect the to-be-measured construct by virtue of processes that are uncontrolled, unintentional, goal independent, purely stimulus driven, autonomous, unconscious, efficient*, or *fast*. When claiming that a measure is implicit, one needs to (1) specify that the measurement outcome is based on processes that possess one or more of these features, (2) do this in a manner in which the exact meaning of the specified features is made explicit, and (3) have arguments or empirical evidence to back up these claims. We now discuss how this can be done for each of the features.

To say that a measure is *uncontrolled* can have several meanings. First, it can refer to the fact that the processes responsible for the translation of the to-be-measured construct into the measurement outcome are not caused by the goal to *engage in* this translation (i.e., the goal to express the construct in the outcome). This means that the goal to engage in the translation is either absent or noncausal. Such a measure can also be called *unintentional*. One can examine this feature by asking participants to report their goals regarding the task or by varying whether participants are instructed to express the to-be-measured construct. As far as we know, such studies have not yet been conducted. Note, however, that these studies would not allow one to assess the presence of *unconscious* goals to express the construct of interest (assuming that such goals can be unconscious).

The second sense in which measures can be uncontrolled is in the sense that participants cannot *change, stop*, or *avoid* the translation of the to-be-measured construct into the outcome. To test this feature, one can examine whether the measurement outcome varies as a function of attempts to change, stop, or avoid the translation. Studies like these have already been conducted. For instance, there is evidence that IAT effects are (relatively) unaffected by instructions to fake a certain attitude (see Steffens, 2004). Again, such studies are limited to assessing the role of conscious goals. It would be interesting to see whether an unconscious activation of goals (e.g., to hide one's true feelings) through subliminal priming or scrambled sentence completion (see Moskowitz, Li, & Kirk, 2004, for a review) has an effect on implicit measures such as IAT effects. Note that in order to demonstrate that a measure is *autonomous*, one needs to show that the measure is uncontrolled in both of the senses we have discussed above.

Measures are *goal independent* if the translation of the to-be-measured construct into the outcome does not depend on any (proximal or remote) goal. It is difficult to demonstrate goal independence, because it implies that every possible goal is irrelevant. However, it might be interesting to examine the role of certain theoretically important goals. For instance, there is evidence that the attitude toward a prime stimulus influences responses in affective priming even when participants do not have the goal to evaluate stimuli in their environment (e.g., Bargh, Chaiken, Raymond, & Hymes, 1996; De Houwer

& Randell, 2004; Spruyt, Hermans, De Houwer, & Eelen, 2002). This is a remote (i.e., process-unrelated) goal because it is not directly related to the translation of the attitude into the affective priming score. Hence, one can say that affective priming effects can be goal independent with regard to the goal of evaluating stimuli in the environment. As far as we know, these studies on the role of evaluative goals in affective priming are the only studies on the goal independence of implicit measures. In fact, with measures such as the IAT, it seems impossible to examine the role of evaluative goals because the evaluation of words is an integral part of the task. As such, it will be difficult to argue that IAT effects can provide an implicit measure in the sense of a goal-independent measure of attitudes. It is even more difficult to demonstrate that the IAT or any other implicit measure is *purely stimulus driven*. This would imply that one would demonstrate not only that the validity of the measure is independent of every possible goal, but also that it does not depend on other factors such as awareness or attention.

As we mentioned earlier in this chapter, the feature unconscious is often mentioned as typical of implicit measures. Unfortunately, it is rarely specified in which sense the measure should be regarded as unconscious. Based on our analysis (see also Bargh, 1994), a measure can be unconscious in the sense that the to-be-measured construct is translated into the outcome even though participants are unaware of (1) the stimuli that activate the construct (e.g., the attitude object that is presented during the task), (2) the construct itself (e.g., the fact that they possess a certain attitude), (3) the fact that the construct influences performance (e.g., that the outcome reflects a certain attitude), or (4) the manner in which the construct influences performance (e.g., that an attitude leads to faster performance in a compatible than in an incompatible IAT block). As Fazio and Olson (2003) pointed out, researchers almost never examine whether an implicit measure reflects constructs of which participants are unaware (meaning 2), whether participants are aware that a measure reflects a certain construct (meaning 3; see Monteith, Voils, & Ashburn-Nardo, 2001, for a notable exception), or whether participants know how the construct influences the outcome (meaning 4; again, see Monteith et al., 2001, for an exception). Nevertheless, it would be easy to examine these issues by simply asking people to express the relevant construct in a conscious manner (meaning 2), to guess which construct is being measured (meaning 3), and to speculate about how the construct could influence performance (e.g., by speeding up performance on some trials as compared to others; meaning 4). Although these studies are feasible, one does need to take into account problems that can arise when assessing conscious knowledge (e.g., the assessment needs to be sensitive enough; see Shanks & St. John, 1994). There are some studies on subliminal affective priming that suggest that participants need not be aware of the attitude object in order to measure the attitude toward that object (meaning 1; see, e.g., Degner, Wentura, Gniewosz, & Noack, 2005). But other implicit measures, such as the IAT, require that participants are aware of the attitude object because otherwise they cannot fulfill the task. To summarize, despite the common claim that implicit measures are unconscious measures, these claims are most often ill specified and lack supporting evidence. More research on this issue is urgently needed.

A measure can be called efficient if the processes translating the construct into the outcome use only a minimal amount of attentional resources. The standard manner to examine efficiency is to use a dual-task method and manipulate the mental load of a secondary task. We know of only two series of studies in which this approach was adopted. Hermans, Crombez, and Eelen (2000) asked participants to perform an affective priming task while simultaneously reciting a series of digits. They found that the magnitude of the affective priming effect was unaffected by the degree of mental load imposed by the secondary task, which suggests that the translation of the attitude in the priming effect was efficient. Quite recently, Schmitz, Teige, Voss, and Klauer (2005) also examined the impact of memory load on the IAT. They found that an increase in memory load led to an increase in the magnitude of the IAT effect but did not influence external correlations with self-reported attitudes. Hence, these initial results suggest that the translation of individual attitudes in IAT scores is efficient. Note that the dual-task approach that is commonly used in studies on efficiency is founded on the single-resource view of attention. Some have argued that there are multiple resources and that the two processes in a dual task might draw on different resources. If this is the case, one might observe that the two tasks do not interfere with each other (and thus appear to be efficient) even though they both rely heavily on attentional resources, albeit different ones. Some caution is therefore needed when interpreting the results of dual-task studies. Finally, efficiency is a gradual feature. For instance, if one does not observe any effect of the mental load imposed by the secondary task, it is always possible that an effect will be found when a more difficult secondary task is used. Hence, one can never conclude that a measure is completely independent of attentional resources.

The features fast and slow are also gradual features. Studies have demonstrated that affective priming effects can be found even when the prime stimulus is presented only briefly before or simultaneous with the target stimulus and target responses are very quick (see, e.g., Hermans, De Houwer, & Eelen, 2001; Klauer, Rossnagel, & Musch, 1997). This suggests that the attitude toward the prime is translated in the measurement outcome even when the stimulus is presented only briefly and little time is available for the translation to occur. Affective priming effects thus seem to depend on relatively fast-acting processes. The same can be said about other reaction-time-based measures such as the IAT and the affective Simon task (e.g., De Houwer & Eelen, 1998).

CONCLUSION

Building on our previous work (De Houwer, 2006; Moors & De Houwer, 2006), we have argued that implicit measures are measurement outcomes that rely on processes that are uncontrolled, unintentional, autonomous, goal independent, purely stimulus driven, unconscious, efficient, or fast. We have defined what these features mean, how they are related to each other, and how they can be assessed. We hope that our analysis will clarify the meaning of the concept *implicit measure* and will allow researchers to examine in more detail the nature of (the processes underlying) these measures. More research regarding the features of implicit measures is desperately needed. This research will not only help increase conceptual clarity but will also help develop much needed theories about the processes that underlie the various measures (see Borsboom, Gideon, & van Heerden, 2004). We urge researchers to take up this challenge and to be more explicit and precise in their use of the term *implicit measure*.

ACKNOWLEDGMENTS

Preparation of this chapter was supported by Grant No. G.0356.03 from the Fund for Scientific Research (Flanders, Belgium).

NOTE

1. Measurement procedures can be described as direct or indirect (see De Houwer, 2006). In direct measurement procedures, participants are asked to self-assess the to-be-measured construct. In indirect measurement procedures, the construct is assessed indirectly on the basis of other behavior.

REFERENCES

Bargh, J. A. (1989). Conditional automaticity: Varieties of automatic influence in social perception and cognition. In J. S. Uleman & J. A. Bargh (Eds.), *Unintended thought* (pp. 3–51). New York: Guilford Press.

Bargh, J. A. (1994). The four horsemen of automaticity: Awareness, intention, efficiency, and control in social cognition. In R. S. Wyer & T. K. Srull (Eds.), *Handbook of social cognition* (Vol. 1, pp. 1–40). Hillsdale, NJ: Erlbaum.

Bargh, J. A., Chaiken, S., Raymond, P., & Hymes, C. (1996). The automatic evaluation effect: Unconditional automatic activation with a pronunciation task. *Journal of Experimental Social Psychology, 32*, 104–128.

Block, N. (1995). On a confusion about a function of consciousness. *Behavioral and Brain Sciences, 18*, 227–287.

Borsboom, D., Gideon, M. J., & van Heerden, J. (2004). The concept of validity. *Psychological Review, 111*, 1061–1071.

Degner, J., Wentura, D., Gniewosz, B., & Noack, P. (2005). *Implicit prejudice in eighth-graders.* Manuscript submitted for publication.

De Houwer, J. (2003). The extrinsic affective Simon task. *Experimental Psychology, 50*, 77–85.

De Houwer, J. (2006). What are implicit measures and why are we using them? In R. W. Wiers & A. W. Stacy (Eds.), *The handbook of implicit cognition and addiction* (pp. 11–28). Thousand Oaks, CA: Sage.

De Houwer, J., & Eelen, P. (1998). An affective variant of the Simon paradigm. *Cognition and Emotion, 12*, 45–61.

De Houwer, J., & Randell, T. (2004). Robust affective priming effects in a conditional pronunciation task: Evidence for the semantic representation of evaluative information. *Cognition and Emotion, 18*, 251–264.

Fazio, R. H., Jackson, J. R., Dunton, B. C., & Williams, C. J. (1995). Variability in automatic activation as an unobtrusive measure of racial attitudes: A bona fide pipeline? *Journal of Personality and Social Psychology, 69*, 1013–1027.

Fazio, R. H., & Olson, M. A. (2003). Implicit measures in social cognition research: Their meaning and use. *Annual Review of Psychology, 54*, 297–327.

Fazio, R. H., Sanbonmatsu, D. M., Powell, M. C., & Kardes, F. R. (1986). On the automatic activation of attitudes. *Journal of Personality and Social Psychology, 50*, 229–238.

Greenwald, A. G., McGhee, D. E., & Schwartz, J. L. K. (1998). Measuring individual differences in implicit cognition: The Implicit Association Test. *Journal of Personality and Social Psychology, 74*, 1464–1480.

Greenwald, A. G., Nosek, B. A., & Banaji, M. R. (2003). Understanding and using the Implicit Association Test: I. An improved scoring algorithm. *Journal of Personality and Social Psychology, 85*, 197–216.

Hermans, D., Crombez, G., & Eelen, P. (2000). Automatic attitude activation and efficiency: The fourth horseman of automaticity. *Psychologica Belgica, 40*, 3–22.

Hermans, D., De Houwer J., & Eelen, P. (2001). A time course analysis of the affective priming effect. *Cognition and Emotion, 15*, 143–165.

Klauer, K. C., Rossnagel, C., & Musch, J. (1997). List context effects in evaluative priming. *Journal of Experimental Psychology: Learning, Memory, and Cognition, 23*, 246–255.

Logan, G. D. (1985). Skill and automaticity: Relations, implications, and future directions. *Canadian Journal of Psychology, 39*, 367–386.

Logan, G. D. (1988). Toward an instance theory of automatization. *Psychological Review, 95*, 492–527.

Logan, G. D. (1989). Automaticity and cognitive control. In J. S. Uleman & J. A. Bargh (Eds.), *Unintended thought* (pp. 52–74). New York: Guilford Press.

Monteith, M. J., Voils, C. I., & Ashburn-Nardo, L. (2001). Taking a look underground: Detecting, interpreting, and reacting to implicit racial bias. *Social Cognition, 19*, 395–417.

Moors, A., & De Houwer, J. (2006). Automaticity: A conceptual and theoretical analysis. *Psychological Bulletin, 132*, 297–326.

Moskowitz, G. B., Li, P., & Kirk, E. R. (2004). The implicit volition model: On the preconscious regulation of temporarily adopted goals. In M. Zanna (Ed.), *Advances in experimental social psychology* (Vol. 34, pp. 317–414). San Diego, CA: Academic Press.

Naccache, L., Blandin, E., & Dehaene, S. (2002). Unconscious masked priming depends on temporal attention. *Psychological Science, 13*, 416–424.

Schmitz, F., Teige, S., Voss, A., & Klauer, K. C. (2005, June). *Working memory load in the IAT.* Paper presented at the fifth Workshop on Implicit Representations and Personality, Berlin, Germany.

Shanks, D. R., & St. John, M. F. (1994). Characteristics of dissociable human learning systems. *Behavioral and Brain Sciences, 17*, 367–447.

Smith, E. R., & Lerner, M. (1986). Development of automatism of social judgements. *Journal of Personality and Social Psychology, 50*, 246–259.

Spruyt, A., Hermans, D., De Houwer, J., & Eelen, P. (2002). On the nature of the affective priming effect: Affective priming of naming responses. *Social Cognition, 20*, 225–254.

Steffens, M. (2004). Is the Implicit Association Test immune to faking? *Experimental Psychology, 51*, 165–179.

8 Paradigms We Live By

A Plea for More Basic Research on the Implicit Association Test

Dirk Wentura
Klaus Rothermund

To arrive at a certain point, you sometimes need to take a detour. So please follow us—we will tell you a fairytale.

Once upon a time there were some colleagues working in the field of selective attention. What were the main questions in this field? Surely one has always been, How does our cognitive apparatus manage to focus on task-relevant information while simultaneously being exposed to distracting irrelevant information? Our colleagues invented a new paradigm to answer this question. In this paradigm, participants had to process a target stimulus (e.g., a word that had to be named), while ignoring a distractor stimulus (e.g., another word) that was presented near to the target. What our colleagues found was that if the distractor of one trial was repeated as the target in the subsequent trial, response latencies were increased (compared to a control condition). They said to themselves, "That's really interesting! It seems that irrelevant information is processed but then inhibited to avoid interference at the level of generating a response. This inhibition can be assessed in the subsequent trial. That must be interesting to lots of colleagues! Let's call it the Inhibition Test, or—even better—the Implicit Inhibition Test, IIT for short, because the effect does not seem to reflect intentional behavior." And, indeed, lots of researchers used this paradigm to test whomever could be tested for this capability (e.g., older people, people with schizophrenia, or depressed people) and whatever could be tested for—whether it could be inhibited or not (e.g., threat stimuli). Results often conformed to expectations, but sometimes they did not, a fact causing lively debates about the kind of inhibition assessed by this tool. But nobody ever questioned whether the IIT in fact measured inhibition . . . and they lived happily ever after.

Those who are somewhat acquainted with research paradigms in cognitive psychology have already recognized that the fairytale is a merger of two real stories: the paradigm is in fact the negative priming paradigm (for reviews, see, e.g., Fox, 1995; May, Kane, & Hasher, 1995; Neill & Valdes, 1996; Tipper, 2001), and some aspects of the story were a caricature of the Implicit Association Test's (IAT) history.

In fact, the most obvious interpretation of the negative priming effect is the assumption of inhibitory processes in selective attention (see, e.g., Houghton & Tipper, 1994; Tipper, 1985, 2001). Thereby, the paradigm is related to theories of selective attention that address problems of wider interest (e.g., see above, the question, "How does our cognitive apparatus manage the problem of focusing on and reacting to task-relevant information while ignoring irrelevant information?"). We might call these theories "large-scale theories."

Meanwhile, however, several alternative theories of the negative priming effect are on the market; for instance, the effect has been related to processes of an automatic memory retrieval of previous stimulus–response episodes (see, e.g., Neill & Valdes, 1996; Rothermund, Wentura, & De Houwer, 2005a). Such an explanation is of comparatively small scale; that is, it first of all focuses on explaining the effect found with the experimental technique, without bothering too much about explaining something in the world outside the laboratory. Of course, in a second step it might possibly be linked to other interesting large-scale phenomena—for example, theories of automatization or common coding of perception and action codes. But that has not been the primary goal.

The lesson to be learned from this story is that we should emphasize the gap between an experimental technique (and the effect that is usually found with it) and the theory that accounts for this effect. In cognitive psychology, the "could it be otherwise?" question is ubiquitous; you will find it not only for the negative priming paradigm, but for the semantic priming paradigm (see, e.g., Neely, 1991), the affective priming paradigm (see, e.g., Klauer & Musch, 2003), the visual search paradigm (see, e.g., Wolfe, 1998), and the Stroop task (see, e.g., MacLeod, 1991), to name just a few. We agree that small-scale, paradigm-oriented research can be disillusioning, and sometimes it may even appear as *l'art-pour-art*. But in our view it is an indispensable step to achieve scientific progress.

What about our caricature of the IAT history? Of course, it *is* a caricature, because in fact there are several studies concerned with the processes that might be involved in producing IAT effects (e.g., Brendl, Markman, & Messner, 2001; De Houwer, 2001; De Houwer, Geldof, & De Bruycker, 2005; Kinoshita & Peek-O'Leary, 2003, 2005; Klauer & Mierke, 2005; Mierke & Klauer, 2001, 2003; Rothermund & Wentura, 2001, 2004). However, the bulk of studies did not make any problem out of the claim that the IAT does in fact measure associations. In these studies, it seems as if not the slightest gap is seen between the theoretical assumption of associative representations and the IAT difference score. We admit that this neglect is supported by an ever growing number of studies that reveal IAT effects with high *prima facie* validity: Categories that intuitively "go together" (e.g., flower and positive; insects and negative; see Greenwald, McGhee, & Schwartz, 1998) are accompanied by shorter categorization latencies if they have to be categorized by the same key (in contrast to the reversed pairing of categories and keys).[1]

A second look reveals, however, that the explanation of IAT effects by associative relations is not an easy task (despite its intuitive plausibility), and that the "could it be otherwise" question can be answered affirmatively, as we have argued elsewhere (Rothermund & Wentura, 2001, 2004). In the following two sections we elaborate on these two points. Both types of theories—that is, the association account as well as our alternative—emphasize the assumption that IAT effects are a result of automatic processes ("automatic" here in the sense of unintentional, uncontrollable, and nonstrategic).[2] A further threat to validity is discussed in a third section. As we argue, in principle some IAT effects are neatly explained by a rather trivial small-scale theory, that is, by assuming simple intentional recoding strategies of participants (e.g., imagine a participant's thoughts for the Compatible block in the flower/insect IAT: "Oh, flowers are positive and insects are negative, so I do not have to bother about these four different categories at all. The only thing I have to do is to use one key for positive words and one for negative ones"). With this example, it is of course not our point to trivialize all results found with the IAT, but to opt for further small-scale-oriented research that searches for procedural recommendations that might differentiate between automatic and strategic components of an IAT effect (again: "automatic," in the sense given above). Finally, we want to discuss why we stress the importance of small-scale theorizing, knowing that others obviously follow a different route: They accept (at least tentatively) the association account and persistently examine matters of convergent and discriminant validity by correlating IAT results with other measures, such as self-reports or behaviors. In contrast, we will argue that a social cognition perspective is intimately tied to measures such as the IAT. To emphasize: A social cognition perspective has no other measures than those measures. Therefore, we should clearly know *what* they measure. And this can be done only by establishing valid small-scale theories (i.e., theories that link an experimental technique with global theories about mental representations and the processes that operate on these representations).

AN IAT ACCOUNT BASED ON ASSOCIATIONS

However intuitively plausible an association account of the IAT might be, spelling out the details is not an easy task. De Houwer (2001) proposed the following small-scale theory within an association account of the IAT, exemplified with an evaluation-based IAT (i.e., the attributes are of positive and negative valence). During the Compatible block of an IAT, the a priori neutral key responses acquire short-term associations with either positive or negative valence, because each response is unequivocally linked to two categories (e.g., flower and positive) sharing the same valence. Categorizing stimuli as belonging to the category *flower* or *positive* automatically activates their positive valence and thus a positive response tendency. Given the background of the affective Simon effect (De Houwer & Eelen, 1998), it can be assumed that executing the required response (e.g., pressing the right key) is facilitated, because the valence of the correct response is similar to the valence of the automatically activated evaluative response tendency. In an incompatible block, however, response keys will not be associated with valence because categories of opposite valence are assigned to the same key. This reduces the facilitatory effects of response compatibility and may even lead to response interference.

This small-scale theory is not entirely convincing (as already noted by De Houwer, 2001), because it localizes IAT effects predominantly at the level of the valence of the category exemplars, although it is known that the categories themselves play the dominant role. This can be easily demonstrated by the results of the following study: De Houwer (2001) conducted (in the United Kingdom) a "British" versus "foreign" evaluation IAT and found—not surprisingly, given other results with the IAT—an ingroup bias for the average participant (i.e., the block with the assignment of "British" and "positive" to the same key yielded lower latencies). However, exemplars for the British versus foreign classification were famous persons, known either for a very positive (e.g., Princess Diana, Albert Einstein) or a very negative reputation (e.g., Donald Shipman [a mass murderer], Adolf Hitler). In fact, the British/foreign dichotomy was orthogonal to valence. Thus, the explanation given above cannot easily be applied, because even in the compatible block the response keys did not unequivocally acquire a valence connotation.

THE SALIENCE ACCOUNT OF THE IAT

As mentioned in the introduction to this chapter, cognitive psychologists love to pose the "could it be otherwise?" question. In this spirit, we proposed our alternative account, termed the figure–ground account or salience asymmetry account (Rothermund & Wentura, 2001, 2004). It is based on three simple assumptions.

The first assumption is a simple proposition that cannot be empirically disproved: Binary classification tasks can in principle be done in an asymmetric way. That is, participants might implicitly solve the classification task not as a "category A" versus "category B" task, but as a "yes (that is an exemplar of the salient category A)" versus "no (that is not an exemplar of A)" task. To elaborate on this point, imagine another well-known experimental task from attention research: the visual search paradigm. In this task, participants are presented with a set of a varying number of distractor stimuli that does or does not include an exemplar of a specified target category. Participants have to respond as fast as possible with "yes" if a target is included, but with "no" if only distractors are present. Thus, binary classification tasks may have the character of a visual search task with a set size of one, that is, either a target or a distractor is presented.

The second assumption is that in fact a lot of binary classifications are done in this asymmetrical way. The underlying rationale is that one pole of a dichotomy is usually the more salient one; it is the figure that stands out from the ground of the other pole. The finding of an asymmetrical processing of binary categorizations is a very general finding across different experimental tasks, which has recently been reviewed extensively by Proctor and Cho (2006).

The third assumption is that if the two asymmetric dichotomies are congruently mapped onto two response keys (i.e., both "figures" are assigned to the same key), categorization on the basis of salience or the "figure-like" character of stimuli can persist, whereas an incongruent mapping requires that salience is suppressed and that the stimuli are processed more deeply.

What evidence can be found for this account? We first give a short review of our own research (Rothermund & Wentura, 2001, 2004) and then add some remarks on studies of others that easily fit with the figure–ground account, but are problematic for an association account.

IAT Effects with Salience Asymmetries in the Absence of Associations

The most straightforward idea to test the salience account against the association account is quite simple. We used an IAT for which a clear average effect can be found that might plausibly be based on associations. Then we replaced the attribute dichotomy by one that is plausibly asymmetric, but clearly not associated with the target dichotomy. In detail, we presented participants with old and young first names (i.e., names that are clearly associated with either old or young persons) as the target dichotomy of "old versus young (persons)." As the attribute category, we used positive and negative adjectives. As expected, we found an IAT effect that fits the usual interpretation of an "ageism" effect; that is, old age seems to be associated with a negative evaluation. Then we replicated this experiment by replacing the positive words with neutral words and the negative words with senseless letter strings. The attribute categorization was now "word versus nonword" instead of "good versus bad." In fact, we found a significant IAT effect that was structurally equivalent to the one found with the evaluation IAT (i.e., shorter latencies if old names and nonwords are assigned to the same key, as compared to the reversed pairing). Obviously, old age is not associated with "nonwordness," nor is young age associated with "wordness." Thus, the result cannot be explained by the association account.[3] However, it can plausibly be claimed that if there is any truth in our rationale, then a dichotomy like word versus nonword should do the job of an asymmetric classification task. Of course, this asymmetry should be shown independently of the IAT.

Diagnosing Salience Asymmetries

Therefore, we introduced a task that was modeled after the visual search task in cognitive psychology. We always presented four different words on the screen, which were chosen from the word/nonword sets. Half of the trials comprised only words or only nonwords, whereas the other half comprised either three words (and one nonword) or three nonwords (and one word). The task was to decide as quickly as possible whether all stimuli belonged to the same category (i.e., all words or all nonwords), or whether one of the stimuli belonged to a different category (e.g., one word among three nonwords or vice versa). If nonwords are more salient, and if salient stimuli automatically draw and/or hold attention, it should take longer to process displays that contain a majority of nonwords (i.e., a display with four or three nonwords as compared to displays with four or three words). That was exactly what we found. Of course, to make the argument complete, it was necessary to show with the same tool that old names were more salient as compared to young names, and that negative words were more salient than positive words. Again, that was exactly what we found. Moreover, we tested a further dichotomy that should plausibly be processed in an asymmetric way, but should not be associated with old and/or young age. In a further search task, multicolored versus single-colored strings of zeroes were presented as stimuli. Not unexpectedly, it turned out that multicolored strings were more salient as compared to single-colored strings. Replacing negative words with multicolored strings and positive words with single-colored ones, another old/young IAT yielded an IAT effect that suggested an association of the category of multicolored strings with older people, if interpreted in terms of an association account.

Manipulating Salience

A further step in accumulating evidence for a salience account is to experimentally manipulate salience while holding everything else constant. In the absence of any a priori salience differences or presumed associations, this can be done by a simple manipulation. We again conducted an old/young IAT with first names as target exemplars, but with neutral words as attribute exemplars, half of which were presented in yellow and half in green. Categorization of color was the task for those stimuli. To manipulate the salience of color, the old/young stimuli were presented either in yellow (thereby making green stimuli the minority and thus more salient) or in green (thereby making yellow stimuli more salient). Knowing from the studies reported above that old names are more salient, we expected and found response latencies to be lower if old names and the salient color category were assigned to the same key.

In a further experiment, we tested whether preexisting differences can be varied by a simple manipulation. Therefore, we replicated the old/young IAT with positive and negative words as the attribute dimension. However, differing from the original procedure, the practice blocks (i.e., the blocks employing only either old/young or positive/negative stimuli) were now realized as go/no-go tasks. For instance, for the old/young practice trials, half of the participants were instructed to press a key only for old names (and to ignore young names). The instruction was reversed for the remaining participants. As far as there is any chance to reverse existing salience asymmetries by a simple manipulation, this instruction should do the job. Of course, we varied the practice instructions for the attribute dimension accordingly. That is, orthogonally to the go/no-go assignment for the target dimension, we varied the go/no-go assignment for the attribute dimension: half of the participants had to press the key for positive words (while ignoring negative ones), whereas the remaining participants had to press the key for negative words (while ignoring positive ones). Note that the main blocks of the IAT (i.e., the blocks employing all four types of stimuli) were essentially the same as in the original version. We expected IAT effects that dominantly reflected the artificially created asymmetries in salience. In fact, if the two go categories of a given participant were assigned the same key, response latencies were lower as compared to the incompatible block, irrespective of any presumed preexisting associations. These experiments show that salience differences can indeed be responsible for IAT effects.

Manipulating Valence

Part of our rationale is that IAT results that were interpreted in terms of an association account might just as well be explained by differences in salience. To lend further support to this claim, we varied the valence of a category while holding salience constant. In detail, we used a known/unknown IAT with names of well-known persons, as well as fictitious names, as the target dimension, and positive and negative words as the attribute dimension. The prediction of the salience account—empirically corroborated by results of our search task (see above)—was that the assignment of unknown names and negative words to the same key will yield lower latencies as compared to the block with the reversed assignment. That was indeed what we found. Interestingly, the essential manipulation was the valence of the known persons: for half of the participants, the set was entirely composed of popular persons; for the remaining participants, the set was entirely composed of unpopular persons. Thus, from the association account, one would clearly expect a moderation of the IAT effect by this variable, which, however, was not found.

The Salience Account and Interindividual Differences

Most of the IAT research to date is concerned with interindividual differences in the strength of IAT effects. A first interesting topic in this regard concerns the diagnostic properties of the IAT. Differences in the strength of IAT effects are taken to indicate that the strength of associations between concepts varies among individuals. To draw this conclusion, that is, to infer strong (weak) associations from strong (weak) IAT effects, presupposes that the IAT is both a reliable and valid measure of associations. IATs typically are characterized by acceptable or even good reliabilities (e.g., Banse, Seise, & Zerbes, 2001; Bosson, Swann, & Pennebaker, 2000; Cunningham, Preacher, & Banaji, 2001; Egloff & Schmukle, 2002), indicating that a large amount of the variance in an IAT indeed reflects systematic and stable interindividual differences rather than random fluctuations. In this regard, the IAT is clearly superior to other implicit measures of associations (e.g., priming, Simon task) that often suffer from a lack of reliability (e.g., Bosson et al., 2000).

High reliability, however, is only one necessary precondition for an interpretation of IAT effects in terms of associations. Besides being reliable, a measure must also be shown to be a valid indicator of what it is purportedly measuring; otherwise it cannot be ruled out that IAT variance may stem from a completely different variable than the one it is assumed to reflect. The traditional strategy of validating a measure is to investigate its correlations with other measures that are already known to be valid indicators of related and unrelated constructs. A clear differentiation in the pattern of correlations—high correlations with indicators of related and low correlations with indicators of unrelated constructs—suggests convergent and discriminant validity, respectively, of the measure under investigation (Campbell & Fiske, 1959).

With only few exceptions (Gawronski, 2002), most of the available evidence to date focused on the convergent validity of the IAT. Because of a lack of other established implicit measures of associations, the IAT has typically been correlated with self-report measures of attitudes, stereotypes, self-concepts, and the like, that were assumed to be theoretical equivalents of the conceptual relations purportedly assessed by the respective IATs. Although these correlations have been mostly positive, relations between IAT effects and self-report variables were, on average, quite moderate. For example, in a recent meta-analysis, Hofmann, Gawronski, Gschwendner, Le, and Schmitt (2005) report an average correlation of only .19 (.24 after correcting for measurement error). In addition, substantial variations in the strength of these correlations have been found (Nosek, 2005). Exactly this pattern of moderately positive correlations, however, is also predicted on the basis of a salience asymmetry account of the IAT. According to this account, evaluative associations and salience asymmetries are often empirically confounded. The reason for such a confound is that evaluations, salience asymmetries, and characteristics of a person's environment can mutually influence each other. For instance, people holding a negative attitude toward African American people may tend to select a neighborhood that is dominated by White people, which in turn makes Black an unfamiliar and thus more salient category for them. In terms of the salience asymmetry account, positive correlations between IAT effects and self-report variables thus reflect a spurious relationship, which is due to an empirical confounding between attitudes, self-concept, or stereotypes, on one hand, and context variables influencing salience asymmetries on the other.

A direct implication of the spuriousness hypothesis is that controlling for salience asymmetries should eliminate the positive relation between IAT effects and self-report measures. In addition, the salience asymmetry account also predicts that similar relations between IAT effects and self-report measures should be obtained for both standard and modified "association-free" variants of the IAT. Empirical support for the spuriousness hypothesis was gathered in two independent experiments (Rothermund & Wentura, 2004, Experiments 2A, 2B). In one study, we investigated the relation between a gender/self-concept IAT (male/female × me/others) and a self-report measure of sex-role identity. Replicating previous findings (e.g., Greenwald & Farnham, 2000), we found a positive correlation between these measures. Interestingly, the gender/self-concept IAT also correlated with a modified version of the IAT, in which the categories me/others were replaced by the word/nonword dichotomy, suggesting a common source of variance of these measures—probably salience asymmetries. This finding indicates a lack of discriminant validity of the IAT as a measure of associations, because self-concept and word/nonword associations with gender should be unrelated. Even more important, introducing a direct measure of salience asymmetries between the male and female categories (search task) as an additional predictor of IAT effects rendered the previous relations of the sex-role identity questionnaire and IAT effects nonsignificant.

Apparently, relations between the IATs and the self-report measure were due to a common source of variance in salience asymmetries. A highly similar pattern of findings was also obtained in a second study that investigated the relations between a measure of ingroup preference for East versus West Germans and different East/West IATs and salience asymmetries for these categories, respectively.

What can we conclude from these findings? A major implication is that positive correlations between self-report measures and IAT effects do not suffice to prove that the systematic variance in the IAT is produced by interindividual differences in the strength of associations. Such a positive relation may instead be due to a confound of associations and salience asymmetries. Of course, having shown a positive relation between IAT effects and self-report measures also justifies the usage of the IAT as an, albeit indirect, indicator of the respective attitude, stereotype, or self-attribute relation. It is important to note, however, that the IAT procedure by itself does not guarantee such a positive relation, as is often presumed by researchers who unquestioningly use the IAT as a measure of associations.

The question of the validity of the IAT as a measure of associations immediately leads to the question of the relation between implicit and explicit measures, and whether self-report questionnaires (of attitudes, self-concept, etc.) should be considered adequate variables for the validation of an implicit measure of associations anyway. After all, an implicit measure of associations is supposed to provide an assessment of cognitive structures, which should be largely independent of strategic or controlled processes that may have a strong influence on responding in self-report measures (Fazio, 1990; Fazio, Jackson, Dunton, & Williams, 1995; Strack & Deutsch, 2004). Furthermore, automatic associations may reflect different sources of experience and may be represented in a different format than personal attitudes and beliefs (Rudman, 2004; Wilson, Lindsey, & Schooler, 2000). We cannot provide sufficient answers to this very complex set of questions here; however, we want to express our concern regarding the practice of evaluating the IAT mainly in terms of its capability of predicting self-report measures, and selecting and prescribing a scoring algorithm on the basis of optimizing this kind of correlation (Greenwald, Nosek, & Banaji, 2003; Greenwald, Nosek, Banaji, & Klauer, 2005). In our opinion, this research strategy in some way runs counter to the original quest for a truly independent implicit assessment of mental processes and may promote the import of strategic elements into the IAT (Rothermund, Wentura, & De Houwer, 2005b; see also our discussion of strategic recoding effects below).

Studies of Other Laboratories

Up to now, we have focused mainly on those research findings relating to the salience asymmetry account that were gathered in our own laboratories. We now briefly summarize the findings of other researchers that provide independent support for the salience asymmetry model.

In an early series of experiments, Brendl and colleagues (2001) investigated whether the IAT can be regarded as a pure measure of automatic prejudice. In one study, they replaced the presumedly positive target category (*flowers* in a flower/insect × pleasant/unpleasant IAT) with the neutral category of nonwords. Interestingly, the previously negative IAT effect for insects (relative to flowers) was reversed when insects were contrasted with nonwords indicating that the effect should be attributed to differences in familiarity rather than valence. To rule out the alternative explanation of their findings that nonwords were evaluated negatively, Brendl and colleagues characterized the nonword category in a very positive manner in another experiment: Nonwords were introduced as positive words that were taken from the language "Lositio"; the term *Lositio* itself was said to have the meaning of "joy." Again, responses were faster when "insects" and "positive" were assigned the same response. These findings are difficult to explain on the basis of evaluative associations between nonwords and unpleasant words. Instead, the pattern of results is compatible with the salience asymmetries account if one assumes that the category of nonwords is more salient than the category of insects.

Effects of salience asymmetry in the IAT were also reported by Kinoshita and Peek-O'Leary (2003) in a series of conceptual replications of our findings; they found compatibility effects for "odd" and "even" as target categories in a good/bad IAT as well as in a word/nonword IAT, indicating salience effects in the absence of any plausible associations between categories. In addition, IAT effects were neutralized or even reversed by previous go/no-go training blocks without changing the stimuli and categories of IATs.

In yet another set of ingenious studies, Mitchell (2004) found that IAT effects could be produced by using asymmetric target categories, such that only one category was specifically described, whereas the opposite category was defined only by negation, that is, a member of the unspecified category was defined simply by not being a member of the specified category (e.g., "can fly"/"cannot fly," "possess teeth"/"does not possess teeth"). Again, the target categories were not conceptually related to the attribute categories ("good" vs.

"bad"). Furthermore, Mitchell (2004) was able to show that the resulting IAT effect depended only on the structural feature of matching a specific description (i.e., being expected/nonsalient) versus deviating from the prespecified category (i.e., being salient): The resulting effect did not depend on the content or valence of the exemplars of the two categories, because the same two sets of target exemplars were used for the two versions of the task. Relabeling the categories, so that members of the prespecified category ("can fly") became the nonmembers ("does not possess teeth") in the second version and vice versa, reversed the resulting IAT effect.

AUTOMATIC PROCESSES OR STRATEGIC RECODING?

A further threat to the validity of an association account is that in at least some cases a strategic recoding of categories may explain the effects (Rothermund et al., 2005b). That is, even if we concede for a moment that associative representations trigger IAT effects, we have to make sure that the results found with the IAT are not due to some kind of strategy used by participants. Take, for example, the study by Gray, MacCulloch, Smith, Morris, and Snowden (2003), who administered an IAT to psychopathic murderers and controls. The IAT consisted of a positive/negative attribute dimension and a violence/nonviolence target dimension, both exemplified by word exemplars. The main result was a tremendous IAT effect (indicating a violence/negative association) that was significantly lower for psychopathic murderers. Does that mean that psychopathic murderers do have a mental representation of violence that is less negatively connoted for them than for others? Maybe, but not necessarily. The easiest way to solve the task is to completely disregard the distinction between the attribute and target dimensions in the Compatible block and to recode the task to a simple positive/negative classification, because presumably all the violence-related items (e.g., *kill*) are negative stimuli. Thus, it may turn out that psychopathic murderers tended to follow such a strategy with a lower probability. This would be an interesting result in itself, but, however, a less spectacular one than initially assumed.

Another example of strong IAT effects indicating strategic recoding in the absence of associations was provided by Mierke and Klauer (2003). In their geometry IAT, participants had to categorize blue and red objects on the basis of their color (target categories: blue vs. red), whereas all other objects had to be categorized on the basis of their size (attribute categories: small vs. large). The key ele-

ment of their experiment was the fact that color was completely confounded with size: all red objects were small, whereas all blue objects
were large. Mierke and Klauer obtained a strong IAT effect; responding was markedly faster when "red" and "small" were assigned to
the same response. This finding reflects the effect of strategic recoding. Because of the redundancy of the color information, responses
could be given on the basis of size alone for all stimuli in the Compatible block (red and small vs. blue and large), whereas such a
recoding was impossible for an incompatible assignment of categories to responses (red and large vs. blue and small). It is important to
note that the effect was obtained although the color and size concepts of the experiment were not associated in any way.

To elaborate on this point, consider a further analogy to research
on a prominent paradigm of cognitive psychology: the semantic
priming paradigm (see Neely, 1991, for a review). In semantic priming experiments, participants have to process target stimuli according
to some simple task (e.g., pronounce the target as quickly as possible). Shortly before each target, another stimulus is presented that is
either associated with the target or not. What is typically found is a
relatedness effect: response times are lower for targets (e.g., *ape*) that
are preceded by an associatively related item (e.g., *banana*) as compared to the control condition (e.g., *tomato*). Does this effect reflect
an automatic spreading of activation in a semantic network? Maybe,
but not necessarily. We can simply assume that participants may realize the contingency and, to speed up their responses, try to build up
expectancies about the target after reading the prime (Becker, 1980).
Fortunately for semantic priming research, it is possible to separate
automatic and strategic priming effects. Using some simple experimental manipulations, Neely (1977) found that expectancies in the
priming paradigm need time to evolve. Thus, priming effects found
with a short time lag between prime onset and target onset (stimulus-
onset asynchrony, SOA) seem to reflect automatic processes.

Going back to IAT research, we can note that to date there is no
equivalent to the SOA manipulation of Neely (1977); that is, we do
not know of any manipulation that might help to separate automatic
and strategic components of IAT effects.

WHY ARE SMALL-SCALE THEORIES SO IMPORTANT?

Using a rough picture, the history of social cognition may be separated into two phases. The first phase was characterized by adopting
the theoretical language of cognitive psychology for social psycho-

logical phenomena. The second one is characterized by adopting the inventory of methods of cognitive psychology.

Essentially, the theoretical language is about functional subsystems of the mind (e.g., long-term memory, working memory, etc.) and processes that operate within and between those subsystems. Most important, it is a language at a subpersonal level: it is about mechanisms that can in principle be simulated on a computer. Theories that are formulated in this language should help us to understand human behavior at a personal level: our intentions, our actions, our decisions, our judgments, and so forth. The theories themselves, however, do not contain those personal terms.

To illustrate these rather abstract considerations, we offer a simple example. We can describe the behavior of judges completely in personal terms: They base their verdicts on a weighing of all evidence that they know of. If we have the impression that there is considerable variance in the severity of sentences (given rather comparable cases), we can proceed in two ways. One way is to find out more about those beliefs and values of the judges that govern their professional behavior. The silver bullet to achieve this is simply to ask them (of course, in a professional way). We are sure that part of the variance can be explained through this procedure. To describe the act of sentencing with reference to personal beliefs and values is an example of what the philosopher Dennett (1987) described as adopting an "intentional stance" in explaining a complex system.

However, for two reasons, we as psychologists cannot be entirely satisfied with the results. First, we are possibly left with the impression that some hidden causes for variance remain undetected. For example, we might wonder whether racial differences in the accused may be associated with differences in the severity of sentences. Racism, we hope, is not part of the explicit beliefs and values of judges. Thus, we will not find out by using our interview techniques.[4] Second and more important, we want to know what mechanisms are behind this complex behavior, which we tend to describe as an intentional act.

Therefore, the second way to find the answer is to formulate at least a partial social-cognitive theory about the mechanisms that finally end up in the utterance of a verdict. In Dennett's terms (1987), we adopt a "design stance" toward the complex system: treat it as a designed mechanism consisting of parts with specific functions that interact to produce characteristic behaviors. To exemplify, we might focus on the last part of our initial description—"they base their verdicts on a weighing of all evidence *that they know of* "—which is a cue for any social-cognitive researcher to the distinction between availability and accessibility (see Higgins, 1996; Tulving & Pearl-stone, 1966). Theories of memory include the difference between availability (i.e., something is stored) and accessibility (i.e., the probability that the stored information will intrude into ongoing information processes is a variable feature). We know that accessibility can be manipulated by simple techniques that do not even depend on conscious, intentional processing by the participant. To render some details of a crime more accessible than others can cause a huge difference in the severity of a sentence (e.g., Englich & Mussweiler, 2001). Assume for a moment—just for the sake of the argument—that you have a process model that has the following chain links: perception of the accused → activation of race → activation of a valence association → adopting an initial hypothesis of either "this is a severe case of, for example, theft" or "this is a mild case of, for example, theft," depending on the activated valence → positive testing renders those details more accessible that conform to the hypothesis → the final verdict is based on those details of the affair that are more accessible.

This causal chain is clearly formulated at a subpersonal level or, to recapitulate Dennett (1987), by using the design stance.[5] Thus, if we want to link these theoretical terms to the empirical world, we need methods that address them—for instance, the automatic evaluation of valence associations. The paradigms of cognitive psychology are those methods, and they are, strictly speaking, the only ones, but at least they are the most *direct* ones to tap those processes. Thus, there is no other way than to deeply explore the link between the data gathered with those experimental techniques and the theoretical terms of the subpersonal level, that is, to develop and test small-scale theories that make plausible why a certain difference score should be interpreted as, for example, automatic activation of an evaluation.

FINAL CONSIDERATIONS

Beyond doubt, cognitive research in general and social cognition in particular profits from the IAT, and the effects found with the IAT are (dominantly) nontrivial. Therefore, our critical remarks should not be understood as destructive. Rather, they are a plea for more basic research with the IAT to obtain deeper insights into the processes that contribute to the effects.

For those who are more inclined to apply the IAT, we have already argued elsewhere (Rothermund & Wentura, 2004) that it might be a good strategy to add salience-based IATs in their research (i.e., for any IAT with, e.g., valence as the attribute dimension, add a word/nonword IAT that is structurally equivalent) or to add our version of the search task (see above).

In linking the salience asymmetry account to other high-level theories of psychological functioning, it may also turn out that salience asymmetries measured with the IAT reveal something even more interesting and more fundamental about the target dimension (and the interindividual differences associated with it), as compared to the assumption of differences in valence or self-relatedness. Attentional asymmetries regarding a specific target dimension indicate asymmetries in the processing of information that can be influenced by certain situations, contexts, habits, and expectancies. Furthermore, interindividual differences in selective attention for certain types of information have already been proposed as a major condition for the emergence and/or maintenance of psychopathological symptoms like anxiety (e.g., Williams, Watts, MacLeod, & Mathews, 1997), phobia (Clark & Wells, 1995; Rinck, Reinecke, Ellwart, Heuer, & Becker, 2005), depression (Gotlib, Krasnoperova, Yue, & Joormann, 2004; Joormann, 2004), obsessive–compulsive disorder (Wegner & Lane, 1995), and addiction (Robinson & Berridge, 2003). Thus, it may finally turn out that the small-scale theory of salience asymmetries can be fruitfully related to large-scale theories of social and personality psychology.

NOTES

1. For a description of the IAT, see Chapter 3, this volume.
2. Of course, as for any response-time based measure, obtaining a valid effect requires intentional behavior of the participants, that is, they have to act according to instructions. However, in the ideal case, the score of interest (e.g., the difference in mean response times between the compatible and incompatible blocks for the IAT) is an unintentional by-product of intentionally behaving according to instructions. The participant as a *person* is a confederate of the experimenter in disclosing something on his or her *subpersonal* level (see page 209 for this term).
3. It might be argued that the response category of *nonword* is negative owing to the negation and therefore the classification is still evaluative. This explanation does not work, because a replication of that experiment with a replacement of the nonword label with "SIWOB," which is an acronym of the German translation of "senseless, but word-like letter string" and, accordingly, the word label with "non-SIWOB," yielded the same results as before.
4. Presumably, readers will murmur, "If they have racist beliefs, they'll not tell you." Of course, that may be true. But it is not our point at the moment that an utterance is an intentional act that may serve different goals besides "giving an honest and truthful answer."

5. Dennett (1987) proposed a third stance or theoretical level: the physical stance: "Treat a complex system as a physical system operating according to the laws of physics." We can easily identify cognitive neuroscience as the endeavor to explore the relations between the design stance and the physical stance.

REFERENCES

Banse, R., Seise, J., & Zerbes, N. (2001). Implicit attitudes towards homosexuality: Reliability, validity, and controllability of the IAT. *Zeitschrift für Experimentelle Psychologie, 48,* 145–160.

Becker, C. A. (1980). Semantic context effects in visual word recognition: An analysis of semantic strategies. *Memory and Cognition, 8,* 493–512.

Bosson, J. K., Swann, W. B., Jr., & Pennebaker, J. W. (2000). Stalking the perfect measure of implicit self-esteem: The blind men and the elephant revisited? *Journal of Personality and Social Psychology, 79,* 631–643.

Brendl, M., Markman, A., & Messner, C. (2001). How do indirect measures of evaluation work? Evaluating the interference of prejudice in the Implicit Association Test. *Journal of Personality and Social Psychology, 81,* 760–773.

Campbell, D. T., & Fiske, D. W. (1959). Convergent and discriminant validation by the multitrait-multimethod matrix. *Psychological Bulletin, 56,* 81–105.

Clark, D. M., & Wells, A. (1995). A cognitive model of social phobia. In R. G. Heimberg, M. R. Liebowitz, D. A. Hope, & F. R. Schneier (Eds.), *Social phobia: Diagnosis, assessment, and treatment* (pp. 69–93). New York: Guilford Press.

Cunningham, W. A., Preacher, K. J., & Banaji, M. R. (2001). Implicit attitude measures: Consistency, stability, and convergent validity. *Psychological Science, 121,* 163–170.

De Houwer, J. (2001). A structural and process analysis of the Implicit Association Test. *Journal of Experimental Social Psychology, 37,* 443–451.

De Houwer, J., & Eelen, P. (1998). An affective variant of the Simon paradigm. *Cognition and Emotion, 8,* 45–61.

De Houwer, J., Geldof, T., & De Bruycker, E. (2005). The Implicit Association Test as a general measure of similarity. *Canadian Journal of Experimental Psychology, 59,* 229–239.

Dennett, D. (1987). *The intentional stance.* Cambridge, MA: MIT Press.

Egloff. B., & Schmukle, S. C. (2002). Predictive validity of an Implicit Association Test for assessing anxiety. *Journal of Personality and Social Psychology, 83,* 1441–1455.

Englich, B., & Mussweiler, T. (2001). Sentencing under uncertainty: Anchoring effects in the courtroom. *Journal of Applied Social Psychology, 31,* 1535–1551.

Fazio, R. H. (1990). Multiple processes by which attitudes guide behavior: The MODE model as an integrative framework. In M. P. Zanna (Ed.), *Advances in experimental psychology* (Vol. 23, pp. 75–109). San Diego, CA: Academic Press.

Fazio, R. H., Jackson, J. R., Dunton, B. C., & Williams, C. J. (1995). Variability in automatic activation as an unobtrusive measure of racial attitudes: A bona fide pipeline? *Journal of Personality and Social Psychology, 69,* 1013–1027.

Fox, E. (1995). Negative priming from ignored distractors in visual selection: A review. *Psychonomic Bulletin and Review, 2,* 145–173.

Gawronski, B. (2002). What does the Implicit Association Test measure?: A test of the convergent and discriminant validity of prejudice-related IATs. *Experimental Psychology, 49,* 171–180.

Gotlib, I. H., Krasnoperova, E., Yue, D. N., & Joormann, J. (2004). Attentional biases for negative interpersonal stimuli in clinical depression. *Journal of Abnormal Psychology, 113,* 127–135.

Gray, N. S., MacCulloch, M. J., Smith, J., Morris, M., & Snowden, R. J. (2003). Violence viewed by psychopathic murderers. *Nature, 423,* 497–498.

Greenwald, A. G., & Farnham, S. D. (2000). Using the Implicit Association Test to measure self-esteem and self-concept. *Journal of Personality and Social Psychology, 79,* 1022–1038.

Greenwald, A. G., McGhee, D. E., & Schwartz, J. L. K. (1998). Measuring individual differences in implicit cognition: The Implicit Association Test. *Journal of Personality and Social Psychology, 74,* 1464–1480.

Greenwald, A. G., Nosek, B. A., & Banaji, M. R. (2003). Understanding and using the Implicit Association Test: I. An improved scoring algorithm. *Journal of Personality and Social Psychology, 85,* 197–216.

Greenwald, A. G., Nosek, B. A., Banaji, M. R., & Klauer, K. C. (2005). Validity of the salience asymmetry interpretation of the IAT: Comment on Rothermund and Wentura (2004). *Journal of Experimental Psychology: General, 134,* 420–425.

Higgins, E. T. (1996). Knowledge activation: Accessibility, applicability, and salience. In E. T. Higgins & A. W. Kruglanski (Eds.), *Social psychology: Handbook of basic principles* (pp. 133–168). New York: Guilford Press.

Hofmann, W., Gawronski, B., Gschwendner, T., Le, H., & Schmitt, M. (2005). A meta-analysis on the correlation between the Implicit Association Test and explicit self-report measures. *Personality and Social Psychology Bulletin, 31,* 1369–1385.

Houghton, G., & Tipper, S. P. (1994). A model of inhibitory mechanisms in selective attention. In D. Dagenbach & T. H. Carr (Eds.), *Inhibitory processes in attention, memory, and language* (pp. 53–112). San Diego, CA: Academic Press.

Joormann, J. (2004). Attentional bias in dysphoria: The role of inhibitory processes. *Cognition and Emotion, 18,* 125–147.

Kinoshita, S., & Peek-O'Leary, M. (2003, November 6–9). *Implicit Association Test (IAT): Support for the salience asymmetry account.* Paper presented at the 44th annual meeting of the Psychonomic Society, Vancouver, BC, Canada.

Kinoshita, S., & Peek-O'Leary, M. (2005). Does the compatibility effect in the race Implicit Association Test (IAT) reflect familiarity or affect? *Psychonomic Bulletin and Review, 12,* 442–452.

Klauer, K. C., & Mierke, J. (2005). Task-set inertia, attitude accessibility, and compatibility-order effects: New evidence for a task-set switching account of the Implicit Association Test effect. *Personality and Social Psychology Bulletin, 31,* 208–217.

Klauer, K. C., & Musch, J. (2003). Affective priming: Findings and theories. In J. Musch & K. C. Klauer (Eds.), *The psychology of evaluation: Affective processes in cognition and emotion* (pp. 7–49). Mahwah, NJ: Erlbaum.

MacLeod, C. M. (1991). Half a century of research on the Stroop effect: An integrative review. *Psychological Bulletin, 109,* 163–203.

May, C. P., Kane, M. J., & Hasher, L. (1995). Determinants of negative priming. *Psychological Bulletin, 118,* 35–54.

Mierke, J., & Klauer, K. C. (2001). Implicit association measurement with the IAT: Evidence for effects of executive control processes. *Zeitschrift für Experimentelle Psychologie, 48,* 107–122.

Mierke, J., & Klauer, K. C. (2003). Method-specific variance in the Implicit Association Test. *Journal of Personality and Social Psychology, 85,* 1180–1192.

Mitchell, C. J. (2004). Mere acceptance produces apparent attitude in the Implicit Association Test. *Journal of Experimental Social Psychology, 40,* 366–373.

Neely, J. H. (1977). Semantic priming and retrieval from lexical memory: Roles of inhibitionless spreading activation and limited-capacity attention. *Journal of Experimental Psychology: General, 106,* 226–254.

Neely, J. H. (1991). Semantic priming effects in visual word recognition: A selective review of current findings and theories. In D. Besner & G. W. Humphreys (Eds.), *Basic processes in reading: Visual word recognition* (pp. 264–336). Hillsdale, NJ: Erlbaum.

Neill, W. T., & Valdes, L. A. (1996). Facilitatory and inhibitory aspects of attention. In A. F. Kramer, M. Coles, & G. D. Logan (Eds.), *Converging operations in the study of visual selective attention* (pp. 77–106). Washington, DC: American Psychological Association.

Nosek, B. A. (2005). Moderators of the relationship between implicit and explicit evaluation. *Journal of Experimental Psychology: General, 134,* 565–584.

Proctor, R. W., & Cho, Y. S. (2006). Polarity correspondence: A general principle for performance of speeded binary classification tasks. *Psychological Bulletin, 132,* 416–442.

Rinck, M., Reinecke, A., Ellwart, T., Heuer, K., & Becker, E. S. (2005). Speeded detection and increased distraction in fear of spiders: Evidence from eye movements. *Journal of Abnormal Psychology, 114,* 235–248.

Robinson, T. E., & Berridge, K. C. (2003). Addiction. *Annual Review of Psychology, 54,* 25–53.

Rothermund, K., & Wentura, D. (2001). Figure–ground asymmetries in the Implicit Association Test (IAT). *Zeitschrift für Experimentelle Psychologie, 48,* 94–106.

Rothermund, K., & Wentura, D. (2004). Underlying processes in the Implicit Association Test (IAT): Dissociating salience from associations. *Journal of Experimental Psychology: General, 133,* 139–165.

Rothermund, K., Wentura, D., & De Houwer, J. (2005a). Retrieval of incidental stimulus–response associations as a source of negative priming. *Journal of Experimental Psychology: Learning, Memory, and Cognition, 31,* 482–495.

Rothermund, K., Wentura, D., & De Houwer, J. (2005b). Validity of the salience asymmetry account of the IAT: Reply to Greenwald, Nosek, Banaji, and Klauer (2005). *Journal of Experimental Psychology: General, 134,* 426–430.

Rudman, L. A. (2004). Sources of implicit attitudes. *Current Directions in Psychological Science, 13*, 79–82.

Strack, F., & Deutsch, R. (2004). Reflective and impulsive determinants of social behavior. *Personality and Social Psychology Review, 8*, 220–247.

Tipper, S. P. (1985). The negative priming effect: Inhibitory priming by ignored objects. *Quarterly Journal of Experimental Psychology, 37A*, 571–590.

Tipper, S. P. (2001). Does negative priming reflect inhibitory mechanisms? A review and integration of conflicting views. *Quarterly Journal of Experimental Psychology: Human Experimental Psychology, 54A*, 321–343.

Tulving, E., & Pearlstone, Z. (1966). Availability versus accessibility of information in memory for words. *Journal of Verbal Learning and Verbal Behavior, 5*, 381–391.

Wegner, D. M., & Lane, J. D. (1995). From secrecy to psychopathology. In J. W. Pennebaker (Ed.), *Emotion, disclosure, and health* (pp. 25–46). Washington, DC: American Psychological Association.

Williams, J. M. G., Watts, F. N., MacLeod, C., & Mathews, A. (1997). *Cognitive psychology and emotional disorders* (2nd ed.). Chichester, UK: Wiley.

Wilson, T. D., Lindsey, S., & Schooler, T. Y. (2000). A model of dual attitudes. *Psychological Review, 107*, 101–126.

Wolfe, J. M. (1998). Visual search. In H. Pashler (Ed.), *Attention* (pp. 14–73). Hove, UK: Psychological Press.

9 Beyond the Attitude Object

Implicit Attitudes Spring from
Object-Centered Contexts

Melissa J. Ferguson
John A. Bargh

Among the most important developments in attitude research over the last two decades has been the advent of measures that
capture people's attitudes in an implicit manner, as this book attests
(see also Banaji, 2001; Bargh, Chaiken, Govender, & Pratto, 1992;
Bassili & Brown, 2005; Blair, 2002; Fazio, 2001; Fazio & Olson,
2003; Fazio, Sanbonmatsu, Powell, & Kardes, 1986; Ferguson, in
press; Greenwald & Banaji, 1995; Greenwald, McGhee, & Schwartz,
1998; Musch & Klauer, 2003). These measures gauge the degree to
which people evaluate a given stimulus as good or bad without being
aware that their attitude toward the stimulus is being measured.
Some implicit measures can capture a person's attitude toward a
stimulus without the person even consciously registering the stimulus
itself, much less realizing that his or her attitude toward it is being assessed (e.g., Greenwald, Klinger, & Liu, 1989).

Implicit attitude measurement stands in contrast to the direct
self-report methodology that has guided much of attitude research
over the last century. Whereas implicit measures gauge attitudes co-
vertly, self-report measures consist of directly asking people to report
their attitudes or evaluations of certain stimuli (see Albarracín, John-

son, & Zanna, 2005; Eagly & Chaiken, 1993). For instance, the standard "feeling thermometer" measure of attitudes requires respondents to report their warmth, from 0 to 100 degrees, toward some group or object. Even many of the subtler attitude measures developed in the 1970s and 1980s required people to explicitly and deliberately report their attitudes. The "bogus pipeline" developed by Jones and Sigall (1971), for example, was predicated on the assumption that people will intentionally report a more truthful attitude if they believe that any fabrication will be detected (see also McCauley & Stitt, 1978; McConahay, 1986). Because such measures allow the respondent to respond strategically (and typically without time constraints), attitudes measured explicitly may reflect respondents' attempts at hiding their true feelings or yielding to what they think the experimenter wants them to feel (see, e.g., Orne, 1962; Rosenberg, 1969).

Contemporary implicit measures that gauge people's attitudes without their awareness thus represent a substantive departure from the ways in which attitudes have characteristically been measured over the last 100 years. Given this rather dramatic shift in measurement techniques, there has been a considerable amount of research directed toward understanding the precise nature of implicit attitudes.[1] Because explicit measures have been found to be highly sensitive to contextual factors at the time of measurement, a great deal of this research has examined how implicit attitudes may similarly depend on the context (e.g., Barden, Maddux, Petty, & Brewer, 2004; Dasgupta & Greenwald, 2001; Ferguson & Bargh, 2004; Karpinski & Hilton, 2001; Livingston & Brewer, 2002; Lowery, Hardin, & Sinclair, 2001; Mitchell, Nosek, & Banaji, 2003; Wittenbrink, Judd, & Park, 2001). In addition, differences between implicit and explicit attitudes have prompted the development (or modification) of theories concerning the representation and generation of evaluative information in memory more generally (e.g., Bassili & Brown, 2005; De Houwer, 2006; Ferguson, in press-b; Gawronski, Strack, & Bodenhausen, in press; Mitchell et al., 2003).

Largely on the basis of this recent research and theory, we argue in this chapter for a reconceptualization of what automatic attitudes reflect. Rather than such an attitude reflecting the unintentionally activated evaluation of an "object," we argue that automatic attitudes would be more appropriately understood as unintentionally activated evaluations of "object-centered contexts." An overt emphasis on the contextual dependence of such attitudes is reasonable, we argue, given the evidence accumulated over the last 5 years especially, and recent theoretical frameworks concerning the generation of evaluations. Moreover, we also speculate that automatic attitudes may be especially reflective of contextual factors as compared with more deliberate attitudes. In what follows, we review the contemporary definition of an automatic attitude, the research and theory suggesting its contextualized nature and relevant issues concerning attitude stability, and finally a consideration of why automatic attitudes may be more context dependent than more deliberately generated attitudes.

WHAT IS AN AUTOMATIC ATTITUDE?

There are arguably three components of the definition of an automatic attitude. The first concerns the attitude itself. From the inception of the construct in the beginning of the 20th century (see, e.g., Albarracín et al., 2005; Eagly & Chaiken, 1993), attitudes have been understood as assessments of whether the corresponding objects are pleasing or displeasing. Although some definitions have included aspects of beliefs and behavior (see, e.g., Fishbein & Ajzen, 1975), they have always stressed the importance of the evaluative dimension, and contemporary definitions seem to rest primarily on the evaluative aspect. For example, one of the most currently widely accepted definitions stipulates that an attitude is a "psychological tendency that is expressed by evaluating a particular entity with some degree of favor or disfavor" (Eagly & Chaiken, 1993). Similarly, Fazio and colleagues (Fazio, 1986, 1995, 2001; Fazio et al., 1986) have argued that an attitude consists of the association in memory between an object and its (positive or negative) evaluation.

The second component refers to the nature of the attitude object. Traditionally, the *object* of an evaluation can consist of whatever the person is thinking about at the time of measurement. The only requisite for an "attitude object" (i.e., an object that is being evaluated) is that it is discriminable, or a subject of thought (Eagly & Chaiken, 1993). Attitude objects have most often consisted of physical, concrete objects (e.g., apple, garbage), individuals or groups of people (e.g., Michael Jordan, Blacks), abstract ideals and values (e.g., equality, freedom), or issues and policies (e.g., abortion, voting). Within the automatic attitude literature, attitudes have most often been measured in response to concrete graspable objects, such as people and items (though see Ferguson, in press-a). This literature suggests overall that an attitude is assumed to reflect a person's evaluation of an object in isolation.

The third component of the definition of an automatic attitude of course entails the implicit way in which the attitude is generated. As mentioned earlier, an attitude can be characterized as implicit when its activation happens unintentionally and spontaneously (see, e.g., Greenwald & Banaji, 1995). Although most of the research in this area has focused on attitudes that are activated unintentionally, there is evidence that attitudes can also be activated without the person being aware of the corresponding stimulus (see, e.g., Bargh, 1997; Ferguson, in press-b). Explicit attitudes, in contrast, necessarily require the respondent's intention, awareness, and control. The two major types of attitude measures currently being used in the field thus differ in terms of the way in which evaluative information about the object is activated in memory. It should be noted that in both types of measures, however, the evaluation is assumed to refer to a single object.

THE INITIAL PROMISE OF AUTOMATIC
ATTITUDES AS CONTEXT DEPENDENT

The development of implicit measures was prompted by the accumulating, extensive evidence that explicitly measured attitudes are highly influenced by the context in which they are assessed (see, e.g., Anderson, 1974; Bem, 1972; Chaiken & Yates, 1985; Fazio, 1987; Feldman & Lynch, 1988; Forgas, 1992; Miller & Tesser, 1986; Olson, 1990; Schuman & Presser, 1981; Schwarz & Bless, 1992; Schwarz & Clore, 1983; Strack, 1992; Tesser, 1978; Tourangeau & Rasinski, 1988; Wilson, Dunn, Draft, & Lisle, 1989; Wilson & Hodges, 1992). Researchers have demonstrated that people's explicit attitudes about the state of their marriages depend in part on whether it is sunny outside at the moment (Schwarz & Clore, 1983) and that a person's self-reported religiosity on a questionnaire depends in part on the nature of the preceding question (Salancik & Conway, 1975), for example. Similarly, respondents who want to be perceived as egalitarian may intentionally report positive attitudes toward a stigmatized group to an experimenter, yet behave in a highly prejudiced manner in less public settings (see, e.g., LaPiere, 1934; McConahay, 1983).

Research demonstrating that explicit attitudes are influenced by observations of one's own behavior, current thoughts, mood, demand effects, and other contextual constraints led some researchers to suggest that explicit attitudes are highly contextually dependent, to the point that they are constructed on the spot (Anderson, 1974; Tesser, 1978). In other words, people may spontaneously construct their attitudes when they are asked to report them, rather than recalling and reporting preexisting attitudes in memory. Because of this constructive process at the time of measurement, contextual factors that may have little to do with the actual attitude itself nevertheless influence the response (see Schwarz & Bohner, 2001 for a review).

Given the inherent difficulties in interpreting data from explicit attitude measures, researchers began to search for less reactive, and therefore more effective, tools of attitude assessment. Implicit measures, which have been included in cognitive psychology methodologies for decades, were first employed to measure attitudes in 1986 by Fazio, Sanbonmatsu, Powell, and Kardes (1986). Fazio and colleagues modified a sequential priming paradigm that was developed by Neely (1976, 1977). Whereas Neely used the priming paradigm to study the automatic activation of semantic information on perception of a stimulus, Fazio and colleagues modified the priming paradigm to examine the automatic activation of solely evaluative information on perception of a stimulus. This paradigm has since been utilized as an implicit attitude measure (e.g., Fazio, Jackson, Dunton, & Williams, 1995; Ferguson & Bargh, 2004; Wittenbrink, Judd, & Park, 1997, 2001), and comprehensive details of this measure are provided by Wittenbrink (Chapter 2, this volume). Since the publication of the evaluative priming paradigm by Fazio and colleagues (Fazio et al., 1986), researchers have developed other means of implicitly assessing attitudes, including the Implicit Association Test (IAT; Greenwald et al., 1998; see also Lane, Banaji, Nosek, & Greenwald, Chapter 3, this volume), various physiological tools and measures (see Ito & Cacioppo, Chapter 5, this volume), and an assortment of other implicit behavioral measures (De Houwer, 2003; De Houwer & Eelen, 1998; Dovidio, Kawakami, Johnson, Johnson, & Howard, 1997; Koole, Dijksterhuis, & van Knippenberg, 2001; Nosek & Banaji, 2001; Payne, Cheng, Govorun, & Stewart, 2005; von Hippel, Sekaquaptewa, & Vargas, 1997).

The development of implicit attitude measures was accompanied by the hope that such measures might prove less reactive and more covert than explicit attitude measures (Banaji, 2001; Fazio et al., 1995). From the beginning, automatic attitudes were assumed to be contextually independent (e.g., Bargh, 1999; Bargh et al., 1992, 1996; Devine, 1989; Fazio et al., 1995; Wilson & Hodges, 1992; Wilson, Lindsey, & Schooler, 2000), to the point that an implicit attitude measure was regarded as a potential "bona fide pipeline" to people's inner attitudes (Fazio et al., 1995). One of the straightforward reasons for such an assumption is that implicit measures tap people's attitudes outside their awareness, and thus without any strategic editing. That is, participants cannot possibly modify their responses if they are not aware of making such responses in the first place. Not only was it presumed that implicit measures are therefore impervious to strategic intentions, it was also assumed that they are able to capture a constant and unchanging summary evaluative index of the object (see Wilson et al., 2000).

Thus, at least initially, implicit measures seemed likely to provide clean, less variable indices of how people feel toward the stimuli in their environment. Researchers in attitude theory, as well as many working on prejudice and stereotyping, therefore initially embraced a view of implicit attitudes as context independent and stable indices of people's "true" evaluations of objects, people, places, and concepts. Researchers studying socially sensitive topics such as prejudice toward various groups therefore began to rely on implicit attitude measures rather than explicit measures (e.g., Devine, 1989; Fazio et al., 1995; Swanson, Rudman, & Greenwald, 2001).

THE CONTEXTUAL DEPENDENCE
OF AUTOMATIC ATTITUDES

Over the last 5 years, in contrast to initial assumptions, there has been a wealth of evidence suggesting that automatic attitudes vary according to a host of factors at the time of measurement. This work suggests that a person's implicit attitude toward a racial group, for example, will depend on that person's recently activated memories about the group (Dasgupta & Greenwald, 2001), task instructions (Mitchell et al., 2003), the race of the experimenter (Lowery et al., 2001), the person's active goals (Ferguson & Bargh, 2004; Sherman, Presson, Chassin, Rose, & Koch, 2003), the person's chronic goals about egalitarianism (Barden et al., 2004; Maddux, Barden, Brewer, & Petty, 2005), and the person's mood (Hermsen, Holland, & van Knippenberg, 2004). We review this evidence of contextual dependence by dividing the research into two broad groups—one group includes those experiments that directly constrained the types of object-relevant information accessible at the time of measurement, and another group that includes experiments that constrained the accessibility of object-relevant information more indirectly through goals and task instructions.

Direct Constraints (Information about Attitude Object
Is Manipulated Physically in Environment)

The first batch of experiments to suggest the contextual dependence of automatic attitudes was published in 2001 in a special issue of the

Journal of Personality and Social Psychology devoted to implicit measures of attitudes and stereotypes. In one of the articles, Dasgupta and Greenwald (2001) demonstrated that the way in which participants implicitly evaluate a racial group depends on which group members are most accessible in memory at the time of measurement. Participants first looked at pictures of either liked White people and disliked Black people (pro-White group) or the reverse (pro-Black group). Participants then completed a race-based IAT (see Lane et al., Chapter 3, this volume), and the results demonstrated that those in the pro-Black group displayed significantly less negative automatic attitudes toward Blacks than those in the pro-White group. Dasgupta and Greenwald showed that this effect also remained 24 hours later when participants came back to the lab to retake the race-based IAT. These findings reinforce the view that a given object is likely associated with a wide array of memories, some of which may differ in their evaluative connotation (e.g., Abelson, 1976, 1981; Barsalou, 1992; Bower, 1981; Fishbein & Ajzen, 1975; Fiske & Pavelchak, 1986; Schank & Abelson, 1977; Smith, 1992; Smith & Zarate, 1992). This means that the particular memories that are active at the time of an attitude measure will likely greatly influence the direction (positive, negative) of the attitude, a view that has also been applied to explicit attitudes (e.g., Schwarz & Bohner, 2001).

In the same volume of the *Journal of Personality and Social Psychology*, Wittenbrink and colleagues (2001) reported evidence that participants' automatic attitudes toward Black people depended on the context in which the people were encountered. When participants saw photos of a Black person in a picnic setting, for instance, they displayed significantly more positive automatic attitudes toward that person as compared with those who saw photos of the same Black person standing by a wall with graffiti on it in an inner-city scene. This work is consistent with that of Dasgupta and Greenwald (2001) and suggests that the attitudes that are activated on perception of a stimulus do not depend solely on the stimulus in isolation—they are heavily influenced by the rich context in which the stimulus is perceived.

Also in the same volume, Lowery and colleagues (2001) demonstrated that one way to alter the accessibility of object-relevant information is to vary the race of the experimenter. In this research, participants completed an implicit attitude measure on race, and the experimenter of the study was either Black or White. When the experimenter was Black, participants displayed significantly less negative automatic attitudes toward Blacks than when the experimenter was White. The authors interpreted these results as evidence that people's automatic attitudes are sensitive to the social pressures in a situation, such as the pressure to avoid being perceived as prejudiced in the presence of a person who belongs to a group that has traditionally been stigmatized. This suggests that interacting with a particular group member right before completing an implicit attitude measure alters a person's automatic attitudes toward that group, just as the research by Dasgupta and Greenwald (2001) and Wittenbrink and colleagues (2001) suggests.

Karpinski and Hilton (2001) also investigated the influence of highly accessible, object-relevant information on automatic attitudes. In their research, however, they experimentally increased the accessibility of pro-elderly and anti-youth information through the repetitive viewing of pro-elderly and anti-youth stimuli. They found that those participants who had viewed the pro-elderly stimuli did in fact exhibit significantly more positive attitudes toward elderly people. This research is consistent with research on implicit stereotyping that shows that people's automatic stereotypes depend on the nature of recently activated and repeatedly viewed stereotype-relevant information (see also Blair, Ma, & Lenton, 2001; Kawakami, Dovidio, Moll, Hermsen, & Russin, 2000; Rudman, Asmore, & Gary, 2001).

Other research has also demonstrated the potency of accessible object-relevant information on automatic attitudes toward an object. Livingston and Brewer (2002), for instance, tested whether the negative automatic evaluation of Black people was primarily due to facial features that were strongly prototypic of Blacks, versus the categorization of a person in terms of race or ethnicity. They found evidence for the former by showing that participants in fact displayed significantly more negative automatic attitudes toward those who possessed facial features that were prototypic of Black people, such as a wide nose and full lips, as compared with less prototypic features (see also Blair, Judd, & Fallman, 2004). This suggests that certain group features are more strongly associated with negativity than others, and that making those features salient influences the type of attitude that is automatically generated toward the group. The degree of negativity of an individual's automatic attitude toward a given Black person, then, depends on the relative accessibility of prototypically Black versus nonprototypically Black features.

Indirect Constraints (Information about Attitude Object Is Manipulated via the Perceiver's Goals)

Research has also demonstrated that the accessibility of object-relevant information can be determined by the type of motivation or goal the person possesses at the time of measurement. Whereas the research reviewed earlier manipulated the accessibility of object information directly—that is, different kinds of information about the attitude object were included (or not) in participants' physical environment (e.g., Dasgupta & Greenwald, 2001; Wittenbrink et al., 2001)—other research has presented the same physical stimulus but altered people's goal or task objective at the time of the measurement. For example, Mitchell and colleagues (2003) recently tested whether participants' automatic attitudes toward Blacks depend on the way in which they are categorized. Participants completed an IAT, having been instructed to classify Black and White persons in terms of either career or race. Whereas the Black targets were all liked athletes, the White targets were all disliked politicians. The results demonstrated that when participants classified the targets in terms of career, they exhibited significantly more positive automatic attitudes toward Blacks than Whites. However, this pattern was reversed, and negativity toward Blacks was demonstrated, when participants classified the targets in terms of race. This research suggests that the categorization task determined the types of memories activated in response to each target person, and consequently the nature of the automatic evaluation toward that person. When Blacks were categorized in terms of their athleticism, more positive memories were presumably activated and thus drove participants' automatic evaluative responses.

Maddux and colleagues (2005) recently demonstrated that people's automatic attitudes toward group members also depend on their chronic goals to avoid being prejudiced. They included participants who were low or high in motivation to respond without prejudice and asked them to complete an implicit attitude measure similar to the one developed and used by Wittenbrink and colleagues (2001). Participants saw photos of Black people who were in either negative (e.g., a prison) or positive (e.g., a church) contexts. The results showed that those who were low in motivation to avoid prejudice demonstrated significantly more negative automatic attitudes toward Black persons in the negative as compared to the positive context. Interestingly, however, those who were high in motivation to avoid prejudice actually showed weaker negative automatic attitudes in the negative as compared to the positive context. For these participants, their negativity toward Blacks was apparently inhibited in response to a context that would normally provoke negativity. These findings suggest that people who have chronic egalitarian goals may be especially sensitive to situations that normatively provoke prejudicial responses toward a group member. And, their automatic evaluations of group members in such situations reflect this sensitivity (see Moskowitz, Gollwitzer, Wasel, & Schaal, 1999).

Ferguson and Bargh (2004) demonstrated that people's currently active goals also influence the automatic evaluation of a range of (nonracial) stimuli, depending on the relation between participants' current goals and the utility of the stimuli. Participants who were pursuing a goal tended to automatically evaluate as positive those objects that could help them achieve the goal, as compared with other objects, unlike those participants who had already reached the goal. For example, those participants who were playing a competitive word game exhibited significantly more positive automatic attitudes toward words that were relevant to the game (e.g., *achieve, win, noun, c*), as compared with those who had finished the game only a minute earlier. This suggests that automatic attitudes can reflect the current or prospective utility of the corresponding objects, rather than solely the retrospective or recent utility (see also Sherman et al., 2003). This work is in line with the classic notion that thinking (and evaluating) is in the service of action (see, e.g., Fiske, 1992; James, 1890).

In similar research, Sherman and colleagues (2003) tested whether participants' automatic attitudes toward smoking paraphernalia would depend on whether they had a current need to smoke. Participants in this study were all habitual smokers and had either just smoked or not. Those who had *not* just smoked were found to automatically evaluate smoking-related objects as significantly more positive than those who had just fulfilled their nicotine needs. This work suggests, along with the work by Ferguson and Bargh (2004), that evaluations that are activated automatically reflect what the perceiver currently wants to do vis-à-vis the objects, rather than solely what the perceiver has just recently done (see also Moors & De Houwer, 2001; Moors, De Houwer, & Eelen, 2004).

THEORIES ON THE GENERATION
OF AUTOMATIC ATTITUDES

As the preceding review indicates, research over the last 5 years suggests that automatic attitudes are actually highly sensitive to a number of contextual factors in place at the time of measurement. These factors include the nature of recently encountered exemplars, the prototypicality of the attitude object itself, the context in which the target object is encountered, the task instructions, and the perceiver's chronic and temporary goals. Given this evidence, we now turn to theories of how attitudes are generated and what they reflect. We first review contemporary theories and then discuss a more constructivist approach.[2] Whereas the contemporary approaches assume that automatic attitudes refer to the respective objects in isolation, a more constructivist approach assumes that an automatic evaluation of an object will never be activated in isolation of other relevant contextual information.

Automatic Attitudes toward Objects in Isolation

There are currently two predominant theories about the representation and generation of automatic attitudes (see, e.g., Bargh et al., 1992; Fazio, 1986, 1995, 2001; Fazio et al., 1986, 1995; Fiske & Pavelchak, 1986; Wilson et al., 2000). Whereas one can be understood as the "single-tag" perspective (e.g., Fazio, 1986, 1990, 2001), the other might be classified as the "dual-tag" perspective (Chaiken & Bargh 1993; Wilson et al., 2000). Both of these theories assume that evaluative information is associated in memory with an object, and importantly, that this is what is captured by implicit (and explicit) attitude measures. These two theories differ primarily in the number of summaries of evaluative information associated with the object and the circumstances under which evaluative information may be activated.

Much of the research on the automatic activation of attitudes is based on the supposition that (many) attitude objects are each associated in memory with a positive or negative evaluative index, or a summary evaluative "tag" (e.g., Bargh et al., 1992; Bargh, Chaiken, Raymond, & Hymes, 1996; Fazio et al., 1986; Fiske & Pavelchak, 1986). After the activation of the object representation, the evaluative tag becomes activated and can then influence subsequent judgment and behavior. From the single-tag perspective, the strength of the association between an object and its evaluation is the main determinant of whether the attitude will be automatically activated in the first place and then influence judgment and thought (Fazio, 1989, 1990; Fazio & Williams, 1986; Petty & Krosnick, 1995).

The single-tag view is largely based on a localist, symbolic model of memory that presupposes an associative network in which isolated nodes represent individual constructs, exemplars, or features of an object (see, e.g., Anderson & Bower, 1973; Collins & Loftus, 1975). These nodes are interconnected according to the amount of semantic relation between the nodes, with activation spreading along these links automatically upon perception of an object (see, e.g., Meyer & Schvaneveldt, 1971; Neely, 1976, 1977; Posner & Snyder, 1975;

Shiffrin & Schneider, 1977). Such models have been referred to as "file drawer" models of memory because the contents of memory remain inert and unchanged (as though stored in a file cabinet) until independent retrieval processes act on them (e.g., see Carlston & Smith, 1996; Smith, 1996).

According to the single-tag perspective, evidence of the contextual dependence of automatic attitudes may be explained through differences in categorization depending on the context. Because categories are likely associated with different summary evaluative tags (see Fiske & Pavelchak, 1986), differences in categorization may lead to differences in automatic attitudes. In this way, the single-tag perspective may explain at least some of the evidence for the contextual dependence of automatic attitudes by suggesting that the attitude objects were categorized in different ways across conditions. For example, from this perspective, one might assume that in the work by Wittenbrink and colleagues (2001), the attitudes of those participants who saw photos of Black persons at a picnic reflected the evaluation of a subtype of Black persons (e.g., "non-city"). In contrast, the automatic attitudes of those who saw the photos of Black persons in inner-city scenes may have reflected a different, more negatively evaluated subtype (see, e.g., Weber & Crocker, 1983). In this way, even though there is variability in the attitudes depending on the context in which the perceiver encounters the object, each attitude is still assumed to reflect the evaluative tag associated with a single object (or category) in memory.

In order to more fully explain the evidence for contextual dependence, the single-tag perspective would have to address evidence suggesting that the accessibility of positive information can be orthogonal to the accessibility of negative information relevant to an object (Cacioppo & Berntson, 1994; Cacioppo, Gardner, & Berntson, 1997). In particular, the findings of Ferguson and Bargh (2004) demonstrated that for participants who were actively pursuing a competitive game, the accessibility of positive material associated with the relevant objects was unchanged, but the negativity associated with relevant objects was inhibited, as compared with those who had already finished the game. In another experiment, automatic attitudes toward objects such as water and juice were compared across thirsty and nonthirsty people. The results showed that whereas the positivity associated with those objects was more accessible for thirsty (vs. nonthirsty) people, the accessibility of the negativity associated with those objects was the same across the two groups. These results are in line with the notion that there are multiple kinds of evaluative information associated with any given stimulus (e.g., Abelson, 1976, 1981; Barsalou, 1992; Bower, 1981; Carlston, 1994; Fishbein & Ajzen, 1975; Schank & Abelson, 1977; Smith, 1992; Smith & Zarate, 1992), rather than a solitary, summary evaluative tag. Furthermore, these types of evaluative information may become more or less accessible in orthogonal ways. That is, whereas some types of evaluative information associated with a given object may become more accessible, other types of evaluative information may become more inhibited. The single-tag perspective seems ill equipped to handle such simultaneous processes (see Chaiken & Bargh, 1993, for a similar argument concerning ambivalent attitudes).

The "dual-tag" view, in comparison, assumes that objects are associated with two attitudes (i.e., evaluative tags), one that becomes activated implicitly and one that becomes activated explicitly (Wilson et al., 2000). In line with much work in social and cognitive psychology (e.g., Bargh, 1984, 1989, 1990; Jastrow, 1906; Schneider & Fisk, 1982; Shiffrin & Dumais, 1981; Shiffrin & Schneider, 1977; Smith & Lerner, 1986; cf. Gollwitzer, 1996, 1999), this second perspective assumes that an integration of recently acquired evaluative information requires conscious effort. Because of this, implicit measures, which operate outside the respondent's awareness, presumably can capture only preexisting, stable attitudes (e.g., Wilson & Hodges, 1992; cf. Bargh, 1999; Duckworth, Bargh, Garcia, & Chaiken, 2002). Explicit measures, however, are assumed to be able to assess more complex integrations of object-relevant and novel information.

Because of the complex integrative processes that can occur during explicit attitude measurement, these researchers argued that the explicit attitude toward a given object is frequently susceptible to a number of contextual parameters, such as social desirability, mood, and temporary goals, and thus can vary considerably across measurement times. The authors argued that the implicit attitude for any object, however, is quite stable and is not generally amenable to modification. Although a person may develop a new explicit attitude toward an object, the old, well-learned, and highly stable implicit attitude continues to exist and may be expressed under some circumstances. For instance, Wilson and colleagues (2000) asserted that, "Explicit attitudes change relatively more easily whereas implicit attitudes, like old habits, change more slowly. Attitude change techniques often change explicit but not implicit attitudes" (p. 4). It should be noted that, according to this perspective, data from explicit versus implicit *measures* reflect explicit versus implicit *attitudes*.

The dual-tag perspective does not seem consistent with the accumulating evidence of the contextual dependence of automatic attitudes. One could bootstrap this perspective by assuming, as with the single-tag perspective, that contextual dependence arises out of varying categorization, but this runs into the same problem of simultaneous inhibition and excitatory processes that the single-tag view faces. Furthermore, it is not clear why there would be only a single implicit and explicit attitude for every object—why not multiple implicit (or explicit) attitudes? This possibility seems to suggest that a given attitude object might hypothetically be associated with numerous implicit and explicit attitudes, which seems a cumbersome solution to the evidence of context sensitivity.[3]

Both the single-tag and dual-tag perspectives assume that an automatic attitude reflects the evaluation of the respective object. For the single-tag perspective, this assumption is consistent with a symbolic model of memory, which assumes that constructs can be retrieved from memory in isolation of other information. Thus, for example, it is possible for an implicit attitude measure to capture the nature of the summary evaluative tag associated with a given object. For the dual-tag perspective, however, implicit attitudes are assumed to emerge out of connectionist, nonsymbolic processes (Wilson et al., 2000; see also Gawronski et al., in press; Smith & DeCoster, 1999). Although such a model of memory would necessarily mean that any attitude would reflect a combination of sources of evaluative information, as we describe later, the dual-tag perspective seems to assume otherwise. In fact, the assumption of this perspective is that an implicit attitude is slow to develop and change and thus should exhibit stability and resistance across contexts. Wilson and colleagues (Wilson et al., 2000, p. 4) assume that implicit attitudes should display less contextual dependence than explicit attitudes.

In sum, both the single-tag and dual-tag perspectives argue that implicit measures capture attitudes that are preexisting. In addition, such evaluations are entirely or primarily in reference to the objects in isolation of other kinds of information. These perspectives assume, in other words, that what is measured during an implicit attitude measure is an approximate 1-to-1 mapping of the *observed response* to the *stored attitude toward that object in memory* (plus measurement error). According to this perspective, it is at least logically possible to directly measure the evaluative tag that is associated in memory with a given attitude object, assuming a lack, or minimum, of measurement error.

It should be noted that the claim that implicitly measured attitudes must be preexisting is in accord with the view in experimental psychology that responses must be repeatedly enacted over time in order to automatically operate, as previously mentioned (Bargh, 1984, 1989, 1990; Fazio, 1986; Jastrow, 1906; Schneider & Fisk, 1982; Shiffrin & Dumais, 1981; Shiffrin & Schneider, 1977; Smith & Lerner, 1986; cf. Bargh, 1999; Duckworth et al., 2002; Gollwitzer, 1996, 1999). This assumption is evident in researchers' attempts to foster new implicitly measured attitudes. For example, in order to change participants' implicitly measured attitudes toward elderly persons, Karpinski and Hilton (2001) exposed participants to more than 200 examples of pro-elderly stimuli. The extreme repetition was assumed to be essential for participants' automatic attitudes to shift (see also Kawakami et al., 2000).

Automatic Attitudes toward Object-Centered Contexts (a Constructivist View)

An alternative theoretical possibility is that the observed response on an implicit attitude measure is instead the result of a computation performed by an evaluative system, on the basis of numerous representations, possibly including multiple categories and exemplars that relate to the attitude object in various ways (Bassili & Brown, 2005; Duckworth et al., 2002; Ferguson, in press-b; Ferguson & Bargh, 2003; Smith, 1997, 2000). In this way, automatic attitudes would be sensitive to whatever evaluative information is contextually relevant at the time of measurement. Accordingly, the attitude that is implicitly measured does not represent the activation of a single evaluative tag as a function of only the attitude object (Fiske & Pavelchak, 1986), but is instead an *integration* across multiple sources of affective information.

An integrative process would technically be compatible with the traditional "file drawer" models of memory in which concepts are represented by nodes, and the nodes are interconnected according to semantic similarity (see, e.g., Smith, 1996). In models of this type, each representation is inert and static when it is not activated. These static representations are periodically manipulated by processes such as encoding, storage, and retrieval, for example. Such a model suggests that a single representation can be activated independently of other activation. It would theoretically be possible for an integrative process to take place across numerous discrete representations.

However, the notion of an integrative process across various sources of evaluative information is directly predicted by parallel distributed processing models of memory (e.g., Anderson & Rosenfeld,

1988; Bechtel & Abrahamsen, 1991; Carlston & Smith, 1996; Smith, 1996; Smith & DeCoster, 1999). Models of such connectionist systems include the assertion that every observable behavior (explicit or implicit) is the result of a fleeting *state* of the mind, wherein all representations are potentially implicated or contributive (see Smith, 1996). An integration across multiple sources of evaluative information would be highly compatible with the assumptions of connectionist systems (see also Arieli, Sterkin, Grinvald, & Aertsen, 1996; Fiedler, 1996).

If attitude generation is supported by connectionist systems, then any observable response would be the result of an integration of information about both the particular object as well as the context in which the object is encountered. Recent publications have suggested this type of approach for explaining findings of contextual dependence of automatic attitudes (see, e.g., Bassili & Brown, 2005; Ferguson & Bargh, 2004; Mitchell et al., 2003) and have also advocated for connectionist modeling more generally, rather than attempting to use underspecified models of associative networks that are difficult to formalize (see, e.g., Smith, 1996, 1997).

OBJECT-CENTERED CONTEXTS

According to the evidence of the contextual dependence of automatic attitudes, and the recent theoretical approaches to attitude generation, we argue that a given attitude object can implicitly evoke multiple potential attitudes, according to the context in which the attitude object is perceived. Implicitly measured attitudes are sensitive to recently acquired information, including goal-relevant expectations, and are each based on an integrative process whereby numerous sources of evaluative information contribute to the observed attitudinal response. To this end, an implicitly measured attitude could be defined as an indication of the relevance of the object for the perceiver as a function of past, current, and future object-relevant circumstances.

Because of the fact that an object is therefore never evaluated in a vacuum, it seems misleading to refer to an implicitly measured attitude as an evaluation of the corresponding *object*. Rather, on the basis of the current argument, an implicitly measured attitude corresponds to an *object-centered context*. This new definition is in contrast to the way in which attitudes and attitude objects are typically discussed in attitude literature. For example, Eagly and Chaiken (1993, pp. 4–5) stated:

An evaluation is always made with respect to some entity or thing that is the object of the evaluation. . . . Virtually anything that is discriminable can be evaluated and therefore function as an attitude object. Some attitude objects are abstract (e.g., liberalism, secular humanism), and others are concrete (e.g., a chair, a shoe). Particular entities (e.g., my green pen) can function as attitude objects, as can classes of entities (e.g., ballpoint pens). Behaviors (e.g., playing volleyball) and classes of behaviors (e.g., participating in athletic activities) can also function as attitude objects. In general, anything that is discriminated or that becomes in some sense an object of thought can serve as an attitude object.

On the basis of this excerpt from the widely influential attitudes text by Eagly and Chaiken (1993), it seems possible to measure a solitary attitude toward a solitary object. For example, the excerpt suggests that it is possible to measure a person's attitude toward a chair. According to the new definition of an attitude as an indication of an object-based context, however, the best one could do to calculate the person's attitude toward chairs *in general* would be to average that person's attitudes toward multiple object-based contexts (a lounge chair, a desk chair, a wooden chair, a chair when someone wants to sit down versus when he or she does not, etc.). However, the utility of such an average may be suspect because the average attitude across time points may not serve as a very accurate predictor of behavior in a given particular context. As has long been argued by attitude theorists (e.g., Fishbein & Ajzen, 1974, 1975; Kelman, 1974; Schuman & Johnson, 1976), increasing the specificity with which one describes an attitude object and object-relevant behavior increases the chance that the (explicit) attitude predicts the relevant behavior. The present research suggests that the same reasoning can be applied to implicitly measured attitudes. Thus, it seems potentially useful to conceptualize the referents of automatic attitudes with greater specificity.

Issues Related to Object-Centered Contexts

The concept of attitude stability is a traditionally important issue in attitude research (see, e.g., Eagly & Chaiken, 1993). There are two points of clarification with regard to stability that are related to the present discussion concerning the contextual dependence of implicitly measured attitudes. The first point of clarification is the distinction between the stability of an attitude, as measured (i.e., observational stability), and the stability of the representations in memory that underlie the attitude expression (i.e., representational stability). The second point of clarification is the distinction between the concept of contextual dependence and each of the two meanings of stability.

According to a perspective that assumes a 1-to-1 mapping of the observed attitude to the stored attitude in memory, the two meanings of attitude stability (representational versus observational) would be isomorphic except for the issue of measurement noise. That is, given the assumption of 1-to-1 mapping, if researchers observed that an attitude was stable across time points (holding categorization constant), they might assume that the attitude construct remained unchanged in memory. If they observed attitude instability across time (again, holding categorization constant), they could assume that either the attitude construct had changed across time, or that some measurement noise of the instrument was obscuring stability, or some combination of the two possibilities. Thus, if one assumes a 1-to-1 mapping, then observational and representational stability would be highly related theoretically, except for the variance from measurement error.

However, according to the claim that an observed attitude (either explicitly or implicitly measured) reflects an integration of multiple sources of evaluative information, these two meanings of attitude stability become orthogonal. That is, because the observed attitude reflects a computation across numerous components, it is impossible to ascertain the individual status of one component of that function, such as the status of the evaluative information associated with one relevant exemplar of the attitude object, for instance. More specifically, even when there is observational stability across time points, it is impossible to infer that the same particular components contributed to the integration, or even in the same way, across time points. It may be that the integration process across time generates a consistently positive attitude, for instance, but this does not indicate anything concerning the representational status of evaluative information associated with each of the components of the integration.

When there is observational instability across time, assuming little measurement noise, it is possible that either the set of particular evaluative memories contributing to the integration has changed, or that the set of evaluative components is the same, but the components themselves have undergone some change. For example, if someone displays a positive attitude toward elderly people on one occasion and a negative attitude toward the same group at a later time, perhaps after some new information, there could be two broad reasons for the instability from Time 1 to Time 2 (not including measurement error). One reason might be that the components involved in the integration changed from Time 1 to Time 2. Assuming a hypothetical array of "elderly" memories that may contribute to the overall integration, whereas elderly memories 4–8 contributed to the integration at Time 1, elderly memories 6–15 may have contributed to the integration at Time 2. A second reason may be that the same elderly memories (4–8) were involved in the integration at both time points, but that the valence of the memories changed. (It should be noted that this possibility assumes that the evaluative information associated with a particular memory can be replaced by different evaluative information.)

The adoption of either the direct mapping or the integration claim influences how freely researchers can generate conclusions about the contents of memory, based on data from attitude measures. Given the assumption of a 1-to-1 mapping, researchers could use attitude measures to generate inferences about the specific organization and contents of memory. For example, if someone demonstrated a positive, implicitly measured attitude toward a certain group, researchers might assume that the perceiver possesses a representation of that group that is associated with a positive evaluative tag. Given the integration claim, however, it is no longer viable to make such inferences. It is difficult, if not impossible, to postulate about individual pieces of information in memory solely on the basis of an integrative function. Although an object may be associated with a valence in memory and this association may be stable across time, that individual association or valence will always be one component that contributes to the overall summary response that is observed. Thus, according to the integrative, or constructivist, perspective, although there may be stability in the memorial representations involving object-related memories and their respective valences, the observable response of a person toward an object will reflect a complex computation, to which many object relevant and irrelevant memories and their associated valences potentially contribute.

Contextual Dependence and Observational Stability

The next consideration is the observational stability of implicitly gauged attitudes. Although the degree of observational stability of an attitude is sometimes interpreted as a proxy for the degree of contextual dependence of the attitude, or vice versa, the current argument is that observational stability and contextual dependence are orthogonal concepts. It is possible that an implicit attitude, even though dependent on the context in which it is measured, can be (observationally) stable or unstable across time.

When will a contextually dependent, implicitly measured attitude be observationally stable across contexts? An object will evoke the same attitude across time points (i.e., demonstrating observational stability) if all object-relevant memories are univalent, if the object-relevant memories that are activated across time points are consistently of the same valence, or if the usefulness of the object (harmful versus helpful) is constant across time. In this way, the stable attitude can be thought of as an indication of stable circumstances or (object-relevant) situational constancy. In contrast, a contextually dependent, implicitly measured attitude will be observationally unstable across contexts if the set of object-relevant memories that is activated across contexts differs in terms of valence, or if the goal-relevance of the object changes across contexts (specifically, from harmful to safe, or vice-versa, for instance).

Observational instability should therefore be somewhat positively related to complex and ambiguous attitude objects. The more object-relevant memories exist, the more likely the object will be able to be perceived in different ways across contexts. As long as some of those object-relevant memories are mixed in valence, the more likely the implicitly invoked attitude will change in direction across time and situations. In general, the more mixed (i.e., both positive and negative) the object-relevant memories, the more likely the implicitly measured attitude will be observationally unstable across time.

Contextual Dependence and Representational Stability

As is the case with observational stability, we argue here that contextual dependence of an attitude does not indicate anything about the representational stability underlying that attitude. Representational stability is somewhat difficult to consider, as the nature (e.g., organization and format) of representations in memory is still far from clear (e.g., Pinker, 1997; Plotkin, 1997). However, it is possible to speculate that the object- and situation-relevant memories that typically contribute to an integration can either remain stable or undergo change. (This is assuming that the evaluative information associated with a memory can change, rather than the idea that a change in evaluation forces a whole novel object representation with the new attitude.)

Accordingly, the contextually dependent, implicitly measured attitude can result from integrations that are based on either stable (static) pieces of evaluative information (although not always the same pieces, and not always weighted in the same way) or pieces of evaluative information that undergo change. In short, the contextual dependence of an attitude does not imply anything about its underlying representational stability.

THE CONTEXT DEPENDENCE OF AUTOMATIC
VERSUS DELIBERATE ATTITUDES

In an argument similar to that proposed in this chapter, researchers have claimed that explicit attitudes are heavily (or entirely) dependent on the context in which the perceiver encounters the corresponding stimuli (e.g., Anderson, 1974; Schwarz & Bohner, 2001; Tesser, 1978). For example, Schwarz and Bohner (2001) identify five steps at which contextual factors may influence the reporting of an attitude, from interpreting the nature of the attitude query to deciding whether to report one's consciously accessible attitude. We wholeheartedly agree that explicit attitudes are likely influenced by a wide array of contextual factors. However, we also assert that the contextual dependence of explicit measures may be somewhat obscured by the metacognitive and introspective thinking that such measures enable (e.g., Cohen & Schooler, 1997). In particular, because a respondent during an explicit measure has to consciously generate and then report his or her attitude, that person's implicit or even explicit theories about the stability of his or her attitudes may encourage stability that would not otherwise emerge. In line with research by Nisbett and Wilson (1977), among others, people's implicit theories about whether they like pizza, for example, may push them toward reporting a more consistently positive (explicit) attitude toward it, even while their automatic attitude may reflect considerably more fluctuation as a function of current goals, expectations, recently encountered information, and the like.

Another possibility is that automatic attitude measures may tap associations and information that are not consciously accessible to the person. This may mean that a greater wealth of information is potentially more influential on the attitude when the person is not consciously thinking about that attitude. This argument is consistent with recent work by Greenwald and colleagues (Greenwald et al., 2002) that suggests that although implicit measures are subject to cognitive consistency pressures (Heider, 1946, 1958), explicit measures do not seem to be. For example, this work suggests that when a woman displays automatic positivity toward herself, and toward females in general, she will likely not display automatic positivity toward math, which is assumed to be dissociated from the concept of females (see also Nosek, Banaji, & Greenwald, 2002). Implicitly measured attitudes, from this perspective, may be sensitive to and influenced by a more extensive set of memories than are explicitly measured attitudes. Future research can undoubtedly shed more light on the comparative degree to which implicit versus explicit measures are dependent on the context in which they are administered, but we put forth at this point the possibility that implicit (versus explicit) measures yield more contextually sensitive attitudes.

CONCLUSION

Research and theory conducted and developed over the last 5 years suggest that automatic attitudes are highly contingent on numerous contextual factors. Specifically, research findings suggest that automatic attitudes vary depending on current goals, task instructions, recently encountered attitude objects and attitude-relevant contexts, and even mood. In line with this evidence, recent theoretical approaches have argued that an automatic attitude is likely the result of an integrative process within a connectionist system. In such a system, the pattern of activation across a set of processing units for any given attitude is re-created each time the attitude object is encountered. Although there are undoubtedly stable sources of evaluative information reflected in the weights that connect the processing units, the resulting attitude is nevertheless based on a constructivist process that incorporates multiple sources of information. In this way, slight changes in the type of evaluative information included in the computation according to the context can potentially change the direction or intensity of the automatic attitude. This research and theory suggest that automatic attitudes should be understood as evaluations of object-centered contexts, rather than objects in isolation.

It is important to note that although implicit measures clearly do not assess attitudes free of the context in which the objects are perceived, they are certainly nevertheless valuable research tools. Implicit attitude measures can effectively gauge a person's response tendency (either approach, if the attitude is positive, or avoidance if the attitude is negative) within certain situations, with regard to a particular object. This is useful to the extent that researchers can show that such implicitly gauged responses are predictive of the person's behavior (either subtle or overt) in a future similar situation. A large body of research now has shown that implicit attitude measures can predict a variety of both nonverbal and overt behaviors toward the attitude object (e.g., for reviews, see Blair, 2002; Fazio & Olson, 2003; Ferguson, in press-a, in press-b; Lane et al., Chapter 3, this volume; Wittenbrink, Chapter 2, this volume).

Furthermore, implicit attitude measurement is also useful because it can indicate various characteristics of nonconscious processing. Whereas the initial assumption in attitude research, and in social psychology in general, was that automatic responses can only be the result of repeated previous experiences with the object (e.g., Bargh, 1984, 1989, 1990; Jastrow, 1906; Schneider & Fisk, 1982; Shiffrin & Dumais, 1981; Shiffrin & Schneider, 1977; Smith & Lerner, 1986; cf. Gollwitzer, 1996, 1999) and cannot reflect recent integrations of new information (e.g., Wilson & Hodges, 1992; Wilson et al., 2000), recent research has challenged these assumptions (see Bargh, 2001; Dijksterhuis, 2004; Duckworth et al., 2002). There is still much to learn about people's ability to automatically assess their environments, and implicit attitude measures represent one valuable tool in this endeavor.

NOTES

1. The terms *implicit attitudes* and *explicit attitudes* should be assumed to reflect the type of measurement, rather than the type of attitude (see DeHouwer, 2006; Fazio & Olson, 2003).
2. The term *constructivist* is used to connote a process whereby an attitude is generated by integration across multiple sources of evaluative information. The term is unrelated to the constructivist philosophy of mathematics.
3. In addition, the proposal that implicit attitudes are distinct from explicit attitudes is not consistent with research suggesting that they are, in fact, related constructs (Hofman, Gawronski, Gschwendner, Le, & Schmitt, 2005; Nosek, 2005).

REFERENCES

Abelson, R. P. (1976). Script processing in attitude formation and decision making. In J. S. Carroll & J. W. Payne (Eds.), *Cognition and social behavior* (pp. 33–45). Hillsdale, NJ: Erlbaum.

Abelson, R. P. (1981). Psychological status of the script concept. *American Psychologist, 36,* 715–729.

Albarracín, D., Johnson, B. T., & Zanna, M. P. (2005). *Handbook of attitudes.* Mahwah, NJ: Erlbaum.

Anderson, J. A., & Rosenfeld, E. (1988). *Neurocomputing: Foundations of research.* Cambridge, MA: MIT Press.

Anderson, J. R., & Bower, G. H. (1973). *Human associative memory.* Washington, DC: Winston.

Anderson, N. H. (1974). Cognitive algebra: Integration theory applied to social attribution. In L. Berkowitz (Ed.), *Advances in experimental social psychology* (Vol. 7, pp. 1–101). New York: Academic Press.

Arieli, A., Sterkin, A., Grinvald, A., & Aertsen, A. (1996). Dynamics of ongoing activity: Explanation of the large variability in evoked cortical responses. *Science, 273,* 1868–1871.

Banaji, M. R. (2001). Implicit attitudes can be measured. In H. L. Roediger, J. S.

Nairne, I. Neither, & A. Surprenant (Eds.), *The nature of remembering: Essays in honor of Robert G. Crowder* (pp. 117–150). Washington, DC: American Psychological Association.

Barden, J., Maddux, W. W., Petty, R. E., & Brewer, M. B. (2004). Contextual moderation of racial bias: The impact of social roles on controlled and automatically activated attitudes. *Journal of Personality and Social Psychology, 87,* 5–22.

Bargh, J. A. (1984). Automatic and conscious processing of social information. In R. S. Wyer Jr. & T. K. Srull (Eds.), *Handbook of social cognition* (Vol. 3, pp. 1–43). Hillsdale, NJ: Erlbaum.

Bargh, J. A. (1989). Conditional automaticity: Varieties of automatic influence in social perception and cognition. In J. S. Ulerman & J. A. Bargh (Eds.), *Unintended thought* (pp. 3–51). New York: Guilford Press.

Bargh, J. A. (1990). Auto-motives: Preconscious determinants of social interaction. In E. T. Higgins & R. M. Sorrentino (Eds.), *Handbook of motivation and cognition: Vol. 2. Foundations of social behavior* (pp. 93–130). New York: Guilford Press.

Bargh, J. A. (1994). The four horsemen of automaticity: Awareness, intention, efficiency, and control in social cognition. In R. J. Wyer & T. K. Srull (Eds.), *Handbook of social cognition* (2nd ed., pp. 1–40). Hillsdale, NJ: Erlbaum.

Bargh, J. A. (1997). The automaticity of everyday life. In R. S. Wyer Jr. (Ed.), *The automaticity of everyday life: Advances in social cognition* (Vol. 10, pp. 1–61). Mahwah, NJ: Erlbaum.

Bargh, J. A. (1999). The cognitive monster: The case against the controllability of automatic stereotype effects. In S. Chaiken & Y. Trope (Eds.), *Dual-process theories in social psychology* (pp. 361–382). New York: Guilford Press.

Bargh, J. A. (2001). Caution: Automatic social cognition may not be habit forming. *Polish Psychological Bulletin, 32,* 1–8.

Bargh, J. A., Chaiken, S., Govender, R., & Pratto, F. (1992). The generality of the automatic attitude activation effect. *Journal of Personality and Social Psychology, 62,* 893–912.

Bargh, J. A., Chaiken, S., Raymond, P., & Hymes, C. (1996). The automatic evaluation effect: Unconditional automatic attitude activation with a pronunciation task. *Journal of Experimental Social Psychology, 32,* 104–128.

Barsalou, L. W. (1992). *Cognitive psychology: An overview for cognitive scientists.* Hillsdale, NJ: Erlbaum.

Bassili, J. N., & Brown, R. D. (2005). Implicit and explicit attitudes: Research, challenges, and theory. In D. Albarracín, B. T. Johnson, & M. P. Zanna (Eds.), *Handbook of attitudes* (pp. 543–574). Mahwah, NJ: Erlbaum.

Bechtel, W., & Abrahamsen, A. (1991). *Connectionism and the mind: An introduction to parallel processing in networks.* Oxford, UK: Blackwell.

Bem, D. J. (1972). Constructing cross-situational consistencies in behavior: Some thoughts on Alker's critique of Mischel. *Journal of Personality, 40,* 17–26.

Blair, I. (2002). The malleability of automatic stereotypes and prejudice. *Personality and Social Psychological Review, 6,* 242–261.

Blair, I. V., Judd, C. M., & Fallman, J. L. (2004). The automaticity of race and

Afrocentric facial features in social judgments. *Journal of Personality and Social Psychology, 87,* 763–778.

Blair, I. V., Ma, J. E., & Lenton, A. P. (2001). Imagining stereotypes away: The moderation of implicit stereotypes through mental imagery. *Journal of Personality and Social Psychology, 81,* 828—841.

Bower, G. H. (1981). Mood and memory. *American Psychologist, 36,* 129–148.

Cacioppo, J. T., & Berntson, G. G. (1994). Relationship between attitudes and evaluative space: A critical review, with emphasis on the separability of positive and negative substrates. *Psychological Bulletin, 115,* 401–423.

Cacioppo, J. T., Gardner, W. L., & Berntson, G. G. (1997). Beyond bipolar conceptualizations and measures: The case of attitudes and evaluative space. *Personality and Social Psychology Review, 1,* 3–25.

Carlston, D. E. (1994). Associated systems theory: A systematic approach to the cognitive representation of persons and events. In R. S. Wyer (Ed.), *Advances in social cognition: Vol. 7. Associated systems theory* (pp. 1–78). Hillsdale, NJ: Erlbaum.

Carlston, D. E., & Smith, E. R. (1996). Principles of mental representation. In E. T. Higgins & A. W. Kruglanski (Eds.), *Social psychology: Handbook of basic principles* (pp. 184–210). New York: Guilford Press.

Chaiken, S., & Bargh, J. A. (1993). Occurrence versus moderation of the automatic attitude activation effect: Reply to Fazio. *Journal of Personality and Social Psychology, 64,* 759–765.

Chaiken, S., & Yates, S. (1985). Affective-cognitive consistency and thought-induced attitude polarization. *Journal of Personality and Social Psychology, 49,* 1470–1481.

Cohen, J. D., & Schooler, J. W. (1997). *Scientific approaches to consciousness.* Hillsdale, NJ: Erlbaum.

Collins, A. M., & Loftus, E. F. (1975). A spreading-activation theory of semantic processing. *Psychological Review, 82,* 407–428.

Dasgupta, N., & Greenwald, A. G. (2001). On the malleability of automatic attitudes: Combating automatic prejudice with images of liked and disliked individuals. *Journal of Personality and Social Psychology, 81,* 800–814.

De Houwer, J. (2003). The extrinsic affective Simon task. *Experimental Psychology, 50,* 77–85.

De Houwer, J. (2006). What are implicit measures and why are we using them? In R. W. Wiers & A. W. Stacy (Eds.), *Handbook of implicit cognition and addiction* (pp. 11–28). Thousand Oaks, CA: Sage.

De Houwer, J., & Eelen, P. (1998). An affective variant of the Simon paradigm. *Cognition and Emotion, 8,* 45–61.

Devine, P. G. (1989). Stereotypes and prejudice: Their automatic and controlled components. *Journal of Personality and Social Psychology, 56,* 5–18.

Dijksterhuis, A. (2004). I like myself but I don't know why: Enhancing implicit self-esteem by subliminal evaluative conditioning. *Journal of Personality and Social Psychology, 86,* 345–355.

Dovidio, J. F., Kawakami, K., Johnson, C., Johnson, B., & Howard, A. (1997). On the nature of prejudice: Automatic and controlled processes. *Journal of Experimental Social Psychology, 33,* 510–540.

Duckworth, K. L., Bargh, J. A., Garcia, M., & Chaiken, S. (2002). The automatic evaluation of novel stimuli. *Psychological Science, 13*, 513–519.

Eagly, A. H., & Chaiken, S. (1993). *The psychology of attitudes.* Fort Worth, TX: Harcourt Brace Jovanovich College.

Fazio, R. H. (1986). How do attitudes guide behavior? In R. M. Sorrentino & E. T. Higgins (Eds.), *Handbook of motivation and cognition: Vol. 1. Foundations of social behavior* (pp. 204–243). New York: Guilford Press.

Fazio, R. H. (1987). Self-perception theory: A current perspective. In M. P. Zanna, J. M. Olson, & P. C. Herman (Eds.), *Social influence: The Ontario Symposium* (Vol. 5, pp. 129–150). Hillsdale, NJ: Erlbaum.

Fazio, R. H. (1989). On the power and functionality of attitudes: The role of attitude accessibility. In A. R. Pratkanis, S. J. Breckler, & A. G. Greenwald (Eds.), *Attitude structure and function* (pp.153–179). Hillsdale, NJ: Erlbaum.

Fazio, R. H. (1990). Multiple processes by which attitudes guide behavior: The MODE model as an integrative framework. In M. P. Zanna (Ed.), *Advances in experimental social psychology* (Vol. 23, pp. 75–109). New York: Academic Press.

Fazio, R. H. (1995). Attitudes as object-evaluation associations: Determinants, consequences, and correlates of attitude accessibility. In R. E. Petty & J. A. Krosnick (Eds.), *Attitude strength: Antecedents and consequences* (pp. 247–282). Hillsdale, NJ: Erlbaum.

Fazio, R. H. (2001). On the automatic activation of associated evaluations: An overview. *Cognition and Emotion, 14*, 1–27.

Fazio, R. H., Jackson, J. R., Dunton, B. C., & Williams, C. J. (1995). Variability in automatic activation as an unobtrusive measure of racial attitudes: A bona fide pipeline? *Journal of Personality and Social Psychology, 69*, 1013–1027.

Fazio, R. H., & Olson, M. A. (2003). Implicit measures in social cognition research: Their meaning and use. *Annual Review of Psychology, 54*, 297–327.

Fazio, R. H., Sanbonmatsu, D. M., Powell, M. C., & Kardes, F. R. (1986). On the automatic activation of attitudes. *Journal of Personality and Social Psychology, 50*, 229–238.

Fazio, R. H., & Williams, C. J. (1986). Attitude accessibility as a moderator of the attitude–perception and attitude–behavior relations: An investigation of the 1984 presidential election. *Journal of Personality and Social Psychology, 51*, 505–514.

Feldman, J. M., & Lynch, J. G. (1988). Self-generated validity and other effects of measurement on belief, attitude, intention, and behavior. *Journal of Applied Psychology, 73*, 421–435.

Ferguson, M. J. (in press-a). On the automatic evaluation of end-states. *Journal of Personality and Social Psychology.*

Ferguson, M. J. (in press-b). The automaticity of evaluation. In J. A. Bargh (Ed.), *Automatic processes in social thinking and behavior.* Hove, UK: Psychology Press.

Ferguson, M. J., & Bargh, J. A. (2003). The constructive nature of automatic evaluation. In J. Musch & K. C. Klauer (Eds.), *The psychology of evaluation: Affective processes in cognition and emotion* (pp.169–188). Mahwah, NJ: Erlbaum.

Ferguson, M. J., & Bargh, J. A. (2004). Liking is for doing: Effects of goal pursuit on automatic evaluation. *Journal of Personality and Social Psychology, 88*, 557–572.

Fiedler, K. (1996). Explaining and simulating judgment biases as an aggregation phenomenon in probabilistic, multiple-cue environments. *Psychological Review, 103*, 193–214.

Fishbein, M., & Ajzen, I. (1974). Attitudes towards objects as predictors of single and multiple behavioral criteria. *Psychological Review, 81*, 59–74.

Fishbein, M., & Ajzen, I. (1975). *Belief, attitude, intention, and behavior: An introduction to theory and research*. Reading, MA: Addison-Wesley.

Fiske, S. T. (1992). Thinking is for doing: Portraits of social cognition from daguerreotype to laserphoto. *Journal of Personality and Social Psychology, 63*, 877–889.

Fiske, S. T., & Pavelchak, M. A. (1986). Category-based versus piecemeal-based affective responses: Development in schema-triggered affect. In R. M. Sorrentino & E. T. Higgins (Eds.), *Handbook of motivation and cognition: Vol. 1. Foundations of social behavior* (pp. 167–203). New York: Guilford Press.

Forgas, J. P. (1992). Affect in social judgments and decisions: A multiprocess model. In M. P. Zanna (Ed.), *Advances in experimental social psychology* (Vol. 25, pp. 227–275). San Diego, CA: Academic Press.

Gawronski, B., Strack, F., & Bodenhausen, G. V. (in press). Attitudes and cognitive consistency: The role of associative and propositional processes. In R. E. Petty, R. H. Fazio, & P. Briñol (Eds.), *Attitudes: Insights from the new wave of implicit measures*.

Gollwitzer, P. M. (1996). The volitional benefits of planning. In P. M. Gollwitzer & J. A. Bargh (Eds.), *The psychology of action: Linking cognition and motivation to behavior* (pp. 287–312). New York: Guilford Press.

Gollwitzer, P. M. (1999). Implementation intentions: Strong effects of simple plans. *American Psychologist, 54*, 493–503.

Greenwald, A. G., & Banaji, M. R. (1995). Implicit social cognition: Attitudes, self-esteem, and stereotypes. *Psychological Review, 102*, 4–27.

Greenwald, A. G., Banaji, M. R., Rudman, L. A., Farnham, S. D., Nosek, B. A., & Mellott, D. S. (2002). A unified theory of implicit attitudes, stereotypes, self-esteem, and self-concept. *Psychological Review, 109*, 3–25.

Greenwald, A. G., Klinger, M. R., & Liu, T. J. (1989). Unconscious processing of dichoptically masked words. *Memory and Cognition, 17*, 35–47.

Greenwald, A. G., McGhee, D. E., & Schwarz, J. L. K. (1998). Measuring individual differences in implicit cognition: The Implicit Association Test. *Journal of Personality and Social Psychology, 74*, 1464–1480.

Heider, F. (1946). Attitudes and cognitive organization. *Journal of Psychology: Interdisciplinary and Applied, 21*,107–112.

Heider, F. (1958). *The psychology of interpersonal relations*. New York: Wiley.

Hermsen, B., Holland, R. W., & van Knippenberg, A. (2004). *The influence of mood on automatic evaluations*. Unpublished manuscript, University of Nijmegen.

Hofmann, W., Gawronski, B., Gschwendner, T., Le, H., & Schmitt, M. (2006). A meta-analysis on the correlation between the Implicit Association Test and explicit self-report measures. *Personality and Social Psychology Bulletin, 31,* 1369–1385.

James, W. (1890). *The principles of psychology* (Vol. 2). New York: Holt.

Jastrow, J. (1906). *The subconscious.* Boston: Houghton-Mifflin.

Jones, E. E., & Sigall, H. (1971). The bogus pipeline: A new paradigm for measuring affect and attitude. *Psychological Bulletin, 76,* 349–364.

Karpinski, A., & Hilton, J. L. (2001). Attitudes and the Implicit Association Test. *Journal of Personality and Social Psychology, 81,* 774–788.

Kawakami, K., Dovidio, J. F., Moll, J., Hermsen, S., & Russin, A. (2000). Just say no (to stereotyping): Effects of training in the negation of stereotypic associations on stereotype activation. *Journal of Personality and Social Psychology, 78,* 871–888.

Kelman, H. C. (1974). Attitudes are alive and well and gainfully employed in the sphere of action. *American Psychologist, 29,* 310–324.

Koole, S. K., Dijksterhuis, A., & van Knippenberg, A. (2001). What's in a name: Implicit self-esteem. *Journal of Personality and Social Psychology, 80,* 614–627.

LaPiere, R. T. (1934). Attitudes vs. actions. *Social Forces, 13,* 230–237.

Livingston, R. W., & Brewer, M. B. (2002). What are we really priming?: Cue-based versus category-based processing of facial stimuli. *Journal of Personality and Social Psychology, 82,* 5–18.

Lowery, B. S., Hardin, C. D., & Sinclair, S. (2001). Social influence on automatic racial prejudice. *Journal of Personality and Social Psychology, 81,* 842–855.

Maddux, W. W., Barden, J., Brewer, M. B., & Petty, R. E. (2005). Saying no to negativity: The effects of context and motivation to control prejudice on automatic evaluative responses. *Journal of Experimental Social Psychology, 41,* 19–35.

McCauley, C., & Stitt, C. L. (1978). An individual and quantitative measure of stereotypes. *Journal of Personality and Social Psychology, 36,* 929–940.

McConahay, J. (1986). Modern racism, ambivalence, and the Modern Racism scale. In J. Dovidio (Ed.), *Prejudice, discrimination, and racism* (pp. 91–125). San Diego, CA: Academic Press.

McConahay, J. B. (1983). Modern racism and modern discrimination: The effects of race, racial attitudes, and context on simulated hiring decisions. *Personality and Social Psychology Bulletin, 9,* 551–558.

Meyer, D. E., & Schvaneveldt, R. W. (1971). Facilitation in recognizing pairs of words: Evidence of a dependence between retrieval operations. *Journal of Experimental Psychology, 90,* 227–234.

Miller, M. G., & Tesser, A. (1986). Thought-induced attitude change: The effects of schema structure and commitment. *Journal of Personality and Social Psychology, 51,* 259–269.

Mitchell, J. P., Nosek, B. A., & Banaji, M. R. (2003). Contextual variations in implicit evaluation. *Journal of Experimental Psychology: General, 132,* 455–469.

Moors, A., & De Houwer, J. (2001). Automatic appraisal of motivational valence: Motivational affective priming and Simon effects. *Cognition and Emotion, 15,* 749–766.

Moors, A., De Houwer, J., & Eelen, P. (2004). Automatic stimulus–goal comparisons: Evidence from motivational affective priming studies. *Cognition and Emotion, 18*, 29–54.

Moskowitz, G. B., Gollwitzer, P. M., Wasel, W., & Schaal, B. (1999). Preconscious control of stereotype activation through chronic egalitarian goals. *Journal of Personality and Social Psychology, 77*, 167–184.

Musch, J., & Klauer, K. C. (2003). *The psychology of evaluation: Affective processes in cognition and emotion.* Mahwah, NJ: Erlbaum.

Neely, J. H. (1976). Semantic priming and retrieval from lexical memory: Evidence for faciliatory and inhibitory processes. *Memory and Cognition, 4*, 648–654.

Neely, J. H. (1977). Semantic priming and retrieval from lexical memory: Roles of inhibitionless spreading activation and limited-capacity attention. *Journal of Experimental Psychology: General, 106*, 225–254.

Nisbett, R., & Wilson, T. (1977). Telling more than we can know: Verbal reports on mental processes. *Psychological Review, 84*, 231–259.

Nosek, B. A. (2005). Moderators of the relationship between implicit and explicit evaluation. *Journal of Experimental Psychology: General, 134*, 565–584.

Nosek, B. A., & Banaji, M. R. (2001). The Go/No-Go Association Task. *Social Cognition, 19*(6), 625–666.

Nosek, B. A., Banaji, M. R., & Greenwald, A. G. (2002). Math = male, me = female, therefore math ≠ me. *Journal of Personality and Social Psychology, 83*, 44–59.

Olson, J. M. (1990). Self-inference processes in emotion. In J. M. Olson & M. P. Zanna (Eds.), *Self-inference processes: The Ontario Symposium* (Vol. 6, pp. 17–42). Hillsdale, NJ: Erlbaum.

Orne, M. T. (1962). On the social psychology of the psychological experiment: With particular reference to demand. *American Psychologist, 17*, 776–783.

Payne, B. K., Cheng, C. M., Govorun, O., & Stewart, B. (2005). An inkblot for attitudes: Attitude misattribution as implicit measurement. *Journal of Personality and Social Psychology, 89*, 277–293.

Petty, R. E., & Krosnick, J. A. (1995). *Attitude strength: Antecedents and consequences.* Hillsdale, NJ: Erlbaum.

Pinker, S. (1997). *How the mind works.* New York: Norton.

Plotkin, H. 1997. *Evolution in mind.* London: Penguin.

Posner, M. I., & Snyder, C. R. R. (1975). Attention and cognitive control. In R. L. Solso (Ed.), *Information processing and cognition: The Loyola Symposium* (pp. 55–85). Hillsdale, NJ: Erlbaum.

Rosenberg, M. J. (1969). The conditions and consequences of evaluation apprehension. In R. Rosenthal & R. Rosnow (Eds.), *Artifact in behavioral research* (pp. 279–349). New York: Academic Press.

Rudman, L. A., Ashmore, R. D., & Gary, M. L. (2001). "Unlearning" automatic biases: The malleability of implicit stereotypes and prejudice. *Journal of Personality and Social Psychology, 81*, 856–868.

Salancik, G. R., & Conway, M. (1975). Attitude inferences from salient and relevant cognitive content about behavior. *Journal of Personality and Social Psychology, 32*, 829–840.

Schank, R. C., & Abelson, R. P. (1977). *Scripts, plans, goals, and understanding: An inquiry into human knowledge structures.* Hillsdale, NJ: Erlbaum.

Schneider, W., & Fisk, A. D. (1982). Degree of consistent training: Improvements in search performance and automatic process development. *Perception and Psychophysics, 31,* 160–168.

Schuman, H., & Johnson, M. P. (1976). Attitudes and behavior. *Annual Review of Sociology, 2,* 161–207.

Schuman, H., & Presser, S. (1981). *Questions and answers in attitude surveys: Experiments on question form, wording, and context.* New York: Academic Press.

Schwarz, N., & Bless, H. (1992). Constructing reality and its alternatives: Assimilation and contrast effects in social judgment. In L. L. Martin & A. Tesser (Eds.), *The construction of social judgment* (pp. 217–245). Hillsdale, NJ: Erlbaum.

Schwarz, N., & Bohner, G. (2001). The construction of attitudes. In A. Tesser & N. Schwarz (Eds.), *Blackwell handbook of social psychology: Intraindividual processes* (Vol.1, pp. 436–457). Oxford, UK: Blackwell.

Schwarz, N., & Clore, G. L. (1983). Mood, misattribution, and judgments of well-being: Informative and directive functions of affective states. *Journal of Personality and Social Psychology, 45,* 513–523.

Sherman, S. J., Presson, C. C., Chassin, L., Rose, J. S., & Koch, K. (2003). Implicit and explicit attitudes toward cigarette smoking: The effects of context and motivation. *Journal of Social and Clinical Psychology, 22,* 13–39.

Shiffrin, R. M., & Dumais, S. T. (1981). The development of automatism. In J. R. Anderson (Ed.), *Cognitive skills and their acquisition* (pp. 111–140). Hillsdale, NJ: Erlbaum.

Shiffrin, R. M., & Schneider, W. (1977). Controlled and automatic human information processing: II. Perceptual learning, automatic attending, and a general theory. *Psychological Review, 84,* 127–190.

Smith, E. R. (1992). The role of exemplars in social judgment. In L. L. Martin & A. Tesser (Eds.), *The construction of social judgment.* Hillsdale, NJ: Erlbaum.

Smith, E. R. (1996). What do connectionism and social psychology offer each other? *Journal of Personality and Social Psychology, 70,* 893–912.

Smith, E. R. (1997). Preconscious automaticity in a modular connectionist system. In R. S. Wyer (Ed.), *Advances in social cognition* (Vol. 10, pp. 181–202). Mahwah, NJ: Erlbaum.

Smith, E. R. (2000, February). *Connectionist representation of evaluation.* Paper presented at the meeting of the Society for Personality and Social Psychology, Nashville, TN.

Smith, E. R., & DeCoster, J. (1999). Associative and rule-based processing: A connectionist interpretation of dual-process models. In S. Chaiken & Y. Trope (Eds.), *Dual-process theories in social psychology* (pp. 323–336). New York: Guilford Press.

Smith, E. R., & Lerner, M. (1986). Development of automatism of social judgments. *Journal of Personality and Social Psychology, 50,* 246–259.

Smith, E. R., & Zarate, M. A. (1992). Exemplar-based model of social judgment. *Psychological Review, 99,* 3–21.

Strack, F. (1992). The different routes to social judgments: Experiential versus informational strategies. In L. L. Martin & A. Tesser (Eds.), *The construction of social judgments* (pp. 249–276). Hillsdale, NJ: Erlbaum.

Swanson, J. E., Rudman, L. A., & Greenwald, A. G. (2001). Using the Implicit Association Test to investigate attitude–behaviour consistency for stigmatised behaviour. *Cognition and Emotion, 15,* 207–230.

Tesser, A. (1978). Self-generated attitude change. In L. Berkowitz (Ed.), *Advances in experimental social psychology* (Vol. 11, pp. 289–338). New York: Academic Press.

Tourangeau, R., & Rasinski, K. A. (1988). Cognitive processes underlying context effects in attitude measurement. *Psychological Bulletin, 103,* 299–314.

von Hippel, W., Sekaquaptewa, D., & Vargas, P. (1997). The linguistic intergroup bias as an implicit indicator of prejudice. *Journal of Experimental Social Psychology, 33,* 490–509.

Weber, R., & Crocker, J. (1983). Cognitive processes in the revision of stereotypic beliefs. *Journal of Personality and Social Psychology, 45,* 961–977.

Wilson, T. D., Dunn, D. S., Kraft, D., & Lisle, D. J. (1989). Introspection, attitude change, and attitude–behavior consistency: The disruptive effects of explaining why we feel the way we do. In L. Berkowitz (Ed.), *Advances in experimental social psychology* (Vol. 22, pp. 287–343). Orlando, FL: Academic Press.

Wilson, T. D., & Hodges, S. D. (1992). Attitudes as temporary constructions. In A. Tesser & L. Martin (Eds.), *The construction of social judgment* (pp. 37–65). Hillsdale, NJ: Erlbaum.

Wilson, T. D., Lindsey, S., & Schooler, T. Y. (2000). A model of dual attitudes. *Psychological Review, 107,* 101–126.

Wittenbrink, B., Judd, C. M., & Park, B. (1997). Evidence for racial prejudice at the implicit level and its relationship with questionnaire measures. *Journal of Personality and Social Psychology, 72,* 262–274.

Wittenbrink, B., Judd, C. M., & Park, B. (2001). Spontaneous prejudice in context: Variability in automatically activated attitudes. *Journal of Personality and Social Psychology, 81,* 815–827.

10 Mental Representations Are States, Not Things

Implications for Implicit and Explicit Measurement

Eliot R. Smith
Frederica R. Conrey

What does an Implicit Association Test (IAT; Greenwald, McGhee, & Schwarz, 1998) score (block compatibility effect) of 35 msec, or a rating of 5 on a 7-point Likert scale, actually mean? Researchers' interpretations of implicit or explicit measurement results usually rest on the fundamental assumption that these observables reveal (with some unavoidable measurement error) properties of the underlying mental representations possessed by the research participant. For example, these measures may be taken to indicate the participant's "implicit attitude" or "explicit attitude" regarding some social object. Even more specifically, the typical assumption is that an attitude is an association between the representation of the attitude object and evaluation (Fazio, Sanbonmatsu, Powell, & Kardes, 1986). Beyond attitudes, other types of implicit and explicit measures have also been conceptualized as tapping associations. The very name of the IAT carries forward the assumption that implicit measures tap evaluative associations, and the idea has become so entrenched among the assumptions of social cognition that stereotypes are often specifically defined as associations between the representations of social groups and various attributes (e.g., traits).

Both semantic and evaluative associations have widely been assumed to be largely static, changing only slowly, and only on the basis of extensive new input or intentional practice (Dovidio, Kawakami, & Beach, 2000; Greenwald & Banaji, 1995; Wilson, Lindsey, & Schooler, 2000). Our purpose in this chapter is to offer an alternative picture of the nature of representation and to explore its implications for the ways explicit and implicit measures can be interpreted.

Our fundamental point is that we believe it is most useful to think of mental representations as states rather than as things. As Smith (1998) outlined, common metaphors for representations owe much to ideas about papers or other physical objects that are "stored," "searched for," and "retrieved" from physical locations like shelves or filing cabinet drawers. This metaphor presupposes that representations are things, and numerous implications follow so immediately that they generally escape critical consideration:

- Representations are static: like a paper put into and then taken out of a file drawer, the representation that is "stored" is the same as the one that is "retrieved" at a later time, potentially impoverished through decay or loss, but not fundamentally different from the original.
- Representations are the same in content and format whether passively stored (sitting in the file drawer) or actively being processed.
- To find the desired representation, one must search through a number of other, irrelevant representations.
- A representation is constructed (comes into existence) at a specific point in time. Representation construction is a qualitatively different process from representation change.
- If people's responses demonstrate context sensitivity or change over time, it must be due to their accessing different representations (e.g., thinking about social desirability concerns), because the target representation is assumed to be unchanging.

Alternatively, representations can be understood as dynamic states rather than static things (Smith, 1998). We focus on the specific model of representations as context-sensitive reconstructions in a connectionist memory system, although that is not the only possible state-like conceptualization of representations (exemplar-based representations are one alternative, for instance). See Smith (1996) for a more extensive introduction to this idea and references to other useful tutorial presentations. In a connectionist system, a number of elementary representational units (loosely analogous to biological neurons) are richly interconnected so that they can send signals to each other. Each unit has an activation level, which can change moment to moment in response to signals that the unit receives over its incoming connections, including input connections that arrive from outside the network (e.g., from sensory organs). In turn, each unit sends output to other units over its outgoing connections.

A concept is represented by a *pattern of activation* across a number of units. The same population of units participate in multiple distinct representations by taking on different patterns of activation. A familiar analogy is a TV or computer screen, in which a fixed number of pixels, by taking on different color and brightness values, can represent a very large number of meaningfully different images—far more images than the number of pixels themselves. The number of concepts that can be represented by files in a drawer, however, is limited by the number of files—one file per concept—because each file is itself a representation of an object. On a TV screen no individual pixel has any meaning by itself; the unit of meaning is the pattern that is defined by combining many different pixels. The number of states that can be represented by a connectionist system is virtually unlimited, constrained by the number of unique patterns that can be activated rather than by the number of nodes in the system. However, no individual node in the system has a meaning—there is no node for "dog," for instance—the unit of meaning is the pattern of nodes and links that is activated.

The activation pattern (representational state) the network forms is jointly determined by the current inputs flowing into the network and by the *weights* on the interunit connections, which gate or modulate the signals flowing from one unit to another. These weights are assumed to change only slowly with time. They therefore serve as the repository of the network's long-term, stable knowledge. The weights are generally assumed to be shaped by a learning process, with each weight being incrementally adjusted as the network processes a stimulus, in order to reduce the error and increase the efficiency with which the network arrives at the appropriate activation pattern (representation) for that stimulus. In this type of model, quite different properties emerge.

- Because many different representations share the same system of nodes and links, representations are not static: as a representation is maintained in memory (in the connection weights), it is changed by learning due to other stimuli the network is processing.

• Representations that are currently active states (activation patterns) exist in a completely different representational format from those that are currently inactive. The latter are represented in the connection weights, but the same set of weights contributes to the construction of *all* the patterns of which the network is capable, so the different patterns are not represented in individuated or isolated form.

• To find a desired representation, there is no need to search through a number of other, irrelevant representations; instead, a representation (pattern) is simply reconstructed by flows of activation in the network given the appropriate inputs.

• A representation is not constructed at a specific point in time, going from nonexistence to existence. Rather, representation construction is an ongoing process, qualitatively the same as representation change, and both are solely due to incremental changes in the network's connection weights.

• If people's responses demonstrate context sensitivity or change over time, it could be because the same focal inputs (e.g., a target stimulus) result in the elicitation of different reconstructed representations, owing to (1) intervening learning or (2) effects of other inputs representing nonfocal or contextual elements of the overall situation.

In this chapter we do not attempt to empirically demonstrate that representations "are" state-like rather than thing-like; see Smith (1998) for relevant discussion. Instead, we simply ask readers to assume, for the sake of argument, that this might be so and to consider with us some of the implications for the ways we think about implicit and explicit measurement in social psychology.

MENTAL REPRESENTATIONS AS CONTEXT-SENSITIVE, RECONSTRUCTED STATES

Specifically, how does a connectionist network learn a concept, such as "dog"? Assume that the network encounters many stimuli from this category. Initially the network will need additional input (such as a verbal label) to learn that a specific stimulus is actually an instance of the "dog" category, but over time it will become able to recognize itself that new stimuli (if sufficiently similar to previously categorized ones) are themselves category members. The important point is that a connectionist network ends up with a representation that is much more than a simple, dumb average or central tendency of all the "dog" stimuli that it has encountered through the learning process. Instead, it will store multiple, contextually specific instances. Thus, "fierce watchdogs" (large, barking, with sharp teeth) and "elderly pet poodles" (fuzzy, probably sleeping on the sofa) and "my boxer Lyla" (carrying a shoe around the house) may be among the context-specific instances that are learned.

The parent concept "dog" refers equally to these and many more variants. Thus, which one is reconstructed in any given case when the concept is invoked depends crucially on contextual information. The relevant context could be a narrative or sentence in which the concept is used, a physical setting, or, in general, any kind of information that suggests one sort of concept instance or another. Thus, in the context of "wore a knitted sweater," the elderly poodle variant may be reconstructed, whereas in the context of "mauled the burglar," the barking Rottweiler variant would be more likely (Clark, 1993, Ch. 2). Barsalou (1987) empirically demonstrated such effects. Clark summarized the properties of connectionist memories thus:

> The upshot is that there need be no context-independent core representation for [a concept]. Instead, there could be a family of states linked merely by a relation of family resemblance. . . . A single . . . [concept] will have a panoply of [specific activation patterns] . . . and which realization is actually present will make a difference to future processing. (1993, p. 24)

The model of context-sensitive representations just outlined should be clearly distinguished from the idea that people *possess* an invariant underlying "core" concept (e.g., of a dog) but *use* it in a way that depends on the current context. Such a suggestion would be comparable to the idea frequently offered within social psychology, that people "have" a single underlying representation (an attitude toward some social object or stereotype of some social group), but may shade the way they explicitly report it on the basis of social desirability or other such considerations. The proposal here is that in fact the reconstructed representation itself is context sensitive; that no stable, cross-contextually fixed knowledge representations exist; and that explicit considerations of social desirability or anything else, although of course they do occur, are not the sole or even the primary reason for observed context sensitivity of attitude or other responses.

Given this picture of the nature of context-sensitive knowledge reconstruction, we now turn to a brief review of evidence that knowledge representations are in fact context sensitive in the ways suggested.

Basic Memory Processes: Evidence from Nonhuman Animals

The proposal that context sensitivity of memory reflects fundamental properties of connectionist network mechanisms implies that context sensitivity should not be limited to humans, but should characterize memory very generally, even in nonhuman species. Indeed, this is the case (Holland & Bouton, 1999). Simple Pavlovian conditioning in rats and other nonhuman species shows context effects (for rats, the effective context is mainly a place). That is, when an animal is exposed to a conditioned stimulus–unconditioned stimulus pairing, it not only learns to associate those two stimuli, but also learns about the context in which the exposure has occurred (Pickens & Holland, 2004). As a result, the effects of conditioning are stronger in the same context than they are in a different context. Context sensitivity is found even for such a "basic," biologically prepared type of learning as conditioned taste aversion, in which an animal avoids a novel taste that has been associated with illness on a single previous occasion (Bills, Smith, Myers, & Schachtman, 2003). A final example: Drug tolerance effects (decreasing effects of a drug that is repeatedly administered) are also context specific: tolerance is greater when the repeated administrations occur in the same situation (Domjan, 2005). All these findings show that context sensitivity is not limited to cognitively sophisticated types of human learning, but characterize learning and memory very generally.

Evidence Regarding Nonsocial Concepts

Barsalou (1987) provided the seminal demonstrations of the context sensitivity of simple nonsocial concepts. His studies found, similarly to our informal "dog" example, that the concept of "bird" is instantiated in one way (e.g., a robin) in a "suburban backyard" context, but in a different way (chicken) in a "barnyard" context. Barsalou also demonstrated that people can report different "point of view" variants of common concepts, such as a bird from the point of view of an Australian, a city dweller, or a sailor. Clearly, these results speak strongly against the idea that people have a single, context-independent version of a concept that they use on all occasions. As Barsalou argued, they also speak against the idea that people have a whole host of *prestored, static* context-specific representations (e.g., of bird-in-barnyard or bird-from-a-sailor's-perspective), because the number of potential contexts times the number of concepts seems quite unrealistically large. The only reasonable model consistent with these data is one in which information about concepts together with the contexts in which they occur is stored in a flexible representational medium (such as connectionist networks) that allow not the retrieval of a statically stored representation but the flexible reconstruction of an appropriately context-sensitive conceptual variant—the very type of model we have outlined in this chapter.

Going beyond Barsalou's original demonstrations, a more recent paper by Yeh and Barsalou (in press) summarizes a variety of evidence supporting the idea that concepts take different form in different contexts. For example, people recall lists of words better in the same physical room in which they previously studied them than they do in different rooms. Words can also be recognized better when they are presented in the same sentence context at test as at study. And people can verify that specific properties are true of an object or concept much faster when the properties are relevant to the situation in which the object is encountered than in a situation that makes the property irrelevant. For example, in a context involving household movers, people would be able to verify quickly that "heavy" is true of the concept "piano," while that property would be more difficult to verify in a concert-hall context. Yeh and Barsalou (in press) argue that these properties of conceptual knowledge are highly functional, because concepts are likely to continue to be relevant in situations where they were relevant on past occasions.

In summary, there are several types of evidence that people do not have a *single* mental representation of a concept (such as "dog") to which various attributes (evaluation, affect, stereotypic traits) become stably "attached" or "associated." Instead, they have multiple, contextually specific versions of such a concept, each of which—like the sleepy poodle and the snarling guard dog—may have a distinct, even completely unrelated set of attributes (such as evaluation) attached to it.

THE EFFECTIVE CONTEXT FOR SOCIAL CONCEPTS

To acknowledge the importance of context to the structure and content of activated representations is not to imply that all aspects of context are equally important. While every context is different, not every context is unique. If every context were unique, the pursuit of generalization through scientific inquiry would be futile. Fortunately, the aspects of context that are most important to social psychology are relatively few. Here we focus on social categories, social relationships, and internal states.

Social Categories

The distinction between ingroups, people who are on my side, and outgroups, people whose intentions toward me I cannot be sure of, is fundamental to our social cognition. It is no surprise, then, that the social group memberships of both perceivers and targets are a fundamental part of the representation context. Assignment to minimal groups produces implicit as well as explicit positivity toward fellow ingroup members (Ashburn-Nardo, Voils, & Monteith, 2001). There is much evidence that how perceivers categorize targets affects both the semantic and affective components of their representations. Macrae, Bodenhausen, and Milne (1995), for instance, demonstrated that participants who saw a Chinese woman using chopsticks activated content consistent with a representation of Chinese people, while participants who saw the same woman using makeup activated content consistent with a representation of women. Mitchell, Nosek, and Banaji (2003) assigned participants to categorize the same set of target persons as either politicians/athletes or as Black/White. Participants who focused on occupation preferred Black athletes to White politicians, but participants who focused on race favored White politicians over Black athletes. Clearly, the representation that a perceiver constructs even for the same individual depends to a great extent on the target person's, and the perceiver's, respective memberships in social categories.

Social Relationships

Another feature of the social context is the specific personal relationship between the perceiver and the target, which can also strongly affect the nature of my representation of another person. Relationships can be null (e.g., when perceivers in a person–perception experiment form impressions of strangers they will never meet), or can be friendly and positive, or can be negative and adversarial. Research demonstrates, for instance, that sharing a goal with another person affects how that person is mentally represented. When subjects believe that they share a common fate, such as winning or losing a competition, with another person, they tend to rely less on categories and more on individuating information about the target in forming an impression of him or her (Neuberg & Fiske, 1987). Identifying personally with a target can also affect the extent to which he or she is associated with positivity. For instance, participants display more positivity toward Black targets when they are in the room with a Black experimenter (Lowery, Hardin, & Sinclair, 2001).

Internal States

Features of our internal states are also important to the content and strength of the representations we activate. Evaluative responses to objects, for instance, are affected by currently active goals and motives. Smokers who are nicotine deprived evaluate cigarettes more positively (Sherman, Rose, Koch, Presson, & Chassin, 2003), and thirsty students evaluate beverages more positively for as long as they are deprived (Ferguson & Bargh, 2004). An important point is that this increased positivity toward goal-relevant objects goes away when the goal is satisfied. Thirsty students allowed to drink before completing the measure of implicit attitudes show less positivity toward beverages. Thus, the perceiver's currently active goals also function as a kind of context that tunes the nature of representations as they are reconstructed.

Affective states and moods may also have profound impacts on the ways in which we represent information. There is much data to suggest that mood has a substantial impact on processing of information. Happiness, for instance, is consistently related to greater use of social stereotypes than is sadness (Bodenhausen, Kramer, & Süsser, 1994), an effect that is attributed to greater local, detail-oriented processing in sad moods (Bless & Fiedler, 1995). There is a growing body of evidence to suggest that mood also affects the content of our activated representations. Much research has explored the hypothesis that depressed people tend to experience a mood-congruent memory bias, remembering negative information more readily than positive information (Barry, Naus, & Lynn, 2004). Mood may interact with other features of the environment to produce changes in affective and cognitive representations as well. Previously depressed people's implicit self-esteem goes down when they experience negative mood, but there is no such effect in never-depressed controls (Gemar, Segal, Sagrati, & Kennedy, 2001). Exactly how mood and motivation affect our representations is still unclear, but that they have profound effects on how we perceive and think about the reconstructed world is indisputable.

IMPLICATIONS OF CONTEXT SENSITIVITY
FOR IMPLICIT MEASURES

Implicit measures are designed to tap representations that are automatically (spontaneously and immediately) activated by a specific stimulus, rather than what the perceiver might deliberately choose to activate. If we assume that implicit measures generally tap evaluative and semantic aspects of the mental representations that are spontaneously activated by a stimulus in a particular context, then it follows from the argument above that implicit measures will display context sensitivity. Many researchers have acknowledged that performance on implicit tasks is context sensitive (Blair, 2002), but interpretations for context effects in the literature vary widely. In our view, context sensitivity in implicit tasks reflects a fundamental feature of the representational system; implicit measures imperfectly tap mental representations that are themselves context sensitive. That scores vary with the context does not reflect a deficiency in the measures, but is an accurate reflection of the changing underlying representations. Nor is context sensitivity a deficiency of the underlying representational system. Instead, as argued above, it is functional; it allows the mind to respond efficiently and accurately to a constantly changing environment that calls for situated knowledge and behaviors. The version of the "dog" concept that is useful in dealing with a sleepy poodle on the sofa is different from the one needed to deal with a snarling guard dog.

While context sensitivity of the measures themselves is not a flaw, interpreting their results becomes trickier when we shift from thinking of representations as static things stored inside the mind to thinking of representations as transient states of activation. Because the specific content of an activated representation will be different every time it is called to mind because of passive change in the system and differences in the cognitive and social context, it is dangerous to interpret any implicit measure as demonstrating that "X is linked to Y," or, for example, "Fear and avoidance tendencies are linked to dogs." Instead, the linkage is conditional, as in "X is linked to Y when . . . ": "Fear and avoidance tendencies are linked to dogs when a particular context leads to the instantiation of the snarling Rottweiler concept variant." As we have said, however, not all features of the context are equally important. Features of the context that matter most for social concepts are social features that affect how we behave toward one another: group memberships, interpersonal relationships, and internal states such as active goals.

This last type of social feature, action motivations, has particularly important implications for the measurement of implicit representations. If representations are influenced by the goals perceivers are motivated to accomplish, such as finishing a chapter or playing in a poker tournament, then representations must also be influenced by the tasks experimenters use to measure them. Implicit measures themselves require participants to complete specific tasks, and so these measures themselves affect the representation and processing of information. For example, in person memory research, impression formation and memorization instructions constitute different task contexts. Participants instructed to memorize information about targets tend to store items in the order they are presented. Participants instructed to form impressions, however, tend to store semantically related items together (Hamilton, Katz, & Leirer, 1980). Gawronski and Bodenhausen (2005) have demonstrated, using implicit measures, that task differences (evaluative tasks versus lexical decision tasks) lead to systematically different patterns in the results.

Considered in this way, the sensitivity of representations to the demands of immediate tasks has a thought-provoking implication. Researchers may ask themselves, "What task can I have subjects perform that will most clearly reveal the content of their mental representations?" This question implies that there is an underlying representation that is invariant across different tasks, an assumption that we have shown is false. Instead, each task that subjects may be assigned can generally be expected to reveal different representations, for representations are constructions that are sensitive to the context, which includes the task. Again, the statement "X is linked to Y" is always less precise than the statement "X is linked to Y when the association is measured with an IAT, which forces subjects into an evaluative task."

IMPLICATIONS OF CONTEXT SENSITIVITY
FOR EXPLICIT JUDGMENTS

It is common for researchers to assume that both implicit and explicit attitudes are internal representations (evaluative associations connected to representations of the attitude object). For example, this model is presupposed by a research question such as, Do implicit and explicit measures access the same representation or two distinct representations? To a first approximation, as noted above, we accept the idea that implicit measures tap spontaneously activated aspects of a representation of the stimulus object, as it is reconstructed in the current context. However, we do not think that it is generally useful to consider explicit measures as accessing a mental representation of "the explicit attitude." Rather, it is more useful to consider how explicit responses arise based on a process rather than on the assumption of tapping an underlying representation.

Our proposal about the process of explicit judgment is as follows. We do not claim any great novelty for this model; in fact, we believe that it is largely mainstream, in that it rests on more or less standard dual-process assumptions (Smith & DeCoster, 2000; Strack & Deutsch, 2004). However, it is rarely made explicit.

1. Confronted with a judgment to be made, such as an attitude judgment, people start with what is spontaneously activated by the target stimulus in the given context (the same material that is assumed to be tapped by implicit measures).
2. Given plenty of time, the initial spontaneous representation may evolve based on features of the cognitive and social context. New representations may be added; currently active representations may decay.
3. On the basis of some intuitive sufficiency criterion, people may also proceed to intentionally activate additional representations that they consider relevant to evaluating the object, even if those are not spontaneously activated.
4. They may engage in complex attributional inferences or propositional/logical reasoning, for example, if they see inconsistencies or contradictions in the material they activate.
5. Finally, they report as their attitude some kind of weighted average of all the material they have come up with.

For example, consider the attitude object "stem cell research." Probably most people who know what this concept means have a positive implicit attitude toward it, based on the attractive idea of powerful new technologies that may permit medical science to save lives and cure terrible diseases. Yet many people report an explicit negative attitude toward the same concept. We suggest that the reason is not that they lack this implicit positive reaction nor that they have a separately stored "explicit attitude" especially for reporting to others, but that they are able to follow logical connections and (in Stages 3 and 4) intentionally activate information indicating that, for them, "stem cell research" is related to "abortion." If they judge that abortion is extremely negative and that its importance in their value system outweighs that of possible medical advances, they will explicitly respond negatively to "stem cell research" on that basis (Stage 5).

Among the representations that may be intentionally accessed in Stages 3 and 4 of making an explicit attitude report are abstract, linguistic/propositional representations. In the dual-process framework advanced by Smith and DeCoster (2000; see also Strack & Deutsch, 2004), systematic or controlled processing is largely driven by linguistically encoded propositions, related by logical principles. In contrast, the representations activated in heuristic or associative processing often include more sensory details and are structured and interrelated by associations rather than by logic. Thus, one of the implications of our model is that abstract, linguistic content may be more likely to be activated in the process of making explicit judgments than in responding to implicit measures.

This principle has an important implication. One and the same abstract and relatively amodal representation may be activated on the basis of its linguistic meaning, in response to a variety of superficially different target stimuli, when the perceiver considers them to be similar *in essence*. For example, a religious conservative may activate the negative concept of "abortion" in response to a variety of specific political issues (sale of birth control pills, stem cell research) that to another perceiver may appear virtually unrelated and elicit widely different evaluations. Consider another example: A Black face or the name "Jamaal" or the label "Blacks" may lead a highly prejudiced person to think explicitly of African Americans and of how much he or she dislikes them. This would be a relatively context-free response (produced in response to a range of specific stimuli in a variety of contexts and situations).

The general point, as suggested by these examples, is that making a context-free response (a response that depends on the core underlying meaning the perceiver thoughtfully attributes to a stimulus, without much influence by the specific details of either the target stimulus or its context) is a highly sophisticated *accomplishment* of the symbolic reasoning system. Clark (1993, p. 31) observes that during the learning process, one might learn abstract concepts that become more and more detached from the specific, contextualized variants with which learning began. This suggestion, that access to a relatively context-free representation is a late accomplishment, inverts the commonsense notion that context-free representations are the simple starting point, and that effects of context are "added in" through separate processes (such as correction of responses based on social desirability concerns). In fact, the most context-independent representations should be expected to be those deployed in response to explicit measures, because the exertion of cognitive control in the construction of a response is so likely to employ abstract, context-independent processing. Given that implicit tasks intentionally limit participants' access to this type of processing, the fact that the representations measured by implicit measures demonstrate a higher degree of context sensitivity seems obvious rather than surprising. There is some evidence supporting this hypothesis. Cunningham, Preacher, and Banaji (2001) found that over-time stability is higher for explicit than for implicit racial attitude measures (after properly controlling for differential reliability).

With sufficient practice, activation of a relevant general, abstract concept may become automatized, so that the person may spontaneously produce that concept in response to a wide range of concrete stimuli. Once this occurs, even an implicit measure could tap a response that is largely context free. In fact, there is evidence using implicit measures that more prejudiced people do activate negatively toned representations of Blacks as a social group when exposed to Black faces, while less prejudiced people have much more highly variable reactions to such faces (depending on their specific appearance, degree of attractiveness, facial expression, etc.) (Olson & Fazio, 2003). Presumably this difference may be due to prejudiced individuals' more extensive practice in thinking about negative aspects of African Americans in a variety of different contexts, which has led to automatization of those responses.

In summary, our perspective has important implications for explicit measurement. Explicit measures, like implicit measures, can be context sensitive; we argue that this is the default. Context sensitivity arises for reasons that are much more fundamental than "social desirability pressures" as often assumed. But under some circumstances, one might find less context sensitivity for explicit measures than for implicit measures, for the reasons just outlined.

SUMMARY OF IMPLICATIONS
AND RECOMMENDATIONS

The considerations discussed in this chapter lead to several specific recommendations, which we list here.

- No measures (implicit or explicit) can in general be interpreted as showing that X (e.g., a social group) is associated with Y (e.g., evaluation or a stereotype). Instead, the proper interpretation is that X is associated with Y in context Z.
- The fundamental elements of social context are social categories, social relationships, and internal states such as moods or

social motives. The latter include, among other things, the tasks that participants are assigned in the research setting.

- Behavioral criteria as well as measurement procedures occur in contexts that influence the representations participants construct. In other words, behaviors as well as implicit and explicit measurement results will display context sensitivity (De Houwer, in press). Thus, the strongest prediction of behavior will occur when measurement takes place in a similar context as that in which the behavior is to be predicted (where, again, context refers to categories, relationships, and internal states).

- To the extent that explicit measures allow and encourage people to respond on the basis of abstract, general representations, explicit measures may permit better cross-contextual prediction of behavior than do implicit measures. But the extent to which this can occur will depend on the nature of the construct being measured, the amount of experience the participants have had in thinking about it, and so forth.

- Considering the reality of context sensitivity should motivate researchers to measure implicit and explicit attitudes (or other constructs) in several contexts within a single study, rather than in just a single context. The purpose is not simply to demonstrate (again) that implicit measures can be context sensitive; we already know that. The purpose is to map out how the reconstructed concept shifts with contexts, and thus to begin to describe theoretically the ways in which relevant behaviors also might flexibly shift and accommodate to social situations. This approach holds the promise of turning context sensitivity from a measurement obstacle into a theoretical gold mine.

There is a natural worry that acknowledging the context sensitivity of social representations puts an end to ecological validity as we know it. If the context, especially the experimental context, pervasively influences the representations we measure, then how can our measurements shed light on representations and behaviors that occur outside the lab? The perspective advanced here, however, is not intended to be simply cautionary. Instead, we hope this perspective leads researchers to explore exactly how social cognition is flexible and situated (Smith & Semin, 2004) rather than inflexible and invariant. Rather than dismissing differences in results as contaminated by differences in the tasks, for instance, Gawronski & Bodenhausen (2005) demonstrated that the differences in measures obtained with lexical decision versus evaluative tasks reflected meaningful differences in the types of processes the different tasks set in motion.

REFERENCES

Ashburn-Nardo, L., Voils, C. I., & Monteith, M. J. (2001). Implicit associations as the seeds of intergroup bias: How easily do they take root? *Journal of Personality and Social Psychology, 81*(5), 789–799.

Barry, E. S., Naus, M. J., & Lynn, P. R. (2004). Depression and implicit memory: Understanding mood congruent memory bias. *Cognitive Therapy and Research, 28,* 387–414.

Barsalou, L. W. (1987). The instability of graded structure: Implications for the nature of concepts. In U. Neisser (Ed.), *Concepts and conceptual development: Ecological and intellectual factors in categorization* (pp. 101–140). New York: Cambridge University Press.

Bills, C., Smith, S., Myers, N., & Schachtman, T. R. (2003). Effects of context exposure during conditioning on conditioned taste aversions. *Learning and Behavior, 31*(4), 369–377.

Blair, I. V. (2002). The malleability of automatic stereotypes and prejudice. *Personality and Social Psychology Review, 6*(3), 242–261.

Bless, H., & Fiedler, K. (1995). Affective states and the influence of activated general knowledge. *Personality and Social Psychology Bulletin, 21,* 766–778.

Bodenhausen, G. V., Kramer, G. P., & Süsser, K. (1994). Happiness and stereotypic thinking in social judgment. *Journal of Personality and Social Psychology, 66,* 621–632.

Clark, A. (1993). *Associative engines: Connectionism, concepts, and representational change.* Cambridge, MA: MIT Press.

Cunningham, W. A., Preacher, K. J., & Banaji, M. R. (2001). Implicit attitude measures: Consistency, stability, and convergent validity. *Psychological Science, 12*(2), 163–170.

De Houwer, J. (in press). What are implicit measures and why are we using them? In R. W. Wiers & A. W. Stacy (Eds.), *The handbook of implicit cognition and addiction.* Thousand Oaks, CA: Sage.

Domjan, M. (2005). Pavlovian conditioning: A functional perspective. *Annual Review of Psychology, 56,* 179–206.

Dovidio, J. F., Kawakami, K., & Beach, K. (2000). Examination of the relationship between implicit and explicit measures of intergroup attitudes. In R. Brown & S. Gaertner (Eds.), *Blackwell handbook in social psychology: Vol. 4. Intergroup relations* (pp. 175–197). Oxford, UK: Blackwell.

Fazio, R. H., Sanbonmatsu, D. M., Powell, M. C., & Kardes, F. R. (1986). On the automatic activation of attitudes. *Journal of Personality and Social Psychology, 50,* 229–238.

Ferguson, M. J., & Bargh, J. A. (2004). Liking is for doing: The effects of goal pursuit on automatic evaluation. *Journal of Personality and Social Psychology, 87*(5), 557–572.

Gawronski, B., & Bodenhausen, G. V. (2005). Accessibility effects on implicit social cognition; The role of knowledge activation and retrieval experiences. *Journal of Personality and Social Psychology*, 89, 672–685.

Gemar, M. C., Segal, Z. V., Sagrati, S., & Kennedy, S. J. (2001). Mood-induced changes on the Implicit Association Test in recovered depressed patients. *Journal of Abnormal Psychology*, 110, 282–289.

Greenwald, A. G., & Banaji, M. R. (1995). Implicit social cognition: Attitudes, self-esteem, and stereotypes. *Psychological Review*, 102(1), 4–27.

Greenwald, A. G., McGhee, D. E., & Schwartz, J. L. K. (1998). Measuring individual differences in implicit cognition: The implicit association test. *Journal of Personality and Social Psychology*, 74(6), 1464–1480.

Hamilton, D. L., Katz, L. B., & Leirer, V. O. (1980). Cognitive representation of personality impressions: Organizational processes in first impression formation. *Journal of Personality and Social Psychology*, 39(1, Suppl. 6), 1050–1063.

Holland, P. C., & Bouton, M. E. (1999). Hippocampus and context in classical conditioning. *Current Opinion in Neurobiology*, 9(2), 195–202.

Lowery, B. S., Hardin, C. D., & Sinclair, S. (2001). Social influence effects on automatic racial prejudice. *Journal of Personality and Social Psychology*, 81(5), 842–855.

Macrae, C. N., Bodenhausen, G. V., & Milne, A. B. (1995). The dissection of selection in person perception: Inhibitory processes in social stereotyping. *Journal of Personality and Social Psychology*, 69(3), 397–407.

Mitchell, J. P., Nosek, B. A., & Banaji, M. R. (2003). Contextual variations in implicit evaluation. *Journal of Experimental Psychology: General*, 132(3), 455–469.

Neuberg, S. L., & Fiske, S. T. (1987). Motivational influences on impression formation: Outcome dependency, accuracy-driven attention, and individuating processes. *Journal of Personality and Social Psychology*, 53(3), 431–444.

Olson, M. A., & Fazio, R. H. (2003). Relations between implicit measures of prejudice: What are we measuring? *Psychological Science*, 14(6), 636–639.

Pickens, C. L., & Holland, P. C. (2004). Conditioning and cognition. *Neuroscience and Biobehavioral Reviews*, 28(7), 651–661.

Sherman, S. J., Rose, J. S., Koch, K., Presson, C. C., & Chassin, L. (2003). Implicit and explicit attitudes toward cigarette smoking: The effects of context and motivation. *Journal of Social and Clinical Psychology*, 22(1), 13–39.

Smith, E. R. (1996). What do connectionism and social psychology offer each other? *Journal of Personality and Social Psychology*, 70(5), 893–912.

Smith, E. R. (1998). Mental representation and memory. In D. T. Gilbert & S. T. Fiske (Eds.), *Handbook of social psychology* (Vol. 2, 4th ed., pp. 391–445). New York: McGraw-Hill.

Smith, E. R., & DeCoster, J. (2000). Dual-process models in social and cognitive psychology: Conceptual integration and links to underlying memory systems. *Personality and Social Psychology Review*, 4(2), 108–131.

Smith, E. R., & Semin, G. R. (2004). Socially situated cognition: Cognition in its social context. *Advances in Experimental Social Psychology*, 36, 53–117.

Strack, F., & Deutsch, R. (2004). Reflective and impulsive determinants of social behavior. *Personality and Social Psychology Review, 8,* 220–247.

Wilson, T. D., Lindsey, S., & Schooler, T. Y. (2000). A model of dual attitudes. *Psychological Review, 107*(1), 101–126.

Yeh, W., & Barsalou, L. W. (in press). The situated nature of concepts. *American Journal of Psychology.*

11 What Do We Know about Implicit Attitude Measures and What Do We Have to Learn?

Bertram Gawronski
Galen V. Bodenhausen

I cannot totally grasp all that I am. . . . For that
darkness is lamentable in which the possibilities in me
are hidden from myself: so that my mind, questioning
itself upon its own powers, feels that it cannot rightly
trust its own report.
—St. Augustine, *Confessions*

In his influential *Confessions*, St. Augustine lamented the evasiveness of full self-understanding, questioning the reliability of our intuitions about our own minds. Although introspection and self-report formed the foundation of the earliest approaches to studying psychology, the development of psychological research over the course of the 20th century led social psychologists steadily back to the view espoused by St. Augustine in the early 5th century. In particular, demonstrations of respondents' lack of introspective access to the causes of their own judgments and behavior (see, e.g., Nisbett & Wilson, 1977) forever shattered the illusion that self-reports would be a sufficient means for illuminating the workings of the mind. Alternatives to self-report began to be formulated, and at the dawn of the 21st century an explosion of research is exploring the usefulness of these new, implicit measures of mental contents and processes (see, e.g., Lane, Banaji, Nosek, & Greenwald, Chapter 3, this volume; Wittenbrink, Chapter 2, this volume). While undeniably exciting, this plethora of new techniques for peering into our inner mental lives raises a number of important questions that will have to be thoroughly researched and satisfactorily answered in order for the promise of these new measures to be fully realized. What is the appropriate theoretical construct corresponding to each measure? Do these measures really provide access to unconscious mental processes? What do the different measures have in common, and what is unique to each particular measure? How are the different measures related to physiological correlates? It is toward these questions that we turn our attention.

CONCEPTUAL CLARITY

The initial enthusiasm for implicit measures seemed to be accompanied by relatively loose and shifting conceptualizations of their meaning. Part of the confusion undoubtedly arises from more fundamental ambiguities and debates about the meaning of relevant theoretical constructs. For example, much of the work on implicit measures has focused on the assessment of attitudes. However, fundamental disagreements still exist concerning the appropriate conceptualization of "attitude." Some theorists view attitudes as enduring structures in long-term memory (e.g., Fazio, 1995), whereas others view them as momentarily constructed evaluations that integrate current contextual information with selective subsets of long-term memory (e.g., Schwarz & Bohner, 2001). Whereas the former approach conceives of attitudes as relatively static and defined by fixed structural properties, the latter emphasizes a dynamic process with minimal structural assumptions. Theorists from these different camps might very well make different assumptions about what an implicit measure of attitudes is capturing— the strength of a stable association in long-term memory on one hand, or the emergent net evaluative implications of contexually activated knowledge and situationally available input on the other. Thus, labeling something as an "attitude measure" does nothing to clarify the matter, because the term *attitude* means different things to different researchers. It is an open question whether implicit measures map well on to a particular conceptualization of "attitude," a question that must be addressed by systematic empirical investigation.

The importance of this issue becomes even more apparent in the context of early theorizing that implicit attitude measures provide direct access to stable evaluative representations that have their roots in long-term socialization experiences (see, e.g., Dovidio, Kawakami, & Beach, 2001; Greenwald & Banaji, 1995; Rudman, 2004; Wilson, Lindsey, & Schooler, 2000). This assumption has been challenged over the last few years by accumulating evidence that implicit measures of attitudes are highly susceptible to contextual influences (for a review, see Blair, 2002). However, even though such findings may be interpreted as evidence for the attitudes-as-constructions account (Schwarz & Bohner, 2001), it is not entirely clear how implicit attitude measures are influenced by the context. Does the context lead to a shift in the measurement of an otherwise stable attitude, or does the context influence how the attitude itself is constructed on the spot? Again, the specific answer to these questions depends on the preferred conceptualization of attitudes as momentary constructions (Schwarz & Bohner, 2001) or stable evaluative representations (Fazio, 1995). Notwithstanding these ambiguities, the fact that implicit attitude measures show a strong susceptibility to contextual influences poses a serious challenge to the original expectation that these measures provide direct and unbiased access to stable evaluative representations in memory.

Another fundamental confusion, noted by several scholars (see especially De Houwer, 2006), concerns the meaning of the term *measure,* which can be used to refer to a measurement *procedure* or to the *outcome* of a measurement procedure. As De Houwer (2006) noted, a measurement procedure can be direct or indirect, whereas the term *implicit* is meaningful only with regard to the outcome of a measurement procedure. Conversely, it does not make sense to call the outcome of measurement procedure direct or indirect, just as it does not make sense to label a measurement procedure explicit or implicit. An important consideration is that whereas the direct versus indirect nature of a measurement procedure can be determined a priori by the objective properties of the task, the explicit versus implicit nature of the outcome of a measurement procedure needs to be established empirically.

In this context, De Houwer (2006) pointed out another, related problem in the way the term *implicit* is used. In particular, he argued that researchers often fail to specify in what sense a particular measure should be regarded as implicit. As originally used in the memory literature on patients with amnesia (see, e.g., Warrington & Weiskrantz, 1968), "implicit" mental processes referred specifically to processes that operated in the absence of conscious awareness. Implicit memory thus was evident in task performance reflecting the residue of previous experience, in the absence of any explicit memory for that experience. In keeping with this precedent, it seems to be commonly the case in the social psychology literature that whenever something is called "implicit," it is assumed to be consciously inaccessible. But as De Houwer (2006) noted, this is an empirical assumption, and it is usually an untested one.

Besides the interpretation of the term *implicit* as "unconscious," implicit attitude measures are sometimes assumed to reflect "automatic" attitudes. Bargh (1994) identified four separate senses in which information processing can be considered automatic, and lack of awareness is but one of these "four horsemen" of automaticity. Many so-called automatic processes happen with awareness (Moors & De Houwer, 2006). At the level of implicit attitude measures, it is thus important to specify which aspect(s) of automaticity one capitalizes on. It may be that awareness covaries with measures, such that for some measures, respondents are consciously aware of the assessed attitude. The same holds for other aspects of automaticity (i.e., controllability, spontaneity, and resource dependency). We argue that it is important to understand how these issues map onto the features of a particular task and whether they remain invariant across different content domains or interact with content. It may be, for example, that the controllability of responses varies across different tasks, across content domains, or as a function of motivation and practice at controlling particular kinds of responses. It is incumbent upon researchers to understand the scope of what they can claim about the implicitness of their measures and to tailor their theoretical conclusions accordingly.

Another major lesson for researchers that will lead to greater conceptual clarity is the loss of innocence regarding our aspiration to create "process-pure" measures. A process-pure measure would be one that cleanly and unambiguously indexes a single construct of interest. Many people using the Implicit Association Test (IAT), for example, functionally regard it as a process-pure measure of the strength of a mental association (or, more accurately, a pair of associations). However, performance on the IAT is clearly influenced by many other factors, some of which are theoretically uninteresting and potentially controllable (e.g., general perceptual–motor skills) and others of which are highly interesting in their own right. The application of process-dissociation techniques (Conrey, Sherman, Gawronski, Hugenberg, & Groom, 2005; Payne, 2001) provides a way of systematically decomposing these theoretically relevant components of performance, and it represents one of the most promising and important directions for research employing implicit attitude measures. For example, Conrey and colleagues (2005), in their Quad-Model, have shown that performance on the IAT (and many other measures) reflects not only the automatic associative bias that has been the focus of most IAT users, but also on several other processes, such as the discriminability of the stimulus, success at overcoming bias, and general guessing biases. Of the other processes in the Quad-Model, the theoretically most relevant is the process of overcoming bias. Multinomial modeling of IAT data has confirmed that the motivation/ability to overcome the automatic associative bias also influences IAT performance systematically. By applying a process-dissociation methodology to the IAT (among other measures), it becomes possible to obtain much more finely tuned estimates of the automatic associative bias by pulling out separate processes that influence overall performance. The important general lesson here is that no measure is process pure, and a major path toward clarity lies in the application of new techniques for decomposing task performance into more specific, conceptually meaningful subcomponents. By defining our terms and specifying our constructs as precisely as possible, rapid progress will be greatly facilitated.

INTROSPECTION AND CONSCIOUSNESS

Does the outcome of an indirect measurement procedure necessarily reflect an implicit attitude in the sense that it is unavailable to introspection or self-report? Not necessarily. As noted by De Houwer (2006), whether or not the construct assessed by a given task is "implicit" (or unconscious) needs to be established empirically. Indeed, attitudes assessed with indirect measures are sometimes highly correlated with self-reported attitudes (e.g., Banse, Seise, & Zerbes, 2001; Dovidio, Kawakami, Johnson, Johnson, & Howard, 1997; Teachman, Gregg, & Woody, 2001). On one hand, these findings may indicate that the attitude reflected in the implicit measure is available to introspection. On the other hand, however, one could object that there might be a separate, implicit aspect to the attitude that just happens to coincide with the explicit aspect in the case of some attitudes. Notwithstanding these two possible interpretations, it seems more parsimonious to assume that the attitude in such cases is available to introspection; yet it may nevertheless influence some other automatic aspects of information processing that are picked up via implicit attitude measures. Someone who detests spiders may be well aware of that fact and may show a rapid, involuntary avoidance response to spiders on an indirect measure of attitudes. Should that response be labeled an "implicit" attitude that is unavailable to introspection, or is it best viewed as a spontaneous, unintentional consequence of a given attitude?

In a similar way, one could ask whether low correlations between self-reported and indirectly assessed attitudes indicate that the indirectly assessed attitude is "implicit" or unconscious. Again, the answer to this question is, not necessarily. Correlations between self-reported and indirectly assessed attitudes would naturally be expected to be low if the indirectly assessed attitude is unconscious (unless there is reason to assume a spurious relation). However, low correlations between the two kinds of measures can arise for a multitude of reasons other than a lack of introspective access (Gawronski, Hofmann, & Wilbur, 2006). In fact, there is now a large body of evidence showing that multiple factors determine whether "implicit" attitudes assessed with indirect measures are related to self-reported "explicit" attitudes. If these factors are controlled, explicit and implicit attitude measures typically show quite substantial correlations.

First, it is often assumed that indirect attitude measures are less affected by individuals' deliberate attempts to control their responses than self-report measures. Such motivationally driven influences are particularly pronounced in socially sensitive domains where social desirability may affect self-reported, but not indirectly assessed attitudes. Consistent with this assumption, several studies have demonstrated that self-reported and indirectly assessed attitudes toward racial minority groups are highly correlated when individual differences in the motivation to control prejudiced reactions are controlled (e.g., Akrami & Ekehammer, 2005; Banse & Gawronski, 2003; Dunton & Fazio, 1997; Fazio, Jackson, Dunton, & Williams, 1995; Gawronski, Geschke, & Banse, 2003; Hofmann, Gschwendner, & Schmitt, 2005). In a similar vein, Nier (2005) demonstrated that correlations between self-reported and indirectly assessed attitudes toward African Americans were significantly higher when participants believed that inaccurate self-reports could be detected by means of a lie detector.

Second, correlations between self-reported and indirectly assessed attitudes have been shown to depend on the degree of cognitive deliberation. Consistent with this assumption, Florack, Scarabis, and Bless (2001) demonstrated that individuals with a strong dispositional tendency to engage in cognitive deliberation (i.e., high need for cognition; see Cacioppo, Petty, Feinstein, & Jarvis, 1996) showed lower correlations between self-reported and indirectly assessed attitudes than individuals with a low tendency to engage in deliberation. In a similar vein, a meta-analysis by Hofmann, Gawronski, Gschwendner, Le, and Schmitt (2005) found that correlations between self-reported and indirectly assessed attitudes generally increase as a function of the spontaneity of self-reports.

Third, self-reports may or may not correspond to indirect measures with regard to the specific aspect of the attitude that is being assessed. As such, correlations between the two are sometimes reduced simply because of such underlying conceptual differences. Banse and colleagues (2001), for example, demonstrated that indirectly assessed attitudes toward homosexuals show higher correlations with self-reported attitudes when the latter involve self-reports on affective responses (e.g., "I feel uncomfortable nearby two men kissing each other") than when they involve self-reports on normative beliefs (e.g., "Gay men should not work with children or adolescents"). These results were corroborated in Hofmann, Gawronski, and colleagues' (2005) meta-analysis, showing that attitudes assessed with the IAT show higher correlations with affective as compared to cognitive self-report measures. In addition, Hofmann et al. found that low correlations can also be due to mismatches in dimensionality (see also Nosek, 2005). The IAT, for example, generally involves a comparison between two attitude objects, thus representing relative rather than absolute evaluations. Thus, it is not very surprising that correlations between the IAT and explicit self-reports are generally higher when the latter involve the same relative rather than absolute evaluations.

Finally, implicit attitude measures often exhibit low internal consistencies (e.g., Banse, 1999; Bosson, Swann, & Pennebaker, 2000; Gawronski, 2002; Olson & Fazio, 2003). Thus, their correlations to self-reported attitudes are often reduced by measurement error. Consistent with this assumption, Cunningham, Preacher, and Banaji (2001) found substantial correlations between self-reported and indirectly assessed attitudes when the impact of measurement error was controlled with latent variable analyses (see also Gawronski, 2002; Hofmann, Gawronski, et al., 2005).

Taken together, these results suggest that indirectly assessed and self-reported attitudes show substantial correlations under certain conditions. If the relevant factors are controlled, the two kinds of attitude measures typically show quite substantial correlations. From this perspective, it seems unwarranted to claim that "implicit" attitudes assessed with indirect measures reflect unconscious attitudes that are unavailable to introspection. To be sure, indirect attitude measures usually do not require introspection for the assessment of an attitude. However, that does not imply that the assessed attitude is unavailable to introspection.

In addition to the assumption that indirectly assessed attitudes themselves are unconscious, there is another interpretation of the term *unconscious* that has been proposed in the context of implicit

attitude measures (Greenwald & Banaji, 1995). Rather than referring to the attitude itself, the term *unconscious* could also refer to the
influence an attitude has on other mental processes. In other words,
indirectly assessed attitudes may be consciously accessible, but they
may influence other psychological processes outside of conscious
awareness (see Nisbett & Wilson, 1977). Even though research on
this question is rather limited, there seems to be at least some evidence for this assumption. For example, Gawronski and colleagues
(2003) demonstrated that people are sometimes unaware of how indirectly assessed attitudes influence their interpretation of ambiguous
information. In this study, German participants were asked to form
an impression of either a German or a Turkish individual on the basis
of evaluatively ambiguous behavior. Consistent with previous research (e.g., Darley & Gross, 1983; Duncan, 1976; Dunning &
Sherman, 1997; Kunda & Sherman-Williams, 1993; Sagar & Schofield,
1980), German participants evaluated the behavior more negatively
when the target was Turkish than when he was German. However,
this effect was moderated by indirectly assessed attitudes, such that
the target's category membership influenced the interpretation of
ambiguous behavior only for participants with negative attitudes toward Turkish people and not for those with neutral attitudes (see
also Hugenberg & Bodenhausen, 2003). More important, the influence of indirectly assessed attitudes on the interpretation of ambiguous behavior was *not* moderated by participants' motivation to control prejudiced reactions. Instead, motivation to control prejudice
affected only the relation between self-reported and indirectly assessed attitudes toward Turkish people, such that self-reported and
indirectly assessed attitudes were highly correlated for participants
low in motivation, but not for those high in motivation to control
prejudice (see also Akrami & Ekehammer, 2005; Banse & Gawronski,
2003; Dunton & Fazio, 1997; Fazio et al., 1995; Hofmann, Gschwendner, & Schmitt, 2005). Self-reported attitudes had no impact on the
interpretation of ambiguous behavior. Thus, given that participants
were generally able to control the influence of indirectly assessed attitudes on their interpretation of ambiguous behavior (i.e., participants were not under time pressure or otherwise cognitively de-
pleted), these results are consistent with the assumption that people
are sometimes unaware of the impact of "implicit" attitudes on the
interpretation of ambiguous behavior. In other words, whereas indirectly assessed attitudes seem to be conscious in the sense that they
are introspectively accessible to self-report, they still seem to involve
an unconscious component, such that they can influence other men-

tal processes outside of conscious awareness. Notwithstanding this finding, much more research is needed to clarify which particular processes are influenced by indirectly assessed attitudes, and which of these influences do or do not occur outside people's conscious awareness.

COMMONALITIES AND DIFFERENCES
BETWEEN IMPLICIT MEASURES

Originally it was a matter of some vexation when two different indirect measures of a particular attitude (e.g., IAT and sequential priming measures of racial attitudes) were found not to correlate particularly strongly (or even not at all). After all, it is not uncommon to find that a Likert scale and a semantic differential scale measuring attitudes toward the same attitude object correlate extremely strongly. If different self-report measures of attitudes correlate in this manner, why should indirect measures not likewise correspond? If the starting assumption is that there is some fixed entity called an "implicit attitude" that can be measured in a variety of different ways, then it would indeed seem disheartening if different measures of this same entity did not correlate with one another. However, as we have argued, if the emphasis is shifted to the idea that it is the *outcome* of a particular measurement procedure that is implicit, and that the implicitness or automaticity of this outcome may depend on specific features of the measurement procedure, then the important question becomes, which automatic aspect(s) of attitude activation can be captured by a particular task? Is it spontaneous approach/avoidance tendencies or the activation of evaluative associations in memory (Neumann, Hülsenbeck, & Seibt, 2004)? Is it the activation of conceptual or evaluative knowledge in memory (Wittenbrink, Judd, & Park, 2001)? Or is it something else? Measures should be expected to correlate strongly only to the extent that they each tap similar information-processing consequences of attitude activation. Different self-report measures typically do assess the very same aspect of processing (i.e., deliberative evaluation of the attitude object), while different indirect measures are likely to assess a broader range of disparate processes. Indeed, recent research has begun to examine these differences, leading toward a typology of indirect attitude measures that will provide researchers with a rich arsenal to draw from in attacking the mysteries of the black box. Ultimately, the target and range appropriate for each of these research tools need to be specified.

Several proposals have been offered to describe and account for the different emphases of the different indirect attitude measures. Olson and Fazio (2003), for example, proposed that available measures differ in the extent to which they tap general categorical responses versus exemplar-based responses. The attitude version of the IAT, for example, requires respondents to categorize a set of exemplars (e.g., names or faces) in terms of their membership in the relevant attitudinal category (e.g., a racial group). As such, the cognitive focus of the task is on the category. This situation can be contrasted with a common version of the affective priming task, which examines the effects of individual exemplars (e.g., faces) on the processing of subsequently encountered words. While the category to which the exemplar belongs is expected to influence this processing, the cognitive focus of the task is not on the category per se. Thus, differences in the way exemplars are evaluated, versus evaluation of the category as a whole, underlie the low correspondence between affective priming measures and the IAT, according to Olson and Fazio. They found that by modifying the affective priming task in a way that encouraged categorization of the exemplars, correlations with the IAT were greatly enhanced. Mitchell, Nosek, and Banaji (2003) provided further evidence that the IAT does indeed operate at the level of categorical evaluations. In their studies, the same set of exemplars (e.g., African American athletes) produced evidence of both negative and positive associations, depending on whether they were categorized by race or by occupation. These studies make it clear that a focus on the category per se, rather than on individual exemplars of the category, can produce marked shifts in implicit attitude measures.

De Houwer (2003) has proposed another useful distinction between various indirect measures. A basic structural property of many indirect measurement procedures is that they involve examining whether information processing is facilitated (speeded) or impaired (slowed) by the presentation of an attitude object (see Lane et al., Chapter 3, this volume; Wittenbrink, Chapter 2, this volume). The crucial question revolves around whether or not the processes triggered by the activation of the attitude are compatible or incompatible with other processing requirements. De Houwer (2003) argued that there are at least two general kinds of compatibility (see also Kornblum, Hasbroucq, & Osman, 1990) and that different tasks vary in the extent to which they draw upon one or the other of these two phenomena. One of these, *response compatibility*, has to do with how the (natural or induced) response tendencies associated with the attitude object map onto the response requirements of the task (see also Stroop, 1935). This issue is important in the IAT, for example (see Lane et al., Chapter 3, this volume). In a race IAT, African American exemplars are supposed to be categorized as "Black." Thus, when an African American face (or name) appears on the screen, there will be a (task-appropriate) tendency to respond by pressing the "Black" button. However, for a respondent who harbors negative associations toward African Americans, there may also be a spontaneous response tendency toward the "Unpleasant" button. For the so-called compatible trial block, the "Unpleasant" button and the "Black" button are one and the same, so the two response tendencies are compatible and performance should be facilitated by the fact of their coinciding. For the incompatible trial block, however, the "Unpleasant" response is *not* the same as the "Black" response, so these two response tendencies will be in conflict. As such, performance should suffer (i.e., slower reactions, more errors).

A very similar logic is at work in the affective priming task proposed by Fazio and colleagues (Fazio et al., 1995; see Wittenbrink, Chapter 2, this volume). In this task, the exemplar prime (e.g., a Black face) may elicit a spontaneous evaluative response tendency. Irrespective of this tendency, the task requirement is to categorize the target words presented after the primes in terms of their valence. For trials in which the spontaneous evaluative response to the prime coincides with the valence of the target word, performance should be facilitated because both the prime and the target potentiate the same response. For trials in which the spontaneous evaluative response to the prime is different from the valence of the target word, performance should be inhibited because of the incompatibility of the response tendencies elicited by prime and target. From the standpoint of this structural characteristic, the IAT and the affective priming task are quite similar.

The other form of compatibility that De Houwer (2003) described is *stimulus compatibility*. The fundamental issue here concerns how semantically similar two sets of stimuli are. The lexical decision task used by Wittenbrink, Judd, and Park (1997) is a good example of an indirect measure that relies on stimulus compatibility (see Wittenbrink, Chapter 2, this volume). In this task, a prime stimulus (e.g., an African American face) precedes a standard lexical decision task, in which respondents must simply categorize a letter string as a word or nonword. The words used as target stimuli in the lexical decision task vary in their stereotypical relation to the prime stimulus (e.g., *hostile* vs. *friendly* as target words that are consistent vs. inconsistent with the negative stereotype of African Americans). For instance, if an African American face activates stereotype-consistent concepts in memory, this reaction will either coincide with or contradict the semantic notion of the target word. When the semantic connotations of the prime and target word coincide, responses should be faster, but they should be slower when they are contradictory. It is important to note that as meaningful target words require responses with the same key irrespective of their semantic connotation, (in)compatibility in the lexical decision task is defined on the level of stimulus features rather than on the level of response tendencies; any response tendency that is created by the prime will be irrelevant to the task-required response, which is "word" irrespective of whether the target word is stereotype consistent or stereotype inconsistent.

De Houwer's (2003) structural analysis leads to the interesting prediction that performance on the IAT and the affective priming task may look more similar to one another than performance on affective versus semantic priming tasks. Indeed, this prediction was borne out in a series of studies by Gawronski and Bodenhausen (2005). These studies also documented another way in which indirect measures differ from one another—in terms of their sensitivity to metacognitive inferences. In research on self-reported attitudes, there is extensive evidence that individuals use metacognitive information to inform their judgments. In this research, two types of influences on judgment are contrasted: the content of activated knowledge versus the experienced ease with which this knowledge was retrieved (for a review, see Schwarz, Bless, Wänke, & Winkielman, 2003). In a typical study, participants are asked to generate a certain number of instances fitting a particular category (e.g., likeable Canadians). For instance, the more likeable Canadians one calls to mind, the more one's activated knowledge is consistent with a positive evaluation of Canadians. However, because it is typically harder to think of more instances than to think of fewer, experiencing the difficulty of trying to think of many likeable Canadians may imply that there are not very many of them, consistent with a more negative evaluation of Canadians. In the realm of self-reported judgments, experienced ease is commonly observed to determine the tone of overall judgments, unless its diagnosticity is explicitly discredited.

Gawronski and Bodenhausen (2005) extended this research to the realm of indirect attitude measures. A common assumption about indirect measures is that they simply tap the activation level of associations in memory. From this standpoint, the more exemplars of a certain type one calls to mind, the more one's implicit evaluation will move in the direction of those exemplars, based on the activated knowledge. Whether or not it was easy or difficult to generate the exemplars should be irrelevant. Thus, performance on a race IAT should reflect more negative evaluations after participants have generated many dislikeable African Americans, as compared to generating just a few dislikeable African Americans. In actuality, however, results were just the opposite. IAT scores reflected the pattern that would be expected if retrieval experiences were guiding responses. Subsequent studies replicated this pattern and showed that it also generalized to an affective priming task as well. Considered from the standpoint of De Houwer's (2003) distinction between response compatibility and stimulus compatibility, we reasoned that a direct reflection of activated knowledge would be most likely in tasks that involve stimulus compatibility. Again, this prediction was borne out. In a direct comparison of two sequential priming tasks assessing implicit prejudice against African Americans, implicit prejudice depended on the experienced ease of retrieving dislikeable African Americans when the task included an evaluative decision task (i.e., response compatibility). In contrast, implicit prejudice was influenced by the overall amount of activated exemplars when the task included a lexical decision task (i.e., stimulus compatibility).

Further evidence for the differential role of stimulus compatibility and response compatibility in indirect attitude measures is implied by research that investigated the impact of multiple primes on sequential priming effects. Balota and Paul (1996), for example, found that two sequentially presented prime stimuli resulted in additive effects in a typical semantic priming paradigm using a lexical decision task. This result is consistent with an interpretation of sequential priming effects in terms of spreading activation (see Collins & Loftus, 1975), implying that increasing stimulation should increase the activation level of corresponding associations in memory. Interestingly, such additive effects turn into contrast effects when the stimulus compatibility structure implied in the lexical decision task is changed into a response compatibility structure. Gawronski, Deutsch, and Seidel (2005), for example, found that affective priming effects in Fazio and colleagues' (1995) paradigm were *more* pronounced when the evaluative prime stimulus was preceded by a context prime of the *opposite* valence. However, affective priming effects were *less* pronounced when the prime stimulus was preceded by a context prime of the *same* valence. This finding stands in contrast to the assumption that affective priming effects in evaluative decision tasks have their roots in the same spreading activation mechanisms that are responsible for semantic priming effects in lexical decision tasks (see, e.g., Fazio, Sanbonmatsu, Powell, & Kardes, 1986; Hermans,

De Houwer, & Eelen, 1994). However, it is consistent with claims that affective priming effects are driven by a response compatibility mechanism (see, e.g., De Houwer, Hermans, Rothermund, & Wentura, 2002; Klauer, Roßnagel, & Musch, 1997; Klinger, Burton, & Pitts, 2000; Wentura, 1999), implying that affective priming effects should be influenced by participants' ability to ignore task-irrelevant features, in this case the valence of the prime (see Besner & Stolz, 1999; Besner, Stolz, & Boutilier, 1997). Applied to the present question, the valence of the second prime may be more salient, and thus more difficult to ignore, when it is evaluatively inconsistent with the valence of the first prime. However, the valence of the second prime may be less salient, and thus easier to ignore, when it is evaluatively consistent with the valence of the first prime (Gawronski, Deutsch, & Strack, 2005).

In summary, the available evidence indicates that the widespread equation of the outcome of different measurement procedures with a single "implicit attitude" construct is quite problematic. Different measures are characterized by very different task structures (e.g., exemplar- vs. category-related responses; stimulus vs. response compatibility). As such, measures that may appear similar on the surface can produce very different results, depending on their underlying task structure. Thus, future research employing indirect attitude measures are well advised to take structural differences between tasks into account in order to avoid theoretical misinterpretations of the obtained results.

PHYSIOLOGICAL CORRELATES

So far, our discussion has primarily addressed measures that are based on response latencies such as the IAT (see Lane et al., Chapter 3, this volume) or sequential priming tasks (see Wittenbrink, Chapter 2, this volume). Even though the vast number of studies using these measures already provide important insights into their underlying mechanisms, and thus into the nature of the constructs assessed with these tasks, many issues are still unresolved, some of which were discussed in the preceding sections of this chapter. A fruitful complement in this endeavor could be the use of physiological measures (see Ito & Cacioppo, Chapter 5, this volume). For instance, by searching for physiological correlates of the performance in indirect attitude measures, physiological measures could provide further insights into both the commonalities and differences between different measures or task properties. In fact, several studies have already investigated the relation between implicit attitude measures and physiological responses. One of the first studies in this area, for example, found that performance on the race IAT was significantly related to amygdala activation in response to Black faces (Phelps et al., 2000). In a similar vein, Chee, Sriram, Soon, and Lee (2000) demonstrated that performance on a flower–insects IAT was significantly related to activation in the left dorsolateral prefrontal cortex. Milne and Grafman (2001) extended these findings by showing that lesions in the ventromedial prefrontal cortex eliminate implicit gender stereotyping in the IAT. A more complex pattern in the relation between implicit attitude measures and physiological responses was demonstrated by Richeson and colleagues (2003). In their study, race bias in the IAT predicted activation in the right dorsolateral prefrontal cortex in response to Black faces, and this activation mediated the relation between race bias in the IAT and performance impairments in the Stroop task resulting from interactions with a Black confederate. Finally, Wheeler and Fiske (2005) have shown that both automatic stereotype activation and amygdala activation in response to Black faces was significantly reduced when participants were asked to focus on a nonracial category (see also Mitchell et al., 2003).

Even though these findings provide first insights into how implicit attitude measures are related to activity in different areas of the brain, the origin and the nature of the obtained relations remain obscure as long as they cannot be matched to the specific psychological mechanisms underlying indirect attitude measures. For example, the available data on the IAT raise the question of why IAT performance is related to both amygdala activation (Phelps et al., 2000) and activation in the dorsolateral prefrontal cortex (Chee et al., 2000; Richeson et al., 2003). Given that amygdala activation reflects automatically activated negativity, whereas activation in the dorsolateral prefrontal cortex reflects deliberate inhibition, these findings suggest that IAT performance is influenced by both automatic and controlled processes. This assumption is consistent with Conrey and colleagues' (2005) claim that performance on indirect attitude measures is not process pure, but influenced by multiple processes. In terms of Conrey and colleagues' Quad-Model, amygdala activation may be related to the associative bias component, whereas activation in the dorsolateral prefrontal cortex may be related to the component reflecting success at overcoming associative bias. However, the mapping of the processes proposed by Conrey et al. and specific physiological correlates is still hypothetical at this stage. Thus, future research on the relation between indirect attitude measures and physiological correlates could provide an even stronger contribution by considering the specific mechanisms underlying different kinds of measures.

WHAT DO WE HAVE TO LEARN?

Given the explosion of research on *implicit attitudes* and *automatic evaluations* (see Wittenbrink, Chapter 2, this volume, Figure 2.1; see also Musch & Klauer, 2003), it is probably not an overstatement to claim that the development of indirect attitude measures brought about, if not a scientific revolution, then at least a substantial reorientation of priorities and perspectives. Certainly, this change has left us not only with important new insights into the psychology of evaluation, but also with some unresolved controversies. These controversies raise a lot of challenging questions that call for answers. Some of the questions we consider to be particularly important are discussed in this chapter. These questions concern (1) the general nature of attitudes as constructions versus stable representations, (2) the "implicitness" of the constructs assessed by indirect attitude measures, (3) the particular processes that are influenced by indirectly assessed attitudes and whether these influences do or do not occur outside of conscious awareness, (4) commonalities and differences between measures as a function of objective task characteristics, and (5) physiological correlates of the processes underlying indirect attitude measures.

Notwithstanding the importance of these issues, the question that we regard as the most important one has not yet been addressed. This question is related to the lack of connection between large-scale theories on the determinants of judgments and behavior, and small-scale theories about what exactly indirect attitude measures assess, how they work, and how they are related to each other. The problem addressed by this question is not so much that we would lack either large-scale theories on human behavior or small-scale theories on indirect attitude measures. Rather, the problem is that the concepts proposed by these two classes of theories do not map onto each other, such that the conceptual terminology of one class of theories could be unambiguously translated into the terminology of the other. For instance, when talking about indirect attitude measures, large-scale theories typically employ abstract theoretical concepts, such as "implicit attitudes" (e.g., Wilson et al., 2000) or "evaluative associations" (e.g., Strack & Deutsch, 2004). Small-scale theories, in contrast, usually refer to concrete operational concepts, such as "response compatibility" (De Houwer, 2003) or "salience asymmetries"

(Rothermund & Wentura, 2004). The challenge that researchers face right now is to find ways to combine the two approaches, such that the relevant concepts can be mapped onto each other and a coherent nomological network can be constructed. A first step in this direction may be Conrey and colleagues' (2005) Quad-Model. This model not only covers some of the theoretical constructs typically proposed by large scale-theories (e.g., automatic attitude activation, cognitive control), but also addresses the mechanisms underlying a specific type of indirect attitude measures (i.e., measures based on response compatibility).

A second question that is directly related to this first one is how physiological processes map onto the constructs proposed by large- and small-scale theories. As outlined above, there is an accumulating body of research that investigated the relation between implicit attitude measures and physiological correlates (e.g., Chee et al., 2000; Milne & Grafman, 2001; Phelps et al., 2000; Richeson et al., 2003; Vanman, Saltz, Nathan, & Warren, 2004; Wheeler & Fiske, 2005). However, compared with the vast number of studies on the mechanisms underlying indirect attitude measures, the available evidence regarding physiological correlates is still very limited. We believe that the proposed mapping of large-scale and small-scale theories could be substantially enriched if this endeavor is associated with a mapping to physiological correlates. Such a multifocus approach would thus include (1) large-scale theories of affect, cognition, and behavior, (2) small-scale theories concerning the mechanisms underlying indirect attitude measures, and (3) theories of physiological functioning. The investigation and integration of this full range of conceptual issues constitutes an ambitious agenda for the next generation of research on "implicit attitudes."

ACKNOWLEDGMENTS

Preparation of this chapter was supported by grants from the Canada Research Chairs Program, the Social Sciences and Humanities Research Council of Canada, and the Academic Development Fund of the University of Western Ontario to Bertram Gawronski.

REFERENCES

Akrami, N., & Ekehammar, B. (2005). The association between implicit and explicit prejudice: The moderating role of motivation to control prejudiced reactions. *Scandinavian Journal of Psychology, 46,* 361–366.

Balota, D. A., & Paul, S. T. (1996). Summation of activation: Evidence from multiple primes that converge and diverge within semantic memory. *Journal of Experimental Psychology: Learning, Memory, and Cognition, 22*, 827–845.

Banse, R. (1999). Automatic evaluation of self and significant others: Affective priming in close relationships. *Journal of Social and Personal Relationships, 16*, 803–821.

Banse, R., & Gawronski, B. (2003). Die Skala Motivation zu vorurteilsfreiem Verhalten: Skaleneigenschaften und Validierung [The scale motivation to act without prejudice: Psychometric properties and validity]. *Diagnostica, 49*, 4–13.

Banse, R., Seise, J., & Zerbes, N. (2001). Implicit attitudes towards homosexuality: Reliability, validity, and controllability of the IAT. *Zeitschrift für Experimentelle Psychologie, 48*, 145–160.

Bargh, J. A. (1994). The four horsemen of automaticity: Awareness, intention, efficiency, and control in social cognition. In R. S. Wyer & T. K. Srull (Eds.), *Handbook of social cognition* (pp. 1–40). Hillsdale, NJ: Erlbaum.

Besner, D., & Stolz, J. A. (1999). Unconsciously controlled processing: The Stroop effect reconsidered. *Psychonomic Bulletin and Review, 6*, 449–455.

Besner, D., Stolz, J. A., & Boutilier, C. (1997). The Stroop effect and the myth of automaticity. *Psychonomic Bulletin and Review, 4*, 221–225.

Blair, I. V. (2002). The malleability of automatic stereotypes and prejudice. *Personality and Social Psychology Review, 6*, 242–261.

Bosson, J. K., Swann, W. B., & Pennebaker, J. W. (2000). Stalking the perfect measure of implicit self-esteem: The blind men and the elephant revisited? *Journal of Personality and Social Psychology, 79*, 631–643.

Cacioppo, J. T., Petty, R. E., Feinstein, J. A., & Jarvis, B. W. (1996). Dispositional differences in cognitive motivation: The life and times of individuals varying in the need for cognition. *Psychological Bulletin, 119*, 197–253.

Chee, M. L., Sriram, N., Soon, C. S., & Lee, K. M. (2000). Dorsolateral prefrontal cortex and the implicit association of concepts and attributes. *Neuroreport for Rapid Communication of Neuroscience Research, 11*, 135–140.

Collins, A. M., & Loftus, E. F. (1975). A spreading-activation theory of semantic processing. *Psychological Review, 82*, 407–428.

Conrey, F. R., Sherman, J. W., Gawronski, B., Hugenberg, K., & Groom, C. (2005). Separating multiple processes in implicit social cognition: The Quad-Model of implicit task performance. *Journal of Personality and Social Psychology, 89*, 469–487.

Cunningham, W. A., Preacher, K. J., & Banaji, M. R. (2001). Implicit attitude measurement: Consistency, stability, and covergent validity. *Psychological Science, 12*, 163–170.

Darley, J. M., & Gross, P. H. (1983). A hypothesis-confirming bias in labeling effects. *Journal of Personality and Social Psychology, 44*, 20–33.

De Houwer, J. (2003). A structural analysis of indirect measures of attitudes. In J. Musch & K. C. Klauer (Eds.), *The psychology of evaluation: Affective processes in cognition and emotion* (pp. 219–244). Mahwah, NJ: Erlbaum.

De Houwer, J. (2006). What are implicit measures and why are we using them? In

R. W. Wiers & A. W. Stacy (Eds.), *The handbook of implicit cognition and addiction* (pp. 11–28). Thousand Oaks, CA: Sage.

De Houwer, J., Hermans, D., Rothermund, K., & Wentura, D. (2002). Affective priming of semantic categorisation responses. *Cognition and Emotion, 16,* 643–666.

Dovidio, J. F., Kawakami, K., & Beach, K. R. (2001). Implicit and explicit attitudes: Examination of the relationship between measures of intergroup bias. In R. Brown & S. L. Gaertner (Eds.), *Blackwell handbook of social psychology: Intergroup processes* (pp. 175–197). Malden, MA: Blackwell.

Dovidio, J. F., Kawakami, K., Johnson, C., Johnson, B., & Howard, A. (1997). On the nature of prejudice: Automatic and controlled processes. *Journal of Experimental Social Psychology, 33,* 510–540.

Duncan, B. L. (1976). Differential perception and attribution of intergroup violence: Testing the lower limits of stereotyping of Blacks. *Journal of Personality and Social Psychology, 34,* 590–598.

Dunning, D., & Sherman, D. A. (1997). Stereotypes and tacit inference. *Journal of Personality and Social Psychology, 73,* 459–471.

Dunton, B. C., & Fazio, R. H. (1997). An individual difference measure of motivation to control prejudiced reactions. *Personality and Social Psychology Bulletin, 23,* 316–326.

Fazio, R. H. (1995). Attitudes as object–evaluation associations: Determinants, consequences, and correlates of attitude accessibility. In R. E. Petty & J. A. Krosnick (Eds.), *Attitude strength* (pp. 247–282). Mahwah, NJ: Erlbaum.

Fazio, R. H., Jackson, J. R., Dunton, B. C., & Williams, C. J. (1995). Variability in automatic activation as an unobtrusive measure of racial attitudes: A bona fide pipeline? *Journal of Personality and Social Psychology, 69,* 1013–1027.

Fazio, R. H., Sanbonmatsu, D. M., Powell, M. C., & Kardes, F. R. (1986). On the automatic activation of attitudes. *Journal of Personality and Social Psychology, 50,* 229–238.

Florack, A., Scarabis, M., & Bless, H. (2001). When do associations matter? The use of automatic associations towards ethnic groups in person judgments. *Journal of Experimental Social Psychology, 37,* 518–524.

Gawronski, B. (2002). What does the Implicit Association Test measure? A test of the convergent and discriminant validity of prejudice-related IATs. *Experimental Psychology, 49,* 171–180.

Gawronski, B., & Bodenhausen, G. V. (2005). Accessibility effects on implicit social cognition: The role of knowledge activation versus retrieval experiences. *Journal of Personality and Social Psychology, 89,* 672–685.

Gawronski, B., Deutsch, R., & Seidel, O. (2005). Contextual influences on implicit evaluation: Additive versus contrastive effects of evaluative context stimuli in affective priming. *Personality and Social Psychology Bulletin, 31,* 1226–1236.

Gawronski, B., Deutsch, R., & Strack, F. (2005). Approach/avoidance-related motor actions and the processing of affective stimuli: Incongruency effects in automatic attention allocation. *Social Cognition, 23,* 182–203.

Gawronski, B., Geschke, D., & Banse, R. (2003). Implicit bias in impression formation: Associations influence the construal of individuating information. *European Journal of Social Psychology, 33,* 573–589.

Gawronski, B., Hofmann, W., & Wilbur, C. J. (2006). Are "implicit" attitudes unconscious? *Consciousness and Cognition, 15,* 485–499.

Greenwald, A. G., & Banaji, M. R. (1995). Implicit social cognition: Attitudes, self-esteem, and stereotypes. *Psychological Review, 102,* 4–27.

Hermans, D., De Houwer, J., Eelen, P. (1994). The affective priming effect: Automatic activation of evaluative information in memory. *Cognition and Emotion, 8,* 515–533.

Hofmann, W., Gawronski, B., Gschwendner, T., Le, H., & Schmitt, M. (2005). A meta-analysis on the correlation between the Implicit Association Test and explicit self-report measure. *Personality and Social Psychology Bulletin, 31,* 1369–1385.

Hofmann, W., Gschwendner, T., & Schmitt, M. (2005). On implicit–explicit consistency: The moderating role of individual differences in awareness and adjustment. *European Journal of Personality, 19,* 25–49.

Hugenberg, K., & Bodenhausen, G. V. (2003). Facing prejudice: Implicit prejudice and the perception of facial threat. *Psychological Science, 14,* 640–643.

Klauer, K. C., Roßnagel, C., & Musch, J. (1997). List-context effects in evaluative priming. *Journal of Experimental Psychology: Learning, Memory, and Cognition, 23,* 246–255.

Klinger, M. R., Burton, P. C., & Pitts, G. S. (2000). Mechanisms of unconscious priming: I. Response competition, not spreading activation. *Journal of Experimental Psychology: Learning, Memory, and Cognition, 26,* 441–455.

Kornblum, S., Hasbroucq, T., & Osman, A. (1990). Dimensional overlap: Cognitive basis for stimulus–response compatibility—a model and taxonomy. *Psychological Review, 97,* 253–270.

Kunda, Z., & Sherman-Williams, B. (1993). Stereotypes and the construal of individuating information. *Personality and Social Psychology Bulletin, 19,* 90–99.

Milne, E., & Grafman, J. (2001). Ventromedial prefrontal cortex lesions in humans eliminate implicit gender stereotyping. *Journal of Neuroscience, 21,* 1–6.

Mitchell, J. P., Nosek, B. A., & Banaji, M. R. (2003). Contextual variations in implicit evaluation. *Journal of Experimental Psychology: General, 132,* 455–469.

Moors, A., & De Houwer, J. (2006). Automaticity: A theoretical and conceptual analysis. *Psychological Bulletin, 132,* 297–326.

Musch, J., & Klauer, K. C. (Eds.). (2003). *Psychology of evaluation: Affective processes in cognition and emotion.* Mahwah, NJ: Erlbaum.

Neumann, R., Hülsenbeck, K., & Seibt, B. (2004). Attitudes toward people with AIDS and avoidance behavior: Automatic and reflective bases of behavior. *Journal of Experimental Social Psychology, 40,* 543–550.

Nier, J. A. (2005). How dissociated are implicit and explicit racial attitudes? A bogus pipeline approach. *Group Processes and Intergroup Relations, 8,* 39–52.

Nisbett, R. E., & Wilson, T. D. (1977). Telling more than we can know: Verbal reports on mental processes. *Psychological Review, 84,* 231–259.

Nosek, B. A. (2005). Moderators of the relationship between implicit and explicit attitudes. *Journal of Experimental Psychology: General, 134.* 565–584.

Olson, M. A., & Fazio, R. H. (2003). Relations between implicit measures of prejudice: What are we measuring? *Psychological Science, 14,* 636–639.

Payne, B. K. (2001). Prejudice and perception: The role of automatic and controlled processes in misperceiving a weapon. *Journal of Personality and Social Psychology, 81,* 181–192.

Phelps, E. A., O'Connor, K. J., Cunningham, W. A., Funayama, E. S., Gatenby, J. C., Gore, J. C., et al. (2000). Performance on indirect measures of race evaluation predicts amygdala activation. *Journal of Cognitive Neuroscience, 12,* 729–738.

Richeson, J. A., Baird, A. A., Gordon, H. L., Heatherton, T. F., Wyland, C. L., Trawalter, S., et al. (2003). An fMRI investigation of the impact of interracial contact on executive function. *Nature Neuroscience, 6,* 1323–1328.

Rothermund, K., & Wentura, D. (2004). Underlying processes in the Implicit Association Test: Dissociating salience from associations. *Journal of Experimental Psychology: General, 133,* 139–165.

Rudman, L. A. (2004). Sources of implicit attitudes. *Current Directions in Psychological Science, 13,* 79–82.

Sagar, H. A., & Schofield, J. W. (1980). Racial and behavioral cues in black and white children's perceptions of ambiguously aggressive acts. *Journal of Personality and Social Psychology, 39,* 590–598.

Schwarz, N., Bless, H., Wänke, M., & Winkielman, P. (2003). Accessibility revisited. In G. V. Bodenhausen & A. J. Lambert (Eds.), *Foundations of social cognition* (pp. 51–77). Mahwah, NJ: Erlbaum.

Schwarz, N., & Bohner, G. (2001). The construction of attitudes. In A. Tesser & N. Schwarz (Eds.), *Blackwell handbook of social psychology: Intraindividual processes* (pp. 436–457). Malden, MA: Blackwell.

Strack, F., & Deutsch, R. (2004). Reflective and impulsive determinants of social behavior. *Personality and Social Psychology Review, 8,* 220–247.

Stroop, J. R. (1935). Studies of interference in serial verbal reactions. *Journal of Experimental Psychology, 28,* 643–662.

Teachman, B. A., Gregg, A. P., & Woody S. R. (2001). Implicit associations for fear-relevant stimuli among individuals with snake and spider fears. *Journal of Abnormal Psychology, 110,* 226–235.

Vanman, E. J., Saltz, J. L., Nathan, L. R., & Warren, J. A. (2004). Racial discrimination by low-prejudiced Whites: Facial movements as implicit measure of attitudes related to behavior. *Psychological Science, 15,* 711–714.

Warrington, E. K., & Weiskrantz, L. (1968). New method of testing long-term retention with special reference to amnesic patients. *Nature, 217,* 972–974.

Wentura, D. (1999). Activation and inhibition of affective information: Evidence for negative priming in the evaluation task. *Cognition and Emotion, 13,* 65–91.

Wheeler, M. E., & Fiske, S. T. (2005). Controlling racial prejudice: Social-cognitive goals affect amygdala and stereotype activation. *Psychological Science, 16,* 56–63.

Wilson, T. D., Lindsey, S., & Schooler, T. Y. (2000). A model of dual attitudes. *Psychological Review, 107,* 101–126.

Wittenbrink, B., Judd, C. M., & Park, B. (1997). Evidence for racial prejudice at the implicit level and its relationships with questionnaire measures. *Journal of Personality and Social Psychology, 72,* 262–274.

Wittenbrink, B., Judd, C. M., & Park, B. (2001). Evaluative versus conceptual judgments in automatic stereotyping and prejudice. *Journal of Experimental Social Psychology, 37,* 244–252.

Index

Page numbers followed by *f* indicate figure; *n*, note; *t*, table.